DICTIONARY OF
THE WAVERLEY NOVELS

Uniform With This Volume
DICTIONARIES TO FAMOUS AUTHORS
Thackeray By I. G. Mudge & M. E. Sears
Scott (Waverley Novels) By M. F. A. Husband
Thomas Hardy By F. Saxelby
Medieval Romance and
    Romance Writers By Lewis Spence

A DICTIONARY

OF THE CHARACTERS IN

THE WAVERLEY NOVELS OF SIR WALTER SCOTT

BY

M. F. A. HUSBAND, B.A.

AUTHOR OF "TALES FROM BARBOUR'S 'BRUCE'"

New York
HUMANITIES PRESS
1962

This is an unaltered and unabridged reprint
of the last (1910) edition.

Reprinted 1962 by
Humanities Press Inc.
by special arrangement with
Routledge & Kegan Paul Ltd.

Printed in the U.S.A.
Noble Offset Printers, Inc.
New York 3, N.Y.

INTRODUCTORY NOTE

THIS book is intended as a work of reference for the student and lover of the Waverley Novels, and, in a minor degree, for the humanist who sees in Scott a noble nature worthy of closer acquaintance. Its aim is that of a Dictionary and not an Encyclopædia—an identification and description, rather than a condensed narrative, of the multitude of characters created by Sir Walter. No fewer than 2836 characters are comprised in the Dictionary, and these include 37 horses and 33 dogs.

Some of the historical errors which appear in the Novels have been corrected in the Dictionary : see, for example, the *Notes* at page 76, col. 2 ; p. 175, col. 1 ; p. 229, col. 1, and p. 271, col. 2. Short notes have been inserted as to the prototype of Jeanie Deans (p. 68), and Old Mortality (p. 198) ; and Scott's acknowledgment of his indebtedness to Mrs. Bethune Baliol in respect of the substratum of his Scottish fictions is reproduced on p. 16.

Comparatively few instances occur in which glossary notes are necessary, and these have, for convenience, been shown immediately after the passages in which the necessity for them arises, instead of being collected to form a Glossary separate from the Dictionary.

In the table of Novels which precedes the Dictionary proper, no attempt has been made to summarise the respective stories. It is hoped, however, that the chronological and other notes therein contained will prove of service in connection with the study of an author whose writings did much to stimulate that " historical sense " which was one of the richest gains of the human mind in the nineteenth century, and whose wide-ranging genius and sunny sympathies continue to win the affectionate attention and admiration of English-speaking readers throughout the world a hundred years after the preparation of his first Novel.

ELDERSLEA,
    MUSSELBURGH, SCOTLAND,
        1910.

A TABLE OF THE WAVERLEY NOVELS

In the following list the novels are taken according to their order in the 1829–33 Edition of 48 volumes. This edition, 'revised and corrected' by the Author, was the first published after Scott's public acknowledgment (in 1827) of his authorship. To the title of each novel is added in brackets the date of original publication. A few general notes are given regarding the period and localities with which each deals.

Vols. I, II, *Waverley; or, 'Tis Sixty Years Since* (1814):
> The story opens in the spring of 1745; it includes the Jacobite rising, 'The Forty-five,' with the battle of Prestonpans, the triumphant occupation of Edinburgh, the march into England, and the return from Derby; it closes a few months after the decisive defeat which occurred at Culloden in April, 1746. Much of the action takes place in the Perthshire Highlands.

Vols. III, IV, *Guy Mannering; or, The Astrologer* (1815):
> The opening scenes take place during the first five years of Harry Bertram's life, 1760–5. The main incidents occur sixteen years later, when Colonel Mannering and Vanbeest Brown return from India, occupying a few months of 1781–2. The scene is chiefly laid in Galloway, but incidents also occur in Westmoreland, Liddesdale, and Edinburgh.

Vols. V, VI, *The Antiquary* (1816):
> The story begins one July near the end of the eighteenth century, and ends in August of the following year. Dealing mainly with the daily life of Monkbarns and his friends, it includes an account of a mistaken alarm of French invasion. With the exception of the opening scenes in Edinburgh and the Hawes Inn, Queensferry, the incidents take place in Forfarshire.

Vols. VII, VIII, *Rob Roy* (1817):
> The story begins a few months before the outbreak of the Jacobite rising in 1715, and closes early in 1716, soon after the collapse of the rebellion. The rising is for the most part described only in its effect on the fortunes of the Osbaldistone family, but indications of the

methods by which it was arranged occur in the course of Frank
Osbaldistone's adventures. He is the central figure whose adventures
in Northumberland, in Glasgow, and in Rob Roy's country among
the mountains of Loch Lomond give continuity to the whole.

Vol. IX (part), *Tales of my Landlord. First Series.*
The Black Dwarf (1816) :

The Black Dwarf is a Border story, and belongs to the period following the Union of the English and Scottish Parliaments in 1707.
' All Scotland was indignant at the terms on which their legislature
had surrendered their natural independence,' and an invasion by
the Pretender was generally expected.

Vols. IX (part), X, XI (part), *Tales of my Landlord. First Series.*
Old Mortality (1816) :

The story opens with the description of a wappenschaw in the
Upper Ward of Clydesdale on 5th May, 1679, two days after the
murder of Archbishop Sharpe. It deals with the defeat of Grahame
of Claverhouse at Drumclog, near Loudon Hill, the march on Glasgow
by the Covenanters, the retreat of Claverhouse to Edinburgh, and
the defeat of the Covenanters at Bothwell Brig by the Duke of Monmouth—the whole occupying about two months. Ten years elapse
and the story draws to a close a few days after the skirmish which
took place at Killiecrankie on 27th July, 1689.

Vols. XI (part), XII, XIII (part), *Tales of my Landlord. Second Series.*
The Heart of Midlothian (1818) :

The events leading up to the Porteous riot, and the riot itself on
14th April, 1736, form the opening scenes of this novel. Some weeks
later take place the trial and sentence to death of Effie Deans for
child-murder, followed by her sister Jeanie's heroic and successful
journey to London to seek a remission of the sentence. The chief
scenes of action are Edinburgh and its neighbourhood, London and
Richmond, the concluding events taking place in Argyleshire in
1751, when Sir George Staunton was murdered. A year later his
widow left Knocktarlitie, and 'after blazing ten years in the fashionable world' retired to a convent.

Vols. XIII (part), XIV, *Tales of my Landlord. Third Series.*
The Bride of Lammermoor (1819) :

The story begins one November, subsequent to the Union of 1707,
with the funeral of Lord Ravenswood, and it recounts the love-
tragedy of Edgar Ravenswood and Lucy Ashton. Sir William Ashton,
after a change of ministry—probably that of August, 1710—no longer
favouring Edgar's suit, Lucy was forced twelve months later into an
engagement with Hayston of Bucklaw. She signed the marriage

contract on St. Jude's Day, 28th October, and the tragedy culminates in November. The whole action takes place in East Lothian, presumably between November, 1709, and November, 1711.

Vol. XV, *Tales of my Landlord. Third Series.*
A Legend of Montrose (1819) :

The opening chapter treats of the political state of Scotland during the Civil War, after the departure to England of the Scottish army under the Earl of Leven. In the summer of 1644 James Grahame, Marquis of Montrose, reached the Highlands in disguise, armed with a commission from Charles I to lead the Royalists. Montrose's successes at Tippermuir, Aberdeen, and Inverary are recounted, and the tale ends soon after his great victory at Inverlochy, Inverness-shire, on 2nd February, 1645. The whole action takes place in the Highlands of Scotland.

Vols. XVI, XVII, *Ivanhoe* (1819) :

This romance contains an historical and social survey of England during the reign of Richard Cœur-de-Lion, marking the hostility between the Saxons and the Normans who ' acknowledged no law but their own wicked pleasure,' and dealing also with the oppression of the Jews. From the opening of the story immediately before the Passage of Arms at Ashby-de-la-Zouch until the trial by combat at Templestowe, about two weeks are occupied of the summer of 1194, after Richard's return from imprisonment in Austria. The incidents take place in Yorkshire and Leicestershire.

Vols. XVIII, XIX, *The Monastery* (1820) :

Simon Glendinning was killed fighting as a vassal of the monks of St. Mary's at the battle of Pinkie in 1547. The story opens immediately afterwards, his son Halbert being then between nine and ten years of age, and it draws to a close when he was nineteen—in 1557. Halbert joined the Protestant forces under Lord James Stewart, whilst Edward took monastic vows, and later became the last Abbot of St. Mary's. The Border Country is the scene of action.

Vols. XX, XXI, *The Abbot ; being the Sequel to the Monastery* (1820) :

Ten years elapse between the action of *The Monastery* and that of *The Abbot.* Roland is spoken of as an infant in 1557 in the closing scenes of *The Monastery*, but is represented as about eighteen when he became Queen Mary's page in July, 1567. Queen Mary's captivity at Lochleven Castle, her abdication, and her escape from the castle are described. The story ends soon after the battle of Langside, 13th May, 1568, when, after a hurried flight to Dundrennan Abbey, Mary confided herself ' to the doubtful faith of England.' The scenes of action are Kennaquhair (Melrose) and neighbourhood, Edinburgh, Lochleven Castle, Kinross, Niddrie Castle, Langside, and Dundrennan.

Vols. XXII, XXIII, *Kenilworth* (1821) :

    The story opens in Cumnor, a village near Oxford, 'two hours' brisk riding' from Woodstock, in the Manor-house of which Amy Robsart was imprisoned. It includes an account of Tressilian's attempts to plead 'the unhappy Amy's cause,' the incident of Sir Walter Raleigh and the cloak, and the rivalry between the Earls of Sussex and Leicester. Queen Elizabeth arrived at Kenilworth Castle for the great revels on 9th July, 1575, and a few days later the tale ends with Amy's tragic death. The incidents take place in Berkshire, Oxfordshire, Devonshire, London, and Kenilworth Castle.
    Note.—Amy Robsart was found dead on 8th September, 1560.

Vols. XXIV, XXV, *The Pirate* (1821) :

    This romance includes a description of life in Zetland in the end of the seventeenth century, and in particular of the family life of Magnus Troil and his daughters Minna and Brenda. Mordaunt was fourteen years old when Mr. Mertoun and he took up their abode in Jarlshof. The incidents occur, however, seven or eight years later, between spring and August, Cleveland being then twenty-five years old, and Mordaunt three or four years younger. The scene is laid in and around the Zetland (or Shetland) and the Orkney Isles.

Vols. XXVI, XXVII, *The Fortunes of Nigel* (1822) :

    The incidents occupy little more than a month beginning in April, between the years 1616—'our Swan of Avon hath sung his last'—and 1618, when Burbage died. Portraits are drawn of James VI of Scotland (I of England) and of his goldsmith, George Heriot, whose wealth 'shall not want inheritors while there are orphan lads in Auld Reekie.' The action takes place almost exclusively in London and Greenwich.

Vols. XXVIII, XXIX, XXX, *Peveril of the Peak* (1823) :

    Sir Geoffrey Peveril was made prisoner at the battle of Worcester, and 'it was chiefly owing to Major Bridgenorth's mediation' that his life was spared. The varying fortunes of the two families—one Cavalier and the other Puritan—are followed. Alice was born in 1658, and in 1660 was removed from Martindale Castle by her father. Four or five years elapse without incident before the unexpected meeting of Lady Peveril and Major Bridgenorth in the avenue of Moultrassie Hall. A further period of many years passes, the later incidents occurring towards the end of the Popish Plot scare in 1680. The scenes are laid in Derbyshire, the Isle of Man, and London, with slight incident in Liverpool.

Vols. XXXI, XXXII, *Quentin Durward* (1823):

The narrative of Quentin's romantic career opens on 'a delicious summer morning' of 1468 with his arrival in Touraine, his accidental meeting with 'Maître Pierre,' and his speedy enrolment as an Archer of the Scottish Guard It draws to a close after the conference between Louis XI and 'his fair cousin of Burgundy,' followed by their united attack on Liège in October, 1468, to avenge the murder of the Bishop of Liège. The action takes place in Plessis-les-Tours, Liège, and Peronne, incidents occurring at Charleroi and Namur while Quentin acted as escort to the Ladies of Croye.

Note.—The Bishop's murder did not take place till 1482.

Vols. XXXIII, XXXIV, *St. Ronan's Well* (1823):

The story begins in a summer very early in the nineteenth century, and ends in November of the same year with several calamities. It describes the petty jealousies and quarrels of 'a party met together for the purposes of health and amusement' in the Fox Hotel, recently erected by a tontine subscription—much to the ire of Meg Dods, mistress of the Cleikum Inn. The action takes place in St. Ronan's Well and Aultoun (Innerleithen), Shaws Castle, and Marchthorn (Peebles).

Vols. XXXV, XXXVI, *Redgauntlet. A Tale of the Eighteenth Century* (1824):

Part of this Jacobite tale is in the epistolary style, part consists of the journal of Darsie Latimer whilst in confinement in Cumberland, and part is the narrative of Alan Fairford. The whole events occupy less than two months of the summer of 1766, ending when Father Buonaventure (Charles Edward Stewart) embarked for France. The scenes of action are Edinburgh, Dumfries and neighbourhood, Annan, the Solway Firth, and Cumberland.

Note.—Charles Edward Stewart paid two or three secret visits to London between 1750 and 1760.

Vol. XXXVII, *Tales of the Crusaders. The Betrothed* (1825):

The story opens in autumn, 1187. At Easter following, Berenger was killed by Gwenwyn, who in turn was killed by Hugo de Lacy. Some months later Hugo, hoping for the remission of his vow to go to the Holy Land, was betrothed to Eveline, but was forced to fulfil his vow—for the shortened period, however, of three years. He was due to return on St. Clement's Day, 23rd November, 1191, but only arrived in the summer of 1192, when he found King Henry with the Princes Richard and John besieging the Castle of the Garde Doloureuse. The borders of England and Wales, and the city of Gloucester are the scenes of action.

Note.—Henry II died in 1189, and Richard joined Philippe on his way to Palestine in 1190.

Vol. XXXVIII, *Tales of the Crusaders. The Talisman* (1825):

The time of this story is not exactly defined, but the whole action takes place within the thirty days' truce between 'the followers of the Cross and of the Crescent,' shortly before Philippe of France left Palestine in 1191. It opens with a duel between Saladin, disguised as Sheerkohf, and the Knight of the Sleeping Leopard which is fought on the oasis, The Diamond of the Desert, and it closes at the same place with the trial by combat between the same Knight and Conrade of Montserrat. The action takes place in the Syrian Desert near the Dead Sea, and in the Crusaders' camp between Jean d'Acre and Ascalon.

Note.—Richard concluded a treaty of peace with Saladin in 1192.

Vols. XXXIX, XL, *Woodstock ; or, The Cavalier* (1826):

The opening scene is in the Parish Church of Woodstock in autumn, 1652, on 'a day appointed for a solemn thanksgiving for the decisive victory at Worcester,' when the Rev. Nehemiah Holdenough, the Presbyterian Divine, was forced to yield his place in the pulpit to the Independent layman, Trusty Tomkins. The main action occupies about a fortnight, and, after the lapse of some years, the closing scene is the Royal Progress from Rochester to London in 1660. Woodstock, Windsor, and Charles II's court at Brussels are the scenes of action.

Note.—The battle of Worcester was fought in 1651.

Vol. XLI, *Chronicles of the Canongate. First Series.*

The Highland Widow (1827):

Hamish MacTavish was killed soon after 1746, Hamish Bean being then a child. The main incidents occur during a length of time not exactly defined, but probably from two to three weeks about twenty years later, when Hamish Bean enlisted. The scenes are on the lower slopes of Ben Cruachan, near the river Awe, in Argyleshire, and in Dumbarton.

The Two Drovers (1827):

Robin McCombich was the grandson of a friend of Rob Roy (1671–1734). The time occupied was that of a drover's journey from Doune to Cumberland, towards the end of the eighteenth century. The scenes are laid in Doune, Perthshire, and in a Cumbrian 'clachan.'

My Aunt Margaret's Mirror (1827):

The length of time of this narrative is not indicated, but it took place early in the eighteenth century, during one of Marlborough's campaigns in Flanders. Edinburgh and Rotterdam are the scenes of action.

The Tapestried Chamber ; or, The Lady in the Sacque (1827):

This ghost-story was the experience of one night in the autumn of 1781 or 1782 in Woodville Castle in one of the western counties of England.

Death of the Laird's Jock (1827):
'The date of the . . . story is about the latter years of Queen Elizabeth's reign; and the events took place in Liddesdale, a hilly and pastoral district of Roxburghshire.'

Vols. XLII, XLIII, *Chronicles of the Canongate. Second Series.*
Saint Valentine's Day; or, *The Fair Maid of Perth* (1828):
The story opens in Perth on St. Valentine's Eve, 13th February, when 'the Scottish sceptre was swayed by the gentle but feeble hand' of Robert III. It closes after Palm Sunday, 30th March, 1396, when there took place the celebrated fight between the clans Chattan and Quhele on the North Inch of Perth. The unhappy King being then informed of the death of the Duke of Rothesay, secluded himself in the Castle of Rothesay in Bute. The concluding chapter tells of the marriage of Henry and Catharine 'within four months after the battle of the North Inch.' Other incidents occur at Kinfauns Castle, Hill of Kinnoull, on the shores of Loch Tay, at Falkland Palace, and at Campsie on the Tay.
Note.—The Duke of Rothesay died in 1402.

Vols. XLIV, XLV, *Anne of Geierstein;* or, *The Maiden of the Mist* (1829):
The greater part of the action takes place in the autumn of 1474, beginning with the journey of the Philipsons from Lucerne to Geierstein in the Canton of Unterwalden. There is little specific reference to 1475, and the concluding events occur from July, 1476, to 'about three months after the battle of Nancy,' Jan., 1477, when Charles the Bold was killed. Other scenes of action are Bâle, La Ferrette, Brisach, Strasburg, Dijon, Aix in Provence, and Salius in Upper Burgundy.

Vols. XLVI, XLVII (part), *Tales of my Landlord. Fourth and Last Series. Count Robert of Paris* (1831):
The main incidents occur during a period of about four weeks in 1097, dealing with Court life and intrigues during the reign of Alexius Comnenus. The concluding chapter tells of the conquest of Jerusalem in 1099, and of the death of Alexius in 1118. The scenes are laid in Constantinople, and in the Crusaders' camp near Scutari.

Vols. XLVII (part), XLVIII (part), *Tales of my Landlord. Fourth and Last Series. Castle Dangerous* (1831):
The story opens on the fourteenth day before Palm Sunday, with the arrival at Hazelside of the minstrel Bertram and Lady Augusta Berkley in disguise. The main incidents end on Palm Sunday, 19th March, 1307, when news was brought of Bruce's victory at Loudon

Hill. 'A singular renewal of intercourse took place, many months afterwards, between Margaret of Hautlieu and her lover, Sir Malcolm Fleming.' All the action takes place in Douglasdale, in Kirkcudbrightshire.

Note.—The battle of Loudon Hill was not fought till 10th May, 1307.

Vol. XLVIII (conclusion), *Chronicles of the Canongate. First Series. The Surgeon's Daughter* (1827) :

The main incidents are covered by Richard Middlemas' life. He was born when the 'Forty-five' was not 'far gone by' in Middlemas, a village 'in one of the midland counties of Scotland.' About twenty-five years later he was trampled to death by an elephant by order of Hyder Ali. The conclusion occurs two years later, when Hartley 'fell a victim to his professional courage.' The scenes are laid in Scotland, Isle of Wight, Madras, Seringapatam, and Bangalore.

DICTIONARY OF THE WAVERLEY NOVELS

A

A—, MARQUIS OF. Leader of the opposition against the administration in which Sir William Ashton held office. He had also a private grievance against Sir William on account of the manner in which Lucy's engagement with his relative, the Master of Ravenswood, was received, and when ministerial changes put him in power he 'drove on . . . an appeal to the British House of Peers against those judgments of the courts of law by which Sir William became possessed of Ravenswood's hereditary property.' These steps, taken during Edgar's absence abroad, were considered to be in his 'true interest,' though 'counter to his inclinations.' A 'sincere but misjudging friend.' *Compare* ATHOLE. *The Bride of Lammermoor.*

ABDALLA. A Saracen slave in the train of Bois-Guilbert. *Ivanhoe.*

ABDALLAH EL HADGI (The Pilgrim). An ambassador from Saladin to King Richard. He arranged all preliminaries for the trial by combat at The Diamond of the Desert. *The Talisman.*

ABERCHALLADER. One of the Highlanders who joined the young Chevalier. *Waverley.*

ABNEY. A young man who reported that he had seen Albert Lee 'a mile from the field' of Worcester. But Sir Henry could not believe that Albert fled 'as early as young Abney.' *Woodstock.*

ACHILLES TATIUS. 'The Acolyte, or Follower' and leader of the Varangians, the imperial bodyguard. Hereward's superior officer, he introduced Hereward to the imperial circle as a soldier 'whose courage and presence of mind could best enable him to remark what passed around him' during the retreat to Laodicea. He conspired with Nicephorus and Agelastes to overthrow Alexius Comnenus, each of the three conspirators having privately determined on his own succession. 'A half-bred, half-acting, half-thinking, half-daring caitiff, whose poorest thoughts—and those which deserve that name must be poor indeed—are not the produce of his own understanding.' *Count Robert of Paris.*

ACLAND, SIR THOMAS. One of those who aided Charles II in his flight from Woodstock Lodge. He and young Knolles undertook to have horses in readiness at Henley. *Woodstock.*

ACUNHA, TERESA D'. A Spanish servant of the Countess of Glenallan. She aided Edward Geraldin Neville in carrying off the newborn child of Eveline Neville. 'If ever there was a fiend on earth in human form, that woman was ane.' *The Antiquary.*

ADAMS. One of the spectators whose greeting the Earl of Leicester returned ' with such ready and condescending courtesy,' as he hurried from the council-chamber ' to attend Her Majesty to her barge.' *Kenilworth.*

ADHEMAR, PRIOR. One of the early Wardours : ' an exemplary prelate ' who, ' from his strictness of morals, rigid execution of penance, joined to the charitable disposition of his mind, and the infirmities endured by his great age and ascetic habits, was called popularly " Hell-in-Harness." ' *The Antiquary.*

ADIE OF AIKENSHAW. One of the neighbours who came to Glendearg at Edward Glendinning's request to ' make amends ' for Halbert's supposed death. *The Monastery.*

ADONBEC EL HAKIM (The Physician). *See* SALADIN.

AGATHA. The name given to the Saxon Bertha by the Lady of Aspramonte as being less ' uncouth ' and ' heathenish.' *Count Robert of Paris.*

AGELASTES. A ' goodly old man, named Michael Agelastes, big, burly, and dressed like an ancient Cynic philosopher.' ' He appears to seek no office—he desires no consideration—he pays suit at court only when positively required to do so.' Yet ' this bookworm—the remnant of old heathen philosophy . . . has topp'd his part so well that he forces his Emperor to dissemble in his presence.' By his ' adroit sycophancy' he enticed Robert of Paris and Brenhilda to his house that the Emperor might gain ' influence ' over the ' tameless bull and unyoked heifer.' Afterwards, by furthering the amorous advances of Nicephorus towards Brenhilda he hoped to gain for himself the first place in the conspiracy against the Emperor. But Sylvanus put an end to all his guile. *Count Robert of Paris.*

AGLIONBY. ' The Recorder.' He presented an address and a ' fair-wrought purse with the twenty gold sovereigns ' to Queen Elizabeth during her progress to Kenilworth Castle. *Kenilworth.*

AIKWOOD, RINGAN. ' The Knockwinnock poinder ' : one of the ' sable personages ' who seized Dousterswivel during the burial service of Countess Joscelin in St. Ruth's. *The Antiquary.*

AIKWOOD, SAUNDERS. Ringan's father : one of Edie Ochiltree's cronies. *The Antiquary.*

AILFORD, ABBOT. *See* MEIGALLOT, CHARLES OF.

AINSLIE, EPPS. The name Maggie Steenson gave herself when tending Darsie Latimer after his injury in the raid on Joshua Geddes' fishing station. *Redgauntlet.*

ALASCO. *See* DOBOOBIE, DR. DEMETRIUS.

ALBANY, DUKE OF. Robert III's brother. ' He was experienced in the ways of courts, calm, cool, and crafty, fixing upon the points which he desired to attain, while they were yet far removed, and never losing sight of them, though the winding paths in which he trode might occasionally seem to point to a different direction.' 'The infirm and timid king was much governed' by his counsels, and he 'had the character of managing the temper of his brother and sovereign, so as might be most injurious to the interests and prospects of the young heir.' Rothesay was starved to death in his castle at Falkland. *The Fair Maid of Perth.*

ALBANY, JOSEPH. A fellow-student in Cambridge University, to whom Nehemiah Holdenough was 'particularly bound in friendship.' Political and religious convictions drove them into opposite camps when the Civil War broke out, and Nehemiah believed himself the indirect cause of Joseph's death during an attack on Clidesthrough Castle. Joseph escaped, however, and under his later title, Dr. Rochecliffe, received Nehemiah's pardon for having appeared to him in the Mirror Chamber as a ghost. 'Thou wert ever a naughty wag.' *Woodstock.*

ALBERICK. Squire to Prince Richard. *The Betrothed.*

ALDRICK, THE JESUIT. The Countess of Derby's confessor. *Peveril of the Peak.*

ALDROVAND, FATHER. 'A black monk of the house of Wenlock,' chaplain to Sir Raymond Berenger. He had been 'squire of the body to Count Stephen Mauleverer for twenty years,' and 'had not entirely forgotten in the cloister his ancient military experience.' Once convinced of Wilkin Flammock's fidelity, he ably seconded his efforts to protect Eveline Berenger and her castle. *The Betrothed.*

ALEXIUS COMNENUS. Emperor of the Greek Empire at the time of the first Crusade. 'By using fair words to one, threats to another, gold to the avaricious, power to the ambitious, and reasons to those that are capable of listening to them,' he secured the allegiance of the leaders as the Crusaders passed through Constantinople. At the same time he showed himself in internal affairs 'a wise and politic prince; his wisdom perhaps too much allied to cunning, but yet aiding him to maintain with great address that empire over the minds of his subjects, which was necessary for their good, and for maintaining his own authority.' 'The disorders of the times were the misfortune and the glory of Alexius.' *Count Robert of Paris.*

ALFAGI, HAMET. A convert who relapsed to the Moslem faith, and was condemned to the stake by the Grand Master. *Ivanhoe.*

ALIBI, TOM. The solicitor who managed the law affairs of Jonathan Grubbet. *Waverley.*

ALICE. 'A dowdy slipshod wench,' the drudge of John Whitecraft's inn. *Peveril of the Peak.*

ALICE. An attendant who, with Rose Flammock, accompanied Eveline Berenger when confined in her own apartment as a prison by Henry II. *The Betrothed.*

ALICE OF BOWER. One of the Black Dwarf's patients. *The Black Dwarf.*

ALICK. One of Sir Arthur Wardour's menservants. *The Antiquary.*

ALISON. One of the two 'aged crones' who kept the Countess of Leicester's apartments in order at Cumnor Place. *Kenilworth.*

ALLAN. One of the Highlanders ordered by Helen MacGregor to bind Bailie Nicol Jarvie and Frank Osbaldistone 'neck and heel together, and throw them into the Highland loch to seek for their Highland kinsfolk.' *Rob Roy.*

ALLAN. A 'cabalist' who served the Earl of Leicester, 'conjuring up the devil.' *Kenilworth.*

ALLAN, MAJOR. 'An old cavalier officer of experience,' next in command to Claverhouse at Drumclog. *Old Mortality.*

ALLAN, MRS. Colonel Mannering's housekeeper at Woodbourne. 'A decent old-fashioned Presbyterian matron.' *Guy Mannering.*

ALLAN, WILLIAM. The name by which Father Eustace was known in his youth. *The Monastery.*

ALLAN-A-DALE. A northern minstrel: one of Locksley's men. It was he who gave to the worthy Prior of Jorvaulx 'usage fit for no hound of good race,' and swore, the Prior complained, 'with many a cruel north-country oath, that he would hang me up on the highest tree in the greenwood.' *Ivanhoe.*

ALLASTER. The minstrel who played the lament when Rob Roy was taken. *Rob Roy.*

ALLEGRE. One of Louis' horsemen. For the hunt which followed Crèvecœur's audience at Plessis-les-Tours, he had harboured a boar that tried 'both dog and man.' *Quentin Durward.*

ALTAMONT, FREDERICK. The name by which Jack Bunce wished to be known, as being somewhat less plebeian than his own. *The Pirate.*

AMAURY, GILES. Grand Master of the Templars. 'Sponsor and most intimate friend' of Conrade of Montserrat, he prompted and furthered his schemes for increasing dissension between the allied princes. 'At the head of that singular body, to whom their order was everything, and their individuality nothing—seeking the advancement of its power, even at the hazard of that very religion which the fraternity were originally associated to protect—accused of heresy and witchcraft, although by their character Christian priests—suspected of secret league with the Soldan, though by oath devoted to the protection of the Holy Temple, or its recovery —the whole order, and the whole personal character of its commander, or Grand Master, was a riddle, at the exposition of which most men shuddered.' *The Talisman.*

AMBROSE. Prior Aymer's attendant monk. When the Prior fell into Locksley's hands, Ambrose was sent to Front-de-Bœuf's castle for help, but the 'dear friends' there had no time to listen. *Ivanhoe.*

AMBROSE, FATHER, and AMBROSIUS, ABBOT. *See* GLENDINNING, EDWARD.

AMBROSE, MR. 'A plausible and respectable-looking old servant, bred in the family, and who had risen from rank to rank in the Arthuret service, till he was become half-physician, half-almoner, half-butler, and entire governor.' He treated Alan Fairford 'with skill and attention.' *Redgauntlet.*

AMELOT. Damian de Lacy's youthful page. 'A forward cockeril for his years, wherever honour is to be won,' he made an attempt to relieve Wenlock when his master lay in the castle of Garde Douloureuse, disabled by wounds. *The Betrothed.*

ANDERSON. The name under which Montrose journeyed in disguise as the Earl of Menteith's attendant, when he came to raise the royal standard in Scotland. *A Legend of Montrose.*

ANDERSON, EPPIE. One of Meg Dods's maids, 'idle limmers—silly sluts,' in scolding whom Meg used considerable 'eloquence and energy.' *St. Ronan's Well.*
(*Limmer*, a woman of loose manners.)

ANDERSON, JOHN. Provost of Edinburgh 'upon the memorable day when your Majesty feasted all the nobles that were at feud together, and made them join hands in your presence.' *The Fortunes of Nigel.*

ANDERTON, THE TOWN-DRUMMER OF. The drummer in Gilfillan's company of Volunteers. Gilfillan refused to allow his followers to march to a profane tune, and ordered the drummer to beat the 119th Psalm! *Waverley.*

ANDREW. Ellangowan's old gardener. *Guy Mannering.*

ANDREW. Ludovic Lesly's servant. *Quentin Durward.*

ANDREW. One of Chrystal Croftangry's servants: 'a handy lad, who can lay the cloth, and take care besides of a pony.' *The Highland Widow.*

ANDREWS. One of the dragoons who were with Sergeant Bothwell at Milnwood when Harry Morton was arrested. *Old Mortality.*

ANGUS, THE 'YERL' (Earl) OF. The commander of a regiment levied by the Covenanters in support of King William, while 'others that stude up for purity of doctrine and freedom of conscience, were determined to hear the breath o' the Jacobites before they took part again them.' This regiment was the first beginning of the celebrated Cameronian Regiment. *Old Mortality.*

ANNA COMNENA, PRINCESS. The 'accomplished' daughter of the Emperor Alexius and his wife Irene, 'known to our times by her literary talents, which record the history of her father's reign.' Against the reproach of partiality in her record she maintains, 'I have been limited by the inviolable fidelity with which I respect the truth.' That she retained some of the weaknesses of the 'fair sex' is indicated by her 'natural desire to please' the comely barbarian Hereward, by her irritation under Count Robert's apparent neglect, and by the changeableness of her attitude towards her husband, Nicephorus, when he fell under the Emperor's displeasure. *Count Robert of Paris.*

Note.— Scott says that Anna 'might be seven-and-twenty' at the time of the main events, (i.e. about 1096). But she was born only in 1083.

ANNABELLA, QUEEN. Consort of Robert III : 'a daughter of the noble house of Drummond, gifted with a depth of sagacity and firmness of mind, which exercised some restraint over the levities of a son who respected her, and sustained on many occasions the wavering resolution of her royal husband.' *The Fair Maid of Perth.*

Note.—Scott has antedated the Queen's death by a few years.

ANNAPLE. Hobbie Elliot's old nurse. *The Black Dwarf.*

ANSELM. One of Front-de-Bœuf's men. He was ordered to 'see that seething pitch and oil are ready to pour on the heads of these audacious traitors' who were attacking the castle. *Ivanhoe.*

ANSELM, PRIOR. Prior of the Dominicans : confessor to King Robert. 'The chief objects which his education and habits taught him to keep in view were the extension of the dominion and the wealth of the church, and the suppression of heresy, both of which he endeavoured to accomplish by all the means which his situation afforded him. But he honoured his religion by the sincerity of his own belief, and by the morality which guided his conduct in all ordinary situations.' *The Fair Maid of Perth.*

ANSTER, HOB. The 'cowardly dog' who remonstrated with Dr. Luke Lundin when told to have Mother Nieneven seized and committed to the tolbooth. *The Abbot.*

ANTHONY. Meg Dods' humpbacked postilion : 'as absolute in his department as Mrs. Dods herself.' On the day of Frank Tyrrel's disappearance he heard 'twa shots gang aff as he was watering the auld naig down at the burn. . . . but he thought it was auld Pirner out wi' the double barrel, and he wasna keen of making himself a witness, in case he suld have been caa'd on in the Poaching Court.' *St. Ronan's Well.*

ANTHONY. One of the English soldiers quartered on Tom Dickson in Hazelside. According to the rules prescribed by Sir John de Walton for the 'out-garrison' he and Bend-the-Bow made enquiry concerning the business of the travellers Bertram and Augustine. They decided to refuse 'free passage into a garrison of a thousand men of all ranks, to a youth who has been so lately attacked by a contagious disorder,' and suggested that Augustine be left at the convent. *Castle Dangerous.*

ANTIQUARY, THE. *See* OLDBUCK, JONATHAN.

ANTON. One of Harry Gow's 'comrades' in the smithy. With Cuthbert, Dingwell, and Ringan, he was left to protect Catharine Glover while Harry went with her father to attend the enquiry into Oliver Proudfute's death. *The Fair Maid of Perth.*

ANTONIO. A youth from the Grison country who acted as guide to Seignor and Arthur Philipson on their journey from Lucerne to Geierstein: 'obtuse in his understanding, but kind and faithful in his disposition.' *Anne of Geierstein.*

ANWOLD. Torchbearer at Rotherwood. *Ivanhoe.*

APOLLYON. Herman von Arnheim's favourite horse, 'jet black, without a hair of white either on his face or feet.' That he bore the name of a foul fiend 'was secretly considered as tending to sanction the evil reports which touched the house of Arnheim.' *Anne of Geierstein.*

ARBROATH, LORD. One of the leaders of Queen Mary's army at Langside. He rode against Lord Seyton to reach the post of danger first—an 'ill-omened haste, and most unhappy strife.' *The Abbot.*

ARCHER. An 'unworthy' friend of Colonel Mannering in India. He was largely responsible for the quarrel with Vanbeest Brown. *Guy Mannering.*

ARCHERFIELD, VISCOUNT. Brother of Archer: 'a poor Scottish peer.' *Guy Mannering.*

ARCHIBALD, DUNCAN. John's cousin —the stabler in Inverary. *The Heart of Midlothian.*

ARCHIBALD, JOHN. The Duke of Argyle's 'groom of the chambers.' He attended Jeanie Deans part of the way to Richmond Park when she was taken by the Duke to see the Queen, and afterwards escorted Jeanie and Mrs. Dutton to Roseneath. 'A decent, elderly gentleman,' whose whole demeanour was marked by a 'solemn courtesy.' *The Heart of Midlothian.*

ARDENVOHR, KNIGHT OF. *See* CAMPBELL, SIR DUNCAN.

ARGENTIN, SIEUR D'. One of the nobles of Burgundy in attendance on Charles the Bold when he retired to Upper Burgundy after the defeat at Morat: 'the future historian of that busy period.' *Anne of Geierstein.*

ARGYLE, ARCHIBALD, MARQUIS OF (8th Earl). 'Gillespie Grumach.' On him as the 'predominating influence' in the West Highlands 'the confidence of the Convention of Estates was reposed with the utmost security,' but 'though possessed of considerable abilities and great power' he showed himself unfit to match Montrose. His paternal territories were ravaged, and a few months later his army was completely routed at Inverlochy. 'This heavy loss was exceeded,' however, by his own 'inglorious conduct' in watching the battle from the safety of a galley on the loch. 'A better man in the cabinet than in the field.' *A Legend of Montrose.*

(*Grumach,* ill-favoured.)

ARGYLE, ARCHIBALD, EARL OF (9th Earl). 'That Argyle that suffered ... in the persecution': grandfather of John, Duke of Argyle and Greenwich. While still Lord of Lorn he was saved from four English troopers by Stephen Butler, and 'having no other present means of recompense' he gave Stephen a letter of acknowledgment. It was this letter that Jeanie Deans received from Reuben Butler, and showed to the Duke John in London. *The Heart of Midlothian.*

ARGYLE AND GREENWICH, JOHN, DUKE OF.

(1) A protector of Rob Roy. His testimonial convinced Squire Inglewood of 'Robert Campbell's' good faith. 'A worthy public-spirited nobleman, and a credit to the country, and a friend and benefactor to the trade o' Glasgow.' *Rob Roy.*

(2) 'A real Scotsman—a true friend to the country.' 'The animated and eloquent opposition which he had offered to the severe measures' proposed against Edinburgh after the Porteous Riot, gave personal offence to Queen Caroline. But it was his 'dearest pride and honour' to stand up in defence of his native country, and he was 'prepared with indifference' for 'the frowns or smiles of a court.' He lent a ready ear to Jeanie Deans' appeal, and, in spite of his strained relations with the Queen, successfully presented his protégée. From this time he proved a beneficent patron to her and her friends. *The Heart of Midlothian.*

ARGYLE, ARCHIBALD, DUKE OF. Brother and successor to John of Argyle and Greenwich. He had not 'the same intimacy' with the Butlers, but 'continued the protection which his brother had extended towards them.' *The Heart of Midlothian.*

ARION. One of the maritime deities in a pageant welcoming Queen Elizabeth to Kenilworth Castle. Michael Lambourne played the part instead of Wayland Smith, whom he had driven from the castle, and played it with an 'unpremeditated buffoonery' which answered the purpose 'probably better than the set speech would have done.' *Kenilworth.*

ARLINGTON, EARL OF. *See* BENNET, HARRY.

ARMSTRONG. One of the commonest clan names in Liddesdale. *Guy Mannering.*

ARMSTRONG, ARCHIE. The celebrated court jester. 'Folly is his best wisdom.' *The Fortunes of Nigel.*

ARMSTRONG, GRACE. Hobbie Elliot's cousin and bride. She was carried off by Willie of Westburnflat when Hobbie's stackyard and steading were burnt, but by the Black Dwarf's orders was taken home again the same day. '"She's twice as clever about the house as my sisters . . . and is the best goer about the toun, now that grannie is off the foot hersell."' *The Black Dwarf.*

ARMSTRONG, JOHN. The Laird's Jock : son of the Laird of Mangerton, and himself afterwards Laird. His youthful title was 'distinguished by so many bold and desperate achievements that he retained it even after his father's death.' With the huge two-handed sword bequeathed to him by Hobbie Noble he was the unrivalled champion of the Border counties. In process of time he became old and helpless and bedridden. But when the English champion, Foster, sent a challenge to the best swordsman in Liddesdale, his heart exulted, and 'to nerve his son to still bolder exertions, he conferred upon him, as champion of his clan and province, the celebrated weapon which he had hitherto retained in his own custody.' 'Wrapt in plaids and blankets,' he was carried out to the place of *rencontre*, but only to see 'his country dishonoured, and his sword, long the terror of their race, in possession of an Englishman.' 'He tossed his arms wildly to Heaven and uttered a cry of indignation, horror, and despair which . . . resembled the cry of a dying lion more than a human sound.' *Death of the Laird's Jock.*

Note.—Scott suggested this 'strong moment of agonizing passion' as a suitable subject for the pencil of an artist.

ARNHEIM, HERMAN VON. The last Baron of Arnheim, Anne of Geierstein's maternal grandfather. Like his ancestors he 'strove to enlarge the boundaries of human knowledge,' but there were 'fools who . . . annexed the idea of witchcraft and sorcery to the possession of knowledge and wisdom.' His mysterious intercourse with Dannischemend and his subsequent marriage with Hermione greatly strengthened the popular notions. But the mysteries arose out of his own and Dannischemend's membership of the Secret Tribunal, the Holy Vehme. *Anne of Geierstein.*

ARNHEIM, HERMIONE, BARONESS VON. Dannischemend's daughter and Baron Herman's wife. 'Amid many excellencies, she had one peculiarity allied to imprudence. She availed herself of her foreign dress and manners, as well as of a beauty, which was said to have been marvellous, and an agility seldom equalled, to impose upon and terrify the ignorant German ladies, who, hearing her speak Persian and Arabic, were already disposed to consider her as over closely connected with unlawful arts. She was of a fanciful and imaginative disposition, and delighted to place herself in such colours and circumstances as might confirm their most ridiculous suspicions, which she considered only as matter of sport.' Her sudden death on the morning appointed for the christening of her daughter Sybilla was ascribed to 'poison, administered by the Baroness Steinfeldt.' *Anne of Geierstein.*

ARNHEIM, SYBILLA. Baron Herman's daughter, and mother of Anne of Geierstein. 'I never heard that the strong imputation of sorcery which attached to her house, prevented numerous applications, from persons of the highest distinctions in the Empire, to her legal guardian, the Emperor, for the rich heiress's hand in marriage. Albert of Geierstein, however, though an exile, obtained the preference.' *Anne of Geierstein.*

ARNISTON. An advocate: a 'clever chield.' *The Heart of Midlothian.*

ARNOT, ANDREW. One of Louis' Scottish Guard. Through the gossip of his groom, Saunders Steed, he was able to inform his comrades that the Countess of Croye and her aunt had arrived at the Castle of Plessis-les-Tours. *Quentin Durward.*

ARTAVAN OF HAUTLIEU. The knight who tried to free the Princess of Zulichium from the Magi's spell. *Count Robert of Paris.*

ARTHURET, THE MISSES SERAPHINA AND ANGELICA. 'The Vestals of Fairladies' under whose care Nanty Ewart placed Alan Fairford. 'Being of a good family,' Nanty explained, 'the old lasses have turned a kind of saints, and nuns and so forth. . . . There are plenty of priests and stout young scholars, and such like about the house—it's a hive of them.' Amongst them at the time of Alan's stay was the 'holy Father Buonaventure,' 'as high in rank as he is eminently endowed with good gifts,' and to him Alan was obliged to give certain undertakings before being allowed to depart. *Redgauntlet.*

ASHLER, JOCK. The St. Ronan's 'stane-mason, that ca's himsell an arkiteck.' *St. Ronan's Well.*

ASHTON, COLONEL SHOLTO DOUGLAS. Lucy's elder brother. He 'trode the path of ambition with a haughtier step than his father,' and shared fully his mother's plans for the family's advancement. In spite of a warm affection for Lucy he subjected her to 'bitter taunts and occasional violence' after her engagement with the Master of Ravenswood, and to the Master himself he swore, 'if you refuse my open challenge, there is no advantage I will not take of you, no indignity with which I will not load you, until the very name of Ravenswood shall be the sign of every thing that is dishonourable.' *The Bride of Lammermoor.*

ASHTON, HENRY. Lucy's younger brother. 'At an age when trifles chiefly occupied his mind,' he 'made her the confidant of all his pleasures and anxieties, his success in field-sports, and his quarrels with his tutor and instructors.' But he was a spoilt boy, and 'was made the instrument of adding to his sister's torments.' *The Bride of Lammermoor.*

ASHTON, LADY. Sir William's wife. 'In the haughtiness of a firmer character, higher birth, and more decided views of aggrandizement, the lady looked with some contempt on her husband,' but his interest and their family's was the motive of all her actions, and she was ever ready to supply 'the courage in which he was deficient.' 'Her proud, vindictive, and predominating spirit' hated the Ravenswood family with such intensity that she scrupled at no means by which she might deceive Lucy into a belief in her lover's unfaithfulness. *The Bride of Lammermoor.*

ASHTON, LUCY. Sir William's daughter. Of a 'gentle, soft, timid, and feminine' nature, she had a 'compliant and easy disposition,' and was 'borne along by the will of others with as little power of opposition as the flower which is flung into a running stream.' Betrayed into loving Ravenswood by the temporizing schemes of her father, and 'exasperated to frenzy by a long tract of unremitting persecution' from her mother, she was finally crushed and broken by her lover's selfish blindness. *The Bride of Lammermoor.*

ASHTON, SIR WILLIAM. Lucy's father. Born of a family which 'had only risen to wealth and political importance during the great civil wars,' he 'contrived to amass considerable sums of money' and to advance to high office in the State. He was a 'cool lawyer and able politician,' and managed through a series of complicated financial transactions to establish himself on the ruins of the Ravenswood family. Subtle and timeserving even in social life he prepared the way for poor Lucy's tragedy by the selfish inconsistency of his intercourse with the Master of Ravenswood. *The Bride of Lammermoor.*

ASKEW, DR. The collector who paid Osborne sixty guineas for the *Game of Chess*, 1474. 'At Dr. Askew's sale, this inestimable treasure blazed forth in its full value, and was purchased by Royalty itself, for £170! *Antiquary.*

ASPRAMONTE. *See* PARIS, COUNTESS OF.

ASPRAMONTE, KNIGHT OF. An old Norman knight who 'amid the general sack of the monastery' of St. Augustin seized upon Bertha and her mother as his prize. 'Struck with her beauty, he designed her as an attendant upon his daughter,' hoping that she might wean Brenhilda from 'those martial amusements which had so sensibly grieved' him. *Count Robert of Paris.*

ASPRAMONTE, LADY OF. Brenhilda's mother. Like her daughter, she had in her youth nourished fancies for 'martial amusements.' 'She had imbibed an idea . . . that the Saxons were heathens . . . or at least heretics, and made a positive point with her husband that the bondswoman and girl who were to attend on her person and that of her daughter, should be qualified for the office by being anew admitted into the Christian church by baptism.' *Count Robert of Paris.*

ASTARTE. One of the white-robed nymphs who acted 'as a species of living book-desk, to support and extend the parchment rolls in which the Princess recorded her own wisdom, or from which she quoted that of others.' *Count Robert of Paris.*

ATHELSTANE, LORD OF CONINGSBURGH. Representative of the Saxon monarchs. Though vain of his descent and 'both stout of heart and strong of person,' he was 'slow, irresolute, procrastinating and unenterprising.' All Cedric's enthusiasm for the restoration of the Saxon line could not rouse him to action. 'Since these plots were set in agitation,' he said, 'I have had nothing but hurried journeys, indigestions, blows and bruises, imprisonments and starvation.' 'Bread and water and a dungeon are marvellous mortifiers of ambition.' *Ivanhoe.*

ATHOLE. One of the chief of Sir William Ashton's political opponents. He 'promised his interest to old Ravenswood,' and Sir William feared he might find in Edgar a 'ready tool' for 'those who are watching the downfall of our administration.' Compare A—, MARQUIS OF. Athole is only incidentally referred to, and that before the Marquis of A— is introduced. The two may be the same. *The Bride of Lammermoor.*

AUCHTERMUCHTY, JOHN. The common carrier of Kinross. 'He never wanted good reasons for stopping upon the road.' His delay at the Keiry-craigs led on one occasion to Roland Graeme's prolonged stay in Kinross, and on another to the squabble between Henry Seyton and Jasper Dryfesdale, which ended in Jasper's death. *The Abbot.*

AUGHTERMUGGITIE, LAIRD OF. A laird in the west from whom Davie Deans bought cows. *The Heart of Midlothian.*

AUGUSTINE. The name under which the Lady Augusta of Berkley travelled when disguised as Bertram's son. *Castle Dangerous.*

AULD AILIE. The ghost of Mucklestane Moor. *The Black Dwarf.*

'AUNT MARGARET.' *See* BOTHWELL, MARGARET.

AUNT PEGGY. One of the few ladies who crossed Mr. Saunders Fairford's threshold. She 'comes to dinner of a Sunday.' *Redgauntlet.*

AUNTIE MEG (*née* Middlemas). Mause Headrigg's 'auld graning tittie' in the Gallowgate of Glasgow. Cuddie bestowed his mother with her when he became Harry Morton's servant. *Old Mortality.*
(*Graning,* groaning. *Tittie,* sister.)

AVENEL FAMILY, THE.

WALTER (1). Baron of Avenel, an ancient Barony 'not very far from the patrimony of St. Mary's.' He was killed in one of the 'bloody and unsparing skirmishes' which showed that the Scots' spirit had not been destroyed at Pinkie. 'A true Scotsman and a good soldier.'

ALICE (1). Baron Walter's Lady. Obliged after her husband's death to take refuge first with Martin and Tibb Tacket, and afterwards with Dame Glendinning, she bore herself with the same meekness and courtesy as she had shown in the days of her prosperity. But her spirit was broken, and before many years had passed she left her daughter Mary to Elspeth's care. 'High in judgment as in rank,' she often read 'good things out of a thick black volume with silver clasps.'

MARY (1). Daughter of the Baron Walter and his Lady. 'She was by nature mild, pensive, and contemplative,' and from her earliest youth was conscious of something in herself 'which fraud flies from and which imposture cannot deceive.' 'I only can judge,' she told Herbert Glendinning, 'of signs, words and actions of little outward import, more truly than those around me,' but at the same time she believed that she had more than once seen the White Lady of Avenel. This mysterious spirit, she thought, guided her, after Halbert's supposed death, to the sacred volume which brought her comfort and 'the serenity of Heaven.'

LADY OF AVENEL (2). During her husband's frequent absences the castle of Avenel was 'as melancholy and solitary a residence for its lady as could well be imagined.' 'To superintend the tasks of numerous female domestics was the principal part of the Lady's daily employment,' and she suffered much from 'the extremity of her desolate feeling.' But the advent of her spirited page, Roland Graeme, brought a warm affection into her daily life, and years later she 'wept for joy' when he was found to be 'the sole surviving branch of her own family.'

KNIGHT OF AVENEL. See GLENDINNING, HALBERT.

JULIAN (1). Walter's younger brother. After his brother's death he seized the house and lands of Avenel, but 'for very shame's sake' he did not allow Mary and her mother to be 'absolutely dependent on the charity of Elspeth Glendinning.' He lived 'a light and evil life,' and was 'a party to almost every dark and mysterious transaction ... in that wild and military frontier.' He was pledged to support Lord James Stewart, but his private animosity against Henry Warden drove him eventually to lead the vassals of St. Mary's against Sir John Foster.

See also CATHERINE OF NEWPORT.

ROLAND. *See* GRAEME, ROLAND.

WHITE LADY OF AVENEL (1). The mysterious spirit associated with the fortunes of the Avenels and 'aye seen to yammer and wail before ony o' that family dies.' She rescued Lady Alice's 'thick black volume with silver clasps' from both Father Philip and Father Eustace, and afterwards took Halbert Glendinning into 'the bowels of the earth,' there to find it lying in a pyramid of fire, yet unconsumed. She did 'mony braw services' besides these, but the union of Halbert with Mary Avenel tied the 'knot of fate,' and she wept as she sang to Edward 'Fall'n is lofty Avenel!'

(*To yammer*, to shriek.)

(2) When Roland Avenel and Catherine Seyton were united, she 'was seen to sport by her haunted well with a zone of gold around her bosom as broad as the baldrick of an Earl.' (1) *The Monastery*, (2) *The Abbot*.

AYLFORD, ALDERMAN. One of the spectators whose greeting the Earl of Leicester returned 'with such ready and condescending courtesy' as he hurried from the council-chamber 'to attend her Majesty to her barge.' *Kenilworth*.

AYLMER, MRS. The lady with whom Alice Lee spent the day following Charles II's flight, when Woodstock Lodge was in Cromwell's hands. *Woodstock*.

AYMER, PRIOR OF JORVAULX ABBEY. 'A free and jovial priest who loves the wine-cup and the bugle-horn better than bell and book.' He accompanied Brian de Bois-Guilbert to the tournament at Ashby-de-la-Zouch, and afterwards fell into Locksley's hands. By a reference, in 'the jargon of chivalry,' to Rebecca as a 'witch of Endor,' he led the Grand Master to deal with her 'as the Christian law and our own high office warrant.' *Ivanhoe.*

B

B—, LORD. One of the 'faithful friends' who met Father Buonaventure at Joe Crackenthorp's inn: a 'fiery young man,' 'with the generous spirit of a young English nobleman.' *Redgauntlet.*

BABBY (Barbara). (1) Mrs. Mailsetter's shop-girl.
(2) Bailie Littlejohn's maid. (1) and (2) *The Antiquary.*

BABIE (Barbara). Old Alice's attendant. *The Bride of Lammermoor.*

BABY CHARLES. See CHARLES, PRINCE OF WALES.

BADGER, WILL. Sir Hugh Robsart's 'huntsman and sworn servant,' 'the old and favourite attendant of the knight who acted alike as squire of his body and superintendent of his sports.' *Kenilworth.*

BAILIE, THE. See TAMLOWRIE, LAIRD OF.

BAILLIE, GABRIEL. Nephew of Meg Merrilies; known amongst the gipsies as Gabriel Faa, and as Tod Gabbie or Hunter Gabbie in Liddesdale. He was pressed into naval service under Captain Pritchard of the *Shark*, but deserted in order to warn Hatteraick of the *Shark's* approach. Later he chanced to sail to the East Indies with Vanbeest Brown, and recognised him then as the lost heir, and again when he saw him in Liddesdale. Obeying his aunt's commands, 'from a belief that she was gifted with supernatural inspirations,' he gave conclusive testimony regarding the identity of Vanbeest Brown with the lost heir. *Guy Mannering.* (*Tod*, fox.)

BAILLIE, GENERAL. 'A Presbyterian officer of skill and fidelity.' He was placed in command of the army raised to help Argyle after Montrose had ravaged his territories. *A Legend of Montrose.*

BAILLIE, GILES. Father of Gabriel. *Guy Mannering.*

BAILLIE, JEAN. See SALMON, PATRICO.

BAILLIE AND WHITTINGTON. A firm whose bill formed one of the assets carried off by Rashleigh Osbaldistone. *Rob Roy.*

BAILZOU, ANNAPLE. A beggar and fortune-teller. Meg Murdockson sold Effie Deans' child to her, and some years later she in turn sold the child to Donacha Dhu. *The Heart of Midlothian.*

BAJAZET. Mistress Chiffinch's 'little heathen Sultan,' 'superbly dressed like an Oriental page, with gold bracelets on his naked arms, and a gold collar around his equally bare neck.' *Peveril of the Peak.*

BALAFRÉ, LE. See LESLY, LUDOVIC.

BALCHRISTIE, MRS. JANET. Jenny, 'the favourite sultana' of the old

Laird of Dumbiedikes, and the young Laird's housekeeper. On the eve of his marriage the Laird found courage to get rid of her and her niece. 'They were a bad pack,' he said, 'steal'd meat and mault, and loot the carters magg the coals.' *The Heart of Midlothian.*
(*Magg*, carry off by stealth.)

BALDER. A 'grisly old wolf-dog,' an 'indulged favourite' of Cedric. *Ivanhoe.*

BALDERSTONE, CALEB. The only male domestic who remained to the house of Ravenswood in Wolf's Crag. Even in this barren refuge he would not acknowledge the family's decay, and he tried by sheer force of words to cover their poverty and want. Alike in providing hospitality and in evading it, he showed an inexhaustible fertility of resource, which was at times, however, more humorous than effective. But in spite of all his brave defiance, his heart was heavy with the portents of fate, and when he saw his master die, his own life lost 'its salt and its savour.' *The Bride of Lammermoor.*

BALDRICK. A Saxon hero, founder of the house of Baldringham. He married Vanda, a fair Briton, but growing weary of her in two years, he caused her to be strangled. In order to secure her wedding ring to show as a token they had done the deed, her murderers were obliged to sever her finger. But long before they returned to Baldrick she herself appeared, and, 'holding up to him her bloody hand, made him fearfully sensible how well his savage commands had been obeyed.' Thereafter she haunted him 'in peace and war, in desert, court, and camp.' *The Betrothed.*

BALDRINGHAM, AELFREID (*Aelfreida?*) OF. Eveline Berenger's Saxon grandparent. *The Betrothed.*

BALDRINGHAM, ERMENGARDE, LADY OF. Sir Raymond Berenger's maternal aunt, a noble Saxon lady who 'looked with contempt and hatred on all innovations that had been introduced since the battle of Hastings.' Eveline spent a night with her when travelling to Gloucester, and was obliged to obey the family traditions by sleeping in the chamber of Redfinger. *The Betrothed.*

BALDWIN. Brother of Godfrey of Bouillon, and after his death King of Jerusalem. 'Remaining in attendance by the Emperor's chair' after swearing allegiance to Alexius Comnenus, he witnessed the 'personal affront' given by Count Robert, and answered the Emperor's enquiries concerning him. *Count Robert of Paris.*

BALDWIN, ARCHBISHOP OF CANTERBURY. Thomas à Becket's successor. 'As he had himself preached the Crusade and brought the Constable and many others into that holy engagement,' he rigidly refused to allow de Lacy to delay his departure. 'The advancement of the Crusade was the chief business of his life, its success the principal cause of his pride; and, if the sense of possessing the powers of eloquent persuasion, and skill to bend the minds of men to his purpose, was blended with his religious zeal, still the tenor of his life, and afterwards his death before Ptolemais, showed that the liberation of the Holy Sepulchre from the infidels was the unfeigned object of all his exertions.' *The Betrothed.*

BALFOUR, JOHN, OF KINLOCH, OR BURLEY. One of the murderers of Archbishop Sharpe: a leader in the Covenanters' army. 'Daring in design, precipitate and violent in execution, and going to the very extremity of the most rigid recusancy,' he yet saw that an insistence on the most violent tenets would bring 'nothing but ruin to the general cause.' Hoping to increase his influence with the more liberal part of the army, he welcomed Harry Morton and furthered his advance. After Bothwell Bridge his spirit remained 'indomitable,' and 'with art equal to his courage and obstinacy,' he continued to work for the cause he had at heart. 'My conduct is open to men and angels,' he said to Harry Morton. 'The deed was not done in a corner; I am here in arms to avow it, and care not where, or by whom, I am called on to do so; whether in the council, the field of battle, the place of execution, or the day of the last great trial.' *Old Mortality.*

BALIOL, MISTRESS MARTHA BETHUNE. A lady of 'quality and fortune' who honoured Mr. Croftangry 'with a great share of her friendship,' and gave him some of the materials for his *Chronicles of the Canongate.* 'Living to the utmost term of human life,' she 'was yet, in gaiety of spirits and admirable sweetness of temper, capable of being agreeable, and even animating society, for those who write themselves in the vanward of youth.' 'Although well acquainted with the customs of other countries, her manners had been chiefly formed in her own, at a time when great folk lived within little space, and when the distinguished names of the highest society gave to Edinburgh the *éclat,* which we now endeavour to derive from the unbounded expense and extended circle of our pleasures.' *The Highland Widow.*

Note.—In this lady the author 'designed to shadow out in its leading points the interesting character of a dear friend,' Mrs. Murray Keith, who died in 1831. 'The author had, on many occasions, been indebted to her vivid memory for the *substratum* of his Scottish fictions.' *The Highland Widow* is given 'very much as the excellent old lady used to tell the story.'

BALIOL, SIR BERNARD BETHUNE. An ancestor of Mistress Martha belonging to James VI's time. *The Highland Widow.*

BALIOL, SIR RICHARD BETHUNE. Mistress Martha's father: one of those who 'had attempted to change the fortunes of Britain in 1715.' *The Highland Widow.*

BALL. Mysie Happer's palfrey.

When Mysie was helping Sir Piercie to escape she pretended to the landlord of the Gled's Nest that Ball had fallen by the way, and so secured from him a nag in Ball's place. *The Monastery.* (*Gled*, kite.)

BALLENKEIROCH. A clansman of Fergus MacIvor. He bore an undying enmity to the Baron of Bradwardine for the death of his son Ronald. *Waverley.*

BALMAWHAPPLE, LAIRD OF. *See* FALCONER, MR.

BALNEAVES. One of the citizens who met together on St. Valentine's Day 'for investigating the affray of the preceding evening.' *The Fair Maid of Perth.*

BALQUIDDER LADS. Redoubtable friends of Rob Roy. *Rob Roy.*

BALRUDDERY, LAIRD OF. Third cousin of the Laird of Ellangowan. Ellangowan earned Sir Thomas Kittlecourt's ill-will by supporting his relative in a parliamentary election. *Guy Mannering.*

BALUE, JOHN OF. Cardinal and Bishop of Auxerre. One of Louis' most influential counsellors. 'Dazzled, doubtless, by the suddenness of his elevation' from an obscure position, he thought unduly well of himself, and in a moment of wounded vanity yielded to Crèvecœur's advances. For so working upon Louis' 'peculiar foibles' as to lead him to visit the Duke of Burgundy in Peronne, he suffered imprisonment for eleven years in one of the iron cages which he himself, 'with horrible ingenuity,' is said to have invented. *Quentin Durward.*

BALVENY, LORD. A kinsman of the Earl of Douglas, and his companion when he dealt summary justice to the criminals in Falkland Castle. *The Fair Maid of Perth.*

BAMBERG, BISHOP OF. An ecclesiastic who gave 'indisputable testimony' in favour of Hermione, Baroness von Arnheim, comparing her to 'a doctor of theology in the dress of an Eastern dancing-girl.' *Anne of Geierstein.*

BAN. One of Bradwardine's deer greyhounds. *Waverley.*

BANDILIER, CAPTAIN. *See* GUNN, DUGALD.

BANDYBRAWL, LAIRD OF. *See* DEILBELICKET.

BANGTEXT, CAPTAIN SALATHIEL. A 'godly gentleman,' whose muster-roll was first handed to the Duke of Argyle by Jeanie Deans instead of Lorne's letter to Stephen Butler. *The Heart of Midlothian.*

BARAK EL HADGI. A Fakir whose physical ailments Adam Hartley treated successfully. In virtue of promises then made Adam applied to him for help when he went to Seringapatam with the hope of saving Menie Gray. But in presence of his superior, Hali ben Khaledoun, Barak affected an 'extreme humility' which for a time deceived Adam. *The Surgeon's Daughter.*

BARBER, NICOL. A friend of Dorothy Glover. Dorothy had recourse to him for comfort when the report of Harry Gow's death sent Catharine running distraught through the streets to see Harry with her own eyes. *The Fair Maid of Perth.*

BARCALDINE. *See* CAMPBELL, CAPTAIN.

BARDON, HUGH. Prince John's scout-master. He supplied the men who went with Fitzurse to make a secret attack on Richard. *Ivanhoe.*

BARESWORD, DOUGALD. *See* DEIL-BELICKET.

BARLOWE. One of the crew of the *Fortune's Favourite* who wished Captain Cleveland well. *The Pirate.*

BARNES. The valet who accompanied Colonel Mannering and Dominie Sampson to Edinburgh; the Dominie's 'pilot in ordinary.' *Guy Mannering.*

BARNES, BETTY. 'Long cook-maid to Mr. Warburton, the painful collector, but ah! the too careless custodier of the largest collection of ancient plays ever known.' Through the intervention of her spirit, the 'Author of Waverley' professed, he became possessed of 'those scraps of old plays' which figure in his pages. *The Fortunes of Nigel.*

BARRATTER, COUNSELLOR. An old Templar who lived in the Chambers immediately below Reginald Lowestoffe, and suffered great annoyance from the young gallant's tunes on the fiddle and French horn. *The Fortunes of Nigel.*

BARRI, GIRALDUS DE. Baldwin's companion, when he preached the Crusade throughout Wales; afterwards Bishop of St. David's. *The Betrothed.*

BARRON, DEACON. A Gandercleugh worthy. He had pronounced the walls of Jedediah Cleishbotham's 'small domicile' incapable of 'enduring such an elevation,' as a second storey with attics. But the 'pleasant turns of fortune' enabled Jedediah to 'simper' when he eventually saw the addition as a reality. For this he thanks 'the best of patrons, a pleased and indulgent reader.' *The Heart of Midlothian.*

BARSTOW, CAPTAIN. 'A Jesuit whose real name was Fenwicke.' One of the letters entrusted to Julian Peveril by the Countess of Derby for delivery in London was addressed to him, but when on the point of discharging this trust, Julian was effectually hindered by Fenella. *Peveril of the Peak.*

BARTHOLOMEW, BROTHER. 'A poor lay brother' who acted as guide to the English merchants Philipson on the first stage of their journey from La Ferette to Strasburg. He was one of a band of outlaws who had determined to rob the merchants, but his purpose was defeated by the appearance of the Black Priest of St. Paul's in the Chapel of the Ferry opposite Kirch-hoff. *Anne of Geierstein.*

BASH. One of the stag-hounds which were 'in at the death' with the King in Greenwich Park. *The Fortunes of Nigel.*

BATTIE. One of the stag-hounds which were 'in at the death' with the King in Greenwich Park. *The Fortunes of Nigel.*

BAULDIE. The old shepherd who told tales about the Black Dwarf to the landlord of the Wallace Inn and his friends. *The Black Dwarf.*

BAULDIE. Joshua Geddes' stable-lad: 'no Quaker, though his intercourse with the family had given him a touch of their prim sobriety of look and manner.' *Redgauntlet.*

BAULDY. The servant sent by Niel Blane to 'drive the pease and bear meal to the camp at Drumclog—he's a whig, and was the auld gudewife's pleughman . . . He maun say it's the last unce o' meal in the house, or, if he scruples to tell a lie, (as it's no likely he will when it's for the gude o' the house) he may wait till Duncan Glen . . . drives up the aitmeal to Tillietudlem.' *Old Mortality.*

(*Bear*, barley.)

BAWTY. The dog that accompanied Donald Bean Lean when he played the part of a pedlar to Gifted Gilfillan. *Waverley.*

BAXTER, PEG. A lass with whom James Wilkinson 'kept company' when in the Fusiliers. *Redgauntlet.*

BAYARD. (1) The palfrey intended by Laurence Goldthred for his bride's use, but converted by Wayland Smith to his own and the Countess of Leicester's service.

(2) The horse Michael Lambourne rode when sent by the Earl of Leicester to overtake Sir Richard Varney with a letter countermanding his orders concerning the Countess. *Kenilworth.*

BEACON, TOM. The groom who attended Chiffinch into the country when he went to meet Edward Christian and Alice Bridgenorth. *Peveril of the Peak.*

BEAN, DONALD. *See* LEAN, DONALD BEAN.

BEARCLIFF, DEACON. 'A man of great importance in the village.' The parcel which Vanbeest Brown received from Meg Merrilies and afterwards left in Mrs. MacCandlish's keeping was, after being 'properly inventoried' in Glossin's presence, deposited with him. *Guy Mannering.*

BEATRICE, SISTER. One of the sisters in St. Bride's convent, 'most of whom have been either sorely misused by time, or their comeliness destroyed by some mishap.' She was 'blessed with a winning gift of making comfits and syllabubs.' *Castle Dangerous.*

BEAUCHAMP. *See* BOHUN, HENRY.

BEAUCHAMP, LADY DIANA VERNON. The name given to Diana Vernon in virtue of her father's 'St. Germain's' title. *Rob Roy.*

(St. Germain, near Paris, was the seat of the Pretender's court.)

BEAUCHAMP, VISCOUNT. The name by which Sir Frederick Vernon was known among the Jacobites. *Rob Roy.*

BEAUFFET. Mrs. Bethune Baliol's butler. 'A full stand, as it is called in Scotland, of garments of a dark colour, gold buckles in his shoes, and at the knees of his breeches, with his hair regularly dressed and powdered, announced him to be a domestic of trust and importance.' 'He now enjoys ease with dignity in as far as his newly-married wife, Tibbie Shortacres, will permit him.' *The Highland Widow.*

BEAUJEU, LADY OF. King Louis' elder daughter, afterwards married to Peter of Bourbon. 'She was tall, and rather handsome, possessed eloquence, talent, and much of her father's sagacity, who reposed great confidence in her, and loved her as well perhaps as he loved any one.' *Quentin Durward.*

BEAUJEU, MONSIEUR DE. A French Count belonging to the young Chevalier's bodyguard. He was deputed to reduce Fergus Mac-Ivor's men to order while his quarrel with Edward Waverley was being settled by the Prince. *Waverley.*

BEAUJEU, MONSIEUR DE. Owner of the ordinary to which Lord Dalgarno introduced Nigel: 'pink of Paris and flower of Gascony— he who can tell the age of his wine by the bare smell—who distils his sauces in an alembic by the aid of Lully's philosophy—who carves with such exquisite precision, that he gives to noble, to knight, and squire, the portion of the pheasant which exactly accords with his rank. . . . the wellknown and general referee in all matters affecting the mysteries of Passage, Hazard, In and In, Penneeck, and Verquire, and what not. Why, Beaujeu is King of the Card-pack, and Duke of the Dice-box!' 'To have been a day in London and not to know Beaujeu is a crime of its own kind.' *The Fortunes of Nigel.*

BEAUMANOIR, LUCAS DE. Grand Master of the Templars. 'Hating sensuality, despising treasure, and pressing forward to that which they call the crown of martyrdom,' he devoted himself without reserve to the purification of his Order. He was 'zealous to slaying,' and when he read the 'goodly stuff' which the Prior Aymer wrote to Bois-Guilbert regarding Rebecca, he welcomed 'the opportunity of bursting the bands of this Delilah . . . this foul witch who hath flung her enchantments over a brother of the Holy Temple.' *Ivanhoe.*

BEAVER, CAPTAIN. Captain of the frigate in which Colonel Talbot sailed from Leith. *Waverley.*

BECK. A 'silly fool' at the Cleikum Inn who brought Mr. Touchwood's port 'into the sun.' *St. Ronan's Well.*

BEDROOKET, LADY. One of the few ladies who crossed Mr. Saunders Fairford's threshold. She 'calls ten times a-year for the quarterly payment of her jointure of four hundred merks.' *Redgauntlet.*

BELASH CASSIM. The Sirdar who accompanied Adam Hartley with a guard on his journey from Seringapatam to Bangalore. *The Surgeon's Daughter.*

BELLENDEN FAMILY, THE. *Old Mortality.*

SIR RALPH. The founder of Tillietudlem in 1350.

SIR ARTHUR. Lady Margaret's 'poor Sir Arthur': brother of Major Bellenden. After Montrose's victory at Kilsythe he 'put twenty whigs' into the dungeon of Tillietudlem. *Compare* SIR RICHARD.

SIR RICHARD. 'The late Sir Richard' who had served under Montrose. *Compare* SIR ARTHUR. *Note.*—Sir Richard is mentioned only once. He may be identical with Sir Arthur.

LADY MARGARET. 'Life-rentrix of the barony of Tillietudlem and others.' She lost her husband and two promising sons in the civil wars, 'but she had received her reward, for . . . Charles the Second had actually breakfasted at the Tower of Tillietudlem; an incident which formed, from that moment, an important era in the life of Lady Margaret.' After the Covenanters' success at Drumclog, Tillietudlem held out under Major Bellenden and Lord Evandale until conquered by mutiny and famine. Just for 'the want o'' some bits of sheep-skin that were lost in the confusion' Tillietudlem passed into the possession of Basil Olifant 'after they had fought a weary sort o' years about it.' But Lady Margaret was able to draw comfort from the thought that 'it has been Heaven's own freewill, as well as those of the kingdom where we live, to take away from us our estate, and from the King his throne.' *See also* TORWOOD, EARL OF.

WILLIE. One of Lady Margaret's sons: Edith's father.

EDITH. Lady Margaret's granddaughter and 'only earthly care.' Her acquaintance with Harry Morton, begun under Major Bellenden's roof, ripened into a warm friendship, and when Harry's life was in danger she saved it through the influence of his rival, Lord Evandale. After he became one of the acknowledged leaders of the Covenanters she 'wept more over his fallen character, blighted prospects, and dishonoured name, than over the distresses of her own house,' and such was the 'waywardness' with which after many years her heart reverted to former times that she could not 'suppress an ominous reluctance' against fulfilling her engagement with Lord Evandale.

MAJOR MILES, OF CHARNWOOD. Lady Margaret's brother-in-law; he did not much 'like the service' on which Claverhouse and his men were engaged, but he was 'one whose sword will not turn back from battle,' and with Lord Evandale he made a gallant resistance against Burley at Tillietudlem. 'He couldna be said to haud up his head after his brother's wife and his niece were turned out o' their ain house.'

BELZIE. Duke Hildebrod's bulldog: 'never flew but at head in his life.' *The Fortunes of Nigel.*

BENARBUCK, LAIRD OF. The 'second-sighted' laird supposed to have had a 'communing' with the Brown Man of the Moors 'some time afore Argyle's landing.' *The Black Dwarf.*

BEND-THE-BOW. *See* ANTHONY (*Castle Dangerous*).

BENEDICT. The sober palfrey on which Abbot Boniface rode to Glendearg. He never quickened his pace beyond 'that which permitted easy conversation and easy digestion.' *The Monastery.*

BENNET, BROTHER. A lay brother of St. Mary's. *The Monastery.*

BENNET, HARRY, EARL OF ARLINGTON. One of Charles II's most attached courtiers during his exile, and after the Restoration Lord Chamberlain and Member of the Privy Council. 'Stiff and formal in manner.' *Peveril of the Peak.*

BENNYGASK. A relative of the Earl of Morton to whom he wished Mary Avenel should be given in marriage. *The Monastery.*

BENSON. One of the crew of the *Fortune's Favourite* who wished Captain Cleveland well. *The Pirate.*

BERENGARIA OF NAVARRE. Queen-Consort of Richard Cœur de Lion. ' One of the most beautiful women of the period . . . she affected, or at least practised, a little childish petulance and wilfulness of manner,' and found amusement in ' idle frolics ' which ill befitted her dignity. Jealous of Edith Plantagenet's ' prudence and wisdom ' she used her name and ring to seduce Kenneth of Scotland from his post on St. George's Mount, intending herself to ' grace him on some future day, to make amends for his wild goose chase.' The consequences of her ' thoughtless prank ' proving more serious than she expected, she found her wiles insufficient to woo Richard from his purpose of punishment. In the end ' the matrimonial dispute ' was settled by transferring the whole blame to her agent, Nectabanus, who was forthwith banished from court. *The Talisman.*

BERENGER—BENEDICTINE ABBESS. The aunt under whose protection Eveline lived for four months in Gloucester. 'Although a nun and a devotee, she held in reverence the holy state of matrimony,' and deeply resented that immediately after his betrothal with Eveline, Hugo de Lacy saw himself bound to fulfil his vow to join the Crusade. She urged Eveline to claim absolution from her engagement. Eveline refusing to be guided by her advice, the Abbess withdrew her protection, urging ' with heat and vehemence ': ' this house is too mean for the residence of the vowed bride of a mighty baron.' *The Betrothed.*

BERENGER, EVELINE. ' The Betrothed ': Sir Raymond's daughter. Endowed with ' a breathing of her father's lofty spirit,' she faced the dangers which surrounded her after his death with courage and ' a resolution to discharge her duty in every emergence.' But Vanda's ominous words of doom weighed on her heart, and when Hugo de Lacy left her to fulfil his vow in the Holy Land, she felt herself ' a creature who must carry distress with her, pass where she will.' Nevertheless, though ' so young—so beset with perils—so much exposed to calumny,' she kept herself free from ' guilt, or falsehood, or ingratitude ' to her betrothed. By her sufferings she atoned for Vanda's wrong, and gained happiness beyond her hopes. *The Betrothed.*

BERENGER, SIR RAYMOND. Seneschal of the Garde Doloureuse, on the marches of Wales. 'Sometimes beaten, sometimes victorious, but never subdued,' he was able to maintain his castle against Gwenwyn's hottest attacks. But when, after his refusal of Gwenwyn's suit, the Welsh marched against him in great numbers, he met them on the plain with only a handful of followers, being bound by a drunken boast to this 'deed next to madness.' He paid the penalty with his life. *The Betrothed.*

BERGEN. The horse Magnus Troil rode when he took his daughters to see Norna : 'a strong, square-made, well-barrelled palfrey, of Norwegian breed, somewhat taller, and yet as stout, as the ordinary ponies of the country.' *The Pirate.*

BERKLEY, LADY AUGUSTA OF. The Lady who promised her hand to Sir John de Walton, if he kept Douglas Castle for a year and a day. Hearing in her lonely castle tidings of the 'constant dangers' to which her lover was exposed, she set out with Bertram, 'determined to take such measures in respect to shortening the term of his trial or otherwise, as a sight of Douglas Castle and . . . of Sir John de Walton might suggest.' At the prospect of being brought face to face with him in her 'masculine disguise,' she fled from the convent of St. Bride's with Sister Ursula—but only to fall into the hands of Sir James Douglas. She then became the gage of battle between Sir James and Sir John.

'What more worthy of a noble heart, possessing riches, beauty, birth, and rank, than to confer them all upon indigent and chivalrous merit ? ' *Castle Dangerous.*

BERNE, THE YOUNG BEAR OF. *See* DONNERHUGEL, RUDOLPH OF.

BERTHA. Aldobrand Oldenbuck's wife. 'Not a bad sample of womanhood, had made a vow she would only marry that man who could work her father's press.' *The Antiquary.*

BERTHA. Daughter of Engelred : 'Agatha,' waiting-woman and female squire to Brenhilda, Countess of Paris. In youth Hereward and she had 'vowed affection,' but on the defeat of the Saxon Foresters, Bertha with her mother was carried off by the Knight of Aspramonte to become the attendant of his daughter Brenhilda. After her mistress' romantic marriage with Count Robert of Paris, Bertha accompanied them to the East, and in the garden of Agelastes found her lost lover Hereward. She acted as his messenger to the Crusaders in Scutari, asking for support to Count Robert in his combat with Nicephorus. When Hereward, fighting in the place of Nicephorus, seemed to be at a disadvantage, her voice stopped the combat. *Count Robert of Paris.*

BERTRAM. Minstrel to the house of Berkley for more than twenty years. He accompanied the Lady Augusta when, disguised as his son, she set out on her 'frolic' to visit Douglas Castle. Leaving Augustine in the convent of St. Bride's, he proceeded to the castle 'under pretence of making some researches after the writings of Thomas of Erceldoun, called the Rhymer.' Nevertheless, he fell under suspicion, and his fidelity to his mistress was tried by 'threats of violence.'

'One of those rare individuals who vindicated the honour of a corrupted profession by their personal good behaviour.' *Castle Dangerous.*

BERTRAM FAMILY, THE.

ALLAN. Laird of Ellangowan in the time of Charles I. 'A steady loyalist,' he lost half of the family estate as a result of his convictions.

CAPTAIN ANDREW. A member of 'the very ancient and honourable house of Ellangowan,' who in the seventeenth century founded the Singleside branch of the family.

DENNIS. Son of Allan. He married the daughter of 'an eminent fanatic,' and 'became enamoured of the lady's principles as well as of her charms.' His politics cost him a large part of the family estate.

DONOHOE. Son of Dennis. He joined Claverhouse at Killiecrankie, and 'at the skirmish of Dunkeld, 1689, he was shot dead by a Cameronian with a silver button (being supposed to have proof from the Evil One against lead and steel), and his grave is still called the "Wicked Laird's Lair."'

LEWIS. Son of Donohoe and father of Godfrey. He was 'full of projects for re-establishing the prosperity of his family,' but in the midst of them 'death claimed his tribute.' It was he who built the 'New Place' of Ellangowan.

GODFREY. Laird of Ellangowan. He succeeded to 'a long pedigree and a short rent-roll,' and under his rule the affairs of the family went from bad to worse. 'He kept neither hunters, nor hounds, nor any other southern preliminaries to ruin; but, as has been observed of his countrymen, he kept *a man of business* who answered the purpose equally well.' By his ill-timed zeal when appointed a justice of the peace he earned the ill-will of a colony of gipsies who had long lived on his land. But Meg Merrilies retained her old loyalty to the family, and was the means of saving the young heir's life, and finally of restoring him to his own.

MRS. BERTRAM. Wife of the Laird of Ellangowan, to whom she brought a portion of about four thousand pounds. After Harry's birth she made a little velvet bag for the scheme of his nativity, and hung it as a charm round the child's neck. It was this bag that conclusively proved Vanbeest Brown to be the lost heir.

HARRY. The son and heir of Godfrey, Laird of Ellangowan. He disappeared on his fifth birthday, and from that time till he was of age, he 'dree'd his weird' as Vanbeest Brown.

'One of the hardiest and most lively children.'

(To *dree one's weird*, to endure one's fate.)

LUCY. Daughter of the Laird of Ellangowan. She was born on the day of her brother Harry's disappearance, and of her mother's death. Her father died when she was about seventeen, leaving her penniless with 'nothing on earth to recommend her but a pretty face, good birth, and a most amiable disposition.' Her 'genuine prudence and good sense' recommended her to Colonel Mannering as a suitable companion for Julia, who found that 'there are few persons to whose consolatory friendship I could have recourse more freely in what are called the *real evils* of life.'

COMMISSIONER BERTRAM. A cousin of the Laird of Ellangowan, through whose influence Godfrey Bertram Hewit got a post on an Excise yacht.

MISTRESS MARGARET. The 'nearest female relation' of Ellangowan : owner of Singleside. She had spent three years as a guest under Ellangowan's roof, but after his death showed little sympathy with Lucy. 'Well assured that he was yet alive in foreign parts,' she left her property to the lost heir. *Guy Mannering.*

BERWICK. The charger that carried Bradwardine at Gladsmuir. *Waverley.*

BERWINE. Attendant to the Lady of Baldringham. She conducted Eveline Berenger to Red-finger's chamber. *The Betrothed.*

BETT. Widow Raine's servant. *Peveril of the Peak.*

BETTY, LADY. The lady who, at a tea-party in the house of an Edinburgh lady of quality, argued in favour of the stability of love. *Waverley.*

BEVIS. Sir Henry Lee's 'faithful mastiff or bloodhound, which in old time had saved his master by his fidelity, and which regularly followed him to church': 'as tractable as he was strong and bold.' In old age 'to lie by Sir Henry's feet in the summer or by the fire in winter, to raise his head to look on him, to lick his withered hand or his shrivelled cheek from time to time, seemed now all that Bevis lived for.' *Woodstock.*

Note.—' Bevis, the gallant hound, one of the handsomest and most active of the ancient Highland deerhounds, had his prototype in a dog called Maida, the gift of the late Chief of Glengarry to the author. A beautiful sketch of him was made by Edwin Landseer and afterwards engraved.'

BIBBET, MASTER. General Harrison's secretary. He was wont to be a little overcome with liquor in the evening, ' not that he is in the least given to ebriety, but simply, that since the Scottish campaign he hath had a perpetual ague, which obliges him so to nourish his frame against the damps of the night.' *Woodstock.*

BICKERTON, MRS. 'Lady of the ascendant of the Seven Stars, in the Castle-gate, York.' An 'exported Scotswoman,' she assisted Jeanie Deans with eagerness, 'furnished her with credentials to her correspondent in London, and to several inns upon the road where she had some influence or interest, reminded her of the precautions she should adopt for concealing her money, and . . . took leave of her very affectionately.' *The Heart of Midlothian.*

BICKERTON, MOSES. Mrs. Bickerton's 'poor man . . . as is i' the kirkyard.' *The Heart of Midlothian.*

BIDDULPH. The husband imposed on Hannah Irwin by the Earl of Etherington. 'A wretch, who maltreated me,' she said on her deathbed, 'plundered me—sold me.' *St. Ronan's Well.*

BIDE-THE-BENT, MR. PETER. The minister before whom Gibbie Girder stood reproved (and 'can a man do mair than stand reproved?') for his strong language on discovering that the chief part of the christening dinner had disappeared. The Rev. Peter was called to Ravenswood Castle to convince Lucy of the wickedness of her engagement with the Master of Ravenswood, but he 'was deeply moved at her distress,' and undertook to despatch for her a letter to the Master. *The Bride of Lammermoor.*

BIDMORE, HON. AUGUSTUS. The Rev. Josiah Cargill's pupil: 'a spoiled though good-humoured lad, of weak health and very ordinary parts.' *St. Ronan's Well.*

BIDMORE, LORD. 'A distinguished connoisseur' who, when consulting the Professor of Theology concerning a tutor for his son and heir, invariably asked, 'Did the candidate understand drawing?' He wished his son 'to maintain that character for hereditary taste which his father and grandfather had acquired at the expense of a considerable estate.' *St. Ronan's Well.*

BIDMORE, MISS AUGUSTA. 'His lordship's only other child,' she also received instruction from the Rev. Josiah Cargill. 'But her progress was as different from that of her brother as the fire of heaven differs from that grosser element which the peasant piles upon his smouldering hearth. Her acquirements in Italian and Spanish literature, in history, in drawing, and in all elegant learning, were such as to enchant her teacher.' *St. Ronan's Well.*

BIEDERMAN, ARNOLD. By birthright Count of Geierstein : Landamman (Chief Magistrate) of Unterwalden, and one of the deputies sent by the Swiss Confederation to remonstrate with the Duke of Burgundy on the aggressions and exactions of von Hagenbach. Characterised by a 'downright and blunt simplicity,' elevated by 'dignity of thought' and 'profound sagacity,' he was 'an especial advocate for peace, while its preservation was compatible with national independence, and the honour of the confederacy.' During the journey of the deputies to Charles the Bold he was able to check the rasher spirits who were led by

Rudolph of Donnerhugel, but his dignified appeal to Charles proved as unavailing as Seignor Philipson's friendly intercession had been. Driven by Charles' taunts to 'welcome war,' he fought with whole-hearted devotion. 'Mirror of ancient faith and integrity . . . noble Arnold . . . soul of truth and candour . . . to whom cowardice, selfishness, and falsehood are alike unknown!' *Anne of Geierstein.*

BIEDERMAN, BERTHA. Arnold's wife, and mother of his 'six stately sons': 'now a saint in Heaven.' *Anne of Geierstein.*

BIEDERMAN, ERNST. Arnold's second son: one of the youths chosen to accompany the Swiss deputies to the court of Charles the Bold. For urging violent measures against the magistrates of Bâle he was sent back to Geierstein, his father telling him, 'Remember that he is not fit to visit strange countries, who cannot rule his tongue before his own countrymen, and to his own father.' *Anne of Geierstein.*

BIEDERMAN, RUDIGER. Arnold's eldest son: one of the youths who accompanied the Swiss deputies to the court of Charles the Bold. He took his part in patrolling the neighbourhood of Graffs-lust, shared Rudolph of Donnerhugel's secret understanding with Count Albert of Geierstein and the Duke of Lorraine, and was employed to expedite the departure of Seignor Philipson and Arthur from La Ferette. He fell before Nancy 'with the banner in his hand,' shot by the only one of 'Colvin's mastiffs' which Campo-Basso had not muzzled. *Anne of Geierstein.*

BIEDERMAN, SIGISMOND. Arnold's third son: one of the youths who accompanied the Swiss deputies to the court of Charles the Bold. He was generally considered 'the most indolent and least spirited of the family of Geierstein,' but he proved himself, 'though with slowness of ideas and expression . . . strong in his principles and sometimes happy in his conceptions.' Twice—in La Ferette and in Charles' deserted tent at Granson —he had the presence of mind to secure Seignor Philipson's precious necklace of diamonds. 'Better to think justly than to think fast.' *Anne of Geierstein.*

BIEDERMAN, ULRICK. One of Arnold's sons. He took part in the 'manly exercises' with his brothers at Geierstein when Rudolph of Donnerhugel first challenged Arthur Philipson. *Anne of Geierstein.*

BIGOT, DE. Prince John's seneschal. He was sent to invite Cedric and his party to the Prince's banquet in Ashby Castle. *Ivanhoe.*

BIGSTAFF, JOHN. The constable on whom John Whitecraft could call in time of need. *Peveril of the Peak.*

BIMBISTER, MARGERY. 'The worthy spouse of the Ranzelman,' Neil Ronaldson. A 'chattering old woman.' *The Pirate.*

BINDLOOSE, MR. 'The copper-nosed sheriff-clerk of the county,' and agent of one of the two national banks lately established in Marchthorn. In her anxiety concerning Frank Tyrrel's disappearance Meg Dods had recourse to him, and in his office became acquainted with Mr. Touchwood. 'Folk miscaa'd ye, and said ye were this, that, and the other thing, and little better than an auld sneck-drawing loon.' *St. Ronan's Well.*

(*Sneck-drawing loon*, a crafty, worthless fellow.)

BINGO. 'A little mongrel cur, with bandy legs, a long back, and huge flapping ears,' belonging to Colonel Mannering. 'Of this uncouth creature he chose to make a favourite.' *Guy Mannering.*

BINKS, LADY (*née* RACHEL BONNYRIGG). Sir Bingo's wife, and 'Leddy Loupengirth's lang-legged daughter.' Naturally 'passionate, ambitious, and thoughtful,' she captivated Sir Bingo by a 'wild, hoydenish, half-mad humour,' which settled into sullenness when she realised after marriage that 'many scrupled to hold intercourse with her in society.' Lord Etherington's advent gave her an opportunity of exciting Sir Bingo's jealousy—this, she had discovered, was 'the most effectual way of tormenting' him. *St. Ronan's Well.*

BINKS, SIR BINGO. 'A sapient English Baronet, who, ashamed, as many thought, to return to his own country, had set him down at the Well of St. Ronan's to enjoy the blessing which the Caledonian Hymen had so kindly forced on him in the person of Miss Rachel Bonnyrigg.' 'Mowbray's convenient shadow and adherent,' he acquired some 'consequence,' when Frank Tyrrel seemed to avoid the duel arranged with him. 'A brute and a fool.' *St. Ronan's Well.*

BISSET,. AILY. The recipient of an opened letter concerning which Mr. Mailsetter 'got an unco rebuke frae the secretary at Edinburgh.' *The Antiquary.*

BITTLEBRAINS, LORD. Owner of the hounds which drew the Master of Ravenswood and Bucklaw from their seclusion in Wolf's Crag. He had obtained his peerage 'by a good deal of plausibility . . . a steady observation of the changes of the times, and the power of rendering certain political services to those who could best reward them.' *The Bride of Lammermoor.*

BLACK, DR. *See* HUME, DAVID.

BLACK-AT-THE-BANE, THE LAIRD OF. The local magnate whose natural son ousted Mr. Butler from the mastership of a school near Dumfries. *The Heart of Midlothian.*

BLACKCHESTER, COUNTESS OF. Lord Dalgarno's sister. She 'aimed at once at superiority in the realms of fashion, of power, and of wit.' *The Fortunes of Nigel.*

BLACK DOUGLAS. The slayer of a former heir of the Osbaldistone family. He surprised the heir on the day after he succeeded to the estate. *Rob Roy.*

BLACK DWARF, THE. 'Elshender the Recluse,' 'Canny Elshie,' 'the Wise Wight of Muckelstane Moor,' or 'the Solitary.' 'A mis-shapen monster' with only a 'distorted resemblance to humanity,' he was thought to be in league with the Devil, but by degrees his skill in cures, his practical wisdom and helpfulness gained him esteem. While professing that he had no object but 'perpetuating the mass of misery,' he acted with constant generosity and 'exuberant' liberality. He was morbidly sensitive concerning his physical deformity, and when to this feeling an acute remorse was added, he became 'the most ingenious self-tormentor of whom I have ever heard.' *The Black Dwarf.* See also MAULEY, SIR EDWARD.

BLACK FELTHAM. One of Captain Colepepper's companions in the attack on Lord Dalgarno at Camlet Moat. *The Fortunes of Nigel.*

BLACKHALL. A victim of Allan, Lord Ravenswood, 'for a wrang word said ower their wine, or brandy, or what not.' *The Bride of Lammermoor.*

BLACK HASTINGS. Sir Geoffrey's war-horse. He 'had but one fault, and that was his wish to turn down Moultrassie avenue.' *Peveril of the Peak.*

BLACK KNIGHT OF THE FETTER-LOCK. See RICHARD CŒUR DE LION (3).

BLACKLEES, TOMALIN. One of the 'reckless warders' who amused themselves by tormenting the Charegite, and were deceived by his pretence of drunkenness. *The Talisman.*

BLACK MOOR. The Master of Ravenswood's led horse which 'cast himself over his halter in the stable' at the Tod's Den when Bucklaw and Craigengelt were awaiting the Master in order to leave for France. *The Bride of Lammermoor.*

BLACK QUENTIN. One of Sir John Ramorny's 'grooms,' or 'chamberlains.' Dwining told 'two or three tattling fools, in deep confidence, that the hand which was found' on the street after the turmoil on St. Valentine's Eve was his. He meanwhile was sent 'privately back to his own county of Fife.' *The Fair Maid of Perth.*

BLACKWELL AND Co. An Exeter firm with whom Osbaldistone and Tresham did business. *Rob Roy.*

BLADDERSKATE, LORD. Dumtoustie's uncle: one of the judges before whom Alan Fairford pleaded Peter Peebles' case. During Alan's speech 'he relaxed the scorn of his features into an expression of profound attention; the highest compliment, and the greatest encouragement, which a judge can render to the counsel addressing him.' *Redgauntlet.*

BLAIR. One of the 'preachers whose talents have done such honour' to Scotland. Guy Mannering made a point of hearing him when in Edinburgh. *Guy Mannering.*

BLAIR, CLEMENT. See CLEMENT, FATHER.

BLAIZE. 'The old reprobate overseer' in the legend of Martin Waldeck. *The Antiquary.*

BLAKENEY, GENERAL. Governor of Stirling. 'A man of honour and humanity.' *Waverley.*

BLAKES, 'MOTHER.' Justice Inglewood's old housekeeper. *Rob Roy.*

BLANCHE. One of the attendants who accompanied Eveline Berenger to the House of Baldringham. *The Betrothed.*

BLANDEVILLE, LADY EMILY. Under parental compulsion engaged for a short time to Sir Everard Waverley. He chivalrously freed her, and used his influence to make her marriage with young Talbot possible when he learnt that this was her real desire. *Waverley.*

BLANE, JENNY. Niel's daughter. After her mother's death she was successfully initiated by Niel 'in those cares which had been faithfully discharged by his wife.' Of her he said, 'a douce woman she was, civil to the customers, and had a good name wi' Whig and Tory, baith up the street and down the street.' She 'could pit up wi' as muckle as maist women.' *Old Mortality.*

BLANE, NIEL. The town-piper, 'a clean, tight, well-timbered, and long-winded fellow.' He won the heart of a jolly widow who kept the principal change-house in the borough, and as 'landlord of the Howff' gave such 'close attention to his helm' that he was able 'to keep his little vessel pretty steady amid the contending tides of faction.' 'If the sodgers draw their swords,' he said to Jenny, 'ye'll cry on the corporal and the guard. If the town folk tak the tangs and poker, ye'll cry on the bailie and town-officers. But in nae event cry on me.' 'The redder gets aye the warst lick in the fray.' *Old Mortality.* (*Howff*, haunt. *Redder*, peacemaker.)

BLATTERGOWL, DR. Minister of Trotcosey, the parish in which Monkbarns and Knockwinnock were situated. 'A dreadful proser,' who 'never reads anything lest he should be suspected of reading his sermons.' *The Antiquary.*

BLATTERGOWL, MISS BECKIE. The minister's sister : Miss Grizzel Oldbuck's friend. *The Antiquary.*

BLAZONBURY, EARL OF. 'Lord Flash and Flame': one of Saddletree's customers. *The Heart of Midlothian.*

BLENKENSOP, LADY. 'A close confederate' of Sarah, Duchess of Marlborough. Through the Duchess 'this Northumbrian cousin' of Bucklaw became 'a crony' of Lady Ashton, and together these two ladies planned the matrimonial alliance between Bucklaw and Lucy Ashton. *The Bride of Lammermoor.*

BLETSON, MR. JOSHUA. One of the Commissioners sent by Parliament to dispose of Woodstock Palace and Park as 'national property': member of Parliament for the borough of Littlefaith (or Littlecreed). 'A true-blue Commonwealth's man . . . with his noddle full of newfangled notions about government,' he at the same time 'came as near the predicament of an atheist as it is perhaps possible for a man to do.' In practical life he was 'cautious' and 'cowardly,' his 'acute self-conceit and worldly learning' finding their most congenial outlet in words. He was driven from Woodstock Lodge by the spiritual apparitions as easily as his colleagues Desborough and Harrison. *Woodstock.*

BLINDAS, JUSTICE. The Justice who issued the warrant to test Wayland Smith as a wizard. *Kenilworth.*

BLINKHOOLIE. *See* BONIFACE.

BLINKINSOP. One of the gang of men who took the *Jumping Jenny's* cargo to Goodman Grist's mill. *Redgauntlet.*

BLOCK, MARTIN. A wealthy butcher and grazier of Dijon. The 'blunt and hardy reply' which he delivered from the Third Estate of Burgundy excited Charles the Bold 'beyond what his nature could endure.' *Anne of Geierstein.*

BLOK, NIKKEL. Chief of the butchers' incorporation of Liège. During the revels in Schonwaldt Castle he occupied a place near William de la Marck, and at his command killed the Bishop 'as if he had been doing his office in the common shambles.' *Quentin Durward.*

BLONDEL DE NESLE. The celebrated minstrel for whom King Richard had an 'enthusiastic admiration.' He entertained the king and his court in camp, flinging away at the king's command 'that newfangled restriction of thine, of terminating in accurate and similar rhymes. They are a constraint on thy flow of fancy, and make thee resemble a man dancing in fetters.' 'Thy noble qualities are like a fire burning within, and compel thee to pour thyself out in music and song.' *The Talisman.*

BLOOD, COLONEL. 'One of those extraordinary characters, who can only arise amid the bloodshed, confusion, destruction of morality, and wide-spreading violence, which take place during civil war.' His most notorious exploit was the theft of the crown from the Tower. For a time he was in high favour with the Duke of Buckingham, who says of him to Jerningham, 'there goes a scoundrel after my own heart, a robber from his cradle, a murderer since he could hold a knife, a profound hypocrite in religion, and a worse and deeper hypocrite in honour— would sell his soul to the devil to accomplish any villainy, and would cut the throat of his brother, did he dare to give the villainy he had so acted its right name.' *Peveril of the Peak.*

BLOUNT, SIR NICHOLAS. Master of the horse to the Earl of Sussex: 'a gentleman of fair estate and ancient name.' 'An honest man of plain common sense' 'without a grain of vivacity or imagination,' he was more at ease on the battlefield than at court. *Kenilworth.*

BLOWER, JOHN. Mrs. Blower's late husband. 'He was a merry man, Doctor; but he had the root of the matter in him, for a' his light way of speaking, as deep as ony skipper that ever loosed anchor from Leith Roads.' *St. Ronan's Well.*

BLOWER, MRS. (*née* PEGGY BRYCE). A widow 'from the Bow-head,

who had come to the Well to carry off the dregs of the *Inflienzie*, which she scorned to term a surfeit.' John 'left me comfortable in warld's gudes'; she confided to the Man of Medicine, 'but comforts hae their cumbers —to be a lone woman is a sair weird.' The doctor's attentions did her 'muckle heart's good.' *St. Ronan's Well.*
(*Cumbers*, vexations. *Weird*, fate.)

BLOWSELINDA or BONSTROPS. An inhabitant of Whitefriars whose room was suggested as a residence for Nigel when he sought sanctuary. Her room had been 'the occasional residence of Slicing Dick of Paddington, who lately suffered at Tyburn, and whose untimely exit had been hitherto mourned by the damsel in solitary widowhood, after the fashion of the turtle-dove.' *The Fortunes of Nigel.*

BOABDIL. The Saracen under the shadow of whose throne Isaac's brother lived safely in Cordova. Isaac and Rebecca sought 'peace and protection' with him after Rebecca's trial, 'for less cruel are the cruelties of the Moors unto the race of Jacob, than the cruelties of the Nazarenes of England.' *Ivanhoe.*

BODACH GLAS. The Grey Spectre which, from the days of Halbert Hall, warned the Vich Ian Vohr of the day of impending disaster. *Waverley.*

BODDERBRAINS, MASTER. A member of Parliament whose speeches secured a sound sleep for Master Charles Topham. *Peveril of the Peak.*

BOHEMOND OF TARENTUM. Son of Robert Guiscard: one of the leaders of the first Crusade; Prince of Antioch. It was when showing 'deference' to Bohemond that Alexius exposed himself to a 'cutting affront' from Robert of Paris. 'A man of undaunted bravery and towering ambition,' he was 'selfish and wily' and held 'his own self-interest to be the devoted guide of his whole conduct.' *Count Robert of Paris.*

BOHUN, HENRY, EARL OF ESSEX. Lord High Constable of England. With other faithful nobles he assembled his men in order that when Richard's return was announced 'he should be at the head of such a force as enemies shall tremble to face, and thus subdue the meditated treason, without even unsheathing a sword.'

The others were Estoteville, Salisbury, Beauchamp, Multon, and Percy. *Ivanhoe.*

BOISGELIN, COUNTESS DE. A 'black-eyed and pretty Provençale' in whose good graces Arthur Philipson made some progress during his visit to Margaret of Anjou at her father's court. *Anne of Geierstein.*

BOIS-GUILBERT, BRIAN DE. 'Commander of the valiant and venerable order of Knights-Templars,' 'valiant as the bravest of his order, but stained with their usual vices, pride, arrogance, cruelty, and voluptuousness; a hard-hearted man who knows neither fear of earth nor awe of heaven.' He was prepared to sacrifice fame, power, and ambition to his passion for Rebecca, but the words 'recreant knight' steeled his heart and drove him into his last encounter with the Knight of Ivanhoe. *Ivanhoe.*

BOLTON, STAWARTH. A Captain in the English army. When, after the battle of Pinkie, he came with a party of men to Glendearg, he was touched by Dame Glendinning's lonely state, and left a sergeant to protect the family. Halbert and he met again about ten years later in the course of Sir John Foster's inroad into Scotland. He was full of 'blunt and unpretending gallantry and generosity.' *The Monastery.*

BONAMICO OF MILAN. The maker of Sir Piercie Shafton's cuirass. *The Monastery.*

BONIFACE. (1) Lord Abbot of St. Mary's. Fond of ease and comfort, good-natured and charitable, he had sought the cloister for 'quiet.' When, instead of this, 'the progress of the reformed doctrines' brought 'turmoil,' his zeal for the Church did not prove sufficient to make him welcome the change. 'It hath cost me no little thought,' he said when at Sir John Foster's approach he transferred his office to Father Eustace, 'no common toil, to keep these weighty matters in such order as you have seen them ... and I warrant me, when every one of you was asleep in your cell, the Abbot hath lain awake for a full hour by the bell, thinking how these matters might be ordered seemly and suitably.'

(2) As Blinkhoolie, the proprietor of a large garden in Kinross, the ex-Abbot had hoped to find amongst his fruit-trees and flowerbeds 'ease and quiet' during the remainder of his days. But after Queen Mary's arrival in Lochleven Castle he was 'dragged into matters where both heading and hanging are like to be the issue.' Again, when the plots for the Queen's release were successful, he was 'hunted round' to Dundrennan Abbey, where he had served his noviciate, and there he witnessed the Queen's fatal departure for England. 'A weary life I have had,' he said, 'for one to whom peace was ever the dearest blessing!' (1) *The Monastery.* (2) *The Abbot.*

BONIFACE, FATHER. The monk of St. Martin's: Ludovic Lesly's 'comrade and confessor.' *Quentin Durward.*

BONNYRIGG, RACHEL. *See* BINKS, LADY.

BONSTETTEN, NICHOLAS. One of the deputies sent by the Swiss Confederation to remonstrate with the Duke of Burgundy on the aggressions and exactions of von Hagenbach. Like Arnold Biederman, he represented a Forest Canton (Schwitz), and he 'seemed to make it his principal object to follow the Landamman's example in everything.' *Anne of Geierstein.*

BONTHRON, ANTONY. Sir John Ramorny's 'dark satellite.' According to a pre-arranged plan he refused to stand the test of bier-right before Oliver Proudfute's body, and after being defeated in combat by Harry Gow, confessed his guilt and named the Duke of Rothesay as the master whom he had served. In return for this false witness Dwining contrived, with Smotherwell's connivance, to save him from death on the gallows. Released at midnight from his perilous position, he was sent down to Falkland Castle, there to play his part in the despatch of the Duke of Rothesay. *The Fair Maid of Perth.*

For bier-right *see* LUNDIN, SIR LOUIS (*Note*).

BOOSHALLOCH, NIEL. Herdsman to the Captain of Clan Quhele. Simon Glover 'had transacted many bargains for hides and furs with him,' and found safety in his cottage when obliged to leave Perth. Niel tried in his loyalty ' to gloss over' the apparent neglect of Simon by Eachin Mac-Ian, ascribing the young Chief's want of hospitality to the ' bad manners' he had learnt in the Low Country. *The Fair Maid of Perth.*

BOTHWELL, EARL OF. James Hepburn, Queen Mary's third husband. Though commonly considered guilty of Darnley's murder, he was married by the Queen three months after Darnley's death. ' A black sight to her, that Bothwell.' *The Abbot.*

BOTHWELL, FRANCIS, EARL OF. (1) Sergeant Bothwell's grandfather. He was ' cousin-german' to James VI and embarrassed the early part of that monarch's reign by his ' turbulence and repeated conspiracies.' He died an exile in great poverty.

(2) An ' unhappy fugitive' in whose train Ralph Olifaunt went abroad. (1) *Old Mortality.* (2) *The Fortunes of Nigel.*

Note.—He was the son of a natural son of James V, and nephew of Queen Mary's husband.

BOTHWELL, SERGEANT. Francis Stewart, a lineal descendant of the last Earl of Bothwell: an officer in Claverhouse's regiment of Life Guards. ' He partook in a great degree of the licentiousness and oppressive disposition' which was ' too general' amongst the soldiers, and he was not ' uniformly so amenable to discipline as the rules of the service require.' He could not forget his pedigree. He had ' great personal strength and dexterity in the use of his arms,' and was no mean opponent of Burley in their wrestling contest at the Howff, and again on the field of Drumclog. He died ' hoping nothing, believing nothing—and FEARING nothing.' *Old Mortality.*

BOTHWELL, LADY. The elder Miss Falconer : ' my aunt Margaret's ' grandmother. A woman of ' high principle' and ' good sense,' she took her sister Jemima under her care when Sir Philip Forester went to the war in Flanders. She tried in vain to dissuade Jemima from consulting Doctor Damiotti, accompanied her in her visit and saw all the wonders of his mirror. ' There were so many difficulties in assigning a natural explanation that, to the day of her death, she remained in great doubt on the subject, and much disposed to cut the Gordian knot, by admitting the existence of supernatural agency.' *My Aunt Margaret's Mirror.*

BOTHWELL, MARGARET. 'My Aunt Margaret.' Her 'solicitude and affection' made her 'the willing slave to the inflictions of a whole nursery' of nephews and nieces. In spite of her 'strong useful common sense,' she confessed herself susceptible to 'the enjoyment of the milder feeling of supernatural awe,' tracing her special 'dislike to look into a mirror in particular times and places' to the story of her grandmother's experiences. This story she told to 'me' when John Clayhudgeons' discovery of a tombstone bearing her name, turned her thoughts to death. *My Aunt Margaret's Mirror.*

BOTHWELL, SIR GEOFFREY. Lady Bothwell's husband : ' an indolent man' who, under his lady's influence, became 'involved in some political matters which had been more wisely let alone.' *My Aunt Margaret's Mirror.*

BOWIE, BESSIE. A cripple born, ' and carried frae door to door . . . begging bawbees.' *The Heart of Midlothian.*

(*Bawbees,* halfpennies.)

BOWYER, MASTER. One of Queen Elizabeth's ushers. He found it difficult to suit his mistress's humour, she, at one moment, chiding a nobleman on his account, and at the next, holding him ' but as the lead-weight that keeps the door fast.' *Kenilworth.*

BRACKEL, ADRIAN. The rope-dancer under whose charge Edward Christian placed Fenella. Later the Countess of Derby rescued her from his brutal treatment. *Peveril of the Peak.*

BRACY, MAURICE DE. Leader of a band of Free Companions or ' mercenaries ' : one of the nobles pledged to support Prince John. He and Bois-Guilbert together planned the 'audacious enterprise' which brought Cedric and his party as captives to Front-de-Bœuf's castle. But in spite of his ' buoyant spirits and bold bearing ' he found that before Rowena's tears he was 'ill-framed' for the part he played. Pardoned by Richard for his share in John's plot, he ' escaped beyond seas.' *Ivanhoe.*

BRADBOURNE, LILIAS. Lady Mary Avenel's handmaiden : ' a spoiled domestic, and often accustomed to take more license than her mistress was at all times willing to encourage.' The favourite page was on ' the frosty side ' of her favour, and though she was ' no tale-bearer,' and ' never envied any one's favour,' she was able to inform the Lady of the boy's misdemeanours. *The Abbot.*

BRADSHAWE, JUDITH. Heiress of Oliver Bradshawe of Highley Park. On her marriage with a member of the junior branch of the Waverley family, the Bradshawe arms (the same as those of Bradshawe the regicide) were quartered with the ancient coat of Waverley. *Waverley.*

BRADWARDINE, COSMO COMYNE. Baron of Bradwardine. A tall, thin, athletic figure, with every muscle rendered as tough as whip-cord by constant exercise, ' he was the very model of the old Scottish cavalier, with all his excellencies and peculiarities.' He was a scholar, ' according to the scholarship of Scotchmen,' with a great zeal for the classic authors. Full of the pride of race and position, he insisted, with great solemnity and pomp, on rendering his humble act of feudal service to the young Chevalier after the battle of Gladsmuir. His anecdotes were ' whimsical from prejudice and pedantry, but often respectable for the good sense and honourable feelings which his narrative displayed, and almost always curious, if not valuable, for the information they contained.' *Waverley.*

BRADWARDINE, GODMUND. A predecessor of the Baron, to whom the family crest (a bear rampant with the motto *Bewar the Bar*) had been assigned by Frederick Red-beard, Emperor of Germany, for prowess in the Holy Land. *Waverley.*

BRADWARDINE, MALCOLM, OF INCH-GRABBIT. Heir male of the Baron of Bradwardine : ' a Whig and a Hanoverian.' He tried ' to avail himself of the old Baron's evil fortune to the full extent.' *Waverley.*

BRADWARDINE, ROSE. Only child of the Baron of Bradwardine, and ' the very apple of his eye.' ' Her very soul is in home, and in the discharge of all those quiet virtues of which home is the centre. Her husband will be to her what her father now is, the object of all her care, solicitude, and affection. She will see nothing, and connect herself with nothing, but by him and through him.' *Waverley.*

BRADWARDINE, SIR JOHN OF. ' Black Sir John,' the common ancestor of the Baron's house and the Inch-Grabbit's. *Waverley.*

BRAN. Fergus MacIvor's greyhound. *Waverley.*

BREADALBANE. A rival of the Duke of Argyle. Between his family and Rob Roy's there was also ' auld ill-will.' *Rob Roy.*

BREAKFAST. A baby saved by Wildrake from ' a parish nurse, who had been paid for the child half a year in advance,' and offered him to Lunsford's Light Horse—' the babe-eaters.' *Woodstock.*

See also LACY.

BRECK, ALISON. A fish-wife, next in age to Elspeth Mucklebackit. She was so impressed by the Antiquary's goodness in helping to carry Steenie to his grave that she ' swore almost aloud, " His honour Monkbarns should never want sax warp of oysters in the season (of which fish he was understood to be fond), if she should gang to sea and dredge for them hersell, in the foulest wind that ever blew." ' *The Antiquary.*

BRECK, ANGUS. One of the two Highlanders who attended Rob

Roy when he went to keep his tryst with Rashleigh Osbaldistone. *Rob Roy.*

BRENGWAIN. Gwenwyn's childless wife. When Gwenwyn became enamoured of Eveline Berenger, Brengwain was removed to a nunnery, and steps were taken to secure a divorce. *The Betrothed.*

BRENHILDA. *See* PARIS, COUNTESS OF.

BREWER, SAM. One of Sir Geoffrey Peveril's menservants. *Peveril of the Peak.*

BRICHAM, DR. Mike Lambourne's 'worthy pedagogue.' 'He passed away in a blessed frame, " *Morior —mortuus sum vel fui*—mori." These were his latest words, and he just added, " my last verb is conjugated." ' *Kenilworth.*

BRIDGENORTH, ALICE. Major Bridgenorth's daughter. After spending her earliest years as Julian Peveril's companion under his mother's care, she learnt to love him again ' in the valleys of Man,' before she knew him as the son ' of him that disgraced and banished ' her father. Though ' bred in solitude and in the quiet and unpretending tastes which solitude encourages,' she bore herself bravely in the purlieus of the court, and on the discovery of Edward Christian's villainous plot she showed 'a strong, firm, concentrated indignation,' which made its realisation impossible. *Peveril of the Peak.*

BRIDGENORTH, MAJOR RALPH. 'A gentleman of middling quality ' whose influence with Cromwell saved Sir Geoffrey Peveril's life.

'Wise and moderate ' in his youth, but ' melancholy by constitution and descent,' he became in middle and later life more and more extreme in his religious and political views. Filled with hatred against the Countess of Derby for the execution of his brother-in-law, William Christian, and alienated at the same time from the Peverils by the stain on his ' worldly honour,' which he could not avenge, he threw himself into the ranks of the ' righters and avengers ' of the profligate times. Conscious of his deep love for his daughter Alice, he distrusted its gratification as a 'worldly indulgence,' but in the midst of his wildest schemes for national regeneration he was never altogether deaf to the dictates of the tender esteem which Lady Peveril had won from him. *Peveril of the Peak.*

BRIDGENORTH, MRS. Alice Christian, Major Bridgenorth's wife. She died at Alice's birth, her constitution having been 'exhausted by maternal grief, and by the anxious and harrowing reflection that from her the children they had lost derived that delicacy of health, which proved unable to undergo the tear and wear of existence.' *Peveril of the Peak.*

BRIDGET, MAY. The woman who brought milk to Falkland Castle. Under cover of her cloak Louise escaped from the Castle and carried news to the Earl of Douglas of the foul play practised on the Duke of Rothesay. *The Fair Maid of Perth.*

BRIDGET, MOTHER. Abbess of the nunnery of St. Catherine, ' till the heretics turned all adrift ' : aunt of Catherine Seyton. After Roland Graeme's dismissal from Avenel Castle he was taken by his grandmother to the ruined nunnery, and there the two elderly women discussed the ' perilous course ' on which Catherine and he were to embark as fellow-travellers. *The Abbot.*

BRIDLESLEY, JOE. The Liverpool horse-dealer from whom Julian Peveril bought a horse for his journey to London. *Peveril of the Peak.*

BRIDOON, CORPORAL. One of Mrs. Nosebag's ' lambs.' *Waverley.*

BRITTSON, SERGEANT. The officer left by Captain Bolton at Glendearg to protect Dame Glendinning and her family. ' A married man, old and steady.' *The Monastery.*

BROAD THORESBY. *See* WETHERAL, STEPHEN.

BROADFOOT, SAUNDERS. The ' honest clown ' who carried to Davie Deans the letter Reuben Butler wrote to him after Jeanie's departure for London. *The Heart of Midlothian.*

BROADWHEEL, JOE. Mrs. Bickerton's waggoner : ' a handy boy, and a wanter and no lad better thought o' on the road.' ' And dinna sneeze at Joe,' Mrs. Bickerton said to Jeanie Deans, ' if he should be for drawing up wi' you . . . the English make good husbands.' *The Heart of Midlothian.* (*A wanter,* a bachelor or widower.)

BROKEN - GIRTH - FLOW, LAIRD OF. One of the guests at Ellieslaw Castle when a Jacobite rising was planned. *The Black Dwarf.*

BROWN, JONATHAN. ' The ruddy-faced host of the Black Bear, in the town of Darlington,' at whose Sunday dinner Frank Osbaldistone met Rob Roy for the first time. *Rob Roy.*

BROWN, ' LIEUTENANT ' VANBEEST. Mate of Dirk Hatteraick's smuggling vessel, and one of the ' brutal tyrants ' of Vanbeest Brown's youth. He was fatally wounded during the smugglers' attack on Woodbourne. When Glossin discovered that Vanbeest Brown was the lost heir of Ellangowan he tried to ruin his cause by identifying him with the ' Lieutenant.' *Guy Mannering.*

BROWN, VANBEEST. The name given to Harry Bertram when he was kidnapped and taken to Holland. He served in India under Colonel Mannering, but for a time incurred the Colonel's serious distrust. ' The obscurity of his birth could alone be objected to him,' for he ' had a fund of principle and honest pride.' Julia Mannering said of him, ' his good-humour, lively conversation, and open gallantry suit my plan of life, as well as his athletic form, handsome features, and high spirit, would accord with a character of chivalry.' After he returned to his own Meg Merrilies predicted, ' and the best laird he shall be that Ellangowan has seen for three hundred years.' *Guy Mannering.*

BROWN MAN OF THE MOORS, THE.

(1) A 'malignant demon,' with whom the Black Dwarf was usually identified. 'He's never permitted but in an ill time.'

(2) 'A being . . . the genuine descendant of the northern dwarfs . . . supposed to be seen' at Glendearg 'when the fogs were thick, and objects not easily distinguished.' 'Savage and capricious.' (1) *The Black Dwarf.* (2) *The Monastery.*

BROWNE, GENERAL RICHARD. The friend on whom Lord Woodville tried his experiment concerning the tapestried chamber. 'Every word marked alike the brave officer and the sensible man who retained possession of his cool judgment under the most imminent dangers,' yet during his night in the tapestried chamber he became 'as very a victim to panic terror as ever was a village girl.' *The Tapestried Chamber.*

BROXMOUTH, JOHNNIE. One of Hob Miller's customers. *The Monastery.*

BRYCE, PEGGY. *See* BLOWER, MRS.

BRYDONE, HALBERT. Dame Glendinning's father: 'portioner of Littledearg.' *The Monastery.*

(*Portioner,* one who owns part of a property which has been divided among co-heirs.)

BUBENBERG, ADRIAN DE. 'A veteran knight of Berne' who 'commanded and maintained the most obstinate defence' in Morat against Charles the Bold. 'One of these stubborn mountain bears of Berne . . . he would not even condescend to shut his gates, but when we summoned the town, returned for answer, we might enter if we pleased—we should be suitably received.' *Anne of Geierstein.*

BUCHANANS, THE. One of the clans 'a' mounted and in order' to make war against Rob. '"It's weel kend their quarrel—and I dinna blame them—naebody likes to lose his kye."' *Rob Roy.*

(*Kye,* cows.)

BUCKERSCHOCKINS, DIEDRICHUS. The erudite foreign scholar who dedicated his treatise on the letter *Tau* to Master Erasmus Holyday. *Kenilworth.*

BUCKINGHAM, DUKE OF (THE FIRST). George Villiers: 'the omnipotent favourite both of the King and the Prince of Wales.' Called 'Steenie' by the king from a fancied resemblance to the Italian pictures of the martyr Stephen, he was 'haughty, violent, and vindictive,' and his 'dear dad and gossip,' the king, 'endured his domination rather from habit, timidity, and a dread of encountering his stormy passions, than from any heartfelt continuation of regard towards him.' 'To ingratiate himself with the youthful Prince, he was obliged to compress within the strictest limits of respectful observance the frolicsome and free humour which captivated his aged father.' *The Fortunes of Nigel.*

BUCKINGHAM, DUKE OF (THE SECOND). (1) George Villiers: one of the 'gallants' of Charles II's 'wandering court,' and present with him in

Brussels when the news came that 'the King shall enjoy his own again.'

(2) George Villiers: a sharer of Charles II's dangers and exile, and treated by the king 'as a friend—a companion—almost an equal.' 'While expending a princely fortune, a strong constitution, and excellent talents, in pursuit of frivolous pleasures, he nevertheless nourished deeper and more extensive designs,' but he had no 'fixed purpose' or 'regulated perseverance.' 'To spoil a well-concerted intrigue by some cross-stroke of your own,' Edward Christian told him, 'would give you more pleasure than to bring it to a successful termination according to the plans of others.' 'Amid the gay and the licentious of the laughing court of Charles . . . the most licentious and most gay.' (1) *Woodstock.* (2) *Peveril of the Peak.*

BUCKINGHAM, COUNTESS OF. Mary, daughter of Thomas, Lord Fairfax. The Isle of Man having been granted to Lord Fairfax in the time of the Commonwealth, Edward Christian tried to engage the Duke of Buckingham against the Countess of Derby by urging him to claim the sovereignty of Man. *Peveril of the Peak.*

BUCKLAW, LAIRD OF. Frank Hayston, Lucy Ashton's 'bonny bridegroom.' Before succeeding to Lady Girnington's wealth he had run through his patrimony and entangled himself with Captain Craigengelt, an adventurer whose influence blunted all his finer feelings. But his honesty of purpose was not wholly destroyed, and he was ready to renounce his engagement with Lucy 'were it so urged as to give' her 'a moment's pain.' His own embarrassment and agitation intervened, however, to prevent him discovering the true state of Lucy's feelings. *The Bride of Lammermoor.*

BUCKSKIN, EPHRAIM. Mrs. Glass's 'old correspondent in Virginia . . . that has supplied the Thistle this forty years with tobacco.' *The Heart of Midlothian.*

BULLOCK, CORPORAL. See POLWARTH, ALICK.

BULLSEGG, MR. Laird of Killancureit: a 'cowardly half-bred swine' who would not 'turn out for the Prince like a gentleman.' *Waverley.*

BULMER, ANN. Mother of the sixth Earl of Etherington ('Valentine Bulmer') by a marriage which took place later than the secret marriage with the Comptesse de Martigny. *St. Ronan's Well.*

BULMER, VALENTINE. See ETHERINGTON, SIXTH EARL OF.

BUMPERQUAIGH, LAIRD OF. The permanent toastmaster and croupier of the Bautherwhillery Club. *Waverley.*

BUNCE, JACK. Lieutenant of the *Fortune's Favourite.* Originally an actor, he was of a less brutal nature than most of the crew, and showed a certain kindliness and sense of justice alike in his domineering treatment of Fletcher and his loyal adherence to Cleveland. *The Pirate.*

BUNCLE, MASTER. A servant of Sir John Ramorny : secret messenger from the Duke of Albany and Sir John to the Earl of Douglas. He helped Dwining and Eviot to release Bonthron from the gallows, but, like Eviot, threw off his allegiance to Sir John when foul play against the Duke of Rothesay was suspected in Falkland Castle. *The Fair Maid of Perth.*

BUNDLEMAN, RAM JOLLI. *See* MANNERING, GUY.

BUNGAY. Sir Hugh Robsart's favourite dog. *Kenilworth.*

BUONAVENTURE, FATHER. *See* STEWART, PRINCE CHARLES EDWARD.

BURBAGE. The 'King Richard' in Shakespeare's play when Lord Dalgarno introduced Nigel to the theatre : 'esteemed the best Richard until Garrick arose.' *The Fortunes of Nigel.*

BURGUNDY, CHARLES THE BOLD, DUKE OF. (1) While Count de Charolais he headed the league of the great vassals of France against Louis XI, and ' placed the French monarchy on the brink of actual destruction,' and as Duke of Burgundy he was ' one of the greatest Princes of Europe,' and ' burned to convert' his ducal coronet 'into a royal and independent regal crown.' But his character was 'the direct contrast' to that of Louis. 'He rushed on danger because he loved it, and on difficulties because he despised them. As Louis never sacrificed his interest to his passion, so Charles, on the other hand, never sacrificed his passion, or even his humour, to any other consideration.' He 'despised the cautious policy of the King, and imputed to the faintness of his courage, that he sought by leagues, purchases, and other indirect means, those advantages which, in his place, the Duke would have snatched with an armed hand.' ' The very soul of bravery . . . Charles the Bold drew into his service almost all the fiery spirits of the age.'

(2) 'His inmost soul . . . set upon extending the dominions of his House in every direction,' he hurried into a quarrel with the Swiss, despising them as 'herdsmen and shepherds.' But his campaign proved more than the 'morning's excursion' he expected. Defeated at Granson and Morat, he became more 'capricious, unreasonable, peremptory, and inconsistent, and rejected every counsel that was offered as if it had been meant in insult.' His 'injured pride' roused him to a last effort in the siege of Nancy, but the effort was rendered unavailing by the treachery of Campo-Basso and his Italian mercenaries. (1) *Quentin Durward.* (2) *Anne of Geierstein.*

BURGUNDY, DUCHESS OF. Wife of Charles the Bold, and sister of Edward IV of England. *Anne of Geierstein.*

BURGUNDY, PHILIP THE GOOD, DUKE OF. Father of Charles the Bold. He showed kindness to Louis when, as Dauphin, he was an exile from his father's court. *Quentin Durward.*

Note.—From *Anne of Geierstein:* 'The memory of Duke Philip, the father of Charles, was dear to the Burgundians, for during twenty years that sage prince had maintained his rank amongst the sovereigns of Europe with much dignity, and had accumulated treasure without exacting or receiving any great increase of supplies from the rich countries which he governed.'

BURLEIGH, LORD. Queen Elizabeth's Lord Treasurer : 'a good and wise servant' whose favour was founded 'on Elizabeth's solid judgment, not on her partiality.' *Kenilworth.*

BURLEY. See BALFOUR, JOHN.

BURNVILLE. A neighbouring laird whose lineage compared unfavourably with Ellangowan's. *Guy Mannering.*

BUSCAR. One of Bradwardine's deer greyhounds. *Waverley.*

BUSKBODY, MISS MARTHA. 'A young lady' who had carried on the profession of mantua-maker at Gandercleugh 'for about forty years.' She had gained experience of 'narratives of this description' by reading through 'the whole stock of three circulating libraries,' and insisted on seeing 'a glimpse of sunshine in the last chapter.' *Old Mortality.*

BUTHAN. The neighbour from whom Higg borrowed a horse to take him to Isaac with Rebecca's letter. *Ivanhoe.*

BUTLER, STEPHEN ('BIBLE BUTLER'). Reuben's grandfather : 'an enthusiastic corporal of Cromwell's dragoons,' and 'a staunch independent.' With General Monk's troop he was quartered in Dalkeith, and when on the eve of the Revolution the troop was remodelled, he withdrew from it, bought the croft Beersheba, and established himself with 'a youthful helpmate.' He once saved the life of the Duke of Argyle's 'unfortunate grandfather,' a circumstance which told in Jeanie Deans' favour when she made her appeal to the Duke. *The Heart of Midlothian.*

BUTLER, JUDITH. Stephen's widow. Left first with her young son to bring up, and afterwards with her grandson, she fell an easy prey to the Laird of Dumbiedikes' extortions. Beersheba was 'fairly wrenched out of her hands.' But the old Laird's feeble death-bed repentance saved her from being turned out, and she was allowed to eke out her existence in her old home, helped by Davie Deans' 'shrewd and sensible advice.' *The Heart of Midlothian.*

BUTLER, BENJAMIN. Stephen's son and Reuben's father. 'A man of few words, and few ideas, but attached to Beersheba with a feeling like that which a vegetable entertains to the spot in which it chances to be planted, he neither remonstrated with the Laird, nor endeavoured to escape from him, but toiling night and day to accomplish the terms of his taskmaster, fell into a burning fever and died.' *The Heart of Midlothian.*

BUTLER, REUBEN. Grandson of

Davie Deans' neighbour, Widow Butler: Jeanie's friend from childhood. Constitutionally weak, and at the same time 'the best scholar at the little parish school,' he was trained for the ministry, Davie Deans urging that the 'puir callant' would never be able to do a 'usefu' day's work, unless it be as an ambassador from our maister.' But after going through his training he did not always show the humble deference that Davie felt to be his due in theological discussion, and had it not been for the Duke of Argyle's opportune presentation of a living, Davie might have hesitated to receive him as a son-in-law.

'A plain character in which worth and good sense and simplicity were the principal ingredients.' *The Heart of Midlothian.*

(*Callant*, a youth.)

BUTLER, DAVID, REUBEN and FEMIE. The children of Reuben Butler and Jeanie Deans. 'The military spirit of Bible Butler seemed to have revived' in David: Reuben followed the law: Femie married a Highland laird. *The Heart of Midlothian.*

BUTLER, JAMES. *See* ORMOND, DUKE OF.

BUTLER, LIEUTENANT JULIUS. Promoted to be captain in Edward Waverley's stead. Edward assumed his name when travelling *vis-à-vis* to Mrs. Nosebag. *Waverley.*

BUTLER, MR. A military chaplain from whom Adam Hartley heard some particulars concerning Madame Montreville's life: 'a little of a coxcomb.' *The Surgeon's Daughter.*

BUTLER, TOM. Master of the buttery in Lidcote Hall. *Kenilworth.*

BUTTON. The owner of a London coffee-house, a 'resort of wit and literature,' into which Frank Osbaldistone had 'insinuated' some of his poetry. *Rob Roy.*

BYNG, or 'BANG.' The admiral who 'bang'd the French ships and the new king aff the coast.' *The Black Dwarf.*

C

CABESTAINY, WILLIAM. A Troubadour, the hero of a lay which Thiebault sang to Arthur Philipson as they approached Provence. He loved 'par amours' Margaret, wife of Baron Raymond de Roussillon. The dishonoured husband assassinated him and ordered his heart to be dressed like that of an animal and served to the lady. After being made to partake of food 'so precious' she maintained that 'no coarser morsel should ever after cross her lips.' The poet 'recorded with vindictive pleasure, how every bold knight and true lover in the south of France assembled to besiege the baron's castle, stormed it by main force, left not one stone upon another, and put the tyrant himself to an ignominious death.' But 'the readiest mode to corrupt a Christian man, is to bestow upon vice the pity and the praise which are due only to virtue.' *Anne of Geierstein.*

CADWALLON. Gwenwyn's chief bard. Distrustful of union between 'the true children of the soil of fair Britain' and the daughters of the 'enslaved Saxon' or the 'rapacious Norman,' he swept away all thoughts of peace from the minds of the Welsh, 'like dust before the whirlwind.' His first scheme for avenging Gwenwyn's death being defeated by Philip Guarine, he accompanied Hugo de Lacy to the Crusades as Renault Vidal, a minstrel, and showed in his master's service 'his faith in doubt—his address in difficulty—his courage in battle—his patience under suffering.' 'Use and wont' divided his feelings towards de Lacy 'between aversion and admiration,' and 'it required,' he confessed to his master, 'that I should have seen you, as I thought, trampling over the field in which you slew my master, in the full pride of Norman insolence, to animate my resolution to strike the blow, which, meant for you, has slain at least one of your usurping race.' *The Betrothed.*

CAILLIACHS. Old women on whom devolved the duty of lamenting for the dead. *Waverley.*

CAIRNS, JENNY. A creditor of Ellangowan. *Guy Mannering.*

CALCOTT. One of the islanders who 'with great zeal and fidelity' helped the Countess of Derby to regain her liberty and the sovereignty of the Isle of Man after the Restoration. *Peveril of the Peak.*

CALDER, QUARTER-MASTER. A friend of Major Mercer. *The Surgeon's Daughter.*

CALEZON. One of the Troubadours present at King René's court. *Anne of Geierstein.*

CALF-GIBBIE. See DUDDEN, GILBERT.

CALISTA OF MONTFAUCON. Queen Berengaria's principal bower-woman. She 'best knew her mistress's temper,' and in ministering to her amusement, helped to plan 'the decoy by which the unfortunate Knight of the Leopard had been induced to desert his post.' *The Talisman.*

CALLUM BEG ('LITTLE'). A page in the service of Fergus MacIvor, who could 'keep his tongue close.' He attended Edward Waverley a short distance on his way from Glennaquoich, and was ready to silence Ebenezer Cruickshanks' inconvenient curiosity by drastic measures. But not many months later he was equally ready, in his master's supposed interest, to kill Edward himself. 'A spirit naturally turned to daring evil, and determined, by the circumstances of his situation, to a particular species of mischief.' *Waverley.*

CALVERT. The 'domestic' who accompanied the Earl of Glenallan during his stay at Monkbarns. *The Antiquary.*

CAMERON, ALLAN BREACK. The sergeant sent with four Highlanders to arrest Hamish MacTavish for failing to appear in Dumbarton at the end of his leave. He was Hamish's 'best friend, who was contriving during the whole march how he could find some way of getting' Hamish off. But, impelled by his mother's taunts, Hamish shot him dead. *The Highland Widow.*

CAMERON, RICHARD. Founder of the Cameronians, the extreme section of the Covenanters: killed at Airds Moss in 1680. His followers ' went the length of disowning the reigning monarch and every one of his successors who should not acknowledge the Solemn League and Covenant,' and in 1690, when Presbyterianism was established in Scotland by Act of Parliament, they formed themselves into a separate church (the Reformed Presbyterian) in order to secure complete spiritual independence. A few congregations of this church still exist. *Old Mortality.*

CAMERONS OF LOCHIEL, THE. One of the clans who, when the battle of Inverlochy was imminent, were summoned by fiery cross. ' As the order was emphatically given, it was speedily and willingly obeyed.' Their chief, the celebrated Evan Dhu, commanded the left column in the battle. *A Legend of Montrose.*

CAMPBELL, CAPTAIN. ' Barcaldine '; ' Green Colin ': the young Chief whose troop Hamish MacTavish joined. Understanding ' the manners and habits of his country . . . he felt the utmost compassion for a youth who had thus fallen a victim to the extravagant and fatal fondness of a parent,' but he was unable to avert Hamish's doom. *The Highland Widow.*

CAMPBELL, GENERAL COLIN. The ' friendly foe ' who, by explaining ' His Majesty's kind purposes,' put an end to the ' headlong enterprise ' which had brought Father Buonaventure to England. *Redgauntlet.*

CAMPBELL, HELEN. *See* MACGREGOR, HELEN.

CAMPBELL (or CAWMILL), ROBERT. The name borne by Rob Roy in consequence of the abolition by Act of Parliament of the name MacGregor. *Rob Roy.*

CAMPBELL, LADY. Wife of the Knight of Ardenvohr: ' a tall, faded, melancholy female dressed in deep mourning ' for her children, whom the Children of the Mist had cruelly destroyed. *A Legend of Montrose.*

CAMPBELL, MURDOCH. The name assumed by the Marquis of Argyle when he visited Dalgetty and Ranald MacEagh in the dungeon of Inverary Castle. *A Legend of Montrose.*

CAMPBELL, SIR DUNCAN. The Knight of Ardenvohr: father of Annot Lyle. A personal friend of Menteith and the McAulays, he was sent by Argyle to the gathering at Darnlinvarach to try to prevent a Highland rising. Failing in this, he fought gallantly, but was wounded at Inverlochy by Ranald MacEagh. ' Brave in war, honest in peace, and true in council.' *A Legend of Montrose.*

CAMPBELL, SIR DUNCAN, OF AUCHENBRECK. ' An experienced and veteran soldier ' whom Argyle ' recalled from the wars of Ireland ' to help in the struggle against Montrose. He took command at Inverlochy after the Chief had sought safety on board a galley, and fell in the course of the battle while endeavouring to restore order. *A Legend of Montrose.*

(A 'historical' character.)

CAMPBELLS, THE. See DIARMID, SONS OF.

CAMPO-BASSO, COUNT. (1) The 'unworthy favourite' of Charles the Bold who was chosen as a husband for the Countess of Croye. But 'with his hypocritical mien, his base treacherous spirit, his wry neck, and his squint,' he became 'more disgustingly hideous than ever' to her after she met Quentin Durward.

(2) Leader of the Italian bands under Charles the Bold. He possessed 'much influence over the Duke's mind, chiefly obtained by accommodating himself to his master's opinions and prejudices, and placing before the Duke specious arguments to justify him for following his own way.' But 'there is no sort of treachery which the heart can devise, or the arm perpetrate, that hath not ready reception in his breast, and prompt execution at his hand.' (1) *Quentin Durward.* (2) *Anne of Geierstein.*

CANNY ELSHIE. See BLACK DWARF, THE.

CANTER, SIMON. A name and character suggested as his own by Edward Christian when travelling with Julian Peveril: 'a poor preacher of the word.' *Peveril of the Peak.*

CANTRIPS, JESS. 'A black-eyed, bouncing wench,' and a good girl till Nanty Ewart and she met. Eventually she 'had the honour to be transported to the plantations for street-walking and pocket picking.' *Redgauntlet.*

CANTRIPS, MRS., OF KITTLEBASKET. Jess's mother : ' cousin five times removed ' to Nanty Ewart. She took the young student to lodge with her, but not even her dignity could prevent Nanty and Jess from getting into mischief. She fell into arrears with her rent ; her landlord, Peter Peebles, 'was a haberdasher, with a heart as rotten as the muslin wares he dealt in. Without respect to her age, or gentle kin, my Lady Kittlebasket was ejected from her airy habitation—her porridge pot, silver posset-dish, silver-mounted spectacles, and Daniel's Cambridge Bible, sold, at the Cross of Edinburgh, to the caddie who would bid highest for them, and she herself driven to the workhouse, where she got in with difficulty, but was easily enough lifted out, at the end of the month, as dead as her friends could desire.' *Redgauntlet.*

CAPSTERN, CAPTAIN. 'The well-known captain of an East Indian vessel,' 'sedulously polite' to Madame Montreville. From him Adam Hartley heard that Menie Gray had come out 'to be a sort of female companion or upper servant, in Madame Montreville's family.' *The Surgeon's Daughter.*

CARADOC OF MENWYGENT. 'A young and ambitious bard ... whose rising fame was likely soon to vie with the established reputation of Cadwallon.' He gained a short-lived popularity by singing the praises of the Norman beauty, Eveline Berenger, when Gwenwyn's wishes failed to rouse Cadwallon. *The Betrothed.*

CAREFOR'T, MRS. Major Bellenden's housekeeper. *Old Mortality.*

CARGILL, DONALD. One of the heroes of the Covenant, executed in 1681. *The Heart of Midlothian.*

CARGILL, REV. JOSIAH. Minister of St. Ronan's : formerly tutor to the Hon. Augustus Bidmore. A disappointed love for his pupil's sister induced 'a melancholy abstraction of mind,' which caused him sometimes to forget, 'amid the luxury of deep and dark investigations,' the ordinary claims of life. 'As for his parishioners, they enjoyed . . . many a hearty laugh at their pastor's expense . . . but all the neighbourhood acknowledged Mr. Cargill's serious and devout discharge of his ministerial duties ; and the poorer parishioners forgave his innocent peculiarities in consideration of his unbounded charity.' He gave the dying Hannah Irwin a refuge in the Manse. *St. Ronan's Well.*

CARLETON, CAPTAIN. The officer in command of the Horse Guards when Buckingham arrived at court to explain Sir Geoffrey Hudson's presence in the violoncello. *Peveril of the Peak.*

CAROLINE, CONSORT OF GEORGE II. Regent during George's absence on the continent in 1736 when the Porteous Riot took place. As a result of the Duke of Argyle's attitude towards some of the measures of vengeance proposed against Edinburgh, her relations with the Duke became somewhat strained, but this did not prevent her receiving his protégée, Jeanie Deans, and granting her petition. 'An accomplished woman . . . proud by nature' but 'ready at repairing any false step,' she 'loved the real possession of power rather than the show of it.' *The Heart of Midlothian.*

CARPENTER, GENERAL. The commanding officer under whom Frank Osbaldistone fought against the rebels of 1715. *Rob Roy.*

CARROL. Deputy Marshal in Kenilworth Castle. He informed Varney that Amy Robsart had been taken to Tressilian's room 'by her own desire.' *Kenilworth.*

CARSLOGIE, LAIRD OF. 'A kend Queen's man,' present at the Kinross fair. 'He would be sure to make a break-out,' Hob Anster urged, 'if the officers meddled with the auld popish witch-wife, who was sae weel friended.' *The Abbot.*

CASPAR. Master of horse to Herman, Baron von Arnheim. To him, Dannischemend's appearance in Apollyon's stall suggested nothing other than the presence of the devil. *Anne of Geierstein.*

CASTLE-CUDDY, LORD. One of Captain Craigengelt's patrons. 'We were hand and glove—I rode his horses —borrowed money, both for him and from him—trained his hawks, and taught him how to lay his bets ; and when he took a fancy of marrying, I married him to Katie Glegg, whom I thought myself as sure of as man could be of woman. Egad, she had me out of the house, as if I had run on wheels, within the first fortnight!' *The Bride of Lammermoor.*

CATERANS. Highland robbers who carried off cattle, and occasionally for the sake of the ransom, people, from the Lowlands. *Waverley.*

CATHERINE OF BRAGANZA. Queen of Charles II. 'Reconciled or humbled to her fate ... she received at her drawing-room, without scruple, and even with encouragement, the Duchesses of Portsmouth and Cleveland, and others, who enjoyed, though in a less avowed character, the credit of having been royal favourites.' *Peveril of the Peak.*

CATHERINE OF NEWPORT. The mother of Julian Avenel's boy. She died beside him on the battlefield, broken-hearted that he had not wed her. Halbert Glendinning saved her child. *The Monastery.* See also PHILIP, FATHER.

CATHLEEN. One of Flora MacIvor's maids. *Waverley.*

CAXON, JACOB. 'The old-fashioned barber who dressed the only three wigs in the parish—the Antiquary's, the minister's, and Sir Arthur Wardour's. He also acted as the Antiquary's 'valley-de-sham.' *The Antiquary.*

CAXON, JENNY. Jacob's daughter: Lieutenant Taffril's sweetheart. 'A girl of uncommon beauty and modesty.' *The Antiquary.*

CECIL. Confidential valet to the fifth Earl of Etherington. *St. Ronan's Well.*

CEDRIC OF ROTHERWOOD. 'The Saxon.' 'Proud, fierce, jealous, and irritable,' he stood up sternly 'for the privileges of his race,' and did not hesitate to disinherit his only son Wilfred 'for lifting his eyes in the way of affection' towards Rowena, whom he destined to marry Athelstane. 'The restoration of the independence of his race was the idol of his heart,' and the 'courage, activity, and energy' which he devoted to the cause 'were unalloyed by the slightest shade of selfishness.' *Ivanhoe.*

CHAMBERLAIN, MATTHEW. Widow Raine's counsellor: 'a bit of a Puritan and no friend to Peveril of the Peak.' *Peveril of the Peak.*

CHAMBERMAID, BEENIE. One of Meg Dods' maids, 'idle limmers— silly sluts,' in scolding whom Meg used considerable 'eloquence and energy.' *St. Ronan's Well.*

(*Limmer*, a woman of loose manners.)

CHAMPAGNE, HENRY, EARL OF. One of King Philip's great vassals. He maintained that Roswal's attack on Conrade of Montserrat was due to 'a stratagem of the Saracens.' *The Talisman.*

CHAREGITE. One of a band of 'desperate and besotted enthusiasts who devote their lives to the advancement of religion.' Disguised as a Turkish marabout, he gained access to the English camp, and after serving as a butt for the soldiers' jests, pretended to be overcome with drink. But Zohauk noticed him creep 'gradually and imperceptibly' nearer the king's tent, and broke the strength of his 'fanatical wrath.' *The Talisman.*

CHARLES, PRINCE OF WALES (afterwards CHARLES I). 'Baby Charles' to King James : 'just and equitable in his sentiments, though cold and stately in his manners, and very obstinate in his most trifling purposes.' *The Fortunes of Nigel.*

Note.—From *Woodstock :* 'The calm pride of that eye might have ruled worlds of crouching Frenchmen, or supple Italians, or formal Spaniards ; but its glances only roused the native courage of the stern Englishman.' And again : ' If moral virtues and religious faith were to be selected as the qualities which merited a crown, no man could plead the possession of them in a higher or more indisputable degree.'

CHARLES II. (1) The 'hunted' king. In the disguise of Louis Kerneguy he quickly won Sir Henry Lee's heart ' by mimicking the manner in which the Scottish divines preached in favour of Ma gude Lord Marquis of Argyle and the Solemn League and Covenant,' and roused Alice's interest and smiles by tales ' told with so much gaiety, and mingled with such a shade of dangerous adventure, and occasionally of serious reflection, as prevented the discourse from being regarded as merely light and frivolous.' Even in moments of 'extreme urgency his courage and composure did not fail,' and he did not forget those who, like Markham Everard, had 'humanity enough' to pity his 'fallen fortunes.' *See also* WILMOT, LORD.

(2) The Merry Monarch : 'Old Rowley' to his intimates. 'Constitutionally brave,' he 'often formed manly and sensible resolutions,' but 'things not connected with his pleasures made a very slight impression on his mind.' 'The most amiable of voluptuaries—the gayest and best-natured of companions—the man that would, of all others, have best sustained his character, had life been a continued banquet, and its only end to enjoy the passing hour, and send it away as pleasantly as might be.' (1) *Woodstock.* (2) *Peveril of the Peak.*

CHARLES THE BOLD. *See* BURGUNDY, CHARLES, DUKE OF.

CHARLES THE SIMPLE. A predecessor of Louis who had been murdered by his treacherous vassal, Herbert, Earl of Vermandois, in the tower where Louis was lodged during his stay in Peronne. *Quentin Durward.*

CHARLES VI OF FRANCE. Grandfather of Louis XI. He 'tore from the fangs of the English lion the more than half-conquered kingdom of France.' *Quentin Durward.*

CHARLIE. The old freebooter who gave his name to Charlieshope. *Guy Mannering.*

CHARLOT. A valet sent to Louis by Quentin to announce the arrival of the Ladies of Croye at Liège. *Quentin Durward.*

CHARLOT. Louise's little French spaniel. *The Fair Maid of Perth.*

CHAROLAIS, COUNT DE. *See* BURGUNDY, CHARLES, DUKE OF.

CHARTERIS, SIR PATRICK, BARON OF KINFAUNS. Provost of Perth. Descended from Thomas de Longueville, whose family had for several generations served the city as Provost, he exerted himself to 'see the freedoms and immunities of the burgh preserved.' In the matter of the affray on Saint Valentine's Eve, and again after the murder of Oliver Proudfute, the citizens did not appeal to him in vain. He helped Simon and Catharine Glover in their flight from Perth, and planned that Catharine should be placed under the protection of the Duchess of Rothesay in Falkland Castle. But he trusted Kitt Henshaw too much. *The Fair Maid of Perth.*

CHATTAN AND QUHELE, CLANS. Two Highland clans by whose 'restless feuds' the country was 'torn to pieces.' At the king's suggestion, thirty champions were chosen from each clan, and a meeting arranged on the North Inch of Perth that their disputes might be finally settled in the presence of the king. So fierce was the fight that out of the sixty champions, only twelve survived. *The Fair Maid of Perth.*

Note.—Clan Quhele is generally held to be Clan Kay.

CHATTERLY, SIMON. A member of the Committee of Management in 'the infant republic of St. Ronan's Well': 'the Man of Religion.' 'The bit prelatical sprig of divinity from the town yonder, that plays at cards and dances six days in the week, and on the seventh reads the Common Prayer-book in the ball-room, with Tam Simson, the drunken barber, for his clerk.' *St. Ronan's Well.*

CHAUBERT, MONSIEUR. The French cook who attended Chiffinch when he went down into the country to meet Edward Christian and Alice Bridgenorth. *Peveril of the Peak.*

CHEVIOT. Diana Vernon's falcon. *Rob Roy.*

CHEYNE, ELSPETH. The maiden name of Elspeth Mucklebackit. *The Antiquary.*

CHEYNE, REGINALD. Father of Elspeth. He 'died to save his master, Lord Glenallan, on the field of Sheriffmuir.' *The Antiquary.*

CHEYNE, ROLAND. One of Elspeth Mucklebackit's forbears. He attended the Great Earl of Glenallan at the battle of Harlaw. 'An awfu' man he was that day in the fight, but specially after the Earl had fa'en; for he blamed himsell for the counsel he gave, to fight before Mar came up wi' Mearns, and Aberdeen, and Angus.' *The Antiquary.*

CHIFFINCH, MISTRESS KATE. Chiffinch's mistress. She had obtained from the king 'a brevet commission to rank as a married woman.' It was under her care that Edward Christian placed his niece Alice when he had persuaded Major Bridgenorth to entrust him with her guardianship. 'She would have been handsome, but for rouge and *minauderie*—would have been civil, but for overstrained airs of patronage and condescension—would have had an agreeable voice, had she spoken in her natural tone—and fine eyes, had she not made such desperate hard use of them.' *Peveril of the Peak.*

CHIFFINCH, TOM. The 'prime master' of the king's pleasures: an 'exquisite critic in beauty and blanc-mange, women and wine.' He was engaged to forward Edward Christian's 'villainous design' concerning Alice Bridgenorth, and was in close touch with Buckingham's intrigues. 'Of too much consequence to be slighted even by the first persons in the state, unless they stood aloof from all manner of politics and Court intrigue.' *Peveril of the Peak.*

CHIRNSIDE, LUCKIE. A tenant of the Ravenswood family. Caleb Balderstone was not very hopeful of getting poultry from her, she maintaining that 'she has paid the kain twice over.' *The Bride of Lammermoor.*

(*Luckie*, a designation given to an old woman. *Kain*, rent paid by a tenant in kind.)

CHOLMONDLEY OF VALE ROYAL. A friend of the Countess of Derby. He made provision for her safety through Cheshire, when the execution of William Christian was under discussion by His Majesty's Council. *Peveril of the Peak.*

CHRISTAL, MARTIN. A 'broker and appraiser' at whose house in the Savoy Julian Peveril expected to deliver the Countess of Derby's letter to Captain Barstow. *Peveril of the Peak.*

CHRISTIAN, DAME. William's widow. Deborah Debbitch and Alice Bridgenorth were enjoined by Major Bridgenorth to consider themselves as under her 'management and guardianship,' even after Deborah had secured their separate residence at Black Fort. She was a 'stern old lady,' 'broken down with premature age, brought on by sorrow.' *Peveril of the Peak.*

CHRISTIAN, EDWARD. William Christian's brother, and Major Bridgenorth's brother-in-law. 'A demon of vengeance,' he trained his daughter Fenella to a course of 'fraud and deception,' and with an equal absence of ordinary humanity he was ready to sacrifice his niece Alice Bridgenorth to a sordid state intrigue. Educated as a Puritan, he retained the confidence of the 'sober' party by a resourceful hypocrisy, while acting as 'a sagacious, artful, and coolheaded instrument and adherent' of Buckingham. But he was false even to his confederates in villainy, and in the end fortune 'cast the balance' against him. *Peveril of the Peak.*

See also GANLESSE, DICK, *and* CANTER, SIMON.

Note.—Of the real Edward Christian, brother of William, Sir Walter writes in his 1831 Introduction: 'As I was not aware that such a person had existed, I could hardly be said to have traduced his character'; and again, 'The Edward Christian of the tale is a mere creature of the imagination.'

CHRISTIAN, WILLIAM. The 'traitor' who, on the Countess of Derby regaining the sovereignty of the Isle of Man after the Restoration, was brought to trial and executed for having led the inhabitants in their surrender to the Parliamentary army. Major Bridgenorth said of him to the Countess, 'He whom thou hast butchered in thy insane vengeance sacrificed for many a year the dictates of his own conscience to the interest of thy family, and did not desert it till thy frantic zeal for royalty had wellnigh brought to utter perdition the little community in which he was born.' *Peveril of the Peak.*

CHRISTIE. The youngest of Johnnie Faa's gang. *Guy Mannering.*

CHRISTIE, DAME NELLY. John's wife: 'a round, buxom, laughter-loving dame.' 'Bewildered with vanity and folly,' she was easily led astray by Lord Dalgarno, but even on their way to the castle in Scotland 'as fine as is in Fairy Land,' he had to reproach her for 'eternally looking back upon your dungeon yonder by the river, which smelt of pitch and old cheese worse than a Welshman does of onions.' *The Fortunes of Nigel.*

CHRISTIE, JOHN. The ship-chandler in whose house Nigel first lodged in London. 'A thriving man and a kind husband.' *The Fortunes of Nigel.*

CHRISTIE, SANDIE. John's father. 'He was an atomy when he came up from the North, and I am sure he died, Saint Barnaby was ten years, at twenty stone weight.' *The Fortunes of Nigel.*

CHRISTIE OF CLINTHILL. Julian Avenel's 'henchman' and 'worthy satellite.' Though formerly 'a little dirty turnspit boy in the house of Avenel that everybody in a frosty morning . . . warmed his fingers by kicking or cuffing,' he was 'bold and forward' and had 'an excellent opinion of himself.' While he had no respect for church or state, he followed his master devotedly through his 'life of expedients and of peril,' was humble and submissive to his every mood, and died by his side when the rest of his men had fled. *The Monastery.*

CHRYSTESON. One of the citizens who met together on St. Valentine's Day 'for investigating the affray of the preceding evening.' *The Fair Maid of Perth.*

CICIPICI. Julia Mannering's Italian teacher: 'that conceited animal.' *Guy Mannering.*

CLANK, DEACON. 'The white-iron smith': a friend of Mrs. Flockhart. *Waverley.*

CLANRANALD. A clan which helped Colkitto when he landed from Ireland. Their Captain, John of Moidart, was esteemed by Montrose as a man of 'sense, practicability and intelligence.' *A Legend of Montrose.*

CLANRONALD. One of the Highland chiefs who joined the young Chevalier. *Waverley.*

CLARENDON, EARL OF. Edward Hyde: one of Charles II's 'sage counsellors,' and a companion of his exile. *Woodstock.*

CLAVERHOUSE. See GRAHAME, COLONEL JOHN.

CLAVERS, JEAN. Third cousin of Jock Jabos, and 'sib to the housekeeper at Woodbourne.' From her Jock could assure Vanbeest Brown that a marriage between Miss Mannering and young Hazelwood was 'for positive and absolute certain.' *Guy Mannering.*
(*Sib*, related by blood.)

CLAWSON. A fisherman of Jarlshof, whose boat, with Peter Grot's, was available to search for Mordaunt Mertoun when his father was alarmed at his long absence. He and Peter had not gone to the fishing, 'for a rabbit ran across the path as they were going on board, and they came back like wise men, kenning they wad be called to other wark this day.' *The Pirate.*

CLAYHUDGEONS, JOHN. The man who cleared out the old chapel of the Bothwells, having, 'it seems, discovered that the stuff within—being, I suppose, the remains of our ancestors—was excellent for top-dressing the meadows.' *My Aunt Margaret's Mirror.*

CLEISHBOTHAM, DOROTHEA. Jedediah's wife. 'In a prerupt and unseemly manner and without due respect either to the language which she made use of or the person to whom she spoke,' she transferred to her husband's ears the calumnious reports which accused him of engaging Paul Pattieson 'to write a new book which is to beat a' the lave that gaed afore it.' *Count Robert of Paris.*

CLEISHBOTHAM, JEDEDIAH. Schoolmaster and parish clerk of Gandercleugh. He 'collected and reported' the *Tales of my Landlord.* While maintaining that his 'information and knowledge of mankind' were 'competent to the task of recording the pleasant narratives,' he disclaimed all responsibility to the critics for them by saying that NOT he, but Mr. Peter Pattieson, wrote them. *Tales of my Landlord.*

CLELAND. One of the Covenanters' leaders at Drumclog; a man 'of military skill.' After the Revolution of 1688 he helped the Earl of Angus to form the Cameronian Regiment. *Old Mortality.*

CLEMENT. One of Front-de-Bœuf's servants. With the others, he was deaf to his master's cries when the castle was on fire. *Ivanhoe.*

CLEMENT, FATHER. Cellarer at St. Mary's. *The Monastery.*

CLEMENT, FATHER. Clement Blair, a Carmelite priest whose teaching exercised a strong influence over Catharine Glover. When he was accused of 'seven rank heresies' she secured his escape to the Highlands under Conachar's protection. 'If you judge Father Clement by what you see him do and hear him say, you will think of him as the best and kindest man in the world, with a comfort for every man's grief, a counsel for every man's difficulty, the rich man's surest guide, and the poor man's best friend. But if you listen to what the Dominicans say of him, he is . . . a foul heretic, who ought by means of earthly flames to be sent to those which burn eternally.' *The Fair Maid of Perth.*

CLERK, JOHN, ESQ., OF ELDIN. See HUME, DAVID.

CLEVELAND, CAPTAIN CLEMENT. 'The Pirate': son of Basil Vaughan and Ulla Troil. While a mere boy, 'his skill and bravery' gained him a separate command as a corsair, and he became 'the daring leader of the bold band whose name was as terrible as a tornado.' 'Bold, haughty, and undaunted, unrestrained by principle, and having only in its room a wild sense of indomitable pride,' he nevertheless impressed Minna Troil as 'one to whom good is naturally more attractive than evil and whom only necessity, example, and habit' forced into his lawless course of life. 'From the moment I came to know you,' he wrote, 'I resolved to detach myself from my hateful comrades.' But he could not separate himself from the consequences of his evil deeds. *The Pirate.*

CLINK, JEM. The turnkey who attended to Julian Peveril in Newgate. At parting 'he exclaimed it went to his heart to take leave of such a kind-natured gentleman, and that he could have turned the key on him for twenty years with pleasure.' *Peveril of the Peak.*

CLINKSCALE. See YELLOWLEY, BARBARA.

CLINTHILL, CHRISTIE OF. See CHRISTIE.

CLIPPURSE, LAWYER. The Waverley family lawyer. When stricken in years he had associated with him a nephew, Hookem, 'a younger vulture.' *Waverley.*

CLUTTERBUCK, CUTHBERT. (1) 'The imaginary editor' of *The Monastery* and *The Abbot:* a retired captain living in Kennaquhair. He guarded himself against ennui by a devotion to the 'lighter and trivial branches of antiquarian study,' and gradually became the local authority concerning the history of the Abbey. He received these 'genuine memoirs of the sixteenth century' from a Benedictine monk who came from France to visit the Abbey and take from its resting-place the heart of the hero of his tale, that it 'should rest no longer in a land of heresy.'

(2) The Prefatory Letter to *Peveril of the Peak* is addressed to him, while he is represented as the editor of *The Fortunes of Nigel*. He also took part in the meeting of shareholders described in the Introduction to *The Betrothed* as being held 'to form a joint stock company, united for the purpose of writing and publishing the class of works called the Waverley Novels.' (1) *The Monastery.* (2) *The Abbot.*

COBB, EPHRAIM. 'A stout bumpkin, lately enlisted' 'from the godly city of Gloucester.' He was drilled by Cromwell in the guardroom at Windsor while Wildrake waited to deliver Markham Everard's letter. *Woodstock.*

COBS. A Northumbrian fiddler. *Rob Roy.*

COCKBURN. The landlord of the George Inn near Bristoport where Colonel Mannering and Dominie Sampson stayed while in Edinburgh. *Guy Mannering.*

COCKPEN, LADY. The victim of some satirical verses by Sir Mungo Malagrowther, which cost him 'a hitch in his gait with which he hobbled to his grave.' *The Fortunes of Nigel.*

COFFINKEY, CAPTAIN. The old captain who taught Bailie Nicol Jarvie the art of making brandy-punch. 'A decent man when I kent him, only he used to swear awfully.' *Rob Roy.*

COGIA, HASSEIN. A Moslem friend of Mr. Touchwood and Frank Tyrrel in Smyrna. *St. Ronan's Well.*

COLEBY, MAJOR. An 'old Worcester friend' of Charles II reduced in his old age to act as a warder in the Tower. He died suddenly during a visit of Charles to the Tower, as a result of his 'tumultuous agitation' on being recognised. *Peveril of the Peak.*

COLEPEPPER (or PEPPERCULL), CAPTAIN JACK. The 'cowardly rascal' who ran with all speed from a sword drawn against him in Beaujeu's bowling-alley. In the sanctuary of Whitefriars he became one of Duke Hildebrod's 'well-beloved counsellors,' and took part with Skurliewhitter in the murder of old Trapbois. He was killed by Richie Moniplies in the affray at Camlet Moat. *The Fortunes of Nigel.*

COLKITTO. See MACDONELL, ALASTER.

COLLEY, MR. The addressee of a letter concerning certain dreadful Apparitions 'seen in the Air on the 26th of July, 1610.' The letter constituted one of the Antiquary's *unique* broadsides. *The Antiquary.*

COLLIER, JEM. One of the gang of men who took the *Jumping Jenny's* cargo to Goodman Grist's mill. *Redgauntlet.*

COLMSLIE, LAIRD OF. One of the Glendinnings' neighbours. *The Monastery.*

COLTHERD, BENJIE. The 'impudent urchin' of about twelve years old, who attached himself to Darsie Latimer at Shepherd's Bush, and played the spy for Cristal Nixon. The 'naughtiest varlet in the whole neighbourhood,' he was guilty of 'every sort of rustic enormity.' He 'had been suspected of snaring partridges—was detected ... liming singing birds —stood fully charged with having worried several cats, by aid of a lurcher which attended him, and which was as lean, and ragged, and mischievous, as his master. Finally, Benjie stood accused of having stolen a duck, to hunt it with the said lurcher, which was as dexterous on water as on land.' *Redgauntlet.*

COLVIN, HENRY. Master of the artillery in Charles the Bold's army. An Englishman and a follower of the Lancaster faction, he was the host of Seignor Philipson and Arthur during their stay in Charles' camp near Dijon. After the disaster at Morat he came to them in Aix ' broken-minded ' and determined to hide his ' disgraced head in a cowl.' But he was dissuaded from this ' act of cowardice,' and gave his life in his master's service when raising the alarm of treachery in the camp at Nancy. *Anne of Geierstein.*

COMINES, PHILIP DES. One of the ' most esteemed counsellors ' of Charles the Bold. He played a prominent part in affairs during Louis' prolonged stay in Peronne, his ' acute and political talents ' being better suited to the king's temper than ' the blunt martial character of Crèvecœur or the feudal haughtiness of d'Hymbercourt.' ' With a profound view of subjects of state ' he had also ' a conscience capable of feeling and discerning between right and wrong.' *Quentin Durward.*

COMNENUS. *See* ALEXIUS.

CONACHAR. The name under which Ian Eachin MacIan served as an apprentice to Simon Glover. *The Fair Maid of Perth.*

CONDIDDLE, SIR COOLIE. A celebrated defendant ' who was tried for theft under trust, of which all the world knew him guilty, and yet was not only acquitted, but lived to sit in judgment on honester folk.' *The Bride of Lammermoor.*

CONINGSBURGH, LORD OF. *See* ATHELSTANE.

CONSTABLE OF CHESTER. *See* LACY, HUGO DE.

CONSTANTINE. The Emperor who first declared Constantinople to be ' the metropolis of the empire.' Having unjustly put his son Crispus to death, he raised an altar to his memory in the Hall of Judgment, and made a vow ' that he himself and his posterity, being reigning Emperors, would stand beside the statue of Crispus, at the time when any individual of their family should be led to execution, and . . . that they should themselves be personally convinced of the truth of the charge under which he suffered.' Nicephorus received pardon from the Emperor Alexius at this shrine. *Count Robert of Paris.*

CONTAY, LORD OF. Gentleman of the chamber to Charles the Bold. After the disaster of Morat he retired with Charles to Upper Burgundy, and there, with Seignor Philipson's help, roused Charles from his despair. *Anne of Geierstein.*

COOK, JOHN. The Earl of Huntinglen's cook. Lord Dalgarno was ashamed that Nigel, ' having been accustomed to eat in saucers abroad . . . should witness our larded capons, our mountains of beef, and oceans of *brewis*, as large as Highland hills and lochs.' *The Fortunes of Nigel.*

COOLIE, CAPTAIN. ' Captain of one of the Honourable East India Company's vessels, which, bound from China homeward, had been driven north-about by stress of weather into Lerwick-bay, and had there contrived to get rid of part of the cargo, without very scrupulously reckoning for the King's duties.' In return for various services he presented Magnus Troil with a punchbowl of enormous size, a 'splendid vehicle of conviviality,' which was named by Magnus and his butler Eric Scambester 'the Jolly Mariner of Canton.' *The Pirate.*

COOPER, ANTHONY ASHLEY. *See* SHAFTESBURY, EARL OF.

COPE, SIR JOHN. King George's commander-in-chief; defeated at Gladsmuir by the young Chevalier. 'Sir John has the commonplace courage of a common soldier,' Major Melville said of him, '. . . but is as fit to act for himself in circumstances of importance, as I, my dear parson, to occupy your pulpit.' *Waverley.*

COPELY, SIR THOMAS. One of those who sought audience from the Earl of Leicester at the Royal Park of Woodstock. *Kenilworth.*

COPMANHURST, CLERK OF. *See* TUCK, FRIAR.

COQUET, CAPTAIN. An officer of the Fairport volunteers; 'him that's to be the new collector.' *The Antiquary.*

CORDERY, MR. Henry Ashton's tutor. *The Bride of Lammermoor.*

CORRINASCHIAN, 'YOUNG.' A young cadet of his clan. He thought a post of honour in the young Chevalier's army his due. *Waverley.*

CORSACKS, THE. Friends of Joshua Geddes in Dumfries. Joshua instructed John Davies to take Miss Rachel there in the event of violence being done to Mount Sharon by the rioters. *Redgauntlet.*

CORSAND, MR. One of the justices of peace before whom Hatteraick was brought. *Guy Mannering.*

CORSE-CLEUGH, GUDEMAN O'. The old man who kept the hiding-place of the Baron of Bradwardine comfortable. *Waverley.*

CORYDON. A shoemaker worthy of contempt from Stephanos as a wrestler. *Count Robert of Paris.*

COSTLETT, CAPTAIN. 'A ready body,' wont to boast of his loyalty to King Charles. Asked by Clerk Pettigrew 'after what manner he served the king, when he was fighting again him at Wor'ster in Cromwell's army,' he answered 'that he served him *after a sort.*' *Rob Roy.*

COTTAH, RAM SING. A 'rich native merchant who, having some reasons for wishing to oblige the Begum Montreville, had relinquished for her accommodation and that of her numerous retinue, almost the whole of his large and sumptuous residence in the Black Town of Madras.' *The Surgeon's Daughter.*

COUCI, INGELRAM DE. 'A great warrior . . . who pretended some claims upon the Duke of Austria.' While fighting against him and his hired warriors, Heinrich of Geierstein gained possession of the great English bow which was afterwards treasured as a trophy. *Anne of Geierstein.*

COVENANTERS, THE. The members of the Scottish nation who in the sixteenth and seventeenth centuries bound themselves by oath to establish and maintain the Presbyterian doctrine and government, to the exclusion of Prelacy and Popery. The National Covenant to renounce Popery and maintain the true Christian faith and doctrine was originally made in 1581, and was sworn and subscribed by all ranks and classes. It was renewed on several occasions and in 1638 was specially directed against the attempts of Charles I to enforce Episcopacy on Scotland. The Solemn League and Covenant was made with England and Ireland in 1643 to maintain the reformed religion throughout the three kingdoms and to secure uniformity in doctrine, worship, and government. Both the National Covenant and the Solemn League and Covenant were sworn to by Charles II in 1650, yet in 1662 they were declared unlawful oaths, and all acts ratifying them were annulled. But the Covenanters maintained their doctrines with the sword until by the Revolution of 1688 a measure of religious freedom was secured. *Old Mortality*, *The Heart of Midlothian*.

See also CAMERON, RICHARD.

COXE, CAPTAIN. The 'celebrated humourist of Coventry' under whose directions one of the pageants at Kenilworth Castle was set forth. 'Worthy he was to be rendered immortal by the pen of Ben Jonson, who, fifty years afterwards, deemed that a masque, exhibited at Kenilworth, could be ushered in by none with so much propriety, as by the ghost of Captain Coxe, mounted upon his redoubted hobbyhorse.' *Kenilworth*.

CRABTREE, MR. The Fairport nurseryman and seedsman. *The Antiquary*.

CRACKENTHORP, DOLL. Joe's daughter : 'a rare wench.' Joe was able to give Doll 'a pretty penny, if he likes the tight fellow that would turn in with her for life.' *Redgauntlet*.

CRACKENTHORP, JOE. Landlord of an inn on the Cumberland coast where people 'on dangerous errands' met. But he kept himself 'clear,' as he told Cristal Nixon, and was no man's 'cat's paw.' 'He is the prince of skinkers,' Nanty Ewart said to Alan Fairford, 'and the father of the free trade—not a stingy hypocritical devil like old Turnpenny Skinflint, that drinks drunk on other folk's cost, and thinks it sin when he has to pay for it—but a real hearty old cock ;—the sharks have been at and about him this many a day, but Father Crackenthorp knows how to trim his sails—never a warrant but he hears of it before the ink's dry. He is *bonus socius* with headborough and constable. The King's Exchequer could not bribe a man to inform against him.' *Redgauntlet*.

(*Skinker*, a drinker.)

CRACKENTHORP, MRS. Joe's wife : 'a canny woman.' *Redgauntlet*.

CRAIGDALLIE, BAILIE ADAM. 'A grave old man,' 'the oldest Bailie of the burgh.' He presided over the meeting of citizens gathered to discuss the affray of St. Valentine's Eve, headed the deputation which made appeal to the Provost, Sir Patrick Charteris, and also took part in the investigation concerning the murder of Oliver Proudfute. Jealous of the burghers' rights and fearless in his guardianship of them, he gave calm and judicious counsel for their preservation. *The Fair Maid of Perth.*

(*Bailie*, a magistrate next in rank to the Provost.)

CRAIGENGELT, CAPTAIN. 'A common gambler and an informer.' He professed to have established 'useful connexions' with Versailles and Saint Germains, and was anxious to introduce Bucklaw and the Master of Ravenswood there. But the change in Bucklaw's fortunes which followed his aunt's death reconciled Craigengelt to an easier life as Bucklaw's boon companion and 'parasite.' He could 'hoist any colours at a pinch.' *The Bride of Lammermoor.*

CRAIG-IN-PERIL. The name with which Pate Maxwell signed the letter he gave to Alan Fairford for Redgauntlet. *Redgauntlet.*

CRAMBAGGE, SIR PAUL. Lady Foljambe's successor: 'a sour fanatic knight,' who turned the two nuns from St. Roque adrift, and spoiled the private chapel. He refrained from destroying the Foljambe apartments only on the ground of unnecessary expense. *The Fortunes of Nigel.*

CRAMFEEZER, LADY. 'The auld laird's widow.' She married young Gilliewhackit, and Donald Bean Lean danced at their wedding. *Waverley.*

CRAMP, CORPORAL. The officer ordered by Captain Thornton to hang 'the Dougal creature' when he pretended that he could not guide the Captain to Rob Roy. *Rob Roy.*

CRANBOURNE, SIR JASPER. An old Cavalier who had had 'a troublesome time of it for many a year.' He had 'sense, as well as spirit and courage,' and helped Lady Peveril through some of the difficulties of her Restoration feast. He was also the bearer of Sir Geoffrey's offer to Major Bridgenorth of 'such satisfaction as is due from one gentleman of condition to another.' *Peveril of the Peak.*

CRANE, DAME ALISON. Mistress of the Crane Inn, Marlborough. On their arrival there Tressilian and Wayland Smith heard the news that 'the devil hath flown away with him they called Wayland Smith ... this very blessed morning.' *Kenilworth.*

CROME, MASTER. Owner of the Crane Inn, Marlborough: 'a mean-looking hop-o'-my-thumb sort of person, whose halting gait, and long neck, and meddling henpecked insignificance, are supposed to have given origin to the celebrated old English tune of "My Dame hath a lame tame Crane."' *Kenilworth.*

CRANK, DAME. 'The papist laundress' of Marlborough. 'Tell me, gentlefolks,' she said to the company in the Crane Inn, 'if the devil ever had such a hand among ye, as to snatch away your smiths and your artists from under your nose, when the good Abbots of Abingdon had their own ? By Our Lady, no!—they had their hallowed tapers, and their holy water, and their relics, and what not, could send the foulest fiends a-packing.—Go ask a heretic parson to do the like.—But ours were a comfortable people.' *Kenilworth.*

CRAON, MONSEIGNEUR DE. One of the nobles of Burgundy who assembled 'to superintend the defence of the country' when Charles the Bold retired to Upper Burgundy after the defeat at Morat. *Anne of Geierstein.*

CRAWFORD, DAVID LINDSAY, EARL OF (THE FIRST). A youth who gave 'patronage' to Sir John Ramorny when Oliver Proudfute's widow made appeal to bier-right. He acted for Clan Quhele in arranging with the Lord High Constable Errol 'all points of etiquette' concerning the combat with Clan Chattan. As a lad of fifteen he had 'the deep passions and fixed purpose of a man of thirty,' and was afterwards known as the Tiger Earl. *The Fair Maid of Perth.*

For bier-right *see* LUNDIN, SIR LOUIS (*Note*).

CRAWFORD, JOHN, LORD. Captain of Louis' Scottish Guard : prudent and dignified, he was held in great respect 'by these proud soldiers, who seemed to respect no one else.' To Louis he was the 'trusty' Crawford, and threw himself between the King and the Duke of Burgundy at a dangerous moment after the banquet in Peronne. He had 'an eye that had looked upon death as his play-fellow in thirty pitched battles, but which, nevertheless, expressed a calm contempt of danger, rather than the ferocious courage of a mercenary soldier.' *Quentin Durward.*

CRENTHEMINACHCRYME. The first of Sir Arthur Wardour's list of Pictish kings, 'well-authenticated' down to Drusterstone, whose death concluded their dynasty. Others were : Drust Macmorachin, Trynel Maclachlin, Gormach Macdonald, Alpin Macmetegus, Drust Mactallargam, Golarge Macchananail, Kenneth Macferedith, Eachan Macfungus. To the Antiquary these were merely a 'bead-roll of unbaptized jargon' : 'mushroom monarchs every one of them.' *The Antiquary.*

CRESSWELL, MOTHER. The subject of the Duke of Buckingham's funeral sermon which won a bet of a thousand pounds from Sir Charles Sedley. *Peveril of the Peak.*

CRÈVECŒUR, COUNTESS OF. The Count's wife, 'a woman of spirit equal to her birth and to the beauty which she preserved even in her matronly years.' She accompanied the Countess of Croye into the presence of Charles the Bold, and protected her against the worst of his passion. *Quentin Durward.*

CRÈVECŒUR DE CORDÉS, PHILIP, COUNT. 'A renowned and undaunted warrior' sent as ambassador by the Duke of Burgundy to demand from Louis the redress of certain wrongs and the restoration of the fugitive Countesses. As a ' climax of audacity ' he charged Louis in the face of his whole court with breach of faith, and defied him in the Duke's name. But when Louis had put himself into the Duke's power by visiting Peronne, Crèvecœur was equally bold in urging his master ' to rein the violence ' of his temper, ' however justly offended,' and ' not to attempt to revenge one horrid murder by another yet worse ! ' *Quentin Durward.*

CRISPUS. *See* CONSTANTINE.

CROFTANGRY, CHRYSTAL. The imaginary editor of *The Chronicles of the Canongate*. As a young man, he ' ran too fast to run long,' and spent his patrimony ' in a few years of idle expense and folly.' Twenty years abroad changed him from ' a haughty, pettish, ignorant, dissipated, broken-down Scottish laird ' to ' an elderly bachelor gentleman.' Finding the family estate in the market, but changed beyond all liking by Mr. Treddles' improvements, he preferred to settle in the Canongate with Janet MacEvoy as his housekeeper. ' A borderer . . . between two generations,' he was ' a mere looker-on ; seldom an unmoved, and sometimes an angry spectator, but still a spectator only, of the pursuits of mankind.' Yet he had ' leisure and reflection ' for literary undertakings, and gladly availed himself of Mrs. Bethune Baliol's manuscripts. *Chronicles of the Canongate.*

CROFTANGRY, GILBERT. An ancestor of Chrystal, killed at Flodden. The estate of Glentanner came into the family through his wife, Tib Sommeril. *The Highland Widow.*

CROFTANGRY, JOHN and WILLIAM. Chrystal's elder brothers : ' hopeful young gentlemen ' who died young. *The Highland Widow.*

CROFTS, MASTER. The young gallant who persisted in making unseasonable references to the ' pretty pageant ' in which Sir Geoffrey Hudson was presented to Henrietta Maria in a pie. He was killed by Sir Geoffrey in a duel. ' Thus fell youth, hopes, and bravery, a sacrifice to a silly and thoughtless jest.' *Peveril of the Peak.*

CROMBIE. The solitary cow left to Mother Bridget and Catherine Seyton in the nunnery of St. Catherine. Roland Graeme found it lodged in the deserted refectory of the convent. *The Abbot.*

CROMWELL, GENERAL OLIVER. ' The person whose valour had made him the darling of the army . . . and who was alone in the situation to *settle the nation*.' ' His demeanour was so blunt as sometimes might be termed clownish, yet there was in his language and manner a force and energy corresponding to his character, which impressed awe, if it did not impose respect ; and there were even times when that dark and subtle spirit expanded itself, so as almost to conciliate affection. The turn for humour, which displayed itself by fits, was broad, and of a low, and sometimes practical character. Something there was in his disposition congenial to that of his countrymen; a contempt of folly, a hatred of affectation, and a dislike of ceremony, which, joined to the strong intrinsic qualities of sense and courage, made him in many respects not an unfit representative of the democracy of England.' 'His deep policy and ardent enthusiasm were intermingled with a strain of hypochondriacal passion' which shook him to his depths, when at times he thought of Charles I's 'cold, calm face' and 'proud, yet complaining eye.' But he could plead to his conscience, 'Not wealth nor power brought me from my obscurity. The oppressed consciences, the injured liberties of England, were the banner that I followed.' *Woodstock.*

CROOKSHANK. One of the citizens who met together on St. Valentine's Day 'for investigating the affray of the preceding evening.' *The Fair Maid of Perth.*

CROSBIE, MRS. JENNY. The Provost's wife and a fourth cousin of Redgauntlet. She 'was supposed to have brought a spice of politics into Mr. Crosbie's household along with her; and the Provost's enemies at the Council-table of the burgh used to observe, that he uttered there many a bold harangue against the Pretender, and in favour of King George and government, of which he dared not have pronounced a syllable in his own bedchamber.' *Redgauntlet.*

CROSBIE, WILLIAM. Provost of Dumfries: a friend of Mr. Saunders Fairford, and writer of the letter concerning Darsie Latimer's disappearance which caused Alan to throw up Peter Peebles' case and hasten to search for his friend. The Provost was cautious and wary and unwilling to take steps against the rioters, but eventually induced Mr. Pate Maxwell to give Alan a letter for Redgauntlet. After acute labour in getting to the point, he gave Alan the parting advice, 'Take a keek into Pate's letter before ye deliver it.' *Redgauntlet.*

(*Keek,* a glance.)

CROSSBITE, MR. One of the learned counsel at the Courts to whom Mr. Saunders Fairford insisted on introducing Alan. *Redgauntlet.*

CROSSMYLOOF, MR. A Counsellor whom Saddletree was fond of quoting. 'A round-spun Presbyterian, and a ruling elder to boot.' *The Heart of Midlothian.*

CROSSPATCH. Jenkin Vincent's tailor. Dame Ursley promised to use her influence with him 'to take a long day' for Jin's bill. *The Fortunes of Nigel.*

CROYE, COUNTESS HAMELINE DE. Aunt and guardian of the young Countess of Croye. A 'blundering, romantic, old match-making and match-seeking idiot,' she fell into the hands of William de la Marck as a result of the selfish scheme by which she hoped to escape with Quentin Durward from Schonwaldt Castle. But 'idiot as she is,' Crèvecœur said, 'she is not quite goose enough to fall in love with the fox who has snapped her, and that in his very den.' She managed to convey to her niece the information concerning 'her William's' coat of arms, which enabled Quentin Durward to penetrate his disguise. *Quentin Durward.*

CROYE, GOTTFRIED (GODFREY) OF. An ancestor of the Countesses Isabelle and Hameline. He won the hand of Isabelle's great-grandmother 'by proving himself the best son of chivalry, at the great tournament of Strasbourg— ten knights were slain in the lists.' 'Something rough-tempered and addicted to the use of Rheinwein.' *Quentin Durward.*

CROYE, ISABELLE, COUNTESS DE. A ward of Charles the Bold. She fled to France with her aunt, Countess Hameline, to escape marriage with Campo - Basso. Louis had promised them protection, but soon he sent them under Quentin Durward's escort to the Bishop of Liège, at the same time informing William de la Marck in order that he might take forcible possession of the young Countess. But by his 'sense, firmness and gallantry' Quentin saved her from treachery, and in their common dangers 'Fate' fostered a love between the two young people, who 'strongly resembled each other in youth, beauty, and the romantic tenderness of an affectionate disposition.' As a punishment for her contumacy in continuing to refuse marriage Charles decreed that 'her fate shall be determined according to the rules of chivalry.

... He that ... brings us the head of the Wild Boar of Ardennes shall claim her hand of us.' *Quentin Durward.*

CROYE, MONSEIGNEUR DE LA. See DURWARD, QUENTIN (2).

CROYE, REINOLD (REGINALD) OF. Countess Isabelle's father: an 'old, valiant and faithful servant' of Philip, Duke of Burgundy, and 'an old companion in arms' of Count Crèvecœur. *Quentin Durward.*

CRUICKSHANKS, EBENEZER. Landlord of *The Seven-branched Golden Candlestick.* His spiritual pride was 'mantled in a sort of supercilious hypocrisy,' and he did not hesitate to profit by Edward Waverley's irregularity in travelling on 'the general fast' 'when the people should be humbled, and the backsliders should return.' *Waverley.*

CRUICKSHANKS, MRS. Wife of Ebenezer. 'The Salique law' extended to the *Golden Candlestick.* *Waverley.*

CRUMMIE. One of Martin Tackett's cows, driven off by the English forayers. *The Monastery.*

CRUMP, CAPTAIN. The 'old cross' captain under whom Nosebag served. *Waverley.*

CUDDIE. A labourer who knew the value of the stock and plenishing that had been 'lifted' from Hobbie Elliot's steading. *The Black Dwarf.*

CUFFABOUT, LAIRD OF. One of the Counsel suggested by Saddletree for Effie Deans' defence, but rejected by her father. 'The fause loon!... he was in his bandaliers to hae joined the ungracious Highlanders in 1715.' *The Heart of Midlothian.*

CUFFCUSHION, MR. An Episcopal clergyman in Wolf's-hope. *The Bride of Lammermoor.*

CULBERTFIELD, JONAS. Son of Sir Everard Waverley's steward: married to Cecilia Stubbs. *Waverley.*

CULLOCH, SAWNEY. 'The travelling merchant, that Rowley Overdees and Jock Penny suffered for at Carlisle twa years since.' *Guy Mannering.*

CULTMALINDIE. See LINKLETTER, LAWRENCE.

CUMBERLAND, DUKE OF. Commander of the army that pursued the young Chevalier out of England. *Waverley.*

CUMMING, MR. An official of the Lyon office in Edinburgh. He found that the Glossins anciently bore the motto, 'He who takes it, makes it.' *Guy Mannering.*

CUMMING, WALTER, OF GUIYOCK. 'A great feudal oppressor' whose violent death became a proverbial curse. *Rob Roy.*

CUNNINGHAM, ARCHIE. One of Louis' Scottish Guard. He cut Quentin's bonds when Trois-Eschelles and Petit-André held him ready for execution. *Quentin Durward.*

CUTHBERT. See ANTON.

CYNTHIA, LADY. A lady whose 'bewitching sorceries' captivated the young Earl of Derby. 'I cannot tell,' he said, 'what makes me dote on her, except that she is as capricious as her whole sex put together.' *Peveril of the Peak.*

CYPRIAN, BROTHER. The monk who at the Duke of Rothesay's command guided Harry Gow and the glee-woman Louise by secret passages from the Dominican cloisters. *The Fair Maid of Perth.*

D

DABBY, MRS. Wife of the 'Worshipful Mr. Deputy Dabby of Farringdon Without': one of the few London ladies to whom Jeanie Deans paid her respects. She 'was dressed twice as grand, and was twice as big, and spoke twice as loud and twice as muckle as the Queen did, but she hadna the same goss-hawk glance that makes the skin creep and the knee bend.' *The Heart of Midlothian.*

(*Goss-hawk*, goose-hawk.)

DADDIE RAT or RATTON. See RATCLIFFE, JAMES.

DAGLEISH, JOHN. 'Finisher of the law in the Scottish metropolis.' *The Heart of Midlothian.*

DAIDLE, EPPIE. Mrs. Howden's granddaughter. She 'had played the truant frae the school ... and had just cruppen to the gallows' foot to see the hanging' of Captain Porteous. *The Heart of Midlothian.*

DAIN, OLIVER. 'The Devil's Oliver': Louis' barber and one of his chief favourites. 'In his whole intercourse with his master, he laid aside that fondling, purring affectation of officiousness and humility which distinguished his conduct to others; and if he still bore some resemblance to a cat, it was when the animal is on its guard—watchful, animated, and alert for sudden exertion.' He was 'able,' yet 'good for nothing but lying, flattering, and suggesting dangerous counsels.' 'His finger was in every man's palm, his mouth was in every man's ear.' *Quentin Durward*.

DALGARNO, LORD. Lord Huntinglen's son. While showing Nigel an 'eager and officious friendship,' and professing to use his influence at court in Nigel's favour, he tried to ruin Nigel by 'inveigling him into houses of ill resort, and giving him evil counsel under pretext of sincere friendship, whereby the inexperienced lad was led to do what was prejudicial to himself, and offensive to us.' When his true character was exposed by Lady Hermione, he bore his disgrace with 'determined effrontery,' and went through the form of marriage with her, only that he might secure the means of 'burning her mother's house to ashes!' *The Fortunes of Nigel*.

DALGETTY, RITT-MASTER DUGALD. Captain in Montrose's army: dubbed 'Sir Dugald' after the battle of Inverlochy. An ex-student of humanity at the Mareschal College of Aberdeen and known as 'a *bonus socius*, a *bon camarado* in all the services of Europe,' he returned to his 'dear native country' in the time of her trouble to give her the advantage of the experience he had gained abroad. Irrepressibly loquacious, conceited, and self-seeking, he yet had a sharpness of insight and a readiness of resource which helped to make him, in Montrose's estimation, 'a man of the times.' *A Legend of Montrose*.

DALTON, MRS. Rev. Robert Staunton's housekeeper. 'A motherly-looking aged person' who was favourably impressed by Jeanie Deans. In her estimation 'order and cleanliness ranked high among personal virtues.' *The Heart of Midlothian*.

DALZELL, GENERAL THOMAS. The Duke of Monmouth's lieutenant-general. 'As much feared for his cruelty and indifference to human life and human sufferings, as respected for his steady loyalty and undaunted valour,' he was 'more feared and hated by the Whigs than even Claverhouse himself.' *Old Mortality*.

DAMAHOY, GRIZEL. 'An ancient seamstress': one of the pleasure-seekers disappointed of their spectacle on the morning of Porteous' reprieve. *The Heart of Midlothian*.

DAMIAN. A noviciate in the Preceptory at Templestowe. He delivered to the Grand Master the letter which Prior Aymer wrote to Bois-Guilbert concerning his own and Isaac's ransom. *Ivanhoe*.

DAMIAN. Count Crèvecœur's squire. *Quentin Durward*.

DAMIOTTI, DOCTOR BAPTISTA. A Paduan Doctor who under the protection of 'some friends of interest and consequence' was able 'to assume, even in the city of Edinburgh, famed as it was for abhorrence of witches and necromancers, the dangerous character of an expounder of futurity.' He was suspected of being an agent of the Chevalier St. George, and 'it certainly seemed probable that intelligence from the continent, which could easily have been transmitted by an active and powerful agent, might have enabled him to prepare such a scene of phantasmagoria' as Lady Bothwell and Lady Forester witnessed in his mysterious mirror. *My Aunt Margaret's Mirror.*

'DAMN-ME-DIKES.' See DUMBIE-DIKES, LAIRD OF.

DAN OF THE HOWLET-HIRST. (1) One of the neighbours who came to Glendearg at Edward Glendinning's request to 'make amends' for Halbert's supposed death.

(*Howlet-Hirst,* a little wood resorted to by owls.)

(2) The masquer who played the 'petulant dragon' under the Abbot of Unreason. (1) *The Monastery.* (2) *The Abbot.*

DANGERFIELD, CAPTAIN. One of Charles Topham's companions in the tour which ended in the arrest of Sir Geoffrey Peveril: a subordinate informer 'who followed the path of Oates with all deference to his superior genius and invention.' *Peveril of the Peak.*

DANNISCHEMEND. 'A brother of the Sacred Fire' who claimed protection from Herman, Baron von Arnheim, 'after the ritual of the Persian Magi' when closely pursued by the agents of the Holy Vehme. The Baron, as President of the Secret Tribunal, became his surety for a year and a day, and they 'studied together during that term, and pushed their researches into the mysteries of nature, as far, in all probability, as men have the power of urging them.' When Dannischemend's time of immunity expired, he left the castle to deliver himself to the Tribunal for judgment. His daughter Hermione had meanwhile become an inmate of the Baron's castle under the protection of Countess Waldstetten. *Anne of Geierstein.*

DAOINE SCHIE. 'Men of peace': the fairies supposed to haunt a beautiful little conical hill in the valley of Aberfoil. *Rob Roy.*

DAREDEVIL, CAPTAIN. Captain of the *Fearnought.* While serving under him Nanty Ewart 'soon learned to fear Satan . . . as little as the toughest Jack on board.' *Redgauntlet.*

DARLET, SAUNDERS. An inhabitant of Kinross who dared to be ill without sending for Dr. Luke Lundin. *The Abbot.*

DARNLEY, LORD. Henry Stewart, Queen Mary's second husband. He took a leading part in the murder of David Rizzio, the queen's favourite, and in less than a year he himself was blown up with gunpowder in a mansion near the Kirk of the Field. *The Abbot.*

Note.—From *The Fair Maid of Perth* : 'The boy Darnley, as goodly in person as vacillating in resolution.'

DARNLINVARACH, LAIRD OF. See MCAULAY, ANGUS.

DAVIDSON. The gentleman who came to the Earl of Murray 'bloody with spurring, fiery red with haste,' to inform him of Sir John Foster's approach. *The Monastery.*

DAVIE. The Milnwood ploughman who was 'ower auld to keep the coulter down.' *Old Mortality.*

DAVIE O' THE STENHOUSE. One of Hobbie Elliot's friends. He and Earnscliff were first to take the chase after the burning of Hobbie's steading and stackyard. *The Black Dwarf.*

DAVIES, JOHN. Superintendent under Joshua Geddes of the Tidenet Fishing Company's station. On the night of the riot, though he was deserted by all but the boy Phil, Joshua and Darsie Latimer found him ready to stand to his weapons. 'One of the best and most faithful creatures that ever was born.' *Redgauntlet.*

DAWFYD, THE ONE-EYED. 'A redoubted freebooter,' who with a 'band of Welsh kites' carried out Randal de Lacy's enterprise of seizing Eveline Berenger. *The Betrothed.*

DAWKINS. One of the Earl of Glenallan's men-servants. *The Antiquary.*

DAWKINS, THE MISSES. Neighbours of Justice Inglewood. *Rob Roy.*

DAWSON. The name assumed by Vanbeest Brown when staying in Westmoreland in order to see Julia Mannering again. *Guy Mannering.*

DAY, FERQUHARD. A young Highlander belonging to Clan Chattan who, in spite of feuds, loved Eva of Clan Quhele, Torquil's only daughter. He was the youngest champion for Chattan, and in the hope that his desertion might allow Eachin MacIan, the youngest for Quhele, to withdraw from the contest, Torquil allowed Eva to give Ferquhard the 'sign of favour' which made him 'forget kith and kin, forsake the field, and fly with her to the desert.' *The Fair Maid of Perth.*

DEANE. The commander of the Parliamentary ships that partly destroyed Ellangowan Castle. *Guy Mannering.*

DEANS, CHRISTIAN. Jeanie's mother: 'that singular Christian woman whose name was savoury to all that knew her for a desirable professor, Christian Menzies.' *The Heart of Midlothian.*

DEANS, DAVID. 'Douce Davie,' father of Jeanie and Effie. 'A staunch Presbyterian of the most rigid and unbending adherence to what he conceived to be the only possible straight line,' he was equally 'firm to inflict and stubborn to endure.' The deepest pain of his daughter's 'open guilt and open shame' lay not in his own and her suffering, but in the thought that 'the lightsome and profane' would 'take up their song and their reproach, when they see that the children of professors are liable to as foul backsliding as the offspring of Belial.' Yet when he came to die he was thankful also for his trials, 'having found them needful . . . to mortify that spiritual pride and confidence in his own gifts, which was the side on which the wily Enemy did most sorely beset him.' *The Heart of Midlothian.*

DEANS, EFFIE. 'The Lily of St. Leonard's': daughter of Douce Davie and half-sister of Jeanie. While still under her father's roof she ' seemed the picture of health, pleasure, and contentment,' but at the same time ' possessed a little fund of self-conceit and obstinacy ' which later proved her undoing. Betrayed by George Robertson and entrusted by him to the tender mercies of Meg Murdockson, she fell under suspicion of having killed her child, and was condemned to death. But Jeanie's heroism saved her life. Unwilling that her father and Jeanie should be 'partakers of her shame,' and unable to listen to her father ' casting up her sins,' she fled with Robertson three days after her release. Education, wealth, and position brought her no peace, and after ' blazing ' for some years ' in the fashionable world as ' Lady Staunton, she retired in her widowhood to ' severe seclusion ' in a convent. *The Heart of Midlothian.*

DEANS, JEANIE. Douce Davie's elder daughter. She was ' in her ordinary habits of life, a docile, quiet, gentle, and even timid country-maiden,' and ' her only peculiar charm was an air of inexpressible serenity, which a good conscience, kind feelings, contented temper, and the regular discharge of all her duties, spread over her features.' In the great trial of her life her soul recoiled from the lie that would have saved Effie's life, but her love found the right means. 'Jeanie was ane, like the angels in heaven, that rather weep for sinners, than reckon their transgressions.' *The Heart of Midlothian.*

Note.—Helen Walker ' the prototype of the imaginary Jeanie Deans,' was the daughter of a small farmer in the parish of Irongray, Dumfriesshire. She was born about 1712, and died in 1791. ' The very day of her sister's condemnation she got a petition drawn up,' and afterwards ' walked the whole distance to London barefoot.' There, with the help of John, Duke of Argyle, she gained a pardon. One of the last acts of Scott's life was to raise a tombstone to her memory in Irongray churchyard.

DEANS, REBECCA. Davie's second wife : Effie's mother. After her death Woodend ' became altogether distasteful ' to Davie. He removed to St. Leonard's Crags, and there employed his ' substance and experience ' as a cow-feeder. *The Heart of Midlothian.*

DEBBITCH, DEBORAH. The nurse who was ' enticed ' away to the Isle of Man from her service at Martindale Castle by Major Bridgenorth that she might look after Alice's nurture according to the plan followed by Lady Peveril. 'Self-willed, obstinate, and coquettish ' she was an indifferent guardian for Alice, being 'considerably biassed' in her line of duty by Julian Peveril's presents and flattery. On her return to Martindale after twenty years' absence her old lover Lance Outram found safety in flight. *Peveril of the Peak.*

DEBORAH. The charwoman who attended to Nigel's wants in Trapbois' house. *The Fortunes of Nigel.*

DEE. A 'cabalist' who served the Earl of Leicester, 'conjuring up the devil.' *Kenilworth.*

Note.—John Dee was a famous mystic and astrologer, and through his influence a Bill was introduced in Parliament in 1585 suggesting that the Gregorian calendar should be adopted in England—a reform not realised until nearly two centuries later.

DEILBELICKET. A friend who did not desert Barbara Clinkscale after her 'horrid and unnatural union' with Jasper Yellowley. He 'would willingly have cemented the friendship by borrowing a little cash' had not the good lady ' put a negative on this advance to intimacy.' Old Dougald Baresword and the Laird of Bandybrawl were friends of the same kind. *The Pirate.*

DELASERRE, CAPTAIN PHILIP. A Swiss gentleman who had a company in Vanbeest Brown's regiment: a 'special friend and confidant' of Brown. *Guy Mannering.*

DEMETRIUS. One of the 'politicians' who watched Tancred's little squadron approach the imperial city from Scutari. 'Rushing down towards the lists at the head of a crowd half desperate with fear, they hastily propagated the appalling news, that the Latins were coming back from Asia with the purpose of landing in arms, pillaging, and burning the city.' *Count Robert of Paris.*

DENNING, SIR FRANCIS. One of the Earl of Leicester's 'zealous dependents.' *Kenilworth.*

DENNIS. The cellarer in Jorvaulx Abbey. *Ivanhoe.*

DENNISON, JENNY. Edith Bellenden's maid: 'a true-bred serving damsell' and a 'complete country coquette.' She knew well how best to turn the admiration of Cuddie Headrigg and Tom Halliday to account with the changing fortunes of her mistress' family. As Cuddie's wife she did not like him to do 'onything aff hand' out of his own head, but aye to 'crack a bit' with her over his affairs. *Old Mortality.*

DERBY, LADY. One of Queen Elizabeth's dames of honour. *Kenilworth.*

DERBY, JAMES, 7TH EARL OF. King of the Island of Man. In 1651 he led a corps from the Isle to help the king, but after the defeat at Worcester he was taken prisoner and executed. *Peveril of the Peak.*

DERBY, COUNTESS OF (*née* Charlotte de la Tremouille). Widow of James, the seventh Earl. Proud and high-spirited, she would have held out 'the little kingdom of Man' 'as long as the sea continued to flow around it,' had not the islanders, under William Christian, yielded to the Parliamentary army. When, at the Restoration, she regained possession of the sovereignty as Regent for her son, she secured a speedy revenge in the execution of William Christian. In their schemes of vengeance against her, Major Bridgenorth and Edward Christian were frustrated mainly through Julian Peveril, whom she had trained in companionship with the young Earl. *Peveril of the Peak.*

Note.—The real Countess on whom this character is based was not a Roman Catholic, as she is represented to have been.

DERBY, PHILIP, 8TH EARL OF. Son of James, the seventh Earl, and his Countess, Charlotte de la Tremouille. Of a 'lighter and more volatile' nature than his friend Julian Peveril, he disappointed his mother by seeming to obey the call of 'the most idle or trivial indulgence' rather than of duty. He was 'deficient in the peculiar and chivalrous disposition which had distinguished his father, and which was so analogous to her own romantic and high-minded character.' *Peveril of the Peak.*

DERMID. Fergus MacIvor's mare. Edward Waverley rode her when he left Glennaquoich. It was this that roused Ebenezer Cruickshanks' suspicions, for he recognised the mare. *Waverley.*

DERRICK, TOM. Quartermaster of the *Fortune's Favourite*: 'an officer of very considerable importance' among the rovers. Though a partisan of Captain Goffe,

he agreed with Hawkins in thinking that Cleveland's skill was necessary to get them out of their difficulties in Kirkwall. *The Pirate.*

DERWENTWATER, LORD. One of the leaders of the 1715 rebellion. *Rob Roy.*

DESBOROUGH, COLONEL. One of the Commissioners sent by Parliament to dispose of Woodstock Palace and Park as 'national property.' 'Desborough, constitutionally stupid, thought nothing about religion at all' and 'only held his consequence as a kinsman of Cromwell.' After two nights in the Lodge which were rendered horrible to him and his colleagues, Harrison and Bletson, by spiritual apparitions, he determined that 'hopes of earthly gain shall never make me run the risk of being carried away bodily by the devil, besides being set upon my head one whole night, and soused with ditch water the next.' *Woodstock.*

'DEUKE'S DAVIE.' One of 'the inferior sort o' people' in Liddesdale who were 'kend by sorts o' bynames.' *Guy Mannering.*

DEVIL'S DICK OF HELLGARTH. The 'gentle Johnstone' with whom Oliver Proudfute had a slight passage of arms when on his way with other leading citizens to Kinfauns Castle. After the affray he found the signet ring which had dropped from the 'trophy' Oliver carried in his pouch. This ring, conveyed to the Earl of Douglas and afterwards to the Duke of Albany, convicted David of Rothesay with his and Sir John Ramorny's part in the turmoil of St. Valentine's Eve. *The Fair Maid of Perth.*

DEVORGOIL, LADY JEAN. A friend of Lady Hazlewood. *Guy Mannering.*

DIAMOND. Sir Halbert Glendinning's favourite falcon. *The Abbot.*

DIARMID, SONS OF. The Highland name of the Campbells. The defeat at Inverlochy was 'the greatest disaster' that ever befell their race, 'it being generally remarked that they were as fortunate in the issue of their undertakings, as they were sagacious in planning, and courageous in executing them.' *A Legend of Montrose.*

DIBBLE, DAVIE. The Antiquary's gardener. *The Antiquary.*

DICCON BEND-THE-BOW. *See* LOCKSLEY.

DICK. The Woolverton miller. *Rob Roy.*

DICK. One of the privates who took part in the mutiny at Tillietudlem. After the Revolution, like Frank Inglis, he was in the pay of Basil Olifant, but he did not share in the treachery to Lord Evandale without scruples. *Old Mortality.*

DICK, PROVOST. Sir William Dick of Braid, at one time the wealthiest man of his day in Scotland. He was a zealous Covenanter, and in 1641 lent one hundred thousand merks to the Scottish Convention of Estates for the payment of the army. During the Commonwealth he 'provoked the displeasure of the ruling party,' and 'was fleeced' of his money, and thrown into prison. There he died in 1655. *The Heart of Midlothian.*

DICK OF THE DINGLE. One of Hobbie Elliot's neighbours. *The Black Dwarf.*

DICKENS, DAME MARTHA. Major Bridgenorth's housekeeper at Moultrassie. She 'has sense,' Lady Peveril said, 'and is careful.' *Peveril of the Peak.*

DICKSON, CHARLES. Tom's son. As Sir John de Walton forced his way out of St. Bride's Church when the alarm was raised on Palm Sunday, Tom met him and 'heaped blow on blow, seconding with all his juvenile courage every effort he could make, in order to attain the prize due to the conqueror of the renowned de Walton.' *Castle Dangerous.*

DICKSON, TOM, OF HAZELSIDE. 'One of the most honest fellows of the dale, and ... as high a warrior ... as any noble gentleman that rode in the band of the Douglas.' Set by Douglas to protect the Lady Augusta of Berkley during the combat at St. Bride's Church on Palm Sunday, he would not allow his attention to be distracted by the dead body of his son 'which lay at his feet, a model of beauty and strength.' 'This youth's death is in no way forgotten,' he said, 'though this be not the time to remember it.' *Castle Dangerous.*

Note.—In reality it was Tom, not his son, who was killed on Palm Sunday.

DIDDLEUM, DR. Sir Hugh Robsart's doctor. His draught 'was emptied out by the housemaid,' Will

Badger preferring to administer Wayland Smith's. *Kenilworth.*

DIETERICK. *See* FLAMMOCK, WILKIN.

DIGGEN. The Woodstock sexton to whom Jocelin Joliffe would gladly have delegated the task of burying Tomkins. *Woodstock.*

DIGGES, MARIA. 'A little miss of fourteen,' 'sweetly communicative' in public of the remarks which Lady Penelope Penfeather made in private. *St. Ronan's Well.*

DIGGORY, FATHER. A Brother in St. Botolph's Priory 'severely afflicted by the toothache, so that he could only eat on one side of his jaws.' *Ivanhoe.*

DINAH. One of the attendants at the table d'hôte in the Fox Hotel : 'a tidy young woman' whom Mr. Winterblossom 'permitted to wait on no one till, as the hymn says, "All his wants were well supplied."' *St. Ronan's Well.*

DINGWALL. 'A sort of aide-de-camp' to Burley. *Old Mortality.*

DINGWALL, DAVIE. The Dunse writer. He upheld the 'feu-charter' rights of the Wolf's-hope feuars against Caleb Balderstone's demands for subsidies of butter and eggs to the Ravenswood family. 'A sly, dry, hard-fisted, shrewd country attorney . . . a principal agent of Sir William Ashton.' *The Bride of Lammermoor.*

DINGWELL. *See* ANTON.

DINMONT, ANDREW (DANDY). The 'honest-hearted' store-farmer whom Vanbeest Brown met for the first time at Tib Mumps' alehouse. 'Like the patriarchs of old,' he was 'cunning in that which belongeth to flocks and herds'; 'the Deuke himsell has sent as far as Charlieshope to get ane o' Dandy Dinmont's Pepper and Mustard terriers.' He proved a good friend to Brown. 'I wish,' he said at a critical time, 'I could mind a bit prayer or I creep after the witch into that hole that she's opening—It wad be a sair thing to leave the blessed sun, and the free air, and gang and be killed, like a tod that's run to earth, in a dungeon like that. But, my sooth, they will be hard-bitten terriers will worry Dandie ; so, as I said, deil hae me if I baulk you.' *Guy Mannering.*

(*Tod*, fox.)

Note.—' Dinmont Junior ' takes part in the meeting of shareholders described in the Introduction to *The Betrothed* as being held to ' form a joint-stock company, united for the purpose of writing and publishing the class of works called the *Waverley Novels.*'

DINMONT, JENNY. Dandy's eleven-year-old daughter. *Guy Mannering.*

DINMONT, MRS. AILIE. Dandy's wife : 'a well-favoured buxom dame.' *Guy Mannering.*

DIOGENES. Slave to Agelastes. He guided Hereward to his master's retreat among the ruins of the temple of Cybele ; attended the guests when 'the poor hermit's larder' afforded food for the Count and Countess of Paris and the Imperial party ; and, after her separation from her husband, secured the Countess' return to the 'secret Cytherean garden-house' by a deceptive promise of help. *Count Robert of Paris.*

DISINHERITED KNIGHT, THE. *See* WILFRID.

DITCHLEY, GAFFER. One of the miners from the Bonadventure mine who helped Lance Outram to release Julian Peveril from Moultrassie Hall. *Peveril of the Peak.*

DITCHLEY, KNIGHT OF. *See* LEE, SIR HENRY (p. 151).

DITTON, TUMMAS. The Rev. Robert Staunton's man-servant. 'That eavesdropping rascal.' *The Heart of Midlothian.*

DIXON. One of Ellieslaw's servants. *The Black Dwarf.*

DOBBIN. Widow Raine's horse. She lent him to Julian Peveril when he was hurrying forward to learn what was amiss at Martindale Castle. *Peveril of the Peak.*

DOBOOBIE, DR. DEMETRIUS. The 'bold, adventurous practioner in physic' from whom Wayland Smith gained his knowledge of the curative arts. 'He cured wounds by salving the weapon instead of the sore—told fortunes by palmistry—discovered stolen goods by the sieve and shears—gathered the right maddow and the male fern seed, through use of which men walk invisible—pretended some advances towards the panacea, or universal elixir, and affected to convert good lead into sorry silver.' As Alasco, the chemist and astrologer, he served the Earl of Leicester in some of his nefarious practices, and at the same time, under Varney's instructions, stimulated the Earl's ambition by forecasts of increasing greatness. *Kenilworth.*

DOCHARTY, FATHER. An Irish priest who sometimes officiated at Osbaldistone Hall. *Rob Roy.*

DOCKET, MR. The Gandercleugh lawyer. *Count Robert of Paris.*

DODDS, JOHNNY, OF FARTHING'S ACRE. A friend of Davie Deans. Davie considered that Johnny with 'ae man mair that shall be nameless,' 'had kept the true testimony . . . avoiding right hand snares and extremes and left hand way-slidings.' *The Heart of Midlothian.*

DODS, MEG. Landlady of the Cleikum Inn, St. Ronan's. 'The most restless and bustling of human creatures,' 'she ruled all matters with a high hand, not only over her men-servants and maid-servants, but over the stranger within her gates,' never hesitating to silence his complaints by a peremptory sentence of banishment. She said of herself 'that her bark was worse than her bite; but what teeth could have matched a tongue, which, when in full career, is vouched to have been heard from the Kirk to the Castle of Saint Ronan's?' With the increasing popularity of the rival hotel at the Well her humour became more capricious, but to favoured travellers like Frank Tyrrel and Mr. Touchwood she could make her inn 'the neatest and most comfortable old-fashioned house in Scotland.' Her oddities 'were merely the rust which had accumulated upon her character, but without impairing its native strength and energy.' *St. Ronan's Well.*

DOGGET. Warder to Damian de Lacy when he was imprisoned on a charge of treason. *The Betrothed.*

DOGUIN. Muleteer at the Fleur-de-Lys Inn, Plessis-les-Tours. He told Saunders Steed the secret of the two ladies whom he had convoyed to the Castle in close litters. *Quentin Durward.*

DOILLY, SIR FOULK. *See* LEICESTER, EARL OF (p. 151).

DONACHA AN AMRIGH. Duncan with the Cap. 'A gifted seer' who had served Donald Bean Lean well. His son Malcolm did not win the same respect. *Waverley.*

DONACHA DHU NA DUNAIGH. Black Duncan the Mischievous, 'the prime pest of the parish of Knocktarlitie' in the troubled times about 1745. Originally a tinker, he bought Effie Deans' son from Annaple Bailzou. Donacha Dhu lost his life in the attack on Sir George Staunton and his party, which also proved fatal to Sir George. *The Heart of Midlothian.*

DONALD. One of the Duke of Argyle's gamekeepers. He gave Lady Staunton and David Butler his protection after their encounter with Donacha Dhu and The Whistler. *The Heart of Midlothian.*

DONALD. An old Highland servant belonging to the McAulay family. *A Legend of Montrose.*

DONALD, LORD OF THE ISLES. Leader of the Highlanders in the battle of Harlaw, when the Great Earl of Glenallan was killed. He claimed the Earldom of Ross, but, though Harlaw was indecisive, he was obliged to retire and renounce his claim. *The Antiquary.*

DONALD NAN ORD (*i.e.* of the Hammer). A Highland Captain 'who used to work at the anvil with a sledge-hammer in each hand.' In admiration of his skill, the Knight of Avenel caused the youth of his household, Roland Graeme amongst them, 'to learn the use of axe and hammer.' *The Abbot.*

DONDERDRECHT, CAPTAIN. Captain of the *Eintracht* of Rotterdam. Magnus Troil hoped he would never hear the story of the whale which came to Burgh-Westra. 'He would swear, donner and blitzen, we were only fit to fish flounders.' *The Pirate.*

DONNERHUGEL, RUDOLPH OF. 'The Young Bear of Berne': one of the deputies sent by the Swiss Confederation to remonstrate with the Duke of Burgundy on the aggressions and exactions of von Hagenbach. 'Brave and highly esteemed by his fellow-citizens ... ambitious ... and desirous of distinction,' he was in league with Count Albert of Geierstein, the Duke of Lorraine, and the young men of Bâle, and was determined that the remonstrance of the deputies should 'pave the way for hostilities.' With the progress of the war 'his services grew more indispensable' and he became 'importunate' in demanding Anne of Geierstein's hand. But to Count Albert he was merely 'a presumptuous young man whose uncle was a domestic in the house of my wife's father,' and the Count welcomed the result of the duel to which he challenged Arthur Philipson. *Anne of Geierstein.*

DONNERHUGEL, STEPHEN OF. Rudolph's father. He 'fought so gloriously at Sempach, abreast with the famous de Winkelried.' *Anne of Geierstein.*

DONNERHUGEL, THEODORE OF. The favourite page of the last Baron von Arnheim : uncle to Rudolph of Donnerhugel. 'He witnessed with his own eyes, and heard with his own ears, great part of the melancholy and mysterious events,' with a recital of which Rudolph tried to influence Arthur Philipson's mind against Anne of Geierstein. *Anne of Geierstein.*

DONNOCHY. The Robertsons of Athole : one of the Highland clans which joined the young Chevalier. *Waverley.*

DOOLITTLE, CAPTAIN. The old captain whose 'happy state of half-pay indolence' induced young Clutterbuck to choose the army as his profession. *The Monastery.*

DOPPLETHUR, JAN. The host of 'the best tavern in Peronne.' There Le Glorieux found Galeotti when sent for him by Louis. *Quentin Durward.*

DORCAS. One of the two 'aged crones' who kept the Countess of Leicester's apartments in order at Cumnor Place. *Kenilworth.*

DORCAS (or CICELY). One of the two servants who waited on Darsie Latimer during his confinement in Cumberland. She treated him like a spoiled child ; 'an arch grin, which she cannot always suppress, seems to acknowledge that she understands perfectly well the game which she is playing, and is determined to keep me in ignorance.' *Redgauntlet.*

DOROTHY. Jedediah Cleishbotham's 'handmaiden' : 'buxom and comely of aspect.' *Old Mortality.*

DOUBAN. 'The experienced leech' under whose care Ursel was placed after his release. His 'medical skill is sufficiently able to counterbalance the weight of years which hang upon him.' *Count Robert of Paris.*

DOUBLEFEE, JACOB. An agent of the Duke of Buckingham. The Duke's gratitude to Jerningham for special service took the form of an order on Jacob 'with two years' interest,' he himself needing his 'loose gold.' *Peveril of the Peak.*

DOUBLEFEE, MISTRESS. Old Sergeant Doublefee's daughter. She 'jumped out of window and was married at Mayfair to a Scotsman with a hard name.' *The Fortunes of Nigel.*

DOUBLEIT, DR. An admirer of St. Duthac's Blessed Bear of Bradwardine, which he called *Ursa Major*. *Waverley.*

DOUBLESTITCH. The tailor who arrayed Master Nicholas Blount in his 'braveries' for court. 'If we must be fools,' Nicholas said, 'ever let us be fools of the first head.' *Kenilworth.*

Douce Davie. *See* Deans, David.

'Dougal creature,' The. *See* Gregor, Dougal.

Dougal-Ciar (*i.e.* Mouse-coloured). The founder of Rob Roy's line. *Rob Roy.*

Douglas, Sholto. 'The first man . . . memorable among those of this mighty line.' With the words 'Sholto Dhu Glass' (see yon dark grey man), he was pointed out to a Scottish king of the eighth century as the man 'whose exertions had gained the battle for his native prince.' *Castle Dangerous.*

Douglas, William the Hardy. Sir James' father. 'He fought in defence of his country, but he had not the good fortune of most of his ancestors, to die on the field of battle. Captivity, sickness, and regret for the misfortunes of his native land, brought his head to the grave in his prison-house, in the land of the stranger.' *Castle Dangerous.*

Douglas, 'The Good' Sir James. The dispossessed owner of Douglas Castle, 'ready to undergo every peril in the cause of Robert the Bruce . . . and sworn and devoted, with such small strength as he can muster, to revenge himself on those Southrons who have for several years . . . possessed themselves of his father's abode.' 'By various devices' he gained possession of his castle several times, but having no garrison was unable to keep it. His attacks were so constant and well planned, however, that the castle was celebrated in song as Castle Dangerous, and there Sir John de Walton hoped to prove himself worthy of his lady's love. But he too was overcome by the stratagems of the Douglas. *Castle Dangerous.*

See also Tomb, Knight of the.

Douglas, Archibald, third Earl of. 'The Grim': one of King Robert's 'powerful and dangerous lords,' 'terrible alike from the extent of his lands, from the numerous offices and jurisdictions with which he was invested, and from his personal qualities of wisdom and valour, mingled with indomitable pride, and more than the feudal love of vengeance.' By offering 'a larger dowry with his daughter Marjory than the Earl of March had proffered,' he secured the Duke of Rothesay as his daughter's husband. But his haughty pride could ill brook the treatment she received, and at times he banded himself with Albany in council. *The Fair Maid of Perth.*

Note.—The Earl did not survive Rothesay as Scott represents: he died in 1401 and Rothesay in 1402. It was his son, not himself as Scott indicates, who married Robert III's daughter.

Douglas, Marjory. The Earl's daughter: Duchess of Rothesay. Catharine Glover found a safe asylum with her in Campsie. 'Duchess Marjory of Rothesay is unfortunate, and therefore splenetic, haughty, and overbearing; conscious of the want of attractive qualities, therefore jealous of those women who possess them. But she is firm in faith, and noble in spirit.' *The Fair Maid of Perth.*

DOUGLAS, JAMES, EARL OF MORTON. (1) The future Regent. He took a leading part in the negotiations with Sir John Foster when the Earl of Murray interposed in the quarrel between Sir John and the Community of St. Mary's. He boasted of the family from which he sprang that 'men have seen it on the tree, but never in the sapling—have seen it in the stream, but never in the fountain.'

(2) One of the 'best generals' in Scotland ; he led the van at Langside. 'Made of iron' and impervious to the 'breath of foolish affection,' he chafed against Murray's wish to remain 'an affectionate brother' towards the Queen in Lochleven Castle, rather than merge this title in the 'bold and determined statesman.' His 'dark strength' and 'tyranny' secured for his own brother, however, the temporalities of St. Mary's Abbey in spite of Edward Glendinning's appointment as Abbot. (1) *The Monastery.* (2) *The Abbot.*

DOUGLAS, GEORGE. 'Youngest son of the Knight of Lochleven, who, during the absence of his father and brethren, acted as Seneschal of the Castle.' He formed a 'deep enthusiastic passion' for Queen Mary and was the 'first deviser and bold executor of the happy scheme' for her freedom. He gloried in having 'deceived the malice of her enemies,' and died in his armour 'as a Douglas should,' happy that he was at least 'pitied by Mary Stewart.' *The Abbot.*

DOUGLAS, LADY MARGARET, OF LOCHLEVEN. Lady Margaret Erskine, mother of Regent Murray, and afterwards wife of Sir William Douglas : Queen Mary's 'amiable hostess.' 'Even while she was proud of the talents, the power, and the station of her son,' the recollection of her 'youthful frailty' gave her 'a painful sense of degradation,' and made her susceptible to the 'cutting sarcasm' with which Queen Mary avenged herself for 'real and substantial injuries.' She had adopted 'uncommonly rigid and severe views of religion' and showed to the Queen the charity which 'giveth to those who are in delirium the medicaments which may avail their health.' *The Abbot.*

DOUGLAS, SIR WILLIAM. Husband of the Lady of Lochleven. 'A man of high rank and interest.' *The Abbot.*

DOUGLAS. 'A Border gentleman' who in the 1715 rebellion commanded a troop almost entirely composed of freebooters. *The Black Dwarf.*

DOUGLAS, MARGARET. Lady Ashton's maiden name. *The Bride of Lammermoor.*

DOUSTERSWIVEL, HERMANN. Agent at the Glen Withershins mining works. For five years he led Sir Arthur Wardour 'by the nose,' and persuaded him to make large advances of money for working the mines. He pretended to have intercourse with the unseen, but was himself frightened and befooled by Edie Ochiltree in the ruins of St. Ruth's Priory. 'An impudent, fraudulent, mendacious quack.' *The Antiquary.* *Note.*—He takes part in the meeting of shareholders described in the Introduction to *The Betrothed* as being held 'to form a joint-stock company, united for the purpose of writing and publishing the class of works called the *Waverley Novels.*'

DOWLAS, DAME. The 'hooded and spectacled old lady' in charge of the set of apartments in the Duke of Buckingham's house usually called 'the Nunnery': 'the trusty depositary of more intrigues than were known to any dozen of her worshipful calling besides.' *Peveril of the Peak.*

DOWNRIGHT DUNSTABLE. *See* MERVYN, ARTHUR.

DRINKWATER, DAME. One of Dame Nelly Christie's friends. *The Fortunes of Nigel.*

DRIVER. Advocate Pleydell's clerk. 'He'll write to my dictating,' the advocate said, ' three nights in the week without sleep, or, what's the same thing, he writes as well and correctly when he's asleep as when he's awake.' ' Sheer ale supports him under everything. It is meat, drink, and cloth, bed, board, and washing.' *Guy Mannering.*

DRIVER, DANIEL. The tradesman from whom George Heriot got 'a copper-gilt pair of spurs' for Sir Mungo Malagrowther, he 'not dealing in the article.' *The Fortunes of Nigel.*

DRIVER, JOCK. A carrier: one of Saddletree's customers. *The Heart of Midlothian.*

DRONSDAUGHTER, TRONDA. Barbara Yellowley's old maid-servant, paid 'twal pennies Scots by the day for working in the house.' 'I trow she works as if the things burned her fingers.' *The Pirate.*

(*A penny Scots*, worth about the twelfth part of a modern penny.)

DROTTLE, JOHNNY. 'The auld doited body' to whom Meg Murdockson had hoped to marry Madge. *The Heart of Midlothian.*

DRUDGEIT, SAUNDERS (or PETER). Lord Bladderskate's clerk: Mr. Saunders Fairford's 'ally.' When Alan lost patience with Peter Peebles' excitement on the day his case was heard Drudgeit gladly followed Mr. Fairford's orders, 'Get him ower to John's Coffee-house, man—gie him his meridian—keep him there, drunk or sober, till the hearing is ower.' *Redgauntlet.*

DRUM, AIKEN. One of the 'kale-suppers o' Fife.' It was his lang Ladle, marked A. D. L. L., which the Antiquary unearthed at the Kaim of Kinprunes, interpreting the letters, *Agricola Dicavit Libens Lubens*. *The Antiquary.*

DRUMMOND, LADY. One of Simon Glover's customers. *The Fair Maid of Perth.*

DRUMMOND, LORD. An ally of the Earl of Douglas. Through his influence the Duchess of Rothesay found a safe retreat in the religious house called Campsie, and there she received Catharine Glover and Louise after Douglas released them from Falkland Castle. *The Fair Maid of Perth.*

DRUMQUAG. See MACCASQUIL.

DRYASDUST, DR. 'A literary friend at York' with whom the Antiquary corresponded concerning the Saxon horn preserved in the Minster. A six years' correspondence secured agreement on the first line of the inscription. *The Antiquary.*

Note.—Ivanhoe is dedicated to this 'grave antiquary,' and the Introductory Epistle to *The Fortunes of Nigel* is addressed to him. He is also represented as the editor of *Peveril of the Peak*, and the writer of the Conclusion to *Redgauntlet.* He takes part in the meeting of shareholders described in the Introduction to *The Betrothed* as being held 'to form a joint-stock company, united for the purpose of writing and publishing the class of works called the *Waverley Novels.*'

DRYFESDALE, MR. JASPER. Steward in Lochleven Castle. 'To redeem the insulted honour' of his master's house he tried to poison Queen Mary. His fatalistic beliefs made him indifferent alike to the Lady of Lochleven's reproaches and to the fear of punishment, and he undertook to be himself the bearer of a letter describing his treachery to his master in Edinburgh. 'Man does nought of himself,' he believed ; 'he is but the foam on the billow, which rises, bubbles, and bursts, not by its own efforts, but by the mightier impulse of fate which urges him.' *The Abbot.*

DUBOURG, CLEMENT. Nephew of M. Dubourg. He was under Mr. Osbaldistone's care in London while Frank was in France. *Rob Roy.*

DUBOURG, MONSIEUR. The French merchant under whose care Frank Osbaldistone was placed that he might be initiated into the mysteries of commerce. He afforded Frank the means of gaining useful knowledge 'without either seeing that he took advantage of them, or reporting' if he did not. *Rob Roy.*

DUCHRAN, LAIRD OF. A relative of Mr. Rubrick, and, more distantly, of the Bradwardines. 'Though he be of Whig principles,' the Baron said of him, 'yet he's not forgetful of auld friendship.' *Waverley.*

DUDDEN, GILBERT. Calf - Gibbie, 'who was whipped through Hamilton for stealing poultry.' 'I am inclined to think him the same with' Goose Gibbie. *Old Mortality.*

DUDLEY. A young English artist with whom Vanbeest Brown took a tour in Westmoreland. Brown assumed his name and profession when staying at Allonby. *Guy Mannering.*

DUDLEY, JOHN, DUKE OF NORTHUMBERLAND. The Earl of Leicester's father, executed for supporting Lady Jane Grey. *Kenilworth.*

DUDLEY, ROBERT. *See* LEICESTER, EARL OF (p. 152).

DUFF, JAMIE. 'An idiot, who, with weepers and cravat made of white paper, attended on every funeral.' *Guy Mannering.*

DUFFER, MRS. 'The master's wife' under whose charge Menie Gray went out to India. *The Surgeon's Daughter.*

DUGWELL, MR. Owen's name for Dougal Gregor. *Rob Roy.*

DUIRWARD, JOHN. Sexton in Gandercleugh. *A Legend of Montrose.*

DULBERRY, DOCTOR. The minister in Middlemas. *The Surgeon's Daughter.*

DUMBIE, LAURENCE. One of Jock's ancestors. His 'mouldering hatchment' hung above the inner entrance to the mansion. *The Heart of Midlothian.*

DUMBIEDIKES, LAIRD OF. (1) 'Damn-me-dikes': the 'grasping landlord' who managed to gain possession of Widow Butler's little croft Beersheba: also Davie Deans' landlord. When on his death-bed, he was attacked by remorse, but his lifelong habits allowed him to go no further than to say to his son 'Dinna let the world get a grip o' ye, Jock—but keep the gear thegither! and whate'er ye do, dispone Beersheba at no rate.'

(2) Jock Dumbie, son of above: 'a tall, gawky, silly-looking boy' when at the age of fourteen or fifteen he succeeded his father: 'close and selfish enough,' but wanting the 'grasping spirit and active mind of his father.' During many years his admiration for Jeanie Deans was satisfied by 'pertinaciously gazing on her with great stupid greenish eyes,' and it was only when she came to borrow from him the money necessary for her journey to London that he awoke to realities. Her refusal did not, however, destroy this accidental impetus to marriage, and in a short time he married the Laird of Lickpelf's daughter. 'She sits next us in the kirk,' he said, 'and that's the way I came to think on 't.' *The Heart of Midlothian.*

DUMBLANE, EPPIE. 'The corporal's wife.' *Old Mortality.*

DUMMERAR, DOCTOR. Vicar of Martindale *cum* Moultrassie before the Rebellion. Deprived of his living during the Commonwealth, he was restored to his charge on the ejection of Mr. Solsgrace after the Restoration. He 'was in high favour with Sir Geoffrey, not merely on account of his sound orthodoxy and deep learning, but his exquisite skill in playing at bowls, and his facetious conversation over a pipe and tankard of October.' *Peveril of the Peak.*

DUMPLE. Dandy Dinmont's galloway pony. 'Dumple could carry six folk, if his back was lang enough.' *Guy Mannering.*

DUMTOUSTIE, DANIEL. A nephew of 'worthy Lord Bladderskate.' He was 'ane of the Poor's Lawyers, and Peter Peebles' process had been remitted to him, of course. But so soon as the harebrained goose saw the pokes . . . he took fright, called for his nag, lap on, and away to the country is he

gone.' Mr. Saunders Fairford and Peter Drudgeit then contrived that Alan should take his place. *Redgauntlet.*
(*Pokes,* process-bags.)

DUN, HUGHIE. A former resident in the Halidome of St. Mary's whose success in life was worthy, Martin Tackett thought, of Halbert Glendinning's emulation. He became body-servant to the Archbishop of St. Andrews, and left ' a good five hundred pounds of Scots money to his only daughter.' *The Monastery.*

DUNBAR AND MARCH, GEORGE, EARL OF. One of King Robert's ' powerful and dangerous lords ' : warden of the Eastern Marches. Burning with ' a desire of vengeance arising out of his disappointed ambition, and the disgrace done to him by the substitution of Marjory Douglas to be bride of the heir-apparent, instead of his betrothed daughter,' he laid himself open to the accusation of calling ' the Southron ' into the Marches. *The Fair Maid of Perth.*

DUNBAR, ELIZABETH OF. The Earl's daughter. She was, ' with the mutual good-will of the young couple, actually contracted to the Duke of Rothesay.' But eventually Marjory Douglas was preferred before her, with no further apology than ' that the espousals . . . had not been approved by the States of Parliament.' *The Fair Maid of Perth.*

DUNBOG. The laird who warned two gipsies off his land. ' He's nae gentleman, nor drap's bluid o' gentleman, wad grudge twa gangrel puir bodies the shelter o' a waste house, and the thristles by the roadside for a bit cuddy, and the bits o' rotten birk to boil their drap parritch wi'. Weel, there's ane abune a'—but we'll see if the red cock craw not in his bonnie barn-yard ae morning before daydawing.' *Guy Mannering.*
(*Gangrel,* wandering. *The red cock,* fire.)

DUNCANSON, GREGOR. Landlord of *The Highlander and the Hawick Gill :* rival of Ebenezer Cruickshanks. *Waverley.*

DUNDEE, VISCOUNT. Grahame of Claverhouse. He fell in the moment of a ' great and decisive victory near Blair of Athole ' (Killiecrankie, 1689). *Old Mortality.*

DUNDER, LAIRD OF. Head of ' ane of the auldest families in Tiviotdale.' ' He's in the tolbooth . . . for a thousand merk he borrowed from Saunders Wyliecoat, the writer.' *The Black Dwarf.*
(*Tolbooth,* prison.)

DUNDERMORE, FATHER. *See* THICKSCULL.

DUNKIESON, DAN. The owner of a pair of plated stirrups borrowed for the ' young Laird's ' use. *Guy Mannering.*

DUNOIS, COUNT DE. Son of the celebrated Dunois, ' the Bastard of Orleans,' who had distinguished himself under the banner of Jeanne d'Arc. He well supported his father's high renown, and with his ' air of conscious worth and nobility,' there went ' such an open, frank loyalty of character ' as endeared him even to the jealous Louis. He suffered a short disgrace for aiding the Duke of Orleans in his attempt to seize the Countess of Croye, but accompanied Louis to Peronne and fought side by side with Quentin Durward against the disguised William de la Marck. *Quentin Durward.*

DUNOVER, MR. Mr. Hardie's 'one and only client.' Obliged by a coach accident to spend a night at the Wallace Inn, Gandercleugh, he entertained his fellow-passengers and Peter Pattieson by relating some of the traditions concerning the tolbooth of Edinburgh which he had heard while imprisoned for debt. This gave Peter some of the material for *The Heart of Midlothian. The Heart of Midlothian.*

DUNTER. A stout journeyman under Harry Gow. He could make a 'prodigious cast' with the hammer, but not quite such an one as Norman nan Ord. *The Fair Maid of Perth.*

DUROCH, DUNCAN. Donald Bean Lean's lieutenant in rescuing Edward Waverley from Gifted Gilfillan, and the leader of the party that conducted him from Janet Gellatley's cottage to the Castle of Doune. *Waverley.*

DURWARD, ALLAN. (1) One of Quentin's ancestors who was High Steward of Scotland.

(2) Quentin's father. 'My mother was left a widow a year since,' Quentin told Ludovic Lesly, 'when Glen-houlakin was harried by the Ogilvies. My father, and my two uncles, and my two elder brothers, and seven of my kinsmen and the harper, and the tasker, and some six more of our people, were killed in defending the castle; and there is not a burning hearth or a standing-stone in all Glenhoulakin.' *Quentin Durward.*

(*Tasker*, a labourer who received his wages in kind.)

DURWARD, QUENTIN. (1) One of King Louis' Scottish Guard. The sole survivor of his family, he was forced to serve in a foreign land,—'somewhere,' he said, 'where a brave deed, were it my hap to do one, might work me a name.' 'Quick, sharp of wit, as well as ardent in fancy,' and 'as shrewd a youth as ever Scottish breeze breathed caution into,' he was selected by Louis to escort the Countess of Croye and her aunt from Plessis-les-Tours to Liège. His fearless courage and truth never forsook him, and he kept a straight course through the tangled schemes of his master while giving him a true and upright adherence.' As her 'faithful and zealous protector' he won the Countess' love, but when the moment came to do the brave deed for which 'both Honour and Love held out the reward,' he obeyed a still higher instinct : with firm resolve, unshaken by his 'unutterable bitterness of feeling,' he gave up 'all the gay hopes which had stimulated his exertion ... through that bloody day.' *See also* HAYRADDIN, *and* PAVILLON, GERTRUDE.

(2) As Monseigneur de la Croye he helped to 'extricate' Charles

the Bold after the disaster at Morat, and 'to superintend the defence of the country' when Charles retired to Upper Burgundy. (1) *Quentin Durward.* (2) *Anne of Geierstein.*

DUSTIEFOOT. Jeanie Deans' little dog. *The Heart of Midlothian.*

DUTTON, ALDERMAN. A colleague of the Mayor of Woodstock. Mrs. Mayor, 'in her love and affection,' suggested that he, rather than her husband, should leave his warm bed at two hours after midnight to lay the ghosts in the Lodge. *Woodstock.*

DUTTON, DOLLY. The Duke of Argyle's dairy-maid. She travelled with Jeanie Deans and Mr. Archibald from London to Roseneath. At first she professed great fear for the 'wild men with their naked knees,' but by degrees she accommodated herself to her surroundings and by and by became Mrs. MacCorkindale. *The Heart of Midlothian.*

DWINING, HENBANE. 'A poor Pottingar,' 'a thin meagre figure of a man, whose diminutive person seemed still more reduced in size, and more assimilated to a shadow, by his efforts to assume an extreme degree of humility, and make himself, to suit his argument, look meaner yet, and yet more insignificant than nature had made him.' While attending to Sir John Ramorny's mutilated arm, he ingratiated himself into his patient's confidence, and suggested revenge against Harry Gow. He directed Bonthron's blow, saved the assassin from the gallows, and aided Sir John in his treacherous schemes against the Duke of Rothesay. 'A sneaking varlet' 'who never threatens till he strikes.' *The Fair Maid of Perth.*

See also LETHAM, MISTRESS JOAN.

(*Pottingar*, an apothecary.)

E

EARNSCLIFF, PATRICK. Son of the Laird who had been fatally stabbed by Sir Edward Mauley during a drunken squabble. Freer from superstition than his friend Hobbie Elliot, he showed humanity and kindness to the Black Dwarf from the first, and found in him a power strong enough to remove all the barriers against his union with Isabel Vere. *The Black Dwarf.*

EBERSON, CARL. A natural son of the ferocious William de la Marck 'towards whom he sometimes showed affection and even tenderness.' When after the murder of the Bishop of Liège in his own Hall, the followers of William de la Marck were on the point of coming to blows with the men of Liège, Quentin Durward averted the danger by a threat of instant retaliation on Carl. *Quentin Durward.*

ECBERT OF RABENWALD. A Knight whose fate foreshadowed that of Martin Waldeck. *The Antiquary.*

ECKIE OF CANNOBIE. A blacksmith. He shod the horse on which Sir Piercie Shafton and Mysie Happer rode to Edinburgh. His shoes gave a 'kenspeckle hoof-mark,' which Christie recognised. *The Monastery.* (*Kenspeckle,* easily recognised.)

EDDERALSHENDRACH. A Highlander who took part in the battle of Gladsmuir. *Waverley.*

EDERIC THE FORESTER. 'Long leader of the insurgent Saxons' against the Normans. Waltheoff and Engelred kept 'as much as possible within the call' of his bugle. *Count Robert of Paris.*

EDGAR. Purse-bearer to the Duke of Rothesay. *The Fair Maid of Perth.*

EDGEIT, MR. One of the visitors to the Well: an artist. *St. Ronan's Well.*

EDITH. Widow of Atheling, and Athelstane's mother. 'Of a dignified mien,' she 'retained the marked remains of majestic beauty.' *Ivanhoe.*

EDRIC. Hereward's military domestic. He served Count Robert of Paris when Hereward gave him a hiding-place in the barracks. *Count Robert of Paris.*

EDRIS OF THE GOBLETS. A Welsh prince, celebrated in song. Eveline Berenger was concealed in the narrow vault where he had been buried, when Randal de Lacy was alarmed by Damian's pursuit. *The Betrothed.*

EDWARD. The attendant under whose charge Lord Lindesay placed Roland Graeme during the journey from Edinburgh to Lochleven Castle. *The Abbot.*

EDWARD. Hereward's elder brother. With a body of the Varangian guard he secured the safe retreat of Alexius Comnenus to Laodicea by keeping Jezdegerd and the Syrians at bay. His devotion cost him his life. *Count Robert of Paris.*

EDWARD IV OF ENGLAND. The first of the Yorkish kings, 'renowned for his numerous victories over the rival House of Lancaster.' Having 'entered into a strict and intimate alliance, offensive and defensive, with the Duke of Burgundy,' his brother-in-law, he invaded France with 'a commodity of bows and bills such as never entered France since King Arthur's time.' But Louis soon found means to persuade him to recross the sea. 'Since he reached, through a bloody path, to the summit of his ambition, he has shown himself rather a sensual debauchee than a valiant knight.' *Anne of Geierstein.*

EINION, FATHER. Gwenwyn's chaplain, 'an able and sagacious man.' He supported Gwenwyn in his wish to wed Eveline Berenger, pointing out to the Welsh chiefs the advantages to be gained by the possession of the castle of Garde Doloureuse. At the same time he hinted that her marriage might prove no more permanent than Brengwain's. *The Betrothed.*

ELCHO, LORD. Commander of the army defeated by Montrose at Tippermuir. *A Legend of Montrose.*

ELFI, BEY. An old friend to Mr. Touchwood, with a fund of 'grave steady attention.' 'You might talk to him in English, or anything he understood least of—you might have read Aristotle to Elfi, and not a muscle would he stir—give him his pipe, and he would sit on his cushion with a listening air as if he took in every word of what you said.' *St. Ronan's Well.*

ELGITHA. Rowena's confidential attendant. *Ivanhoe.*

ELIZABETH, QUEEN OF ENGLAND. ' Queen Elizabeth had a character strangely compounded of the strongest masculine sense, with those foibles which are chiefly supposed proper to the female sex. Her subjects had the full benefit of her virtues, which far predominated over her weaknesses ; but her courtiers, and those about her person, had often to sustain sudden and embarrassing turns of caprice, and the sallies of a temper which was both jealous and despotic.' To the Earl of Leicester she showed ' all those light and changeable gales of caprice and humour, which thwart or favour the progress of a lover in the favour of his mistress, and she, too, a mistress who was ever and anon becoming fearful lest she should forget the dignity, or compromise the authority, of the Queen, while she indulged the affections of the woman.' Yet, when by his own confession he was ' doubly false,' and ' doubly forsworn,' she forgave him, and saw in him, after the Countess' tragic death, ' the object rather of compassion than resentment.' *Kenilworth.*

ELLANGOWAN, THE LAIRD OF. *See* BERTRAM, GODFREY.

ELLESMERE, MISTRESS. Housekeeper at Martindale Castle, ' a person of great trust in the family.' In her old age she made up all her quarrels with Deborah Debbitch and took her to share her cottage, ' for Naunt,' Lance Outram said, ' though high enough when any of *your* folks are concerned, hath some look to the main chance ; and it seems Mistress Deb is as rich as a Jew.' *Peveril of the Peak.*

ELLIESLAW, LAIRD OF. *See* VERE, RICHARD.

ELLIOT. One of the commonest clan names in Liddesdale. *Guy Mannering.*

ELLIOT, HALBERT. ' Hobbie of the Heugh-foot ' : a substantial Border farmer, young, gallant, and frank, ' though blunt, plain of speech, and hot of disposition.' He was ' deeply read ' in all the legends of the district, and not without some belief in supernatural appearances. But when evil came to him and his house there was that in his breast ' that would owermaister a' the warlocks on earth, and a' the devils in hell.' *The Black Dwarf.*

ELLIOT, JOHN and HARRY. Hobbie's brothers. *The Black Dwarf.*

ELLIOT, LILIAS, JEAN, and ANNOT. Hobbie's sisters. ' Rustic coquettes.' *The Black Dwarf.*

ELLIOT, MARTIN. One of Hobbie's ancestors, ' noted in Border story and song.' *The Black Dwarf.*

ELLIOT, MRS. Hobbie's grandmother : a ' venerable old dame, the mistress of the family . . . the lady as well as the farmer's wife.' *The Black Dwarf.*

Ellis. Lady Staunton's maid. She accompanied her mistress to Knocktarlitie. *The Heart of Midlothian.*

Elphin. Harry Morton's 'small cocking spaniel.' The animal recognised him after his return from exile, and so disclosed his identity to Mistress Wilson. *Old Mortality.*

Elshender the Recluse. *See* Black Dwarf, The.

Elspat. Callum Beg's mother. *Waverley.*

Elspeth. (1) An inmate of Charlieshope who told tales and ballads to the Dinmont children.

(2) 'The bedral's widow' to whom Dandy Dinmont suggested the new cottage at Derncleugh should be given. 'The like o' them's used wi' graves and ghaists, and thae things.' (1) and (2) *Guy Mannering.*

(*Bedral*, sexton.)

Elstracke, Reginald. The painter of a print showing Aldobrand Oldenbuck ' pulling the press with his own hand, as it works off the sheets of his scarce edition of the Augsburg Confession.' *The Antiquary.*

Emberson, Helen. A fisherman's wife who tried in vain to fight against her husband's fate when he was fey. *The Pirate.*

(*Fey*, shown by unaccountable actions to be on the verge of death.)

Empson. A person of the royal retinue to whose music Fenella danced 'with wonderful grace and agility' before the king. He afterwards conducted Julian Peveril and Fenella to Mistress Chiffinch's, and when they were leaving with Alice Bridgenorth he carried Buckingham's message to Jerningham to 'make sure' of Alice at any rate. *Peveril of the Peak.*

Engaddi, Hermit of. *See* Theodorick.

Engelbrecht. The Varangian sentinel who explained to Hereward the trumpet calls which alarmed him as he returned to barracks from his private interview with the Emperor. *Count Robert of Paris.*

Engelred. A squire in attendance on Front-de-Bœuf in Torquilstone Castle when the letter of defiance from Gurth and Wamba was under discussion. *Ivanhoe.*

Engelred. Bertha's father. He and Waltheoff as leaders of the Foresters 'were among the last bold men who asserted the independence of the Saxon race of England.' William Rufus 'brought an overpowering force' upon their bands, and both the 'unfortunate chiefs remained dead on the field.' *Count Robert of Paris.*

Enguerrand. Brother to Conrade of Montserrat. He commanded a division of the Marquis' vassals as they marched past St. George's Mount in token of 'regard and amity' to the English flag. *The Talisman.*

Eppie. Bailie Macwheeble's cook. *Waverley.*

Eppie. One of the Rev. Josiah Cargill's maid-servants. 'A barelegged, shock-headed, thick-ankled, red-armed wench,' she became under Mr. Touchwood's 'system of rewards and surveillance,' 'a damsel so trig and neat that some said she was too handsome for the service of a bachelor divine.' *St. Ronan's Well.*

EPPS. Mr. Saunders Fairford's cook. *Redgauntlet.*

ERCELDOUN, THOMAS OF. 'The Rhymer . . . whose intimacy, it is said, became so great with the gifted people, called the Faëry folk, that he could, like them, foretell the future deed before it came to pass, and united in his own person the quality of bard and of soothsayer.' He predicted to Hugo Hugonet that as the Douglasses 'have not spared to burn and destroy their own house and that of their fathers in the Bruce's cause, so it is the doom of Heaven, that as often as the walls of Douglas Castle shall be burnt to the ground, they shall be again rebuilt still more stately and more magnificent than before.' *Castle Dangerous.*

See also THOMAS THE RHYMER.

ERICKSON, SWEYN. A fisherman of Jarlshof : a 'confederate' of Swertha in making as much profit as possible out of Mr. Mertoun. *The Pirate.*

ERICSON, LAWRENCE. One of the young islanders who were favourite guests at Magnus Troil's. *The Pirate.*

ERNEST THE APULIAN. Prince Tancred's favourite page : one of the youths whom Bertha encountered on her way to the Crusaders' camp at Scutari. *Count Robert of Paris.*

ERNHOLD. Herald of Peolphan. *The Antiquary.*

ERROL, GILBERT HAY, EARL OF. Lord High Constable. He presided at the trial by combat between Harry Gow and Bonthron, and after Bonthron's accusation against the Duke of Rothesay was given a temporary wardship over the Duke. He acted for Clan Chattan in arranging with the Earl of Crawford 'all points of etiquette' concerning the combat with Clan Quhele. *The Fair Maid of Perth.*

ERSKINE. Dr. Robertson's colleague. Colonel Mannering heard him preach in Edinburgh. 'The Calvinism of the Kirk of Scotland was ably supported, yet made the basis of a sound system of practical morals.' *Guy Mannering.*

ERSKINE, LADY MARGARET. See DOUGLAS, LADY MARGARET.

ESDALE, MR. A friend from whom Adam Hartley received a more reassuring account of Madame Montreville's life than he had heard from Major Mercer and Mr. Butler. Esdale tried to dissuade Adam from appealing to Hyder Ali for justice to Menie Gray. 'A rising man, calm, steady, and deliberate in forming his opinions.' *The Surgeon's Daughter.*

ESSEX, EARL OF. See BOHUN, HENRY.

ESTOTEVILLE. See BOHUN, HENRY.

ETHERINGTON, FRANCIS (or JOHN), FIFTH EARL OF. Father of Francis Tyrrel and Francis Valentine Bulmer Tyrrel—of the former by a secret marriage with Marie, Comptesse of Martigny, and of the latter by a public (but later) marriage with Ann Bulmer of Bulmer Hall. 'In the face of propriety,' he brought up the two boys together. *St. Ronan's Well.*

ETHERINGTON, SIXTH EARL OF. Valentine Bulmer, Frank Tyrrel's half-brother. Jealous and ambitious, he possessed himself by unscrupulous 'deception and intrigue' of his brother's intended bride, his rank, and his fortune. To the fashionable company at St. Ronan's Well 'his manners and person were infinitely captivating,' while with 'good temper and excellent spirits' unmarred by any touch of pity or remorse, he pursued his heartless wooing of Clara Mowbray. 'Had there been passion in his conduct, it had been the act of a man—a wicked man, indeed, but still a human creature, acting under the influence of human feelings—but his was the deed of a calm, cold, calculating demon, actuated by the basest and most sordid motives of self-interest, joined, as I firmly believe, to an early and inveterate hatred of one whose claims he considered as at variance with his own.' *St. Ronan's Well.*

EUSTACE. One of Front-de-Bœuf's servants. With the others, he was deaf to his master's cries when the castle was on fire. *Ivanhoe.*

EUSTACE, FATHER ('WILLIAM ALLAN'). (1) Sub-Prior of St. Mary's. 'A man of parts and knowledge, devoted to the service of the Catholic Church,' he was sent to St. Mary's by the 'sharp-witted Primate of St. Andrews' to supply the deficiencies of Abbot Boniface. He was at first prone to deride the inexperience and follies of the brethren, but his 'strange visitation' from the White Lady led him to humble his pride and distrust his 'gifts and carnal wisdom.' Thereafter, 'his whole demeanour seemed to bespeak, not the mere ordinary man, but the organ of the Church, in which she had vested her high power for delivering sinners from their load of iniquity.'

(2) Abbot of St. Mary's, Kennaquhair. Notwithstanding 'the nearly total downfall of their faith,' he was permitted with a few monks, chief amongst whom was Father Ambrose, 'to linger in the cloisters.' He died at a time of 'deep crisis,' when his 'far-fetched experience, his self-devoted zeal, his consummate wisdom, and his undaunted courage,' seemed 'indispensable' for the service of the Queen and her faith. (1) *The Monastery.* (2) *The Abbot.*

EVANDALE, LORD. See MAXWELL, WILLIAM.

EVAN DHU. See MACCOMBICH, EVAN DHU.

EVAN DHU OF LOCHIEL. One of the Highland Chiefs who attended the gathering at Darnlinvarach, and put themselves under Montrose. He deprecated personal jealousies amongst the Chiefs regarding precedence. 'My voice,' he said, 'shall be for that general whom the King shall name.' *A Legend of Montrose.*

See also CAMERONS OF LOCHIEL.

EVANS, EVAN. A 'thorough-paced' Welshman in attendance on the Earl of Sussex. On the occasion of the Queen's unexpected visit to Say's Court, Raleigh feared she should find him breakfasting off his 'leek porridge and toasted cheese—and she detests, they say, all coarse meats, evil smells, and strong wines.' *Kenilworth.*

EVERARD, MARKHAM. Sir Henry Lee's nephew. As a 'bright-haired boy' he had been much loved by his uncle, but when he became 'a distinguished and successful soldier' he was denounced by Sir Henry as 'a rebel more detestable on account of his success, the more infamous through the plundered wealth with which he hopes to gild his villany.' Though naturally 'hot, keen, earnest, impatient,' he acquiesced in Alice's dutiful submission to her father, while using his influence to secure their safety in Woodstock Lodge. He saw in Cromwell the best hope that 'the nation should have repose under a firmly-established government of strength sufficient to protect property, and of lenity enough to encourage the return of tranquillity.' But at no time did he favour extreme measures, and he regained his uncle's respect and affection by loyally guarding the secret of Louis Kerneguy's identity, after Louis had revealed himself as the King. *Woodstock.*

EVERARD, UNCLE. Markham's father and Alice Lee's uncle. 'He had been, till partly laid aside by continued indisposition, an active and leading member of the Long Parliament,' but was 'not disposed ... to the extreme of enthusiasm.' His friendship to Sir Henry was unshaken by their political differences. *Woodstock.*

Note.—He is sometimes indicated as the husband of Sir Henry's sister, sometimes as the brother of Sir Henry's wife. Markham's soliloquy before Victor Lee's portrait points to the former as the relationship really intended.

EVERETT, MASTER. One of Charles Topham's companions in the tour which ended in the arrest of Sir Geoffrey Peveril: a subordinate informer 'who followed the path of Oates with all deference to his superior genius and invention.' *Peveril of the Peak.*

EVIOT. Sir John Ramorny's page. Though acquainted with the facts of the murder, he stood the test of bier-right before Oliver Proudfute's dead body, helped Dwining and Buncle to release Bonthron from the gallows, and accompanied his master when the Duke of Rothesay was enticed to Falkland Castle. But at the report of foul play to the Duke, he threw off his allegiance. 'I have followed you long, my lord,' he said, 'but here I draw bridle.' *The Fair Maid of Perth.*

For bier-right see LUNDIN, SIR LOUIS (*Note*).

EWAN OF BRIGGLANDS. The soldier to whom Rob Roy was strapped with a horse-belt. When fording a river he set Rob free. 'Never weigh a MacGregor's bluid,' Rob whispered to him, 'against a broken whang o' leather, for there will be another accounting to gie for it baith here and hereafter.' *Rob Roy.*

EWART, NANTY (ANTONY). Captain of the *Jumping Jenny*, the brig in which Alan Fairford sailed from Annan to Cumberland. A minister's son, he brought ruin to Mrs. Cantrips' household while a student; took service in the West Indies; became a slave to 'that valiant liquor rum'; sailed under the black flag; and finally 'took French leave, and came in upon the proclamation.' Owner of a tenth share in the *Jumping Jenny*, he sailed under orders—chiefly Redgauntlet's—and had brought Father Buonaventure from Dunkirk. His good impulses were not all dead; he showed some kindness to Alan Fairford, and turned with contempt from Cristal Nixon's invitation to treachery. *Redgauntlet.*

EXETER, BISHOP OF. One of the Bishops in attendance on the King. *The Fortunes of Nigel.*

F

FABIAN ('called FABIAN HARBOTHEL'). A 'smart young stripling ... become very proud of late, in consequence of obtaining the name of Sir Aymer's squire.' He had 'bravery, but as little steadiness in him as a bottle of fermented small beer,' and by repeating to his master scraps of conversation which he overheard between Sir John de Walton and Greenleaf, he sowed the seeds of distrust and discontent in Sir Aymer's heart. *Castle Dangerous.*

FAGGOT, NICHOLAS. Squire Foxley's clerk, 'a smart underbred-looking man' who, 'having some petty provincial situation ... deemed himself bound to be zealous for Government.' But 'something besides empty compliment passed betwixt him and Mr. Herries.' *Redgauntlet.*

FAIRBROTHER, MR. Effie Deans' counsel: 'a man of considerable fame in his profession.' 'Compelled to admit the accuracy of the indictment under the statute,' he yet suspected in his heart that Jeanie would save her sister by bearing 'false witness' in her cause. But when Jeanie destroyed 'the proof which he expected to lead' 'he fought his losing cause with courage and constancy.' *The Heart of Midlothian.*

FAIRFORD, ALAN. Darsie Latimer's bosom friend. 'Thou hadst ever, with the gravest sentiments in thy mouth, and the most starched reserve in thy manner, a kind of lumbering proclivity towards mischief,' Darsie wrote to him. But, knowing the high hopes his father cherished, 'he conformed with the utmost docility ... to his father's anxious and severe restrictions,' and 'laboured hard in silence and solitude.' It was only when Darsie disappeared that he 'threw everything aside ... forgetting fame and fortune, and hazarding even the serious displeasure of his father to rescue' his friend. 'Steady, sedate, persevering and undaunted,' he pursued his quest unflinchingly through the midst of smugglers, outlaws, and political firebrands. *Redgauntlet.*

FAIRFORD, MR. Alan's grandfather. As town clerk to the ancient burgh of Birlthegroat, he signed 'a bitter protest against the Union.' *Redgauntlet.*

FAIRFORD, MR. SAUNDERS. Alan's father. His 'anxious, devoted, and unremitting affection and zeal' for Alan's 'improvement,' led him to take 'a troublesome and incessant charge' of his son's motions. But the whole pleasure of his life centred round Alan; he could be 'indulgent as well as strict,' and allowed Darsie Latimer to be an inmate of his house while thinking him 'over-waggish . . . and somewhat scatter-brained.' He was 'a man of business of the old school, moderate in his charges, economical and even niggardly in his expenditure, strictly honest in conducting his own affairs, and those of his clients, but taught by long experience to be wary and suspicious in observing the motions of others.' 'He used to protest, even till the day of his death, that he never had been guilty of such an inaccuracy as giving a paper out of his hand without looking at the docketing, except on that unhappy occasion' when, at a critical moment in Alan's conduct of the notable case, *Peter Peebles against Plainstanes*, he handed him Provost Crosbie's letter about Darsie Latimer 'without observing the blunder.' *Redgauntlet.*

FAIRFORD, PETER. A cousin from the west. Mr. Saunders Fairford gave his presence as a reason why he could not ask Darsie Latimer to come back from Dumfries, in order to attend the 'bit chack of dinner' given in honour of Alan's admission as an Advocate. *Redgauntlet.*
(*Chack*, a snack.)

FAIRFORD, FATHER. A friend of the Misses Arthuret to whom they supposed Alan was related. *Redgauntlet.*

FAIRSCRIBE, MR. The solicitor who helped Mr. Sommerville to free Mr. Croftangry from the evils threatened by his creditors. He was still in business when Mr. Croftangry returned from abroad, and was prepared to help him in the re-purchase of his family estate. Mr. Croftangry submitted some of his 'idle manuscripts' to Mr. Fairscribe's judgment, but received no flattery. *The Chronicles of the Canongate.*

FAIRSCRIBE, MR. JAMES. Mr. Fairscribe's handsome young son, 'who, though fairly buckled to the desk, is every now and then looking over his shoulders at a smart uniform.' He had 'the ease of a youngster that would be thought a man of fashion rather than of business.' *The Surgeon's Daughter.*

FAIRSCRIBE, MISS KATIE. Mr. Croftangry's 'little siren.' She could sing 'a Scots song without foreign graces.' It was from her that Mr. Croftangry heard the story of Menie Gray. *The Chronicles of the Canongate.*

FAIRSCRIEVE, MR. Magistrate's clerk in Edinburgh. *The Heart of Midlothian.*

FAIRSERVICE, ANDREW. The gardener at Osbaldistone Hall. He had been 'flitting every term these four and twenty years,' and when Frank Osbaldistone left the Hall, Andrew went as his servant, and shared most of his adventures. He was consumed with ignorant vanity, and thought himself the 'carefu' body' whom Frank needed to look after him; but in times of real danger his own safety ranked first. *Rob Roy.*

(*To flit,* to remove.)

FAIRY. The handsome Manx pony which Julian Peveril rode when going to see Alice Bridgenorth at Black Fort. She 'came of a high-spirited mountain breed, remarkable alike for hardiness, for longevity, and for a degree of sagacity approaching to that of the dog.' *Peveril of the Peak.*

FALCONER, CORNET. Brother of the Laird of Balmawhapple. He carried the standard in his brother's troop. *Waverley.*

FALCONER, MR. The Laird of Balmawhapple, and a neighbour of the Baron of Bradwardine. He suffered punishment from the Baron for a drunken insult to Edward Waverley. Later, he acted as captain of Edward's escort from the Castle of Doune to Holyrood. 'Further attempts at conversation with any of the party would only give Balmawhapple a wished-for opportunity to display the insolence of authority and the sulky spite of a temper naturally dogged, and rendered more so by habits of low indulgence and the incense of servile adulation.' *Waverley.*

FALCONER, CAPTAIN. Half-brother to Lady Bothwell and Lady Forester. Taken by a Dutch acquaintance in Rotterdam 'to see a countryman of his own married to the daughter of a wealthy burgomaster,' he found in the intending bridegroom his brother-in-law, Sir Philip Forester. He 'proclaimed his villany on the spot... accepted a challenge from him, and in the rencounter received a mortal wound.' *My Aunt Margaret's Mirror.*

FALCONER, JEMIMA. *See* FORESTER, LADY.

FALCONER, MISS. *See* BOTHWELL, LADY.

FANGS. Gurth's dog: 'a ragged wolfish-looking dog, a sort of lurcher, half-mastiff, half-greyhound,' but a 'faithful adherent.' *Ivanhoe.*

FATHER ADAM. The name given to Edie Ochiltree during the colloquy before the duel between Lovel and Hector McIntyre. *The Antiquary.*

FATHER DENNET. One of the crowd who waited round the lists at Templestowe to see Rebecca's fate. He entertained his friends with the story of Athelstane's return from the tomb. *Ivanhoe.*

FATSIDES, FATHER. The priest whom Dalgetty consulted, over

'six flasks of Rhenish, and about two mutchkins of Kirschenwasser,' concerning the propriety of a Protestant attending Mass. *A Legend of Montrose.*

FAUSTA. Constantine's wife. Crispus 'fell a victim to the guilt' of her, his step-mother. *Count Robert of Paris.*

FEA, EUPHANE. Magnus Troil's housekeeper: 'well versed in all the simple pharmacy used by the natives of Zetland.' *The Pirate.*

FEA, JOHNNIE. A youthful friend of Swertha. He 'slept sound among the frozen waves of Greenland for this many a year.' *The Pirate.*

FEATHERHEAD, EARL OF. Lady Penelope Penfeather's father. 'A man of judgment—did little in his family but by rule of medicine.' *St. Ronan's Well.*

FEATHERHEAD, JOHN. The successful opponent of Sir Thomas Kittlecourt in the parliamentary election. *Guy Mannering.*

FENELLA. Edward Christian's daughter. Trained by him in the belief that she was William Christian's daughter, and that to avenge her father's death was her 'first great duty on earth,' she lived for years in the Countess of Derby's household as a deaf mute —and 'base eavesdropper' on the lady's 'dearest and most secret concerns.' Enduring 'insolence without notice, admiration without answer, and sarcasm without reply,' she formed a deep attachment to Julian Peveril in return for his 'uniform kindness.' She followed him to London, visited him in prison, and planned his escape. As Zarah, the 'Moorish sorceress' and dancing-girl, she took Alice Bridgenorth's place under the Duke of Buckingham's roof, laughing at the dangers involved, but the knowledge of Christian's base intrigues led her to throw off his authority, and eventually to discover that she was his daughter and 'a forlorn outcast.' 'The creature is not on earth, being mere mortal woman, that would have undergone the thirtieth part of thy self-denial.' *Peveril of the Peak.*

Note.—As a justification for the hard task he gave to Fenella, Sir Walter in his 1831 Introduction quotes the case of a wandering woman resident in his grandfather's house, who was believed to have feigned deafness and dumbness for some years. But the evidence of her deceit rests solely on the testimony of 'a mischievous shepherd boy.'

FENWICKE. *See* BARSTOW, CAPTAIN.

FERGUSON. One of those Covenanters who, once 'King James' greatest foes,' were on his side after the Revolution. *Old Mortality.*

FERGUSON, DR. *See* HUME, DAVID.

FERRERS, LORD. The nobleman to whom the forfeited lands of William Peveril were granted in King John's 'stormy days.' *Peveril of the Peak.*

FETTERLOCK, KNIGHT OF THE. *See* RICHARD CŒUR DE LION (3).

FIBBET. The 'ingenious nickname'

given to Joseph Tomkins, 'who was in the habit of being voucher for his master upon all occasions.' *Woodstock.*

FINLAYSON, LUCKIE. Keeper of a tavern in the Cowgate where Advocate Pleydell's caddie was to be found. *Guy Mannering.* (*Luckie*, a designation given to an elderly woman.)

FINNISTON, DUNCAN. Luckie's goodman. *Guy Mannering.*

FINNISTON, LUCKIE. One of Ellangowan's tenants who paid part of her rent in hens 'that were a shame to be seen.' *Guy Mannering.* (*Luckie*, a designation given to an elderly woman.)

FISH, ZEDEKIAH. Owner of the vessel *Good Hope*, bound for Massachusetts. Edward Christian advised Major Bridgenorth to escape with him when the outbreak planned with Buckingham failed. *Peveril of the Peak.*

FISHER, RALPH. A young peasant from the hamlet of Avenel who sometimes shared Roland Graeme's sports 'in the subordinate character of assistant.' After Roland's dismissal he made a rough show of friendship, but was somewhat relieved when it was refused. *The Abbot.*

FITZ-ALDIN. *See* REDGAUNTLET, ALBERICK.

FITZDOTTEREL, JACQUES. One of Isaac's clients. His patrimony was devoured by the Jew's exactions. *Ivanhoe.*

FITZURSE, ALICIA. Waldemar's daughter. Richard had roused her father's revenge by scorning alliance with her. *Ivanhoe.*

FITZURSE, WALDEMAR. 'One of the oldest and most important of John's followers.' 'Ambition' was his 'pursuit,' and he hoped to make even Prince John a tool in his hands. But after his unsuccessful attempt on Richard's life, he was unmasked by the king and banished. *Ivanhoe.*

FLAMMOCK, ROSE. Wilkin's daughter : Eveline Berenger's bowerwoman. 'By nature one of the most disinterested and affectionate maidens that ever breathed,' she was equally jealous of her father's honour and of Eveline's. She was Eveline's constant companion ; acquainted with her most inward thoughts ; quick and alert to save her from every appearance of wrong. 'No one who did not know thee would think that soft and childish exterior covered such a soul of fire.' *The Betrothed.*

FLAMMOCK, WILKIN. 'Son of Dieterick, the Cramer of Antwerp' : a Flemish weaver who held his mills on condition of paying manservice in defending the castle of Garde Doloureuse. Commissioned by Sir Raymond Berenger to hold the castle until relieved by Hugo de Lacy, he showed while doing so 'the properties of a good mastiff,' with 'some rude sagacity and a stout hand' to boot. 'His solid sense and sound judgment' were always at Eveline's command during Hugo de Lacy's absence in the Crusade, though the expedition was to him 'little save folly' : thrift and industry were the main objects of life. 'I hate poor people,' he said to Rose, 'and I would the devil had every man who cannot keep himself by the work of his own hand!' *The Betrothed.*

FLEECEBUMPKIN, JOHN. Mr. Ireby's bailiff. His honesty not being above suspicion, he had orders to refer all enquirers about grassland to the Squire himself. But in his master's temporary absence he let an enclosure to Harry Wakefield. He felt aggrieved when Harry had to give way, and made the quarrel his own, stimulating Harry's ill-feelings when good ones were reasserting themselves. *The Two Drovers.*

FLEMING, LADY MARY. The elder of Queen Mary's female attendants. Her 'sense of dignity and love of form' sometimes outraged her young companion. 'She loves her mistress,' Catherine Seyton said, 'yet knows so little how to express her love, that were the Queen to ask her for very poison, she would deem it a point of duty not to resist her commands.' 'That that piece of weaved tapestry should be a woman, and yet not have wit enough to tell a lie!' *The Abbot.*

FLEMING, MALCOLM, OF BIGGAR. Margaret de Hautlieu's lover: one of the most distinguished of the 'soldiers of the soil' who joined the patriot Wallace. Faithless to Margaret when she lost her beauty, he learnt to appreciate her in adventurous freedom. *Castle Dangerous.*

FLEMING, REV. ARCHDEACON. The Carlisle clergyman who received Meg Murdockson's confession after she was sentenced to be hung. Some years later, he was able to give Sir George Staunton a clue to the fate of his and Effie's child. *The Heart of Midlothian.*

FLEMING, WILL. One of Madge Wildfire's 'joes.' *The Heart of Midlothian.*

(*Joes*, sweethearts.)

FLETCHER, DICK. One of the crew of the *Fortune's Favourite*: 'an admirer and adherent' of Jack Bunce. He took part in the seizure of Magnus Troil's brig, and was afterwards wounded fatally in the skirmish with Mordaunt Mertoun. 'A bulldog of the true British breed, and, with a better counsellor, would have been a better man.' *The Pirate.*

FLETCHER, GILES. One of Hob Miller's neighbours. When Father Philip lay groaning near the sluice of the mill, Hob thought the sound came from one of Giles' hogs. 'He never shuts his gate.' *The Monastery.*

FLIBBERTIGIBBET. See SLUDGE, DICKIE.

FLOATING ISLE, LADY OF THE. The Lady of the Lake, who in one of the pageants at Kenilworth Castle came in homage and duty to welcome the peerless Elizabeth to all sport, which the Castle and its environs, which lake or land, could afford.' *Kenilworth.*

FLOCKHART, MRS. The buxom widow with whom Fergus MacIvor

lodged in Edinburgh. 'A person with whom good looks and good humour were sure to secure an interest.' *Waverley.*

FLORISE. One of Queen Berengaria's ladies. She and Calista told the Queen of Lady Edith Plantagenet dropping two rosebuds to Sir Kenneth in the chapel at Engaddi. *The Talisman.*

FLYING HIGHWAYMAN. A 'Beggar's Opera' hero. *Rob Roy.*

FLYTER, LUCKIE. The 'jolly hostler wife' with whom Frank Osbaldistone and Andrew Fairservice took up their abode in Glasgow. *Rob Roy.*

(*Luckie*, a designation given to an elderly woman.)

FOLJAMBE, LADY. A former owner of George Heriot's house. The rooms known as the 'Foljambe apartments' had been prepared by her as a sanctuary for the Abbess of Saint Roque and two vestal sisters. *The Fortunes of Nigel.*

FORBES, DUNCAN. President of the Court of Session : a friend of John, Duke of Argyle. *The Heart of Midlothian.*

FORESTER, LADY. Sir Philip's wife, née Jemima Falconer : Lady Bothwell's sister. A woman of tender heart and weak judgment, she remained 'passionately attached' to her husband, in spite of his callous indifference. 'Obstinate and reckless' under the suspense which her husband's silence caused her, she determined to seek information concerning his fate, 'even were the powers which offer it unhallowed and infernal.' In Doctor Damiotti's mysterious mirror she saw her husband on the point of being married to a young and beautiful girl. The 'next packet' from the continent confirming this scene, she was overcome by 'superstitious terror,' and 'never recovered the shock of this dismal intelligence.' *My Aunt Margaret's Mirror.*

FORESTER, SIR PHILIP. Jemima Falconer's husband, and Lady Bothwell's brother-in-law. A man of 'wit, gallantry, and dissipation,' 'renowned for the number of duels he had fought and the successful intrigues which he had carried on,' he married Jemima for her money. But in time he became 'inconvenienced in his money affairs and tired even of the short time which he spent in his own dull house.' He joined the war in Flanders, ceased communications with his wife, and wooed a beautiful young Dutch heiress. In a duel arising out of this, he killed Captain Falconer, his wife's half-brother. *My Aunt Margaret's Mirror.*

FORSTER, GENERAL. One of the leaders of the 1715 rebellion. *Rob Roy.*

FORSTER, JUSTICE. The justice who had warrants out in Cumberland for the arrest of Meg Merrilies. *Guy Mannering.*

FOSTER. The English champion who defeated the Laird's Jock's son, and took possession of the famous two-handed sword. *Death of the Laird's Jock.*

FOSTER, ANTHONY. Amy Robsart's sullen guardian in Cumnor Place: a pliant tool in Richard Varney's hands. To Michael Lambourne he was 'Tony Fire-the-Fagot, papist, puritan, hypocrite, miser, profligate, devil ... old reprobate, hypocritical dog, whom God struck out of the book of life, but tormented with the constant wish to be restored to it.' Even his love for Janet did not redeem him. *Kenilworth.*

FOSTER, JANET. Anthony's daughter. Guarded jealously by her father from entering his own and Varney's crooked paths, she was 'the kindest and best companion' of Amy Robsart's solitude in Cumnor Place, and helped her to escape under Wayland Smith's protection. *Kenilworth.*

FOSTER, CAPTAIN. The officer in charge of the government troops encamped at Tully-Veolan. *Waverley.*

FOSTER, CHARLIE. 'Charlie Cheat-the-Woodie,' the proposed guardian of Grace Armstrong, after she had been kidnapped. 'A rough customer.' *The Black Dwarf.*
(*Woodie*, gallows.)

FOSTER, SIR JOHN. One of the English Wardens of the Marches. 'Stung with the news that Piercie Shafton was openly residing within the Halidome ... he determined to execute the commands of his mistress ... to make himself master of the Euphuist's person.' But in the moment of his victory over Julian Avenel and the kirk vassals, he was obliged by the arrival of Murray and Morton to forego its results. *The Monastery.*

FOXLEY, SQUIRE. The magistrate whom Redgauntlet brought to his Cumberland mansion in answer to Darsie Latimer's appeal for justice. 'There was an air of importance in his manner which corresponded to the rural dignity of his exterior, and a habit which he had of throwing out a number of interjectional sounds, uttered with a strange variety of intonation, running from bass up to treble in a very extraordinary manner, or breaking off his sentences with a whiff of his pipe, seemed adopted to give an air of thought and mature deliberation to his opinions and decisions. Notwithstanding all this, Alan, it might be *dooted,* as our old Professor used to say, whether the Justice was anything more than an ass.' *Redgauntlet.*

FRANCIE O' FOWLSHEUGH. 'The best craigsman that ever speel'd heugh (mair by token, he brake his neck upon the Dunbuy of Slaines).' *The Antiquary.*
(*To speel*, to climb. *Heugh,* crag).

FRANCIS, FATHER. A friar in the Franciscan convent near Namur in which Quentin Durward and the Ladies of Croye rested for a night. In spite of his Prior's dread of William de la Marck, he tried to persuade Quentin to follow his original plan, and travel by the right bank of the Maes. *Quentin Durward.*

FRANCIS, FATHER. A priest in King Richard's camp. *The Talisman.*

FRANCIS, FATHER. A Dominican priest, Catharine Glover's confessor. He 'urged and provoked' Catharine to talk of such matters as he judged she was 'likely to have learnt something of' from Father Clement. But he 'assumed not his real aspect, and betrayed not his secret purpose, until he had learned all that' she had to tell him. *The Fair Maid of Perth.*

FRONT-DE-BŒUF, REGINALD. A Norman noble 'whose life had been spent in public war or in private feuds and broils.' He lent his castle of Torquilstone to Brian de Bois-Guilbert and Maurice de Bracy for the imprisonment of Cedric and his party. Wounded when defending the castle against the Black Knight's attack, he died in the ruins, forgotten by all but Ulrica. 'A powerful limb lopped off Prince John's enterprise.' *Ivanhoe.*

FRUGAL, SIR FAITHFUL. One of George Heriot's old friends. His money casket was passed on to Nigel by the goldsmith. *The Fortunes of Nigel.*

FURABOSCO, SIGNOR. The antiquarian in Rome from whom the Earl of Derby purchased his seal, a 'cameo Cupid, riding on a flying fish.' *Peveril of the Peak.*

G

GABBLEWOOD, GAFFER. The farmer in whose wheat-close Madge Wildfire put her horse to graze. *The Heart of Midlothian.*

GADABOUT, MANAGER. An actor-manager in whose company Jack Bunce and Claud Halcro were engaged at the same time. *The Pirate.*

GAETHROUGHWI'T, GIBBY. The piper of Cupar. *Waverley.*

GAITA. Wife of Robert Guiscard and 'the parent of a most heroic race of sons.' She 'first took upon her to distinguish herself by manly deeds of emprise, and rival her husband, as well in the front of battle as at the dancing-room or banquet.' She 'makes a conspicuous figure in Anna Comnena's account of her father's campaigns against Robert Guiscard.' *Count Robert of Paris.*

GAIUS THE PUBLICAN. The name given to Niel Blane's predecessor by the Presbyterians, amongst whom he was a man of note. *Old Mortality.*

GALBRAITH, DUNCAN, OF GARSCHATTACHIN. Major of the Lennox militiamen. He captured Rob Roy after Rob had been deceived by Rashleigh Osbaldistone's treacherous message. *Rob Roy.*

GALEOTTI. See MARTIVALLE.

GANDELYN. A leader under whom the Miller had formerly served. He had 'no such scruples of conscience' as Locksley showed in his treatment of Gurth. *Ivanhoe.*

GANDERCLEUGH, LAIRD OF. One of the proprietors whose estates were divided by Mr. Pattieson's 'favourite brook.' He and his neighbour, the Laird of Gusetub, 'fell into discord concerning two roods of marshy ground, near the cove called the Bedral's Beild.' *Old Mortality*. (*Bedral*, sexton. *Beild*, shelter.)

GANLESSE, DICK. The name under which Edward Christian travelled as a Roman Catholic priest with Julian Peveril. Under the mask of friendship he and Will Smith found an opportunity of getting possession of the Countess of Derby's letters. *Peveril of the Peak*.

GARDENER, DICK. Porter to the Misses Arthuret at Fairladies. At the close of Alan Fairford's stay there he guided Alan back to Joe Crackenthorp's inn. 'A forward, talkative fellow.' *Redgauntlet*.

GARDINER, COLONEL. Edward Waverley's commanding officer at Dundee. Very gay in his youth, he had been suddenly converted 'from doubt, if not infidelity, to a serious and even enthusiastic turn of mind.' He was killed at Gladsmuir, but not before recognising Edward in the rebels' ranks. 'Paternal remonstrance was mingled with military authority.' *Waverley*.

GARR, DUGALD. A Highland freebooter who was 'playing the devil in the Garioch' during Dalgetty's youth. *A Legend of Montrose*.

GARSCHATTACHIN. *See* GALBRAITH, DUNCAN.

GATHERAL. The Duke of Buckingham's steward. *Peveril of the Peak*.

GATHERILL. Sir Geoffrey Peveril's bailiff. When Whitaker 'threatened the sacrifice of a fine yoke of young bullocks' for the Restoration feast, Gatherill 'pleaded the necessity of their agricultural services.' *Peveril of the Peak*.

GAUNTLET. The nag which Simon Glover rode from Kinfauns to Niel Booshalloch's cottage. *The Fair Maid of Perth*.

GEDDES, JOSHUA. A Quaker who showed Darsie Latimer kindness, entertaining him in his home, Mount Sharon—an 'Eden of beauty, comfort, and peace.' He was one of the principal partners of the Tide-net Fishing Company, whose innovations roused the ill-will of the Solway fishermen. Though peaceful as became his religious views, he still felt promptings of the 'ancient Adam,' and, with Darsie's help, made some resistance when the fishing station was attacked. He afterwards blamed himself for Darsie's disappearance, and with his galloway Solomon searched the whole coast of the Solway for him. 'Neither the floods of water, nor the fear of the snare, nor the drawn sword of the adversary brandished in the path,' could overcome his purpose. *Redgauntlet*.

GEDDES, PHILIP. (1) Joshua's grandfather. His ancestors had become more and more 'Ged-like, slaying, leading into captivity, and dividing the spoil, until the place where they dwelt obtained the name of Sharing-Knowe, from the booty which was there divided amongst them and their accomplices.' But he received a 'better judgment,' having obtained 'a spark from the lamp of the blessed George Fox.'

(2) Joshua's father. He connected himself by marriage 'with a wealthy family of Quakers in Lancashire, engaged successfully in various branches of commerce, and redeemed the remnants of the property, changing its name in sense, without much alteration of sound, from the Border appellation of Sharing-Knowe to the evangelical appellation of Mount Sharon.' (1) and (2) *Redgauntlet*.

(*Ged*, the pike fish—the 'shark of fresh waters.')

GEDDES, RACHEL. Joshua's sister. 'Her appearance is remarkably pleasing, and although her age is certainly thirty at least, she still retains the shape and motion of an earlier period.' Her smile 'seemed to wish good here and hereafter to every one she spoke to.' *Redgauntlet*.

GEIERSTEIN, ANNE OF. Count Albert's daughter. Entrusted at an early age to the care of her uncle, Arnold Biederman, she was inured by him to all 'mountain exercises,' and while she excelled the damsels of the district in these, her ' blue eyes, lovely features, and dignified simplicity of expression, implied at once a character of gentleness, and of the self-relying resolution of a mind too virtuous to suspect evil, and too noble to fear it.' Her instinct divined that Arthur Philipson was 'well-qualified to gain deservedly a lady's favour,' and she did not 'neglect the opportunity' which Fate, in the person of Annette Veilchen, gave her in her own castle of Arnheim 'to disabuse our English friend of the absurd report' which he had heard from Rudolph of Donnerhugel concerning her supposed supernatural powers. But, on the morrow, she 'queened' it over Ital Schreckenwald, played 'countess and baroness with a witness,' and began 'to tyrannize over her own natural feelings.' *See also* ARNHEIM, HERMAN, HERMIONE, and SYBILLA VON. *Anne of Geierstein*.

GEIERSTEIN, COUNT ALBERT OF. Anne of Geierstein's father: Arnold Biederman's younger brother. Despising 'the prejudices of his countrymen,' and regarding 'form, pomp, and magnificence' as 'the consummation of earthly splendour,' he readily profited by his brother's simple tastes, and, though the younger, became count. Devoting himself to 'courtly intrigues and ambitious plans,' he gained a widespread influence and power. As the Black Priest of St. Paul's, he released Arthur Philipson from the dungeon in La Ferette, 'in order to establish communication betwixt the Swiss without the fortress and the soldiers within'; he secured the execution of von Hagenbach; he accompanied Seignor Philipson during part of his journey to Strasburg, directed him to Ian Mengs' inn, and presided over his weird trial before the Judges of the Vehmgericht; he also acted as speaker for the clergy when the Estates of Burgundy refused to vote Charles supplies. Convinced then that 'being a clergyman would be no longer his protection,' he threw off his allegiance and fought for Lorraine and the Swiss. As a Carmelite monk he learnt from Arthur Philipson the secret negotiations between Charles and Margaret of Anjou concerning Lorraine; and finally, disguised as one of Charles' guard, and attended by his faithful tool, Ital Schreckenwald, he wrought on Charles the vengeance of the Secret Tribunal. 'An able man he is, and knows more of every man's business than the man does himself.' *Anne of Geierstein.*

GEIERSTEIN, HEINRICH OF. Grandfather of Arnold Biederman and Count Albert. While fighting against Ingelram de Couci and his roving bands, he gained possession of the great English bow which gave Arthur Philipson the opportunity of convincing the Swiss youths of Geierstein that he was no mean sportsman. *Anne of Geierstein.*

GEIERSTEIN, WILLIEWALD OF. Father of Arnold Biederman and Count Albert. 'Possessed, as he felt himself, of a species of double character, he was desirous . . . that one of his sons should succeed him in his Lordship of Geierstein, and the other support the less ostentatious, though not . . . less honourable condition, of a free citizen of Unterwalden.' The natural tastes of the brothers determined that the younger should 'wear the coronet.' *Anne of Geierstein.*

GEISLAER, PETERKIN. Syndic Pavillon's lieutenant, 'the person upon whom, on all pressing occasions, whether of war, politics, or commerce, Pavillon was most accustomed to repose confidence.' He seconded the Syndic in helping Quentin Durward and the Countess of Croye to escape from Schonwaldt Castle, and on the following day guided them out of Liège. *Quentin Durward.*

GELLATLEY, DAVIE. 'An innocent,' dependent on the charity of the Baron of Bradwardine. 'Simply a crack-brained knave, who could execute very well any commission which jumped with his own humour, and made his folly a plea for avoiding every other.' *Waverley.*

GELLATLEY, JAMIE. Brother of Davie. The Baron of Bradwardine had kept him 'at school and college, and even at the Ha'-house, till he gaed to a better place.' *Waverley.*

GELLATLEY, JANET. The widowed mother of Davie and Jamie. Like them, she owed much to the Baron of Bradwardine. 'She was suspected to be a witch, on the infallible grounds that she was very old, very ugly, very poor, and had two sons, one of whom was a poet, and the other a fool.' *Waverley.*

GEMMELS, LUCKIE. One of Edie Ochiltree's cronies. *The Antiquary.*

(*Luckie*, a designation given to an elderly woman.)

GENTLEMAN GEORDIE. *See* ROBERTSON, GEORGE.

GENVIL, RALPH. Damian de Lacy's bannerman. 'A veteran whose face was seamed with many a scar,' he helped the youthful

Amelot in his attempt to relieve Wenlock. *The Betrothed.*

GEOFFREY. Ostler in Ian Mengs' inn: 'a very old lame man, who neither put his hand to wisp nor curry-comb, but sat weighing forth hay by the pound, and counting out corn, as it seemed, by the grain, so anxiously did he bend over his task, by the aid of a blinking light enclosed within a horn lantern.' *Anne of Geierstein.*

GEORGE. One of the yeomen of the Queen's guard who interrupted the Earl of Leicester's duel with Tressilian. *Kenilworth.*

GEORGE, DUKE OF CLARENCE. Brother to Edward IV. Used as a tool by his father-in-law, the Earl of Warwick, he afterwards betrayed the Earl. He himself was privately executed in the Tower in 1478, drowned, tradition says, in a butt of Malmsey wine. *Anne of Geierstein.*

GERALDIN, AYMER DE. The first of the Glenallan family. He 'sat in parliament at Perth in the reign of Alexander II,' and 'plausible tradition' said he was descended from the Marmor of Clochnaben. *The Antiquary.*

GERALDIN, WILLIAM, LORD. See LOVEL, MR.

GERARD. One of Sir Patrick Charteris' servants. *The Fair Maid of Perth.*

GERVIS, FATHER. The confessor who attended an Edinburgh Burn-the-wind with whom Harry Gow had measured swords. *The Fair Maid of Perth.*

(*Burn-the-wind*, an old name for a blacksmith.)

GIBBET. The name given by Bletson to his secretary Gideon, 'to make up the holy trefoil with another rhyme,' the secretaries of his colleagues being Bibbet and Fibbet. *Woodstock.*

GIBBON. The Earl of Derby's pet monkey. *Peveril of the Peak.*

GIBBS, GAFFER. One of the Willingham congregation. He looked at Jeanie Deans all the time of service, and told the beadle that she 'could not turn up a single lesson like a Christian.' *The Heart of Midlothian.*

GIBSON, JENNY. The orphan who lived with Mistress Bertram as 'a sort of humble companion.' At the reading of the will 'she was the only person present who seemed really to feel sorrow for the deceased.' *Guy Mannering.*

GIDEON. See GIBBET.

GILBERT. One of Locksley's men. When searching with Wibbald among the ruins of Front-de-Bœuf's castle he found 'the runlet of sack half empty, the Jew half dead, and the Friar more than half—exhausted, as he calls it.' *Ivanhoe.*

GILBERT. Sir Patrick Charteris' butler. *The Fair Maid of Perth.*

GILBERT OF CRANBERRY MOOR. The owner of lands which lay 'intersected with' Julian Avenel's. Julian made the transfer of these lands a condition of service first to the Earl of Murray and afterwards to the Community of St. Mary's. *The Monastery.*

GILBERTSCLEUGH. A 'cousin' of Lady Margaret Bellenden. *Old Mortality.*

GILES. The elder of the two boys acting as turnspit at Gibbie Girder's on the day of the christening dinner. After sending him on an errand to Luckie Sma'trash's, Caleb Balderstone marched off with the goose and ducks, overcoming any possible outcry from the younger turnspit by looking him 'gravely and steadily in the face.' *The Bride of Lammermoor.*

GILES. One of Front-de-Bœuf's menials. With the others, he was deaf to his master's cries when the castle was on fire. *Ivanhoe.*

GILES. Claud Halcro's 'imp of a boy': 'a barefooted, yellow-haired Zetland boy, who acted occasionally as a kind of page to Claud Halcro, bearing his fiddle on his shoulder, saddling his pony, and rendering him similar duties of kindly observance.' *The Pirate.*

GILES. The warder in the Tower who brought Margaret Ramsay, the supposed page, to share Nigel's confinement. *The Fortunes of Nigel.*

GILES, DEAN. One of the king's divines who gave dry discourses on the penitentiary psalms. *The Fortunes of Nigel.*

GILFILLAN, HABAKKUK. A leader of the Cameronians, called 'Gifted Gilfillan.' He commanded the small party of volunteers under whose escort Major Melville placed Edward Waverley. 'It was impossible to behold him without imagination placing him in some strange crisis, where religious zeal was the ruling principle.' *Waverley.*

GILLESPIE GRUMACH (i.e. Ill-favoured). The personal distinction given to the Marquis of Argyle because of an obliquity in his eyes. *A Legend of Montrose.*

GILLESPIE, MASS JOHN. A Scottish divine who as an act of grace allowed King Charles 'to do penance in mine own privy chamber, instead of the face of the congregation.' *Woodstock.*

GILLIAN, DAME. Raoul's wife, a comely middle-aged dame: Eveline Berenger's tire-woman. ⁋She 'used to make it her boast, that she could please everybody with her gossip, when she chose it, from Raymond Berenger down to Robin the horse-boy.' But she had 'neither sense, nor courage, nor principle,' and from her ready tongue Randal de Lacy heard all the gossip he wanted to hear. *The Betrothed.*

GILLIEWHACKIT, 'YOUNG.' Shortly before his marriage with Lady Cramfeezer, he was carried off by Donald Bean Lean on the prospect of a ransom. This Donald fixed at a thousand pounds, but the young man caught small-pox, and in the end Donald was glad to get rid of him for whatever the bride chose to give. 'Between the free open air in the cove and the fresh whey, deil an he did not recover may be as weel as if he had been closed in a glazed chamber and a bed with curtains, and fed with red wine and white meat.' *Waverley.*

GILLIE-WHITEFOOT. 'An imp of the devil' from the printing office, who came to torment Mr. Croftangry for copy. *The Two Drovers.*

GILLON-A-NAILLIE. 'The lads with the kilts.' *Rob Roy.*

GILRY, TAM. One of the 'few lads' Jenny Dennison knew 'to speak to.' *Old Mortality.*

GILSLAND, LORD OF. *See* MULTON, THOMAS DE.

GINGHAM, MRS. Lady Binks' attendant. *St. Ronan's Well.*

GIRDER, GIBBIE. The Wolf's-hope cooper. He 'had headed the insurrection in the matter of the egg and butter subsidy' to the Ravenswood family, and bore 'a decided resentment' to Caleb Balderstone for his attempted extortions. But all ill-will was banished when Caleb's raid on the christening dinner was justified, to Caleb's joyful surprise, by Gibbie's appointment as Queen's Cooper. 'Gudewill, man, is a geizen'd tub, that hauds in nae liquor—but gude deed's like the cask, tight, round, and sound, that will haud liquor for the king.' *The Bride of Lammermoor.*

(*Geizen'd tub,* one that has become leaky for want of moisture.)

GIRDINGBURST, LAIRD OF. One of Saddletree's customers. *The Heart of Midlothian.*

GIRNINGTON, LADY. Bucklaw's grand-aunt. She left 'extensive property' and 'considerable wealth besides' to him. 'An excellent person, excepting that her inveterate ill-nature rendered her intolerable to the whole world.' *The Bride of Lammermoor.*

GLADSMOOR, MR. The Earl of Glenallan's almoner. 'A scholar and a man of the world.' *The Antiquary.*

GLAIKET, CHRISTIE. One of 'the inferior sort o' people' in Liddesdale who were 'kend by sorts o' bynames.' *Guy Mannering.*

GLASBY, HARRY. A pirate whose life was spared by Government because he 'did what was called good service in betraying his comrades.' *The Pirate.*

GLASGOW, BISHOP OF. The prelate who, 'with the utmost solemnity,' performed the ceremonies proper to the day, in St. Bride's Church on Palm Sunday. He also administered comfort to Michael Turnbull as he lay dying. *Castle Dangerous.*

Note.—The Bishop of Glasgow (1272–1317) was Robert Wishart, who, for his devotion to the cause of Bruce, spent some years in an English prison. He was released after the battle of Bannockburn.

GLASS. One of the citizens who met together on St. Valentine's Day, 'for investigating the affray of the preceding evening.' *The Fair Maid of Perth.*

GLASS, MISTRESS MARGARET. 'The tobacconist, at the sign o' the Thistle': the relative with whom Jeanie stayed in London. Her shop was 'then well-known to all Scottish folk of high and low degree,' and amongst her patrons she numbered the Duke of Argyle. She had 'a braw house,' and lived 'bien and warm, wi' twa servant lasses, and a man and a callant in the shop,' but to Jeanie all this did not seem worth 'sitting sneezing all her life in this stifling room.' *The Heart of Midlothian*. (*Bien*, well-provided. *A callant*, a youth.)

GLEGG, KATIE. *See* CASTLE-CUDDY, LORD.

GLEN, DUNCAN. 'The auld drucken trooper' sent by Niel Blane with 'the aitmeal to Tillietudlem, wi' my dutiful service to my Leddy and the Major, and I haena as muckle left as will mak my parritch.' *Old Mortality*.

GLEN, GEORGE. 'The dammer and sinker' at Glen Withershins mines. Edie Ochiltree gave him the old horn which was afterwards imposed as a venerable relic on the Antiquary by Dousterswivel. *The Antiquary*.

GLENALLAN, EARL OF (WILLIAM). Elder son of the Countess Joscelin, and father of 'Mr. Lovel.' For twenty years he lived a life of seclusion, doing penance for the horrible crime which he believed himself to have committed in marrying Eveline Neville. It was only after the Countess' death that old Elspeth Mucklebackit had courage to confess the deception practised on him. 'I have been a man miserable beyond the power of description,' he said, 'and who looks forward at this moment to an untimely grave as to a haven of rest.' *The Antiquary*.

GLENALLAN, JOSCELIN, COUNTESS OF. Mother of the Earl of Glenallan: the lady whose burial at midnight in the ruins of St. Ruth's priory caused terror to the treasure seekers. Countess in her own right, she inherited the 'stern, fierce, and unbending character' of her family. Anxious to prevent her elder son's marriage with Eveline Neville, and ignorant that it had already taken place, she convinced him that Eveline was a natural daughter of his own father. She witnessed her son's misery for twenty years without flinching. *The Antiquary*.

GLENALLAN, LORD. The Countess' father. At Sheriffmuir his life was saved by Reginald Cheyne, father of Elspeth Mucklebackit. *The Antiquary*.

GLENALLAN, THE GREAT EARL OF. One of the leaders of the Saxon and Norman nobility in their resistance against Donald of the Isles. He was killed in the battle of Harlaw, but his mother would allow no lamentation to be made for him. She 'had him laid in the silence o' midnight in his place o' rest, without either drinking the dirge, or crying the lament. —She said he had killed enow that day he died, for the widows and daughters o' the Highlanders he had slain to cry the coronach for them they had lost and for her son too.' *The Antiquary*. (*Coronach*, lament.)

GLENCAIRN, EARL OF. 'A worthy and professing nobleman' from whom Gilfillan had received his commission. *Waverley*.

GLENDALE, SIR RICHARD. One of the 'faithful friends' who met Father Buonaventure at Joe Crackenthorp's inn. He 'seemed personally known to Charles Edward, who received him with a mixture of dignity and affection, and seemed to sympathize with the tears which rushed into that gentleman's eyes as he bid his Majesty welcome to his native kingdom.' But it was his lot to speak 'unwilling truths.' *Redgauntlet*.

GLENDINNING, EDWARD. (1) Simon's younger son. He was 'of softer nature' than Halbert, but 'at once acute and industrious, alert, and accurate,' and retained more of Father Eustace's teaching. Though 'constitutionally shy, respectful, and even timid,' he was capable when need arose, of a generous courage, which had no 'fiery rashness,' but 'reason' to guide it. Halbert's supposed death showed him the depths of ill-feeling to which his love for Mary of Avenel could drag him, and in horror at the discovery he retired to the Monastery, there 'to tame this rebellious heart' or 'tear it out of my bosom.'

(2) Father Ambrose, 'the worthy pupil of the sainted Eustatius'; last Abbot of St. Mary's. In the 'days of tribulation' which had 'wrenched asunder the allegiance of Christians to the Church,' he was 'turned out of house and homestead,' and deprived of 'the temporalities of that noble house of God.' But with undiminished zeal he devoted himself to Queen Mary's release, not scorning to 'wear the garb of a base sworder, and run the risk of dying the death of a traitor.' (1) *The Monastery*. (2) *The Abbot*.

GLENDINNING, ELSPETH. Simon's wife. Left early a widow, with two young boys, she was yet able to receive the Lady of Avenel and Mary into her household, and to order her home with comfort and free hospitality. Though 'jealous of her own consequence,' she admired the Lady of Avenel while alive, and 'idolized her after her death.' But she had an ignorant dread of heresy, and her position as a 'kirk-vassal' seemed to oblige her to give Father Philip the fateful 'black volume with silver clasps.' *The Monastery*.

GLENDINNING, HALBERT. (1) Simon's elder son. From his childhood he was 'hasty, wild, and inconsiderate, rude, and prompt to speak at the volley and without reflection,' and he early determined to 'call none lord, but him who wears a sword to make his title good.' His intercourse with the mysterious White Lady of Avenel gave definiteness and dignity to his ambition, and soon afterwards his duel with Piercie Shafton decided him to leave home and seek the Queen's service. 'A youth of no common spirit, but much like those (in my weak judgment) whom God raises up among a people when He meaneth that their deliverance shall be wrought out with strength of hand and valour of heart.'

(2) The Knight of Avenel, 'a kind and beneficent overlord.' He 'proved what Murray expected of him, a steady friend, strong in battle and wise in council.' Murray was so confident of his 'sure truth and approved worth,' that

he chose for the delicate position of page to Queen Mary in Lochleven Castle, Roland Graeme, formerly page to the Lady of Avenel. (1) *The Monastery.* (2) *The Abbot.*

GLENDINNING, SIMON. Father of Halbert and Edward. He 'boasted his connexion by blood to that ancient family of Glendonwyne,' and in the 'dolourous slaughter of Pinkie . . . bit the dust, no way disparaging in his death that ancient race from which he claimed descent.' *The Monastery.*

GLENFINLAS. Redoubtable friends of Rob Roy. *Rob Roy.*

GLENGALLACHER, LAIRD OF. A Highland friend who gave Darsie Latimer an invitation to shoot a buck in his 'country.' But Mr. Fairford's outcry against the proposal led Darsie to go to Dumfries instead. *Redgauntlet.*

GLENGIBBER, EARL OF. A favourite of James the Sixth, to whom was granted the 'original Charter of Erection of the Abbey, Abbey lands, and so forth, of Trotcosey, comprehending Monkbarns and others.' *The Antiquary.*

GLENGUBBLE, LAIRD OF. A relative of the Bertram family, and also of Frank Kennedy. *Guy Mannering.*

GLENGYLEFOLK. Redoubtable friends of Rob Roy. *Rob Roy.*

GLENMORRISON. One of the Highlanders who fought under Montrose at Inverlochy. *A Legend of Montrose.*

GLENPROSING, LADY. A gossip who at the time of his birth destined Triptolemus Yellowley to 'be a dainty curate—and say he should live to be a bishop, what the waur wad he be?' *The Pirate.*

GLENSTRAE. An ancestor of Rob Roy: chief of the clan in the celebrated conflict at Glenfruin (the Glen of Sorrow). *Rob Roy.*

GLENVARLOCH, LORD. *See* OLIFAUNT, NIGEL and RANDAL.

GLIBLAD. A merchant whose bill formed one of the assets carried off by Rashleigh Osbaldistone. *Rob Roy.*

GLORIEUX, LE. Tiel Wetzweiler, jester to Charles the Bold. His folly, 'however grossly it was sometimes displayed, covered more than the usual quantity of shrewd and caustic observation proper to his class.' *Quentin Durward.*

GLOSSIN, GILBERT. Ellangowan's agent. He 'would have been a pretty lawyer, had he not had such a turn for the roguish part of the profession.' The 'wily scoundrel' was treacherous alike to Ellangowan and Dirk Hatteraick. 'Out of my sight, ye viper!' the laird said in his wrath, 'ye frozen viper, that I warmed till ye stung me!' *Guy Mannering.*

GLOUCESTER, DUKE OF. Charles II's brother Henry. He rode by the king's side in the royal progress from Rochester to London. *Woodstock.*

GLOUCESTER, EARL OF. The celebrated earl' who supported Prince Richard in his sudden attack on the castle of Garde Doloureuse. *The Betrothed.*

GLOVER, HANS. Gertrude Pavillon's 'bachelor.' He guided Quentin Durward and the Countess of Croye on their journey from Liège until they met Count Crèvecœur. He 'conducted himself like a person of reflection and discretion.' *Quentin Durward.*

GLOVER, CATHARINE. 'The Fair Maid of Perth,' 'universally acknowledged to be the most beautiful young woman of the city or its vicinity.' 'Rather allied to reserve than to gaiety,' and earnest in 'the exercises of devotion,' she avoided the addresses of the court gallants, and busied herself in trying to wean the apprentice Conachar 'from his rude Highland habits,' and to convince her lover, Henry Gow, who lived 'in a perfect atmosphere of strife, blood, and quarrels,' that 'vanity and wrath' were his besetting sins. While she was secretly proud of his attachment, she felt forced to reject his suit, partly through fear of Sir John Ramorny's threatened revenge, and partly on account of 'the notions about peace and forgiveness' which she had learnt from Father Clement. But experience brought her to see 'that men rarely advance in civilisation or refinement beyond the ideas of their own age, and that a headlong and exuberant courage, like that of Henry Smith, was, in the iron days in which they lived, preferable to the deficiency which had led to Conachar's catastrophe.' *The Fair Maid of Perth.*

GLOVER, DOROTHY. Simon's housekeeper. 'Dorothy, otherwise an industrious, faithful, and even affectionate creature, had that strong appetite for collecting and retailing sinister intelligence, which is often to be marked in the lower classes.' *The Fair Maid of Perth.*

Note.—'She also took name from the trade she practised under her master's auspices.'

GLOVER, SIMON. Catharine's father: one of the leading burgesses of the city. Proud of his craft, and content with his sphere, he had no wish for a 'son-in-law that thinks himself better than me.' He furthered Henry Gow's suit in every way he could, urging always greater boldness in the wooing. He had little sympathy with Catharine's extreme religious views, but in course of Sir John Ramorny's revenge he was indicted with her for having 'spoken irreverent discourses of the doctrines of holy Church.' With the help of Sir Patrick Charteris he escaped to the Highlands. But he had 'no heart to be a martyr.' His life was that 'of a hale old man of sixty who is in no haste to bring it to a close,' and he was soon 'minded to go back to Perth, sue out my pardon in the spiritual court, carry my fagot to the gallows' foot, in token of recantation, and purchase myself once more the name of a good Catholic, were it at the price of all the worldly wealth that remains to me.' *The Fair Maid of Perth.*

GLOWROWRUM, LADY. A relative of Minna and Brenda Troil, through their mother, 'a canny Scotswoman, like herself.' 'The worst tongue in Zetland,' she confirmed the reports against Mordaunt Mertoun which Bryce Snailsfoot carried to Magnus Troil. *The Pirate.*

GODFREY OF BOUILLON. Duke of Lorraine, and afterwards proclaimed king of Jerusalem: one of the leaders of the first Crusade who, when passing through Constantinople, promised allegiance to Alexius Comnenus. 'The princes and counts esteem him, because he is the foremost in the ranks of those whom they fantastically call knights, and also on account of the good faith and generosity which he practises in all his transactions. The clergy give him credit for the highest zeal for the doctrines of religion, and a corresponding respect for the church and its dignitaries. Justice, liberality, and frankness, have equally attached to this Godfrey the lower class of the people. His general attention to moral obligations is a pledge to them that his religion is real.' *Count Robert of Paris.*

GODOLPHIN. The English statesman who foresaw 'that there was no other mode of avoiding the probable extremity of a civil war' after Queen Anne's death, 'but by carrying through an incorporating union.' *The Black Dwarf.*

GOFFE, CAPTAIN. Captain of Cleveland's consort, the *Fortune's Favourite.* 'Black-haired, bull-necked, and beetle-browed, his clumsy strength and ferocious countenance contrasted strongly with the manly figure and open countenance of Cleveland.' He was brutal and drunken, and 'when he has his grog abroad,' Hawkins said, 'he is so d—d funny with his cranks and his jests, that there is no living with him.' Jealous because the crew thought Cleveland's seamanship more trustworthy, he would have left him wholly at the mercy of the Kirkwall magistrates, had not Jack Bunce intervened. *The Pirate.*

GOLDEN FARMER. A highwayman: a 'Beggar's Opera' hero. *Rob Roy.*

GOLDIE, SANDIE. An Edinburgh silversmith. *Waverley.*

GOLDIEBIRD. The holder of a bond in virtue of which Greenhorn and Grinderson were instructed 'to proceed *peremptorie* and *sine mora*' against Sir Arthur Wardour. *The Antiquary.*

GOLDIEWORD. A creditor of Sir Arthur Wardour to the extent of six hundred. *The Antiquary.*

GOLDTHRED, LAURENCE. 'The cutting mercer of Abingdon.' He affected 'a ruffianly vapouring humour,' and talked 'of breaking parks, and taking the highway, in such fashion that you would think he haunted every night betwixt Hounslow and London; when, in fact, he may be found sound asleep on his feather-bed, with a candle placed beside him on one side, and a Bible on the other, to fright away the goblins.' *Kenilworth.*

See also THACKHAM, JANE.

GOLIGHTLY, GIBBIE. 'The galloping groom' from whom Lovel bought a horse. *The Antiquary.*

GONZAGO, LOUISA. Mordaunt Mertoun's mother. 'She proved faithless' to Vaughan, but he 'did that which made an instant flight from Hispaniola necessary.' *The Pirate.*

GOODFELLOW, ROBIN. 'The original Puck of the Shaws dramaticals.' 'A queer-looking, small-eyed boy of the Aultoun of St. Ronan's,' in whom Captain Jekyl easily recognised 'one of that hopeful class of imps, who pick up a precarious livelihood about places of public resort, by going errands, brushing shoes, doing the groom's and coachman's work in the stables, driving donkeys, opening gates, and so forth, for about one-tenth part of their time, spending the rest in gambling, sleeping in the sun, and otherwise qualifying themselves to exercise the profession of thieves and pickpockets, either separately, or in conjunction with those [sic] of waiters, grooms, and postilions.' *St. Ronan's Well.*

GOODRICHE, MR. The Roman Catholic gentleman 'reported to be in orders,' who was brought to Dr. Gray's house by Major Tresham to baptize Richard Middlemas. *The Surgeon's Daughter.*

GOODSIRE, JOHNNIE. The weaver at the Castletown to whom Mrs. Dinmont entrusted the weaving of a plaid for Vanbeest Brown. *Guy Mannering.*

GOOSE GIBBIE. 'A half-witted lad, of very small stature, who had a kind of charge of the poultry' at Tillietudlem. Armed and mounted to take Cuddie Headrigg's place in Lady Margaret's muster at the wappenschaw, he lost control of his horse at a critical moment, and was thrown, unmasked, before the eyes of his astonished lady and the rest of the gentry. Lady Margaret never forgave the affront, and at a momentous time in Lord Evandale's career dismissed poor Gibbie without receiving a message that might have saved her friend. *Old Mortality.*
See also DUDDEN, GILBERT.

GORDON, FRANCIS. 'A drunken trooper of the Royal Guards.' Without definitely committing himself, David Deans was ready to receive honour for having removed 'this wicked persecutor from the face of the earth.' *The Heart of Midlothian.*

GORDON, LORD LEWIS. One of the Highland chieftains who joined the young Chevalier. *Waverley.*

GORDON, MR. The chaplain who was preaching in an adjacent gallery during Wildrake's interview with Cromwell in Windsor Castle. *Woodstock.*

GORGON. A brache belonging to Charles the Bold. He likened Margaret of Anjou to her: she 'compels whatsoever hound is coupled with her to go the way she chooses, or she strangles him if he resists.' *Anne of Geierstein.* (*Brache,* a hunting bitch.)

GOSLING, CICELY. Giles' daughter, 'the beauty of the bar.' *Kenilworth.*

GOSLING, GILES. Landlord of the

Black Bear in Cumnor : Michael Lambourne's uncle. He was ' a man of a goodly person, and of somewhat round belly ; fifty years of age and upwards, moderate in his reckonings, prompt in his payments, having a cellar of sound liquor, a ready wit, and a pretty daughter.' To the curiosity which belonged to his calling he joined ' a reasonable degree of discretion, and this he exercised for some time towards Edmund Tressilian and Wayland Smith. But after Amy Robsart's escape he told Foster the manner of her flight, for, said he, ' Varney has interest enough with the justices to dismount my noble emblem from the post on which he swings so gallantly, to call in my license, and ruin me from garret to cellar.' *Kenilworth.*

GOSLINN, GILBERT, OF GANDERCLEUGH. The ' good-humoured visitor ' at whose intercession was given the half-holiday which enabled Peter Pattieson to witness the stage-coach accident, and as a result to form the acquaintance of Hardie, Halkit, and Dunover. *The Heart of Midlothian.*

GOUKTHRAPPLE, MAISTER. A ' chosen vessel ' : rival of Jabesh Rentowel. *Waverley.*

GOURLAY, AILSHIE. Sir Anthony Wardour's jester : perhaps ' the last privileged fool, or jester, maintained by any family of distinction in Scotland.' *The Antiquary.*

GOURLAY, AILSIE. ' The wise woman of Bowden.' She had a considerable reputation among the ignorant for her supposed cures, and ' spaed fortunes, read dreams, composed philtres, discovered stolen goods, and made and dissolved matches.' Employed by Lady Ashton to wait on Lucy, she excited Lucy's imagination to such an extent that Sir William at last dismissed her, promising her ' a bonny red gown . . . a stake, and a chain and a tar barrel.' She was ' burned on the top of North Berwick Law by sentence of a commission from the Privy Council.' *The Bride of Lammermoor.*

GOW, NATHANIEL. Leader of the orchestra in the dramatic entertainment at Shaws Castle : Scotland's ' gifted minstrel ' and ' his father's own son.' *St. Ronan's Well.*

GOW, or SMITH, HENRY. ' Gow Chrom ' (the bandy-legged smith): ' Hal of the Wynd.' ' A burgher of wealth and consideration,' he was ' known to Highland and Lowland as the best armourer that ever made sword, and the truest soldier that ever drew one.' ' His professional jealousy, personal strength, and skill in the use of arms, brought him into many quarrels . . . but with these qualities were united the simple good nature of a child and . . . an imaginative and enthusiastic temper,' which exalted his sentiments towards Catharine Glover ' as if they had been fixed upon an actual angel.' But even the dread of her displeasure could not stifle his chivalrous feelings towards the ' defenceless creature,' Louise, and the widowed Maudie Proudfute, while the fear that Simon had promised her hand to Eachin MacIan drove him to espouse the cause of Clan Chattan with a ferocity which vanquished the dauntless Torquil and left Eachin a prey to superstitious terror. *The Fair Maid of Perth.*

Note.—From *Rob Roy:* ' Rob is for his ain hand, as Henry Wynd feught—he'll take the side that suits him best.'

GOWANS. Jeanie Deans' 'brockit cow ' (i.e. the cow with black and white spots or streaks on her face). *The Heart of Midlothian.*

GRAEME, CATHERINE. *See* CATHERINE OF NEWPORT.

GRAEME, MAGDALEN. Roland's grandmother, 'come of the Graemes of Heathergill . . . a people of ancient blood,' and descended from Malise, Earl of Strathern. Full of zeal and ' ecstatic devotion ' for the old faith, she regarded herself as a minister sent down from Heaven to work His will—a minister ' before whom shall be humbled the wisdom of Murray and the dark strength of Morton.' Roland was ' the jewel ' of her life, but him too she was prepared to devote to the good cause, ' flesh and fell, sinew and limb, body and soul ! ' Her zeal was not ' altogether according to knowledge,' however ; at times ' the mist ' came upon her, and her ' wisdom ' was ' folly.' *The Abbot.*

GRAEME, ROLAND. Son of Julian Avenel and Catherine of Newport. When rescued by Wolf from the loch of Avenel he already showed, at the age of ten, a certain ' contempt of danger and impatience of restraint,' and during the years he spent at the castle as the Lady's page, his character became ' bold, peremptory, decisive, and overbearing ; generous, if neither withstood nor contradicted ; vehement and passionate, if censured or opposed.' In spite of the Protestant influences under which he spent these years, his grandmother's early training kept him attached to the old faith, and when, as her page, he had the opportunity of rendering bold and dangerous service to Queen Mary, the ' quicksilver ' in his veins answered readily to Catherine Seyton's magnetic influence. *The Abbot.*

GRAEME, WILLIAM. *See* WILLIE OF WESTBURNFLAT.

GRAHAME, BAILIE. A friend whose ridicule Bailie Nicol Jarvie feared. *Rob Roy.*

(*Bailie*, the magistrate second in rank in a royal burgh.)

GRAHAME, COLONEL JOHN, OF CLAVERHOUSE. One of the military commission appointed by the Scottish Privy Council to carry out their measures against the Covenanters. While possessing ' such a countenance as limners love to paint and ladies to look upon,' with a ' gentleness and gaiety of expression,' that seemed also ' to inspire his actions and gestures,' he was ' cool and collected in danger, fierce and ardent in pursuing success, careless of facing death himself, and ruthless in inflicting it on others.' ' When I think of death, Mr. Morton, as a thing worth thinking of,' he said, 'it is in the hope of pressing one day some well-fought and hard-won field of battle, and dying with the shout of victory in my ear— —*that* would be worth dying for, and more, it would be worth having lived for!' *Old Mortality.* See also DUNDEE, VISCOUNT.

GRAHAME, CORNET RICHARD. Claverhouse's nephew and apparent heir. He was chosen by his uncle to be the bearer of a summons to the Covenanters' army to lay down their arms, but refused to parley with Balfour of Burley. When he persisted in addressing the army, to the neglect of its officers, Balfour shot him dead. The 'youngest and hottest' of Claverhouse's officers, he feared 'shot or steel as little as if the devil had given him armour of proof against it.' *Old Mortality.*

GRAHAME, JAMES. See MONTROSE, EARL OF.

GRAHAMES, THE. One of the clans 'a' mounted and in order' to make war against Rob. 'It's well kend their quarrel—and I dinna blame them—naebody likes to lose his kye.' *Rob Roy.* (*Kye*, cows.)

GRANEANGOWL, MR. The Marquis of Argyle's chaplain. By skilful flattery and effrontery Dalgetty enlisted his aid when escaping from Inverary Castle. *A Legend of Montrose.*

GRANGE, LAIRD OF. See KIRKCALDY.

GRANTMESNIL, HUGH DE. One of the challengers in the tournament at Ashby-de-la-Zouch : 'a noble baron in the vicinity, whose ancestor had been Lord High Steward of England in the time of the Conqueror and his son William Rufus.' *Ivanhoe.*

GRATIAN, FATHER. One of the guests in Ian Mengs' inn. He made friendly advances to Seignor Philipson, and secured the payment of his reckoning by the Englishman, giving him in return 'many a blessing in good German and bad Latin.' *Anne of Geierstein.*

GRAY, ALICE. 'Old Alice,' an 'ancient domestic' of the Ravenswoods. She continued to live in her old cottage under Sir William Ashton's protection, and to Lucy she became 'the very empress of old women, and queen of gossips, so far as legendary lore is concerned. She is blind, poor old soul, but when she speaks to you, you would think she has some way of looking into your very heart.' Her 'strong sense, deep reflection,' and full experience showed her that between the Ashtons and the Master of Ravenswood, bitter enmity and close friendship were equally to be dreaded, but all her warnings were made in vain, and she died oppressed with the sense of a heavy impending fate. *The Bride of Lammermoor.*

GRAY, HABBIE. Old Alice's husband. *The Bride of Lammermoor.*

GRAY, GIDEON. Surgeon in the village of Middlemas : Menie's father and Richard Middlemas' guardian. He led 'the rough, active, and ill-rewarded course of life' of a rural man of medicine, his income approaching two hundred pounds a year, ' for which he travelled about five thousand miles on horseback, in the course of the twelve months.' ' A plain, blunt man,' he was ' devoted to his profession ' and ' clear-sighted ' when dealing with the ordinary affairs of life. *The Surgeon's Daughter.*

GRAY, MENIE. Dr. Gray's daughter : ' she is a noble-hearted girl . . . and for her frankness alone, even without her beauty, and her good sense, deserves an emperor.' But she preferred Richard Middlemas before Adam Hartley, and continued to trust him even when reason whispered doubts. After her father's death she went to India, to ' share his reviving fortunes,' was met in Madras by Madame Montreville, and was conveyed to Bangalore, there to be presented to Tippoo Sahib, ' a lily from Frangistan, to plant within the recesses of the secret garden of thy pleasures.' *The Surgeon's Daughter.*

GRAY, MRS. Jean Watson, the doctor's wife : ' the cherry-cheeked daughter of an honest farmer, who being herself one of twelve children who had been brought up on an income of fourscore pounds a year, never thought there could be poverty in more than double the sum.' She died at Menie's birth, four years after the arrival of Richard Middlemas in the household. *The Surgeon's Daughter.*

GRAYLESS OF THE INNER TEMPLE. A friend with whom Wildrake fought his ' most desperate duel,' Grayless having ' taken the wall of the Reverend Dr. Bunce.' *Woodstock.*

GRAYSTEEL, DR. One of Mr. Oldbuck's antiquarian friends. *The Antiquary.*

GREEN COLIN. *See* CAMPBELL, CAPTAIN.

GREEN, GOODY. The woman at whose house Charles II ' shifted himself out of a woman's into a man's dress . . . and gave Goody Green's Dolly a gold-piece to say nothing about it.' *Woodstock.*

GREENHALGH. The messenger who brought to the Isle of Man ' a parcel of tracts about Protestants and Papists,' and the news that the Countess of Derby was accused of being an agent in the Popish Plot. *Peveril of the Peak.*

GREENHORN, GILBERT. Son and successor of Girnigo. During his absence at the Lamberton races, his partner Grinderson took active steps to recover moneys due by Sir Arthur Wardour to the firm and to clients, and suggested that ' Mr. Greenhorn will accommodate you by taking your service of plate, or the bay horses, if sound in wind and limb, at a fair appreciation, in part payment of your accompt.' Greenhorn's grandfather had been a ' scoundrelly blacksmith ' to the Wardours. *The Antiquary.*

GREENHORN, GIRNIGO. Sir Arthur Wardour's ' late correspondent and man of business.' *The Antiquary.*

GREENLEAF, GILBERT. An old archer ' whose gravity, sagacity, and skill in his vocation, while they gained him the confidence of all in the castle, subjected him, as he himself said, occasionally to the ridicule of the young coxcombs; and at the same time, we may add, rendered him somewhat pragmatic and punctilious towards those who stood higher than himself in birth and rank.' Jealous of the forwardness and inexperience of Sir Aymer de Valence's youth, he increased the misunderstanding between him and Sir John de Walton by fostering Sir John's suspicions of Bertram. *Castle Dangerous.*

GREEN MANTLE. See REDGAUNTLET, LILIAS.

GREENSIDE. A neighbouring laird whose lineage compared unfavourably with Ellangowan's. *Guy Mannering.*

GREGOR. A Highlander who twitted Evan Dhu with Clan Mac Ivor's reception of Edward Waverley. *Waverley.*

GREGOR, CLAN. Part of a reinforcement raised by Colkitto after Montrose had retired from Aberdeen. *A Legend of Montrose.*

GREGOR, DOUGAL. The 'Dougal creature.' Formerly a prisoner in the Tolbooth of Glasgow, he found favour in the jailer's eyes, and was retained as a turnkey. He admitted Frank Osbaldistone with his mysterious guide on their midnight visit to Owen. Devoted to Rob Roy as an 'uncouth, wild, and ugly savage' to 'the idol of his tribe,' he led Captain Thornton into an ambush by assuming a convincing air of treachery to Rob.

'Wha wad hae thought there had been as muckle sense in his tatty pow, that ne'er had a better covering than his ain shaggy hassock of hair?' *Rob Roy.*
(*Tatty,* matted. *Pow,* head. *Hassock,* besom.)

GREGORY. The armourer in Lochleven Castle. Roland Graeme used sometimes to work with him, and after Gregory's dismissal, made false keys to aid in Queen Mary's escape. *The Abbot.*

GREGSON, GILBERT. The jockey who delivered to Redgauntlet the letter in which Father Buonaventure appointed a meeting at Joe Crackenthorp's inn. *Redgauntlet.*

GREGSON, WIDOW. The 'notably clean Englishwoman' at whose inn Darsie Latimer stayed while in Shepherd's Bush, near Dumfries. *Redgauntlet.*

GREY, GILBERT. One of Bucklaw's horses: 'cost me twenty Jacobuses.' *The Bride of Lammermoor.*
(*Jacobus,* a gold coin worth twenty-five shillings.)

GRIEVE, JOCKEY. A friend of Dandy Dinmont. Dandy recommended Vanbeest Brown to stay a night with him on his way from Tib Mumps' to Charlieshope. *Guy Mannering.*

GRIEVE AND SCOTT, MESSRS. Owners of the 'repository' in which Jedediah Cleishbotham bought his hats. *Count Robert of Paris.*

GRIFFIN, ALLAN. Master of the Griffin Inn. He was the 'early citizen' who, on his way to mass on the morning of Ash Wednesday, 'saw the body of the luckless Oliver Proudfute lying on its face, across the kennel.' *The Fair Maid of Perth.* (*Kennel*, gutter.)

GRIFFIN, MASTER. A preacher who with the Bailiff and Aglionby, the Recorder, was graciously received by Queen Elizabeth during her Progress to Kenilworth Castle. *Kenilworth.*

GRIFFITHS. One of the Earl of Derby's menservants. *Peveril of the Peak.*

GRIFFITHS, SAMUEL. A London banker whom Lady Darsie Redgauntlet entrusted with the execution of her last will. He followed her injunctions of secrecy, and enjoined Darsie to refrain from visiting England until his twenty-fifth year was over. 'Honest Griffiths, citizen and broker, who never bestows more than the needful upon his quarterly epistles.' *Redgauntlet.*

GRIGG THE GRINNER. A water-cock 'who never pulls but he shows all his teeth from ear to ear, as if he were grimacing through a horse-collar.' *The Fortunes of Nigel.*

GRIMESBY, GAFFER. One of the company in Dame Crane's inn who discussed the news that 'the devil hath flown away with him they called Wayland Smith.' *Kenilworth.*

GRIMSLEES, MRS. Captain Clutterbuck's landlady in Kennaquhair. *The Monastery.*

GRINDERSON, GABRIEL. For many years Parliament House clerk to Girnigo Greenhorn. He was taken into partnership by Girnigo's son Gilbert, and during his partner's absence at the Lamberton races brought Sir Arthur Wardour's affairs to a crisis. 'There is some use in having two attorneys in one firm. . . . When it is fair weather with the client, out comes the gentleman-partner to fawn like a spaniel; when it is foul, forth bolts the operative brother to pin like a bull-dog.' *The Antiquary.*

GRINDSTONE, PEGGY. 'The miller's daughter at Sillermills': one of Sir Philip Forester's victims, who died of 'heartbreak.' *My Aunt Margaret's Mirror.*

GRISELDA. A 'counterfeit old woman' whose part as nurse Dwining played when Catharine Glover was received by the Duke of Rothesay in Falkland Castle. *The Fair Maid of Perth.*

GRIST, GOODMAN. The miller from whom Jem Collier was told to take orders regarding the *Jumping Jenny's* cargo. *Redgauntlet.*

GRIZZEL. (1) One of Ellangowan's servants.
(2) Mrs. MacCandlish's servant. (1) and (2) *Guy Mannering.*

GRIZZIE. Mrs. Saddletree's servant. *The Heart of Midlothian.*

GRIZZLECLEUGH, SIR GILBERT. See TAMLOWRIE, LAIRD OF.

GRIZZY. One of Martin Tackett's cows, driven off by the English forayers. *The Monastery.*

GRIZZY. One of the Rev. Josiah Cargill's maidservants, whom Mr. Touchwood lectured on the duty of wearing shoes and stockings. 'As his advice came fortified by a present of six pair of white cotton hose, and two pair of stout leathern shoes, it was received, not with respect only, but with gratitude.' *St. Ronan's Well.*

GROATSETTARS, MADDIE and CLARA. Lady Glowrowrum's nieces, 'esteemed considerable fortunes in the island.' During the festivities at Burgh Westra, 'they were both blithe enough to get Mordaunt to sit betwixt them at dinner,' and 'were soon engaged in a gay conversation, to which, as usual on such occasions, the gentleman contributed wit, or what passes for such, and the ladies their prompt laughter and liberal applause.' *The Pirate.*

GROT, PETER. *See* CLAWSON.

GRUB AND GRINDER. A firm whose bill formed one of the assets carried off by Rashleigh Osbaldistone. *Rob Roy.*

GRUBBET, JONATHAN. Mr. Pembroke's bookseller in Little Britain. He boasted of having published for Drake, Lawton, and Amhurst, but could not risk Mr. Pembroke's treatises. 'Not but what I would go to—(what was I going to say?) to the Plantations for the Church with pleasure,' he said, ' —but, dear doctor, I have a wife and family.' *Waverley.*

GRUMBALL, DOCTOR. One of the 'faithful friends' who met Father Buonaventure at Joe Crackenthorp's inn: 'the representative of Oxford, the mother of learning and loyalty.' *Redgauntlet.*

GUARDOVER, GAMELYN DE. One of Sir Arthur Wardour's ancestors. 'He kept company with Bruce and Wallace.' *The Antiquary.*

GUARINE, PHILIP. Squire to Hugo de Lacy. Like 'an old mastiff of the true breed' he loved his master, but could not endure some of those whom he favoured. He felt an 'instinctive suspicion and aversion' towards Renault Vidal, and by his vigilance saved his master from death on the first night of Renault's service. *The Betrothed.*

GUDYILL, JOHN. The 'old drunken cavaliering butler who had served with Sir Richard under Montrose, and stunned the family nightly with his exploits.' '"When I can find a true friend to the king and his cause, and a moderate episcopacy; when I find a man, as I say, that will stand by church and crown as I did mysell in my master's life, and all through Montrose's time, I think there's naething in the cellar ower gude to be spared on him."' *Old Mortality.*

GUELDRES, ADOLPHUS, DUKE OF. 'One of the most atrocious characters of his time.' 'Hell gapes for him,' Quentin said when Maître Pierre suggested his service to the 'young hot-blood.' *Quentin Durward.*

GUENEVRA. *See* NECTABANUS.

GUISCARD, ROBERT. Archduke of Apulia, and father of Bohemond of Tarentum. 'A wily statesman and a brave warrior, he became the terror of Europe, from being a knight whose Norman castle would have been easily garrisoned by six crossbows and as many lances.' *Count Robert of Paris*. See also GAITA.

GUMBLEGUMPTION. One of the names which Claverhouse read to Harry Morton from a curate's list of 'pictures': 'aged 50, indulged, close, sly and so forth.' *Old Mortality*.

GUNN, DUGALD. An old fellow-soldier of Edie Ochiltree. He came off ill 'for letting loose his tongue about the Major's leddy and Captain Bandilier.' *The Antiquary*.

GURTH. 'Son of Beowulph' and 'born thrall of Cedric of Rotherwood.' 'He was wont to be a faithful and cautious drudge,' but forsook his herd of swine to attend his master's disinherited son at Ashby-de-la-Zouch. There he played 'the personage of a Norman squire-at-arms' 'not ill,' and afterwards, with Wamba, took a leading part in the attack on Front-de-Bœuf's castle. Freed in gratitude by Cedric, he was, he said, 'a man changed to myself and all around.' 'There is a free spirit in my breast.' *Ivanhoe*.

GUSETUB, LAIRD OF. *See* GANDERCLEUGH, LAIRD OF.

GUSTAVUS. Dalgetty's horse, named after 'my invincible master.' 'An experienced traveller both by water and land,' he slept 'in the bed of honour' after the battle of Inverlochy. *A Legend of Montrose*.

GUTHRIE, JOHNNY. One of the band of Louis' Scottish Guard who were prepared to defend Quentin after his escape from the hands of Trois-Eschelles and Petit-André. *Quentin Durward*.

GUYOT, BERTRAND. A Gascon : one of the guard who accompanied Quentin Durward in attendance on the Ladies of Croye. He was killed during the attack by the Duke of Orleans and Dunois, fighting 'for the honour of Gascony.' *Quentin Durward*.

GWENWYN ('or more properly GWENWYNWEN'). Prince of Powys and son of Cyverliock : a British prince descended from Mervyn, youngest of the three sons who shared the sovereignty of Wales after Roderick Mawr's death. Notwithstanding Cadwallon's warnings, 'his deeply sworn hatred' against the Normans yielded for a time to the good offices of Baldwin and to his own wish to wed Eveline Berenger. But the denial of his suit roused him to fury, and in the midst of a bloody battle he slew Sir Raymond with his own hand. Two days later he himself was slain by Hugo de Lacy. *The Betrothed*.

GWILLYM. An authority regarding 'the grim hieroglyphics of heraldry' sometimes studied by Sir Hildebrand Osbaldistone to beguile the Sunday *ennui*. *Rob Roy*.

H

HAAGEN. An old man who had been pressed into Montrose's service about 1651. The doughty young people at Magnus Troil's festivities could not make him 'ashamed that he was not killed some scores of years since.' 'I was there with no choice of my own; and, besides, what good could I have done?—all the rest were running like sheep, and why should I have staid?', *The Pirate.*

HACK, WILL. 'The Duke's rider.' *Guy Mannering.*

HACKSTON OF RATHILLET. A spectator of the murder of Archbishop Sharpe: one of the leaders of the Covenanters at Drumclog. *Old Mortality.*

HACKUM, CAPTAIN. 'The Englishman that killed Lady Colgrain's gudeman': one of the reprieved prisoners mentioned by Mrs. Saddletree to Jeanie Deans. *The Heart of Midlothian.*

HACON GOLDEMUND. Claud Halcro's great ancestor 'the Golden-mouthed.' *The Pirate.*

HADAWAY, JACK. A lad from the same parish as Nanty Ewart, who gave Nanty home news from time to time: 'the second person these ten years that has cared a tobacco-stopper for Nanty Ewart.' *Redgauntlet.*

HADAWAY, MISS JEAN. The lady whom the Laird of Glengubble met at Harrogate. *Guy Mannering.*

HADOWAY, MRS. The widow with whom Lovel lodged in Fairport, 'reduced by her husband's untimely death to that state of straitened and embarrassed circumstances in which the widows of the Scotch clergy are too often found.' *The Antiquary.*

HAGENBACH, ARCHIBALD VON. A German noble, 'one of the fiercest and most lawless of that frontier nobility known by the name of Robber-knights and Robber-counts.' Appointed Governor of La Ferette by Charles of Burgundy, he exercised the powers of his position without scruple. Having robbed the English merchants Philipson of the precious packet destined for Charles, and thrown them into dungeons, he barricaded the town and prepared 'to beat into submission' the peaceful embassy of 'Swiss bullies.' But the citizens of La Ferette were in league with the Black Priest of St. Paul's, Lawrenz Neipperg, and the youths of Bâle; von Hagenbach himself became the victim of Steinernherz's sword. *Anne of Geierstein.*

HALBERT, SIR HEW. Third cousin of the Baron of Bradwardine. He had to answer to the Baron for his uncivil jest in explaining the family name as *Bear-warden*—thereby ignoring the exploits of the heroic Godmund. *Waverley.*

HALCRO, CLAUD. The Zetland poet: 'a little slight-made old man whose eye retained all the vivacity of spirit which had supported him under the thousand vicissitudes of a changeful and precarious life.' He had 'knocked about the world,' fought his way and paid his way—'either with money or wit,'—till a cousin left him a 'wee bit island' with 'a penny to spend, a penny to keep in my purse, a penny to give to the poor.' His thoughtless gaiety made him a favourite with the young, and though the elders wearied of his unending reminiscences of the 'glorious John Dryden,' they trusted his ' good old Norse heart ' through all his fiddling and folly. *The Pirate.*

HALDANE, BET. A grog-seller on Kirkwall Quay patronised by Jack Bunce. *The Pirate.*

HALDIMUND, SIR EWES. One of the Prince of Wales' train. He was with Lord Dalgarno in St. James' Park when Nigel made his fateful attack on Dalgarno. *The Fortunes of Nigel.*

HALFTEXT, JOHN. A curate. ' Four men of Belial, called dragoons,' were quartered on Widow Maclure because she would not ' wait upon the thowless, thriftless, fissenless, ministry of that carnal man.' *Old Mortality.*

(*Thowless*, unprofitable. *Fissenless*, pithless.)

HALI BEN KHALEDOUN. *See* HYDER ALI.

HALKIT, JACK. *See* HARDIE, MR.

HALL, HALBERT. A Southland Chief who accompanied Ian nan Chaistel in a raid into Northumberland, and was killed in a quarrel about the division of spoil. *Waverley.*

See BODACH GLAS.

HALL, SIR CHRISTOPHER. A gentleman ' of name and quality ' from the north of England. He attended the Highland gathering at Darnlinvarach and afterwards took part in Montrose's campaign. *A Legend of Montrose.*

HALLIDAY, TOM. A private in Claverhouse's regiment of Life Guards. At one time wounded 'by the hill folk ' he lay at Tillietudlem ' while he was under cure.' There he made the acquaintance of Jenny Dennison, who was glad to make use of him from time to time as far as she could. But he remained true to his colours, whether there was question of a prisoner's escape, or a mutiny of the troops. ' An intrepid fellow.' *Old Mortality.*

HAMAKO. The name by which Theodorick was known amongst the Turks and Arabs. *The Talisman.*

HAMET. A Saracen slave in the train of Bois-Guilbert. *Ivanhoe.*

HAMILTON. Commander of a regiment of horse sent to oppose the young Chevalier's advance to the south of Stirling. *Waverley.*

HAMILTON, LADY EMILY. Lord Evandale's sister. She could not understand Edith's unwillingness to fulfil her engagement, ' being one of those damsels who think there is nothing either wonderful or terrible in matrimony.' *Old Mortality.*

HAMMERLEIN, CLAUS. ' President of the mystery of the workers in iron ' in Liège : one of the excited crowd which gathered round Quentin Durward when his badge had raised false hopes of a message from Louis. *Quentin Durward.*

HAMMORGAW, MR. The precentor in St. Enoch's Kirk. He took Andrew Fairservice to Bailie Nicol Jarvie when Andrew wanted ' to send the crier through the town ' for his master. *Rob Roy.*

(*Bailie*, a magistrate next in rank to the Provost.)

HANDIE-DANDIE. *See* WILSON, AN-
DREW. *The Heart of Midlothian.*

HANNAH. Mr. Bindloose's housekeeper. *St. Ronan's Well.*

HANNAH. Mr. Saunders Fairford's
housekeeper : ' an exception to all
Scottish housekeepers, and stands
unparalleled for cleanliness among
the women of Auld Reekie.' *Redgauntlet.*

HANSEN, NEIL. One of the Flem-
ings who helped Wilkin Flammock
to outwit the Welsh in his defence
of the castle of Garde Doloureuse.
The Betrothed.

HANSON, ADRIAN. A Dutchman
described, in Major Bridgenorth's
story of Richard Whalley, as being
shot and scalped by the Indians
' as a judgment.' *Peveril of the
Peak.*

HAPPER. ' Hob Miller,' Mysie's
father. All the cultivators in the
Halidome had to bring their corn
to be ground in his mill, and his
' utmost vigilance ' was exercised
' to prevent evasions of his right
of monopoly.' *The Monastery.*

HAPPER, KATE. Mysie's aunt : ' a
canty quean . . . twenty years
syne.' *The Monastery.*

(*Canty quean,* lively young
woman.)

HAPPER, MYSIE. The Miller's
daughter, ' a dark-eyed, laughter-
loving wench,' who ' sang and
laughed from morning to night.'
' She was of a simple and affectionate ' character, and was ' completely dazzled and bewildered '
by Sir Piercie Shafton's gallantry
of dress and language. But she
was ' alert and enterprising,' ' possessing more than female strength
of body and more than female
courage,' and her devotion was
content to express itself in honest
service. ' If,' said Sir Piercie,
' the purest sentiments of a
generous mind, streaming forth
like the rays of the sun reflected
by a diamond, may ennoble one,
who is in some sort the daughter
of a molendinary mechanic—.'
The Monastery.

HARDIE, MR. An Edinburgh advocate detained at the Wallace
Inn, Gandercleugh, by a coach-
accident. With him were his
friend Halkit, a young lawyer, and
Mr. Dunover. Entertainment took
the form of a discussion of various
causes célèbres, and from this conversation Peter Pattieson got
some of the material for *The Heart
of Midlothian. The Heart of
Midlothian.*

HARDWICKE, LORD. Lord Chancellor. During the debate on the
' Porteous Bill ' he insinuated
that the Duke of Argyle ' had
stated himself in this case rather
as a party than as a judge.' *The
Heart of Midlothian.*

HARLEWALLS, DEACON. A Fairport
worthy who suggested putting
' the auld stanes ' from Donagild's
chapel on the front of the new
council-house. ' It will be very
tastefu', and just in the style of
modern Gothic.' *The Antiquary.*

HARLEY. Leader of the English
High Church Party which ' affected to separate their principles
from those of the Jacobites and,
on that account, obtained the

denomination of Whimsicals.' *The Bride of Lammermoor.*

HARPAX. The centurion in command of the guard at the Golden Gate when Sebastes made an attempt on Hereward's life. Dishonest in his office, he was also a 'veteran and unbending conspirator.' He was one of the first 'to thunder forth their gratitude for the clemency of the Emperor' in regarding the offence of the conspirators as 'a transient delusion,' but he failed not to strengthen 'for some future renewal of their enterprise the failing spirits of Stephanos.' *Count Robert of Paris.*

HARPER, WILL. Ludovic Lesly's page. Quentin shared his 'cabin' when put under his uncle's protection by Lord Crawford. *Quentin Durward.*

HARRISON, HUGH. Lady Margaret Bellenden's steward. 'To complete the quota which her barony ought to furnish for the muster' at the wappenschaw, he was pushed to sore straits. He was obliged to arm and mount Goose Gibbie as a substitute for Cuddie Headrigg, with results disastrous to Lady Margaret's dignity. *Old Mortality.*

HARRISON, GENERAL. One of the Commissioners sent by Parliament to dispose of Woodstock Palace and Park as 'national property.' Unlike his colleagues Desborough and Bletson, he had risen to a high position in the army 'by his dauntless courage . . . and . . . his exalted enthusiasm.' But 'after a victory . . . Harrison was one of the most cruel and pitiless men,' and this, combined with his fanatical beliefs, made him an easy prey to his fears when the slaughtered Dick Robison appeared before him. *Woodstock.*

HARTLEY, ADAM. Dr. Gray's second apprentice, closely associated with Richard Middlemas in his studies. Making up by 'soundness of judgment' for Richard Middlemas' 'quicker parts,' he was preferred by Dr. Gray as a probable successor, but gave way when Menie refused all encouragement to his hopes. As surgeon in the fever hospital of Ryde he was able to secure General Witherington's interest on Richard's behalf, but he was estranged by Richard's perverse selfishness, and when chance threw them together in India he 'saw neither propriety nor comfort in maintaining a show of friendly intercourse, to conceal hate, contempt, and mutual dislike.' Through his friendship with Barak el Hadgi he was able to defeat Richard's foul plot for the disposal of Menie Gray. *The Surgeon's Daughter.*

HASSAN. The storyteller who beguiled the way as Adonbec and Kenneth rode through the desert. He told 'a tale of love and magic, intermixed with feats of warlike achievement, and ornamented with abundant quotations from the Persian poets.' *The Talisman.*

HASTIE, ROBIN. Landlord of the inn in which Tom Trumbull and Nanty Ewart had a drunken carouse on the night before Alan Fairford sailed with Nanty for Cumberland. *Redgauntlet.*

HASWELL. A *protégé* of Isabel Vere. *The Black Dwarf.*

HATTERAICK, DIRK. Captain of the *Yungfrauw Hagenslaapen:* 'the terror of all the excise and custom house cruisers.' Forced by Glossin's knowledge of his share in Frank Kennedy's death to make terms, he was in the end ruined by the selfish scheming of his associate. But he took an ample revenge. As Jans Jansen he was one of 'the brutal tyrants' of Vanbeest Brown's youth.

'It shall never be said Dirk Hatteraick feared either dog or devil!' *Guy Mannering.*

HAUTLIEU, MARQUIS DE. The fictitious character in whose family memorials the Author of Waverley professed to have found the 'curious particulars respecting the connexion' between France and Scotland, which he incorporated in *Quentin Durward. Quentin Durward.*

HAUTLIEU, MARGARET DE. Sister Ursula in St. Bride's convent. Augustine confided her secret to this sister and together they escaped to the haunts of the Douglas. As Margaret de Hautlieu, Ursula had been 'distinguished among the great and fair of the land.' She was immured within the convent by her father when her attachment to Malcolm Fleming was discovered, and in an attempted rescue by Malcolm and his leader Wallace, received wounds and scars which left her a 'disfigured wretch.' After her escape with Augustine she rose superior to the 'faithlessness of her betrothed knight,' and used her freedom 'to follow her adventurous spirit through dangers not usually encountered by those of her sex.' Soon, beauty seemed to return, for her expression partook 'of the high and passionate character of her soul.' *Castle Dangerous.*

HAUTLIEU (or HATTELY), MAURICE DE. Margaret's father: 'a noble Norman who, like many of his countrymen, sought and found fortune at the court of the King of Scotland.' In the 'unfortunate feuds of Bruce and Baliol' he 'embraced with passion the faction of the English interest,' and 'was furious' when he discovered his daughter's attachment to Malcolm Fleming. *Castle Dangerous.*

HAWKINS. Boatswain of the *Fortune's Favourite.* Both he and Captain Goffe bore Cleveland 'ill-will for keeping them from sinking the Spanish brig with the poor devils of negroes on board.' But he knew Cleveland to be 'a man of thought and action' and in the general council of the ship's crew proposed that he should be 'Captain from one, *post meridiem,* to five *a.m.*, during which time Goffe is always drunk.' *The Pirate.*

HAY, COLONEL. A 'gallant friend' sent by Montrose after the victory at Inverlochy to win the Earl of Seaforth to the Royalist cause. *A Legend of Montrose.*

HAY, JOHN. A fisherman who supplied Ellangowan's table. *Guy Mannering.*

HAY, GILBERT. *See* ERROL, EARL OF.

HAYRADDIN, MAUGRABIN. Quentin's guide on his journey to Liège. In gratitude for Quentin's humane treatment of his brother Zamet, he acted with a certain degree of fidelity, while still prepared to follow the secret instructions which would have placed the little party at the mercy of William de la Marck. But Quentin defeated this purpose as well as the scheme, made through Marthon, which would have left the Countess of Croye alone in the Castle of Schonwaldt. 'Moved by a great reward from de la Marck, and hoping a yet mightier one from King Louis,' Hayraddin went to Peronne in the garb of a herald 'Rouge Sanglier,' 'not merely to bear the message of defiance' to the Duke of Burgundy, but to inform Louis secretly of de la Marck's plans. When at the point of death, he bequeathed the 'important secret' to Quentin Durward with a request for kindness to poor Klepper, his palfrey, 'the only living thing that may miss me.' *Quentin Durward.*

(*Maugrabin,* the African Moor.)

HAYSTON, FRANK. *See* BUCKLAW, LAIRD OF.

HAZELDINE, PHIL. *See* TOMKINS, JOSEPH.

HAZLEWOOD, CHARLES. Son of Sir Robert: in spite of his father's disapproval, the lover and friend of Lucy Bertram.

'Upon my word,' said Pleydell (aside), 'to be a sprig, whom I remember with a whey face and a satchel not so very many years ago, I think young Hazlewood grows a fine fellow.' *Guy Mannering.*

HAZLEWOOD, LADY. Wife of Sir Robert. *Guy Mannering.*

HAZLEWOOD, SIR ROBERT. 'The head of an ancient and powerful interest in the county, which had in the decadence of the Ellangowan family gradually succeeded to much of their authority and influence.' He was ' powerful, wealthy, ambitious, and vindictive, and looked for both fortune and title in any connexion which his son might form.' He narrowly escaped being a tool in Glossin's hands.

'These are dreadful days indeed,' he lamented, ' . . .—days when the bulwarks of society are shaken to their mighty base, and that rank, which forms, as it were, its highest grace and ornament, is mingled and confused with the viler parts of the architecture.' *Guy Mannering.*

HEADRIGG, CUDDIE (Cuthbert). The ploughman at Tillietudlem: an honest fellow. The differences between the episcopalian and the presbyterian doctrines which, to his mother, Mause, were clear as daylight, were 'clean beyond' his comprehension, and it was only through 'a sense of filial piety,' and devotion to Harry Morton, that he was drawn into the Covenanters' army. But he had 'considerable shrewdness,' and his countenance showed the 'mixture of apparent dulness with occasional sparkles, which indicated the craft so often found in the clouted shoe.' He had no ambition to 'testify for the truth gloriously with his mouth in council' and gladly accepted a free pardon. See also DENNISON, JENNY. *Old Mortality*. (*Clouted*, patched.)

HEADRIGG, CUDDIE (junior). 'A white headed rogue of four years' whom Harry Morton saw at Fairy-Knowe when he returned from exile. *Old Mortality*.

HEADRIGG, JENNY. 'A girl of about five years old': eldest child of Cuddie, the ploughman, and Jenny Dennison. *Old Mortality*.

HEADRIGG, JUDDEN. Cuddie's father: 'a douce honest man, though somewhat warldly in his dealings, and cumbered about earthly things.' *Old Mortality*.

HEADRIGG, MAUSE (née MIDDLEMAS). Cuddie's mother: 'an ancient domestic in the family,' and 'a sort of favourite' with Lady Margaret Bellenden. But the dictates of her conscience conflicted with Lady Margaret's commands regarding Cuddie's attendance at the wappenschaw, and so with Cuddie she had to 'leave a' — cot, kale-yard, and cow's grass.' At all times she was 'e'en ready to suffer for righteousness' sake,' and when a prisoner in Bothwell's hands, she poured forth vivid Biblical denunciations against the instruments of oppression with a zeal that knew nothing of fear. *Old Mortality*.

HEATHERBLUTTER, JOHN. 'The auld game-keeper' of the Baron of Bradwardine. He was suspected of interfering with Jamie Howie when lifting the rents for Inch-Grabbit. *Waverley*.

HEATHERCAT. One of the names which Claverhouse read to Harry Morton from a curate's list of 'pictures': 'outlawed — a preacher — a zealous Cameronian — keeps a conventicle among the Campsie hills.' *Old Mortality*.

HEAVYSTERNE, REV. DR. A learned professor from Utrecht. During his visit to Monkbarns he suffered much injury by inadvertently sitting down on three ancient calthrops dug from the field of Bannockburn, and in the night he further 'dree'd pain and dolour' in the haunted Green Room. *The Antiquary*.
(*To dree*, to endure.)

HECTOR OF THE MIST. A leader of the outlawed Children of the Mist. He was one of those who had murdered the McAulays' maternal uncle 'with every circumstance of inventive cruelty.' He died in like manner by Allan's hand. *A Legend of Montrose*.

HEGGIE, ANNIE. See IRWIN, HANNAH.

HEINRICK. The German adventurer with whom Quentin Durward overheard Hayraddin arrange an ambuscade 'at the Cross of the Three Kings,' for the seizure of the Ladies of Croye. *Quentin Durward*.

HELL-IN-HARNESS. See ADHEMAR, PRIOR.

HEMP. Benjie Coltherd's lurcher. *Redgauntlet*.

HEMPSEED, HAL. One of Michael Lambourne's early comrades. 'He was a sort of a gentleman, and would meddle in state matters, and so he got into the mire about the Duke of Norfolk's affair these two or three years since, fled the country with a pursuivant's warrant at his heels, and has never since been heard of.' *Kenilworth.*

HEMPSFIELD, JACK. The companion of Captain Colepepper and Andrew Skurliewhitter in the attack on old Trapbois. He was shot by Nigel. *The Fortunes of Nigel.*

HENDERSON, ELIAS. The Lady of Lochleven's chaplain : a man ' possessed of good natural points, carefully improved by the best education which those times afforded.' He had ' a faculty of close and terse reasoning ' with ' a flow of happy illustration and natural eloquence,' and for a time his teaching was attentively followed by Roland Graeme. *The Abbot.*

HENRY. One of the ' preachers whose talents have done such honour ' to Scotland. Guy Mannering made a point of hearing him when in Edinburgh. *Guy Mannering.*

HENRY, DUKE OF RICHMOND. ' The undoubted heir of the house of Lancaster ' : afterwards Henry VII. During the reign of Edward IV he found refuge in Brittany. *Anne of Geierstein.*

HENRY THE SECOND. A king, ' than whom no wiser, or, generally speaking, more fortunate monarch, ever sat upon the throne of England ; yet whose life is a striking illustration how family dissensions can tarnish the most brilliant lot to which Heaven permits humanity to aspire ; and how little gratified ambition, ex'ended power, and the highest reputation in war and peace can do towards curing the wounds of domestic affliction.' Misled by Randal de Lacy, he judged the castle of Garde Doloureuse to be ' a nest of traitors.' *The Betrothed.*

HENSHAW, EDIE. Goose - Gibbie's master after he left Tillietudlem. *Old Mortality.*

HENSHAW (or STENSHAW), KITT. A Tay boatman whom Sir Patrick Charteris ' highly trusted.' But he was in the pay of Sir John Ramorny, and interposed so many ' obstacles and delays ' to Catharine Glover's journey from Kinfauns to Falkland that when at last she arrived in Falkland she found that the Duchess of Rothesay was no longer there. *The Fair Maid of Perth.*

HERBERT, SIR WILLIAM. Hugo de Lacy's host on the night which Eveline Berenger spent with the Lady of Baldringham. *The Betrothed.*

HEREFORD, DEAN OF. The dignitary through whom Hugo de Lacy approached Baldwin, with a view to gaining a dispensation for delay in his departure to the Holy Land. *The Betrothed.*

HEREWARD OF HAMPTON. Son of Waltheoff : a sergeant in the bodyguard of Alexius Comnenus. ' A poor exile . . . who endeavours to fix his faith upon Heaven, and to perform his duty to the world he lives in, and to the prince in whose service he is engaged,' he resisted all the blandishments of Achilles Tatius and Agelastes, and by his valour and 'good faith' gained increasing confidence from the Emperor. After freeing Count Robert of Paris from his dungeon, and affording him temporary protection, he met the Count in the lists as the representative of Nicephorus. As his only reward from the Emperor he asked his discharge from the Varangian guard, and immediately afterwards, for Bertha's sake, attached himself to the Count's service. Free from artificial politeness, he valued 'men and things not according to the false estimate ascribed to them in the world, but to their real importance and actual value.' *Count Robert of Paris.*

HEREWARD OF ROTHERWOOD. Cedric's father. *Ivanhoe.*

HERIOT, GEORGE. 'Jingling Geordie'—goldsmith to the royal household of James I: Margaret Ramsay's godfather. As an old friend of Nigel's father, he proved a benevolent and sagacious adviser to Nigel in London, and being in general 'no meddler in intrigues or party affairs,' he was trusted by James I as an 'old and faithful servant.' But the king grumbled that he was 'so damnably ready with his gold-ends of wisdom and sae accursedly backward with his gold-ends of siller.' *The Fortunes of Nigel.*

Note.—The real George Heriot, court jeweller and banker to James, left the bulk of his fortune (about £24,000) to found and endow a school for the sons of poor burghers in Edinburgh. The scope of the Trust has several times been enlarged, the annual income being now more than £32,000.

HERIOT, JUDITH. George's sister: 'a decent, elderly, somewhat severe-looking female in a coif who, by the name of Aunt Judith, did the honours of his house and table.' She was 'a woman of a strong Scottish understanding, more inclined towards the Puritans than was her brother George ... attached to him in the strongest degree, and sedulously attentive to all his comforts.' But to Margaret Ramsay she complained 'the follies of the young people of this generation would drive mad an old brain like mine.' *The Fortunes of Nigel.*

HERMAN OF GOODALRICKE. A Preceptor of the Order of the Temple. He took part in Rebecca's trial, and made a direct appeal to Bois-Guilbert to say 'with what eye he himself now regards his unhappy intercourse with this Jewish maiden?' *Ivanhoe.*

HERMIGILD, COUNTESS. The 'Galwegian maid of honour' to the Duchess of Rothesay. The Duke proposed that Sir John Ramorny should play her part when Catharine Glover arrived in Falkland Castle. *The Fair Maid of Perth.*

HERMIONE, LADY. George Heriot's 'ghost': daughter of Giovanni Pauletti, a wealthy merchant of Genoa and Lady Maud Olifaunt. Deceived by Lord Dalgarno and deserted by him when she seemed to have lost her fortune, she found a refuge under the roof of her father's old business friend George Heriot. After two years' retirement in the 'Foljambe' apartments, attended only by Monna Paula, she appealed to the king, and her honour was vindicated. By unfolding Lord Dalgarno's infamy, she helped to reinstate Lord Glenvarloch in the king's favour, proving herself 'a safer and wiser counsellor than the barber woman' to Margaret Ramsay. *The Fortunes of Nigel.*

HERON, SIR GEORGE, OF CHIPCHASE. One of the gentlemen who attended Sir John Foster during his conference with the Earl of Murray. *The Monastery.*

HERRIES, LORD. One of Queen Mary's devoted supporters: a 'faithful knight and true noble,' who 'never knew guile or dishonour.' *The Abbot.*

HERRIES, HERBERT. A maternal ancestor of Redgauntlet. He forfeited the family property for following 'his kinsman, the Earl of Derwentwater, to the Preston affair in 1715.' *Redgauntlet.*

HERRIES, LORD ROBIN. 'The Philosopher': a maternal ancestor of Redgauntlet. At his death in 1667 the elder branch of the family merged in the house of Nithesdale. *Redgauntlet.*

HERRIES, MR., OF BIRRENSWORK. The name by which Redgauntlet was generally known in Dumfries and Edinburgh. *Redgauntlet.*

HESKETT, DAME. Ralph's wife. 'A blithe, bustling housewife,' who did not approve of 'fighting in her house.' *The Two Drovers.*

HESKETT, RALPH. Landlord of the Cumbrian alehouse in which the misunderstanding between Robin McCombich and Harry Wakefield was brought to a head. *The Two Drovers.*

HETTLY, MAY. 'An ancient servant or rather cottar' under whose care Jeanie left her father before starting for London. She afterwards accompanied David to Roseneath. Her 'fidelity was worthy of full confidence.' *The Heart of Midlothian.*

HEUKBANE, MRS. The Fairport butcher's wife: one of Mrs. Mailsetter's friends. *The Antiquary.*

HEWCREED, LIEUTENANT. An officer at 'the great battle of Dunbar in Scotland.' Cromwell himself 'held a pistol to the head of Lieutenant Hewcreed, threatening to shoot him through the brain if he did not give up holding forth, and put his squadron in line to the front.' *Woodstock.*

HEWIT. A shipwright in Annan, married to Janet Lightoheel. *Guy Mannering.*

HEWIT, GODFREY BERTRAM. A natural son of the Laird of Ellangowan. Glossin's attempt to identify Harry Bertram with him was defeated by his timely return from the West Indies. *Guy Mannering.*

HIGG, THE SON OF SNELL. A witness against Rebecca, being 'a bedridden man whom the prisoner had restored to the perfect use of his limbs, by a miraculous balsam.'

But he did not bear witness against her willingly, and afterwards undertook to deliver her letter to Isaac. 'Alas!' he said, 'when I boasted of thy charity, I little thought I was leading thee into danger!' *Ivanhoe.*

HIGHLAND WIDOW, THE. *See* MACTAVISH, ELSPAT.

HILARIUS, BROTHER. Refectioner at St. Mary's. With the Kitchener he accompanied Abbot Boniface to Glendearg, taking a 'sumpter-mule, loaded with provisions,' 'to aid the poor vassals ... in making a suitable collation.' *The Monastery.*

HILDEBRAND. The watch on the tower of Lochleven Castle on the night of Queen Mary's escape. 'A heavy-headed knave who holds a can of ale to be the best headpiece upon a night-watch.' *The Abbot.*

HILDEBRAND, HEW. The Master of Ravenswood's 'outrider.' *The Bride of Lammermoor.*

HILDEBROD, DUKE JACOB. 'Grand Protector of the liberties of Alsatia.' He received Nigel into the Sanctuary of Whitefriars with all the rites and ceremonies of his court, and suggested marriage with Martha Trapbois as a means by which Nigel might gain possession of the money necessary to solve his difficulties—'always deducting from the main sum some five thousand pounds for our princely advice and countenance.' 'An absolute sandbed, capable of absorbing any given quantity of liquid, without being either vivi- fied or overflowed.' *The Fortunes of Nigel.*

HILLARY, TOM. Mr. Lawford's apprentice: 'a whipper-snapper ... run away from Newcastle.' 'Certain circumstances' severed his connexion with Mr. Lawford in a few months, but he returned to the village some years later, a Captain in the East India Company's service, and dazzled his old friend Richard Middlemas with stories of Oriental fortunes. Through his good offices Richard found himself robbed and consigned to a fever hospital in Ryde, while Tom was 'jigging it away in London.' *The Surgeon's Daughter.*

HINCHUP, DAME. One of the crowd that watched Meg Murdockson being hung. *The Heart of Midlothian.*

HIRPLEHOOLY, LORD. A bedridden Privy Councillor. 'For fashion's sake' he was associated with Sir William Ashton in dealing with the Master of Ravenswood concerning the disturbance at his father's funeral. 'One to be a quorum.' *The Bride of Lammermoor.*

HISLOP, JOHN. The old-established carrier of St. Ronan's by whom Meg Dods wished all letters to be sent to her. 'Though he was not just sae fast' he 'was far surer than ony post of them a', or express either.' *St. Ronan's Well.*

HOB MILLER. *See* HAPPER.

HOBBIE O' SORBIETREES. A Liddesdale farmer. *Guy Mannering.*

'HOBBIE OF THE HEUGH-FOOT.' *See* ELLIOT, HALBERT.

HOBBLER, DR. The clergyman engaged to marry Sir Frederick Langley and Isabel Vere. *The Black Dwarf.*

HOBSON, GIL. 'The souple tailor frae Burgh.' One of the men at the Brokenburn dance thought Darsie Latimer was he. *Redgauntlet.*

HOCHSPRINGEN, DUKE OF. One of the 'most indefatigable' dancers in Germany. After being partner to Hermione, Baroness von Arnheim, for half an hour, he 'was compelled to break off the dance, and throw himself, totally exhausted, on a couch, exclaiming he had been dancing not with a woman, but with an *ignis fatuus.*' *Anne of Geierstein.*

HODGE. One of Luke Lundin's 'redoubted bodyguard' during the revels at Kinross. He was sent out with Toby Telford towards the Keiry-craigs to get tidings of John Auchtermuchty with his 'stuff of the honourable household' in Lochleven Castle. *The Abbot.*

HODGES, JOE. Landlord of the inn near Mervyn Hall in which Vanbeest Brown stayed under the name of Dawson. 'But I told him nought of your vagaries, and going out a-laking in the mere a-noights,' he said, 'not I—an I can make no sport I'se spoil none—and Squoire Mervyn's as cross as poy-crust too, mon.' *Guy Mannering.*

HODGES, JOHN. A servant of Edward Waverley who remained in the regiment after the mutiny and was taken prisoner at Gladsmuir, He managed to convey letters from Edward to his father and uncle. *Waverley.*

HODGESON, GAFFER. One of the Puritan guests at Lady Peveril's Restoration Feast. *Peveril of the Peak.*

HOLDENOUGH, NEHEMIAH. The Presbyterian minister who succeeded Dr. Rochecliffe in the rectory of Woodstock. While believing that devils or evil spirits were actually showing themselves in Woodstock Lodge, he went against them, bearing 'in his bosom the word of truth' with which to 'pack them off as with a vengeance to the uttermost parts of Assyria.' Nor did his courage fail until the appearance of Joseph Albany in the Mirror Chamber raised in his conscience 'the full tide of remorseful passion.' 'Thou wert so bold, Nehemiah,' Dr. Rochecliffe said afterwards, 'that our whole scheme would have been shipwrecked, had I not appeared to thee in the shape of a departed friend.' A 'watchful jealousy of his consequence ... joined with a natural heat of temper which he could not always subdue, were the good man's only faults.' *Woodstock.*

HOLDFAST CLEGG. A millwright of Derby who had been active at the siege of Martindale Castle, and recalled it ' with a grim smile ' as he proceeded to Lady Peveril's Restoration Feast. *Peveril of the Peak.*

HOLDFORTH, MASTER. 'The afternoon's lecturer of Saint Antonlin's.' Janet Foster followed his 'precious' doctrines. *Kenilworth.*

HOLYDAY, MASTER ERASMUS. Dickie Sludge's teacher : a voluble, Latin-quoting dominie, 'in arranging pageants, morris-dances, May-day festivities, and such like holiday delights . . . the purest and most inventive brain in England.' 'He is not half the fool you would take him for,' Dickie said, ' when he gets to work he understands ; and so he can spout verses like a play-actor, when, God wot, if you set him to steal a goose's egg, he would be drubbed by the gander.' *Kenilworth.*

HOME, JOHN, ESQ. *See* HUME, DAVID.

HONEST JOE. *See* TOMKINS, JOSEPH.

HONEYWOOD. Commander of a party of dragoons with whom Diana Vernon and her father came into contact during their flight from Preston. *Rob Roy.*

HOOD, ROBIN. *See* LOCKSLEY.

HOOKEM. *See* CLIPPURSE.

HOOPER AND GIRDER. The Newcastle firm on which the bill sent by Owen to Frank at Osbaldistone Hall was drawn. *Rob Roy.*

HORSINGTON. A groom at Ellieslaw Castle. *The Black Dwarf.*

HOSTLER, JACK. Hostler at Dame Crane's Inn. He had perilled ' his own soul to cure the bowels of a nag,' and upheld Wayland Smith's skill as a farrier. *Kenilworth.*

HOSTLER, WILL. One of the 'myrmidons of the bonny Black Bear' in Cumnor. *Kenilworth.*

HOUGHTON, HUMPHRY. Sergeant in Edward Waverley's troop of dragoons at Dundee. He was misled for a time by Will Ruthven, but died at Gladsmuir, fighting for King George. *Waverley.*

HOUGHTON, JOB. Father of Humphry : a tenant of Sir Edward Waverley. *Waverley.*

HOUKHAM, HUGH. The gardener at Lochleven Castle. Blinkhoolie credited him with 'little skill of his craft.' *The Abbot.*

HOWARD, LORD HENRY. *See* NORTHAMPTON, EARL OF.

HOWATSON, LUCKIE. The midwife who attended Mrs. Bertram. *Guy Mannering.*

(*Luckie,* a designation given to an elderly woman.)

HOWDEN, DAVIE. Mrs. Howden's husband. *The Heart of Midlothian.*

HOWDEN, JOCK. One of the Black Dwarf's patients who, after being cured once, died of 'the very same disorder.' *The Black Dwarf.*

HOWDEN, MRS. The ' rouping-wife ' : one of the pleasure-seekers disappointed of their spectacle on the morning of Porteous' reprieve. ' " And sic a comfortable window as I had gotten too, just within a penny-stane-cast of the scaffold —I could hae heard every word the minister said—and to pay twalpennies for my stand, and a' for naething ! " ' *The Heart of Midlothian.*

(*Rouping-wife,* female auctioneer. *Penny-stane,* a stone quoit.)

HOWIE, JAMIE. Inch - Grabbit's ' Bailie ' (*i.e.* deputy). *Waverley.*

HOWIE, JOHNNIE. The ' bonnet-laird' who owned the Kaim of Kinprunes, where, according to the Antiquary, the final conflict between Agricola and the Caledonians had taken place. To secure possession—for it was a 'national concern'— the Antiquary brought his mind to give acre for acre of his good corn land for the barren spot. *The Antiquary.*

(*Bonnet-laird*, a petty proprietor dressed like a yeoman.)

HOWIE, WILLIE. One of Edie Ochiltree's friends. To Sir Arthur Wardour's great offence, Edie said to Caxon that 'Willie Howie's Kilmarnock cowl covered more sense than all the three wigs in the parish'—thereby 'spreading disaffection against church and state through the whole parish.' *The Antiquary.*

HOWISONS, THE FIVE. Five of the 'few lads' Jenny Dennison knew 'to speak to.' *Old Mortality.*

HOWLAGLASS, MASTER. Master Maulstatute's minister. *Peveril of the Peak.*

HOWLEGLAS, FATHER. *See* UNREASON, ABBOT OF.

HUBBLE-DE-SHUFF. The nickname of the Colonel under whom Nosebag served. *Waverley.*

HUBERT. 'Sir Philip de Malvoisin's keeper of the chase.' He was the champion archer in the tournament at Ashby-de-la-Zouch until Locksley entered. 'A man can but do his best,' he said. *Ivanhoe.*

HUDSON, TAM. 'The Deuke's' keeper who was sent to Charlieshope to get one of Dandy Dinmont's terriers. *Guy Mannering.*

HUDSON, SIR GEOFFREY. The 'celebrated dwarf of Henrietta Maria,' and 'the favoured servant of three successive sovereigns,' he fell upon 'evil tongues and evil days' at the time of the Popish Plot. Julian Peveril shared his cell in Newgate, and to him he loved to tell stories showing that he had been a 'very model of valour and gallantry.' In reality he had considerable dignity of spirit, and both by his duel with Master Crofts and his exploits in the Civil War showed skill in arms. But his vanity exposed him to the practical jokes of the courtiers. After his release from prison he was persuaded by Fenella to take the place of the 'pistols, daggers, and ammunition' in the violoncello 'destined to surprise the Court of the unwary Charles.' *Peveril of the Peak.*

HUFFCAP, MOTHER. Owner of a house patronised by Nehemiah Holdenough and Joseph Albany in their student days at Cambridge. *Woodstock.*

HUGH, THE BLACKSMITH OF RINGLEBURN. One of Hobbie Elliot's neighbours. *The Black Dwarf.*

HUGH, THE GREAT COUNT. *See* VERMANDOIS.

HUGO. A squire who attended Bois-Guilbert as he journeyed to Ashby-de-la-Zouch. *Ivanhoe.*

HUGO, FATHER. The name by which Redgauntlet was known amongst his brethren in the monastery to which he retired. He 'displayed in the latter part of his life a strong sense of the duties of religion, which in his earlier days he had too much neglected, being altogether engaged in political speculations and intrigues.' But he never forgot the 'sufferings and injuries' of his House. *Redgauntlet.*

HUGONET, HUGO. 'A sworn minstrel, the ancient friend and servant of the house of Douglas.' He told Bertram the story of the Douglas Larder, and of the vision which appeared to him on that 'night of terror,' when preparing to put into safety the 'parchment volume' containing the poems of Thomas of Erceldoun. *Castle Dangerous.*

HUME, DAVID, ESQ. One of the 'literary characters of Scotland' to whom Advocate Pleydell gave Colonel Mannering an introduction. The others were John Home, Esq., Dr. Ferguson, Dr. Black, Lord Kaimes, Mr. Hutton, John Clerk, Esq., of Eldin, Adam Smith, Esq., and Dr. Robertson. 'Names pretty widely blown.' *Guy Mannering.*

HUMGUDGEON, CORPORAL. The officer stationed by Cromwell on the platform of the window in Rosamund's Tower, in order to guard by 'constant vigilance' against the escape of the supposed king from Love's Ladder. But while Pearson was finally adjusting the mine at the foot of the Ladder, 'the attention of the corporal on the tower became irresistibly and exclusively riveted upon the preparations for the explosion.' Albert Lee seized this instant to spring beside him and 'threw the surprised soldier from his precarious stand.' *Woodstock.*

HUMPHREY ETTERCAP. The 'tinkler' that perished in the moss on Mucklestane Moor 'five years syne.' Hobbie Elliot was at first inclined to think the Black Dwarf was his ghost. *The Black Dwarf.* (*Ettercap*, the poison-spider: hence, an ill-disposed person.)

HUNDEBERT. 'A sort of majordomo' at Rotherwood. *Ivanhoe.*

HUNDLESLOPE, LADY. One of the 'gude and waled Christians' reproached by 'the gracious Saunders Peden' because they 'wad greet mair for a bit drowned calf or stirk, than for a' the defections and oppressions of the day.' *The Heart of Midlothian.* (*Waled*, chosen.)

HUNDWOLF. Steward to the Lady of Baldringham. *The Betrothed.*

HUNSDON, LORD. One of the English Wardens of the Marches. *The Monastery.*

HUNSDON, LORD. 'A rough old noble, who, from his relationship to the Boleyns, was accustomed to use more freedom with the Queen than almost any other dared to do.' *Kenilworth.*

HUNTER, GABBIE. See BAILLIE, GABRIEL.

HUNTINGDON, DAVID, EARL OF. See KENNETH OF SCOTLAND.

HUNTINGDON, EARL OF. Brother-in-law of the Earl of Leicester. He sang the praises of Alasco to Queen Elizabeth when there was question of the genuineness of his certificate concerning Amy Robsart's illness. *Kenilworth.*

HUNTINGLEN, COUNTESS OF. The Earl's wife. She was 'something of a puritan, and kept more company with ministers than was altogether agreeable' to her husband. *The Fortunes of Nigel.*

HUNTINGLEN, EARL. Lord Dalgarno's father. He had been an 'old opponent' of Nigel's father, but gave the young lord a 'ready and efficient friendship,' and tried to forward his cause at court. 'The Earl is the vera soul of honour and cares nae mair for warld's gear than a noble hound for the quest of a foulmart.' *The Fortunes of Nigel.*

(*Foulmart*, a foul marten, or weasel.)

HUNTLY, MARQUIS OF. Chief of the Gordons, a nobleman 'equally loyal and powerful.' He 'was determined to exert his utmost energy' in the King's cause, but his zeal was 'effectually bridled by a large body of Covenanters commanded by the Lord Burleigh.' *A Legend of Montrose.*

HURRY, SIR JOHN. *See* URRIE, SIR JOHN.

HUTCHEON. One of Julian Avenel's Border-riders: 'constant at his feast,' he fled at the fray. *The Monastery.*

HUTCHEON. The old fellow-servant who sat with Dougal MacCallum on the night before Sir Robert Redgauntlet's funeral till the silver whistle sounded 'as sharp and shrill as if Sir Robert was blowing it.' *Redgauntlet.*

HUTCHINSON. Mackitchinson's opponent in the 'weel-kenned' law case about the backyard of the inn. *The Antiquary.*

HUTTON, MR. *See* HUME, DAVID.

HYDE. *See* CLARENDON.

HYDER ALI. Ruler of Mysore: an 'able and sagacious prince.' He 'was one of the wisest that Hindostan could boast; and amidst great crimes, perpetrated to gratify his ambition, displayed many instances of princely generosity, and, what was a little more surprising, of even-handed justice.' Disguised as the holy Scheik Hali ben Khaledoun, the superior of Barak's convent, he heard from Adam Hartley the fate prepared for Menie Gray. He interposed at the moment of Richard Middlemas' apparent success, to give him the reward he deserved and prevent Tippoo Sahib from bartering the safety of his capital 'for the possession of a white slave.' *The Surgeon's Daughter.*

HYMBERCOURT, SIEUR D'. One of the 'principal and most favoured counsellors' of Charles the Bold and one of the leaders 'whose names were then the praise and dread of war.' He played a prominent part in affairs during Louis' prolonged stay in Peronne, and acted with great gallantry in the attack on Liège by the combined forces of France and Burgundy. *Quentin Durward.*

HYNDMAN. Usher of the Council Chamber in Holyrood Palace. 'Too knowing' for his post. *The Abbot.*

I

IAN NAN CHAISTEL. *See* MACIVOR, IAN.

IAN OF GLENROY. One of the Highlanders who went 'out for intelligence' of Argyle's forces before Inverlochy. *A Legend of Montrose.*

IAN ROY CEAN. 'Red John the Warrior, a name personal and proper in the Highlands to John, Duke of Argyle and Greenwich, as MacCummin was that of his race or dignity.' *The Heart of Midlothian.*

ILAY, LORD. The Duke of Argyle's brother. *Rob Roy.*

ILDERIM OF KURDISTAN. *See* SALADIN.

ILDERTON, LUCY. Isabel Vere's cousin and confidante. The Black Dwarf foretold her fortune as 'an endless chase through life after follies not worth catching, and, when caught, successively thrown away.' *The Black Dwarf.*

ILDERTON, NANCY. Isabel Vere's 'timid' cousin. *The Black Dwarf.*

INCH-GRABBIT. *See* BRADWARDINE, MALCOLM.

INDAGATOR. One of the Antiquary's *noms-de-guerre. The Antiquary.*

INGILRAM, ABBOT. Abbot Boniface's 'venerable predecessor,' under whom Father Nicholas served. He was 'a merry man,' and used to say when he saw a party of Borderers approaching with their spoil from England, 'There come the tithes of the spoilers of the Egyptians!' *The Monastery.*

INGLEWOOD, SQUIRE. 'A whitewashed Jacobite,' who had 'qualified himself to act as a justice by taking the oaths to Government.' The sharpness of his clerk Jobson gave him more business than he bargained for.

'Gleams of sense and feeling ... escaped from the Justice through the vapours of sloth and self-indulgence.' *Rob Roy.*

INGLIS, FRANK. A corporal in Claverhouse's regiment of Life Guards. He headed the mutiny at Tillietudlem, and in later years became a 'favourite' of Basil Olifant and a tool in his hands. *Old Mortality.*

INGOLDSBY, SQUIRE. The name by which Redgauntlet was generally known in Cumberland. *Redgauntlet.*

INNERQUHARITY, KNIGHT OF. The 'feudal enemy' who stormed Glenhoulakim and cut off all the Durwards save Quentin. *Quentin Durward.*

INVERASHALLOCH. One of the Highlanders whom Bailie Nicol Jarvie and Frank Osbaldistone met in Jeanie MacAlpine's public-house. He was bent on fighting against 'the red MacGregor that killed my cousin seven times removed, Duncan MacLaren of Invernenty.' *Rob Roy.*

(*Bailie*, the magistrate second in rank in a royal burgh.)

INVERAUGHLIN. A Highlander who took part in the battle of Gladsmuir. *Waverley.*

IREBY, MR. The Cumbrian squire who let a piece of grass land to Robin McCombich and arrived with him to discover that, contrary to orders, his bailiff Fleecebumpkin had let it to Harry Wakefield. *The Two Drovers.*

IRENE, EMPRESS. Wife of Alexius Comnenus, and mother of Anna Comnena. Intimately acquainted with the real character of the Emperor, she judged that he had 'lived a hypocrite' and would not fail to die one. The Empress, 'like most mothers who do not possess much talent themselves, and are not very capable of estimating it in others, was, nevertheless, a great admirer of her favourite daughter's accomplishments, and ready to draw them out on all occasions.' *Count Robert of Paris.*

IRVING, DR. The king's chirurgeon. Raredrench, the apothecary, did 'not object to consult' with him when he was suggested by George Heriot for Richie Moniplies' wounds, though 'he hath had his degrees in Edinburgh.' *The Fortunes of Nigel.*

IRWIN, HANNAH. A relative and companion of Clara Mowbray, and 'the guilty confidant of the false Frank Tyrrel.' When the trick by which he hoped to secure Clara failed, Hannah disappeared, but some years later returned to St. Ronan's 'to unmask' the Earl of Etherington when she heard of his suit to Clara. As Annie Heggie, she was the recipient of charity from Lady Penelope Penfeather, who discovered enough of her story to spread a false report. *St. Ronan's Well.*

ISAAC OF YORK. 'The son of Adonikam': Rebecca's father. 'Detested by the credulous and prejudiced vulgar, and persecuted by the greedy and rapacious nobility,' he found that in wealth lay 'the only road to power and influence.' But while following this road he was 'trampled down like the shorn grass, and mixed with the mire of the ways.' *Ivanhoe.*

ISABELLA. One of Queen Catherine's Portuguese ladies of honour. *Peveril of the Peak.*

ISABELLE, CANONESS OF TRIERS. Sister of the Bishop of Liège. The Ladies of Croye were put under her care during their stay in the Castle of Schonwaldt. *Quentin Durward.*

ISMAIL THE INFIDEL. One of the soldiers on guard at the Golden Gate when Sebastes made an attempt on Hereward's life. Like the rest of the guard he had 'stood by' Harpax in weighty matters 'without tale-telling.' *Count Robert of Paris.*

IVANHOE, KNIGHT OF. *See* WILFRED.

IVERACH. *See* STEWART, ALLAN.

IVOR, SLIOCHD NAN. The race of Ivor. The clan of Ian nan Chaistel took this name to distinguish it from the clan from which it had seceded. *Waverley.*

J

JABOS, JAMES. Father of Jock. *Guy Mannering.*

JABOS, JOCK. Guy's guide to Ellangowan on his first visit there. Later, he was a postilion in the service of Mrs. MacCandlish of the Gordon Arms, and gave testimony to the truth on several important occasions. His 'hard-headed and uncultivated shrewdness seemed sometimes to start the game when others beat the bush.' *Guy Mannering.*

JACK. One of the party of ruffians whom Vanbeest Brown watched from his hiding place behind Meg Merrilies in Derncleugh. *Guy Mannering.*

JACK. One of the watermen who gave Julian Peveril information about Alice Bridgenorth's fate while Julian fought Jenkins. *Peveril of the Peak.*

JACK IN THE GREEN. The name given to Jenkin Vincent by Nigel when Jim rowed him down the river from Whitefriars. *The Fortunes of Nigel.*

JACOB. Dr. Dryasdust's servant. *Peveril of the Peak.*

JACOB BEN TUDELA, RABBI. One of Isaac's friends. Isaac feared his blame when Rebecca suggested that they should take the wounded Ivanhoe to Ashby-de-la-Zouch, and tend him. *Ivanhoe.*

JACOMO. 'The violer that used to scrape on the fiddle to us when he came to Geierstein in his rounds.' Sigismund Biederman found that King René looked 'somewhat like' him. *Anne of Geierstein.*

JACQUELINE. The name borne by the Countess of Croye when staying under Louis' protection in Plessis-les-Tours. *Quentin Durward.*

JAMES I OF THE UNITED KINGDOM. 'He was deeply learned, without possessing useful knowledge; sagacious in many individual cases, without having real wisdom; fond of his power, and desirous to maintain and augment it, yet willing to resign the direction of that, and of himself, to the most unworthy favourites; a big and bold assertor of his rights in words, yet one who tamely saw them trampled on in deeds; a lover of negotiations, in which he was always outwitted; and one who feared war, where conquest might have been easy.' 'He was laborious in trifles, and a trifler where serious labour was required; devout in his sentiments, and yet too often profane in his language; just and beneficent by nature, he yet gave way to the iniquities and oppression of others.' He 'was so utterly devoid of "firm resolve" . . . that even his virtues and his good meaning became laughable, from the whimsical uncertainty of his conduct.' 'The wisest fool in Christendom.' *The Fortunes of Nigel.*

JAMIESON. 'The Caledonian Vandyke.' *Guy Mannering.*

JAMIESON, BET. Peg Thomson's good-daughter: Richard Middlemas' nurse. After Mrs. Gray's death 'she gradually obtained the principal superintendence of the whole household; and being an honest and capable manager, was a person of very great importance in the family.' 'Bold in her temper, violent in her feelings,' she 'had the handsome enjoyment of her tongue and was disposed to use it liberally.' 'Partly to please and interest the boy, partly to indulge her own talent for amplification,' she told Richard the story of his birth 'with so many additional circumstances and gratuitous commentaries' as to raise in his mind 'a hundred flattering edifices,' all of them doomed to demolition. *The Surgeon's Daughter.*

JANET. The Scots laundress, who had been a 'faithful drudge' to Margaret Ramsay since she was a bairn. *The Fortunes of Nigel.*

JANNIKIN. Harry Gow's little apprentice. He was sent to 'scout up and down the wynd' when Harry and Simon Glover were obliged to leave Catharine under Dame Shoolbred's care while they attended the enquiry concerning Oliver Proudfute's death. *The Fair Maid of Perth.*
(*Wynd*, an alley.)

JANSEN, JANS. The name assumed by Dirk Hatteraick after the murder of Frank Kennedy. *Guy Mannering.*

JARDINE. Sir William Ashton's gardener. *The Bride of Lammermoor.*

JARVIE, BAILIE NICOL. A Glasgow magistrate and merchant deeply impressed with a sense of his own importance. Unlike MacVittie, MacFin & Co. he helped Osbaldistone and Tresham in their temporary difficulties and accompanied Frank into Rob Roy's country. A kinsman of Rob, he could 'wink as hard at a friend's failings as onybody,' and his 'Hieland blude' warmed at the tales of Rob's deeds. 'And whiles I like better to hear them,' he confessed, 'than a word o' profit, gude forgie me!—But they are vanities — sinfu' vanities — and, moreover, again the statute law—

again the statute and gospel law.' *Rob Roy.*
(*Bailie*, the magistrate second in rank in a royal burgh.)

JARVIE, DEACON NICOL. The Bailie's father and exemplar of all the virtues : a peaceful man who 'quarrelled wi' nane out o' the town-council.' *Rob Roy.*

JASPER. An old ploughman at Glendearg. *The Monastery.*

JAUP, ALISON. One of the old women who competed to announce to Dr. Gray the approach of interesting strangers. After their installation she 'was hired to assist in the increased drudgery of the family.' *The Surgeon's Daughter.*

JAUP, SAUNDERS. 'A feuar of some importance who held his land free and caredna a bodle for any one.' He resisted Mr. Touchwood's innovations in St. Ronan's, and maintained his right to have a 'filthy puddle' in front of his house. *St. Ronan's Well.*
(*Bodle*, a copper coin worth about the third part of a penny.)

JEAN-QUI-PLEURE. *See* TROIS-ESCHELLES.

JEAN-QUI-RIT. *See* PETIT-ANDRÉ.

JEHOIACHIM. One of Joshua Geddes' menservants. *Redgauntlet.*

JEKYL, CAPTAIN HARRY. Confidential friend to the Earl of Etherington : 'one of those fine gentlemen whom we pay for polishing the pavement in Bond Street, and looking at a thick shoe and a pair of worsted stockings, as if the wearer were none of their paymasters.' But 'in a long train of fashionable follies, his heart had not been utterly hardened,' and he counselled moderation towards Frank Tyrrel and the Mowbrays. *St. Ronan's Well.*

JELLICOT, JOAN. Jocelin's ' old dame.' Though ' parcel blind and more than parcel deaf,' she made Sir Henry and Alice Lee comfortable for the night in her hut, and attended them when they returned to the Lodge. *Woodstock.*
(*Parcel*, in part. *Archaic.*)

JEMIMA. One of the Earl of Glenallan's brood mares. *The Antiquary.*

JENKIN. One of Julian Avenel's attendants. *The Monastery.*

JENKINS, JACK. One of the crew of the *Fortune's Favourite.* He lost a leg as a result of Captain Goffe's ' pleasantry ' in firing off his pistol under the table. *The Pirate.*

JENKINS, JACK. One of the Duke of Buckingham's men : ' a master of the noble science of defence,' he was run through the body by Julian Peveril for interfering with him as he escorted Alice Bridgenorth and Fenella from Mistress Chiffinch's. *Peveril of the Peak.*

JENNY. One of the Elliots' servants. *The Black Dwarf.*

JEPHSON. One of the gang of men who disposed of the *Jumping Jenny's* cargo. ' The best-natured brute amongst them,' he helped Nanty Ewart to take Alan Fairford towards Fairladies. *Redgauntlet.*

JEREMY. Lord Saville's principal attendant. *Peveril of the Peak.*

JEREMY. One of the Shrove Tuesday revellers : a friend of Oliver Proudfute. *The Fair Maid of Perth.*

JERNINGHAM, TOM. The Duke of Buckingham's confidential attendant. ' If old Nick were to arise in our presence,' the Duke said to him after he had ' made sure ' of Alice Bridgenorth, ' and offer me his best imp as a familiar in thy room, I would hold it but a poor compliment.' *Peveril of the Peak.*

JEROME, ABBOT. Abbot of St. Bride's Convent. In consideration of ' an acknowledgment in name of alms ' he received Augustine into the convent as a guest, while Bertram proceeded to Douglas Castle. Loving his ' ease and ... comfortable repose,' he inwardly resented the agitations caused by Sir John de Walton's and Sir Aymer de Valence's suspicions of the young man. He dared not show this, however, for he and his monks depended on the English garrison ' for every indulgence they experienced, as well as for the subsistence and protection necessary to them in so perilous a period.' *Castle Dangerous.*

JERVIE, PROVOST. The last provost of Fairport who wore a wig—' and he had a quean of a servant-lass that dressed it hersell wi' the doup o' a candle and a drudging-box.' *The Antiquary.*
(*Quean*, a young woman. *Doup*, end.)

JESSY. Clara Mowbray's waiting-maid. *St. Ronan's Well.*

JEUNESSE, LA. The solitary attendant of the Marquis of Hautlieu.

He 'seemed to multiply himself with the necessities of the occasion, and discharged his several tasks with such promptitude and assiduity, that farther attendance than his was neither missed nor wished for.' *Quentin Durward.*

JEZABEL (*for* ISABEL). Oliver Proudfute's mount, 'a great trampling Flemish mare, with a nose turned up in the air like a camel, a huge fleece of hair at each foot, and every hoof full as large in circumference as a frying-pan.' *The Fair Maid of Perth.*

JEZDEGERD. The 'dreaded opponent' of Alexius Comnenus during the retreat to Laodicea which is described in a 'curious fragment' of Princess Anna's history, not published elsewhere. During the attack by the Varangian guard Jezdegerd went 'where brave men are who fall in their duty.' *Count Robert of Paris.*

JIM. Reginald Lowestoffe's boy. 'Worth gold in this quarter—he serves six masters—four of them in distinct Numbers, and you would think him present like a fairy at the mere wish of him that for the time most needs his attendance.' *The Fortunes of Nigel.*

JINGLING GEORDIE. *See* HERIOT, GEORGE.

JINGLING JOCK. One of the few who knew the secret cave to which Edie Ochiltree guided Lovel after his duel with Hector McIntyre. *The Antiquary.*

JINKER, JAMIE. A horse-dealer: lieutenant of Edward Waverley's escort from the Castle of Doune to Holyrood.

'Ye see that through-ganging thing that Balmawhapple's on; I selled her till him. She was bred out of Lick-the-Ladle, that wan the King's plate at Caverton-Edge, by Duke Hamilton's White-Foot, &c., &c., &c.' *Waverley.*

JOAN, PRINCESS OF FRANCE. Louis' younger daughter, and the destined bride of the Duke of Orleans. Conscious that she was 'an object of abhorrence' to the Duke, she was unable through timidity 'to make any of those attempts to mend by manners or by art what nature had left amiss, or in any other way to exert a power of pleasing.' *Quentin Durward.*

JOBSON, MR. JOSEPH. Squire Inglewood's clerk. 'A prodigious zealot for the Protestant religion, and a great friend to the present establishment in church and state,' he often talked 'big about reporting his principal to the Secretary of State for the Home Department.' He played a part more to his liking as Squire Standish's clerk.

'And, for the taking away of your good name,' Diana said, 'I pity the poor fellow who gets it, and wish you joy at losing it with all my heart.' *Rob Roy.*

JOCELYN. One of Front-de-Bœuf's squires. He was able to vouch that Father Ambrose, unlike Wamba, was a real monk. *Ivanhoe.*

JOCELYN. A chamberlain in close attendance on King Richard. *The Talisman.*

JOCK. The 'callant' who attended

to Mr. Heukbane's pony. *The Antiquary.*

JOCK O' DAWSTON CLEUGH. A Liddesdale farmer whose land marched with Dandy Dinmont's. 'He's a camsteary chield, and fasheous about marches, and we've had some bits o' splores thegither; but deil o' me if I wad wrang Jock o' Dawston neither.' *Guy Mannering.*

(*Camsteary*, perverse. *Fasheous*, troublesome. *Splores*, quarrels.)

JOCK OF MILCH. The 'tight huntsman' on whom suspicion fell when six of the king's Bluebanders harried the Lady of Loganhouse's 'dowcot and poultry-yard.' 'When I think of these wild passages,' the king said to George Heriot, ' in my conscience, I am not sure but we lived merrier in auld Holyrood in those shifting days, than now when we are dwelling at heck and manger.' *The Fortunes of Nigel.*

(*At heck and manger*, in great fulness.)

JOHN. One of Ellangowan's servants. *Guy Mannering.*

JOHN. Driver of the Queensferry Diligence. He was ' not entitled to make any stop or to suffer prejudice ' by such an accident as the casting of a horse's shoe. This was Jamie Martingale's department. *The Antiquary.*

JOHN. One of the two servants who waited on Darsie Latimer during his confinement in Cumberland. He and Dorcas were ' of the true Joan and Hodge school, thinking of little and desiring nothing, beyond the very limited sphere of their own duties or enjoyments, and having no curiosity whatever about the affairs of others.' *Redgauntlet.*

JOHN. Mr. Sommerville's old domestic. *The Highland Widow.*

JOHN DHU. The ' grim and valiant corporal ' of the old Town Guard of Edinburgh who with his men was ' the alternate terror and derision of the petulant brood of the High School ' in the days of Sir Walter Scott's youth. *The Heart of Midlothian.*

JOHN OF ACQUA MORTIS. One of the Troubadours present at King René's court. *Anne of Geierstein.*

JOHN OF ANJOU. (1) Son of Henry II. He accompanied his father to the siege of the castle of Garde Douloureuse. But not even Richard's taunts roused him to take an active part in it. ' How I should delight to see thee on the highest round,' Richard said,—' thy knees shaking—thy hands grasping convulsively, like those of one in an ague fit—all air around thee, save a baton or two of wood—the moat below—half a dozen pikes at thy throat.'

(2) Brother of Richard Cœur de Lion, whom he succeeded on the throne. ' Light, profligate, and perfidious,' he tried, during Richard's absence abroad, to supplant him at home. But his mind ' was a strange mixture of carelessness and presumption with low artifice and cunning,' and ' his levity and petulance were perpetually . . . undoing all that had been gained by his previous dis-

simulation.' He was 'too weak to be a determined monarch, too tyrannical to be an easy monarch, too insolent and presumptuous to be a popular monarch, and too fickle and timid to be long a monarch of any kind.' (1) *The Betrothed.* (2) *Ivanhoe.*

JOHN OF MOIDART. See CLANRANALD.

JOHN O' THE GIRNELL (i.e. GRANARY). The last bailiff of the abbey who lived at Monkbarns; called the 'Jolly Abbot.' The Antiquary was never known to refrain from telling his story to anyone who visited Monkbarns. *The Antiquary.*

JOHN THE ARMSTRONG. A famous Borderer of Father Nicholas' young days. 'A fair man he was, and a goodly, the more pity that hemp was ever heckled for him.' *The Monastery.*
(To *heckle,* to dress flax.)

JOHNNIE FAA. 'The upright man': leader of a gang of gipsies, when men were men and 'fought other in the open field.' *Guy Mannering.*

JOHNSTONE, DICK. The 'Devil's Dick of Hellgarth.' He followed 'the stout Laird of Wamphray, who rides with his kinsman the redoubted Lord of Johnstone, who is banded with the doughty Earl of Douglas.' *The Fair Maid of Perth.*

JOHNSTONE, PEGGY. Daughter of Willie: laundrymaid at Woodbourne. *Guy Mannering.*

JOHNSTONE, WILLIE. Owner and steersman of the boat in which Vanbeest Brown crossed from Portanferry to Allonby after his encounter with young Hazlewood. Through him and his daughter Brown was able to send an expression of regret to Julia Mannering. *Guy Mannering.*

JOLIFFE. One of the attendants at the Well. *St. Ronan's Well.*

JOLIFFE, JOCELIN. 'One of the underkeepers of the walk' at Woodstock Lodge. Commissioned by Sir Henry to 'make surrender ... of the Lodge and household stuff' to Joseph Tomkins, he found in Joseph his old acquaintance Phil Hazeldine, who professed to be a 'good King's man.' Together with Dr. Rochecliffe and Phœbe Mayflower they played the part of the spiritual apparitions which frightened the Lords Commissioners from the Lodge. But Jocelin, being a 'very shrewd fellow,' never fully trusted Joseph and 'kept a strict, though unostentatious watch' over him. Jealous and watchful on Phœbe's account too, he was able to save her from Tomkins' frenzied passion and at the same time free the Lodge from a 'double-hearted villain.' *Woodstock.*

See also ROBISON, DICK.

JONATHAN. One of Lord Saville's attendants. While the others went forward with his lordship to the Tutbury races, he had to ride back to London 'for life and death,' with the letters containing Chiffinch's drunken confidences. *Peveril of the Peak.*

JONATHAN. One of the servants who helped General Harrison to his apartment in Woodstock Lodge when the frenzy roused by Dick

Robison's ghost had spent itself. *Woodstock.*

JONES, MRS. Lady Penelope Penfeather's maid. From her John Mowbray learned Lady Penelope's light gossip concerning Clara. *St. Ronan's Well.*

JOP, JENNY. *See* POLWARTH, ALICK.

JOPSON, CICELY. Daughter of Jacob. *Waverley.*

JOPSON, JACOB. The farmer who sheltered Edward Waverley on the night after the skirmish at Clifton. *Waverley.*

JORWORTH AP JEVAN. The messenger sent by Gwenwyn to Sir Raymond Berenger with an offer of alliance. He was also sent to the castle of Garde Douloureuse to treat of surrender after Sir Raymond's death, and was outwitted by Wilkin Flammock. *The Betrothed.*

JUNO. Hector McIntyre's spaniel: the cause of some discord between uncle and nephew. *The Antiquary.*

K

KAIMES, LORD. *See* HUME, DAVID.

KAMMERMAISTER, SEBASTIAN. Patron of Wolfbrand Oldenbuck. *The Antiquary.*

KATE. One of Mrs. Flockhart's maids. The 'limmer' went off with one of Hawley's dragoons. *Waverley.*
(*Limmer*, a woman of loose manners.)

KEELAVINE, MR. One of the visitors to the Well. 'I trust your pencil is busy,' Clara Mowbray said to him. *St. Ronan's Well.*
(*Keelavine*, a black-lead pencil.)

KELTIE. Landlord of John Auchtermuchty's favourite resting-place at Keiry-craigs. He 'has bestowed his name on a bridge in the neighbourhood of his quondam dwelling.' *The Abbot.*

KEMP, REV. ZADOCK. Chaplain to the British Embassy at Paris. He celebrated the marriage between 'Marie de Belleroche, Comtesse de Martigny, and the Right Honourable John, Lord Oakendale.' *St. Ronan's Well.*

KENELM. Hereward's grandfather: prior of the convent of St. Augustin. When William Rufus overcame the Saxon Foresters, Bertha and her mother found refuge for a time with Kenelm, but soon 'their place of retreat was completely sacked and burnt to the ground.' *Count Robert of Paris.*

KENMURE, LORD. One of the leaders of the 1715 rebellion. Lewis Bertram went 'out' with him. (1) *Guy Mannering.* (2) *Rob Roy.*

KENNEDY, ALLAN. One of the Highland gillies who with Evan Dhu accompanied Edward Waverley from Tully-Veolan to Donald Bean Lean's cave. *Waverley.*

KENNEDY, FRANK. A supervisor 'who had made seizures to a great amount, and was proportionally hated by those who had an interest in the *fair trade.*' Against the 'old fox Dirk Hatteraick' he made special endeavours, but these cost him his life. The circumstances of his death, and of the disappearance of little Harry Bertram, who was with him at the time, long remained a mystery. *Guy Mannering.*

KENNETH. One of the men who kept watch on St. Valentine's Eve while the Duke of Rothesay and Sir John Ramorny tried to enter Catharine Glover's chamber. *The Fair Maid of Perth.*

KENNETH OF SCOTLAND, KNIGHT OF THE LEOPARD. 'An obscure and nameless adventurer' who, after a two-years' campaign, was 'full well spoken of' for his bravery and prowess. Sent by the Council of the Crusade on a secret mission to Theodorick, the hermit of Engaddi, he brought with him on his return to camp the physician Adonbec, whose good offices earned King Richard's favour. As a 'boon' he was entrusted with the guardianship of the banner of England on a night of special danger, but was enticed from his post by an idle frolic of Queen Berengaria. Hardly caring to live dishonoured, he was given to Adonbec by the King as a bondslave. Soon he returned to camp disguised as the mute Nubian slave, Zohauk, a gift from Saladin. He saved Richard's life from the Charegite's dagger, and with the help of his faithful hound Roswal, detected Conrade of Montserrat as the thief of the banner. After wounding Conrade in the trial by combat, when as the Knight of the Leopard he championed Richard's cause, he was acclaimed by the King in his true title, David, Earl of Huntingdon, brother of William the Lion. In this capacity he was able to express to Edith Plantagenet 'the passion to which he had so often before found it difficult to give words.' *The Talisman.*

KEPPOCH, CHIEF OF. One of the Chiefs who when the battle of Inverlochy was imminent summoned their vassals by the fiery cross. 'As the order was emphatically given, it was speedily and willingly obeyed.' *A Legend of Montrose.*

KERNEGUY, LOUIS. The name which disguised Charles II as Albert Lee's page : 'his father was Lord Killstewers, of Kincardineshire.' At times 'too courteous and civil for a young page,' at times 'too rude,' he 'could not weigh even the thoughts of his safety against the enjoyment of his jest.' *Woodstock.*

KETTLEDRUMMLE, GABRIEL. 'An absolute Boanerges, or son of thunder, in the pulpit.' Unlike Peter Poundtext, he had not availed himself of the Government's 'indulgence' to gain a licence to preach, and was arrested at a conventicle. He regained his liberty after the victory at Drumclog, and was one of the most uncompromising members in the council of the Covenanters. *Old Mortality.*

KILDERKIN. Keeper of an eating-house in Greenwich. Nigel tried in vain to get information from him concerning Sir Mungo Malagrowther's time of arrival for breakfast. He 'spoke as a banker writes, only touching the needful.' *The Fortunes of Nigel.*

KILIAN OF KERSBERG. 'A stout hard-favoured man-at-arms, a Bavarian by birth, and by rank the personal squire of the Governor' of La Ferette, von Hagenbach. The promise of 'a purse of ducats to jingle at his girdle' was sufficient to disarm his scruples against interfering with the English merchants Philipson and the peaceful Swiss embassy. But when the town was in the hands of the Swiss he was one of those 'whom pride prevented from flying, and despair from asking quarter.' *Anne of Geierstein.*

KILLANCUREIT, GIRNIGO OF. The former laird whose widow married her steward, one Bullsegg, 'from the wrong side of the border.' *Waverley.*

KILLANCUREIT, LAIRD OF. *See* BULLSEGG, MR.

KILLBRACKLIN, LADY. Captain MacTurk's great-grandmother, from whom he inherited a watch true to the 'twentieth part of the fraction of a second.' *St. Ronan's Well.*

KILLBUCK. Hobbie Elliot's greyhound that killed one of the Black Dwarf's goats. 'A goat's like first cousin to a deer, sae he acted but according to his nature after a'.' *The Black Dwarf.*

KILL-DOWN, DR. Gaffer Rutledge's medical attendant. *Rob Roy.*

KILLIGREW. One of the 'open debauchers and ruffianly swordsmen' who were 'a terror to peaceable men and a scandal' to the Earl of Leicester's service. They 'bear gallows in their face and murder in their right hand.' *Kenilworth.*

KILLSTEWERS, LORD. *See* KERNEGUY, LOUIS.

KILSYTHE. Major Bellenden's horse. *Old Mortality.*

KILTSTOUP, CURATE. A 'prelatical divine' who 'wad hae read half the Prayer Book' to the Laird of Dumbiedikes, if he had been asked. *The Heart of Midlothian.*

KINFAUNS, BARON OF. *See* CHARTERIS, SIR PATRICK.

KINFAUNS, THE OLD KEMPE (CHAMPION) OF. Sir Patrick Charteris' father: grandson of Tom of Longueville. He gave the youthful Simon Glover a lesson in courage when the Fair City had to be defended against 'the Southron.' *The Fair Maid of Perth.*

KING. A friend of the young buck who, after Mistress Bertram's death, was sorry he ever 'plagued' himself about her. *Guy Mannering.*

KING OF THE WASTE AND OF THE MINE, THE. The Harz demon from whom Martin Waldeck received fateful gifts. *The Antiquary.*

KIRJATH-JAIRAM OF LOMBARY. A rich Jew living in Leicester. By Isaac's order he equipped Wilfred of Ivanhoe for the tournament. *Ivanhoe.*

KIRK, JOHN, ESQ. Chancellor of the jury which tried Effie Deans. 'He wussed them just to get the king's mercy, and nae mair about it.' *The Heart of Midlothian.*

KIRKCALDY, LAIRD OF GRANGE. One of the Protestant leaders at Langside: 'named by the Constable Montmorency the first soldier in Europe.' *The Abbot.*

KITKITBROECK, BARON. A Dutch

acquaintance of the Baron of Bradwardine. *Waverley.*

KITTLECOURT, SIR THOMAS. A political opponent of the Laird of Ellangowan. *Guy Mannering.*

KITTLELOOF, SIR THOMAS. Mrs. Elliot's third cousin by the mother's side. 'He has come by a hantle siller, and been made a knight-baronet into the bargain, for being ane o' the commissioners at the Union.' *The Black Dwarf.*
(*Hantle*, a good deal.)

KITTLEPUNT. One of the counsel suggested by Saddletree for Effie Deans' defence, but rejected by her father as 'an Arminian.' *The Heart of Midlothian.*

KITTLESIDE, MARGERY. One of Reuben Butler's parishioners. She and Rory MacRand 'southered sin wi' marriage.' *The Heart of Midlothian.*
(*South.red*, soldered.)

KLEANCOGG, STEPHEN. The fiddler at Papastow who, in Claud Halcro's opinion, had the same 'soft, full, thoughtful yet penetrating glance,' as the 'glorious John Dryden.' *The Pirate.*

KLEPPER. Hayraddin Maugrabin's 'little, active, and wild-looking jennet.' When leaving him as a dying bequest to Quentin, his master said, 'He will never fail you at need—night and day, rough and smooth, fair and foul, warm stables, and the winter sky, are the same to Klepper.' *Quentin Durward.*

KLINKERMAN. One of Wilkin Flammock's neighbours. *The Betrothed.*

KNIGHTON. The Duke of Buckingham's servant who brought back to George Heriot the salver he had carried to Whitehall, 'flung it into the entrance as if it had been an old pewter platter, and bade me tell you the King would have none of your trumpery.' *The Fortunes of Nigel.*

KNOCK, DUNCAN. Captain of Knockdunder, Laird of Knocktarlitie, and Bailie to the Duke of Argyle: 'a person of first-rate importance in the island of Roseneath and the continental parishes of Knocktarlitie, Kilmun, and so forth,' whose bearing was 'brief, bluff, and consequential.' Davie Deans described him to Jeanie as 'ane Hieland gentleman, tarred wi' the same stick ... as mony of them, namely, a hasty and choleric temper, and a neglect of the higher things that belong to salvation, and also a gripping unto the things of this world, without muckle distinction of property; but, however, ane gude hospitable gentleman with whom it would be a part of wisdom to live on a gude understanding.' *The Heart of Midlothian.*
(*Bailie*, deputy.)

KNOCKWINNOCK, SYBIL. Mother of Malcolm the Usurper, and wife of Sir Richard Wardour. 'Laith, laith was she to gae into the match, for she had fa'en a wee ower thick wi' a cousin o' her ain that her father had some ill-will to.' *The Antiquary.*
(*Laith*, loath.)

KNOLLES. *See* ACLAND, SIR THOMAS.

KYLE, DAVID. Landlord of the George Inn in Kennaquhair. When recommending the Benedictine monk to the kind attentions of Captain Clutterbuck, he said, ' I haena seen the like o' him my very sell since I saw the great Doctor Samuel Johnson on his tower through Scotland, whilk tower is lying in my back-parlour for the amusement of my guests, wi' the twa boards torn aff.' *The Monastery.*

L

LACHLAN. A Highlander in Duncan Knock's service. *The Heart of Midlothian.*

LACKLAND, CAPTAIN. *See* MARSPORT, MUNGO.

LACY. An old play-actor, and a fellow-officer with Wildrake in Lunsford's Light Horse. He ' made drollery ... in a play ' on the scandal which attributed cannibalism to the Troop. *Woodstock.*

LACY, DAMIAN DE. The Constable's ' valued ' nephew. ' Renowned for his early feats of chivalry ' he was chosen by his uncle to lead his forces to the Crusade, but eventually was left as Eveline Berenger's guardian during his uncle's enforced absence. Himself deeply in love with her, and feeling keenly the difficulties of his trust, he observed a strict formality in all their intercourse, but, through Randal de Lacy's machinations, they became involved in a charge of treachery and dishonour. ' Single-hearted and high-souled.' *The Betrothed.*

See also WENLOCK *and* MONTHERMER, GUY DE.

LACY, HUGO DE. Constable of Chester and Lord of the Marches : ' one of the most redoubted warriors of the time.' He avenged Sir Raymond Berenger's death, relieved the castle of Garde Doloureuse, and escorted Lady Eveline to her aunt in Gloucester. Though ' past that period of life when the wise are captivated by outward form,' he became enamoured of ' the beauty and the amiable qualities of the fair orphan,' and they were betrothed ' with all civil and religious solemnity.' But Baldwin insisted on the immediate fulfilment of his vow to join the Crusade. He left his betrothed under the protection of his nephew Damian, and returned after three years to find himself bereft, Renault Vidal informed him, of ' love, dominion, high office, and bright fame.' But he remained ' lord of his own mind,' unshaken by adversity, and determined to bear his impending fate ' like a man.' *The Betrothed.*

LACY, RANDAL DE. A remote kinsman of Hugo de Lacy : a ' decayed reveller,' ' totally worthless, and undeserving of honourable confidence.' Disguised as a pedlar, he ingratiated himself into Dame Gillian's favour, and from her learnt incidents regarding Eveline Berenger and Damian de Lacy which gave him a starting-point for calumny against them. Again, as the merchant of falcons who enticed Eveline to the disastrous

hunting-party, he proved 'the master-mover' in her sorrows. After her castle was taken, 'he appeared daily to rise in the King's grace,' but on the day of his first public appearance as Constable of Chester, he was killed by Cadwallon, whose eyes 'were cheated with those baubles, a plumed cap and a lacquered baton!' *The Betrothed.*
See also DAWFYD *and* EDRIS OF THE GOBLETS.

LAGG, LAIRD OF. A boon companion of Donohoe Bertram. *Guy Mannering.*

LAIDER, DONALD. One of Vanbeest Brown's fellow-prisoners in Portanferry jail 'that's in for sheep-stealing, that should sleep with you by rule, and he'll expect clean strae, and may be some whisky beside.' *Guy Mannering.*

LAIRD'S JOCK, THE. *See* ARMSTRONG, JOHN.

LAMBERT. One of the suite who attended Margaret of Anjou to Strasburg, where, disguised as a beggar, she had an interview with Seignor Philipson. *Anne of Geierstein.*

LAMBOURNE, BENEDICT. Husband of Mike Lambourne's mother. *Kenilworth.*

LAMBOURNE, MICHAEL. Giles Gosling's nephew. As tapster's boy he wellnigh ruined his uncle with his 'misreckonings, miscarriages, mistakes and misdemeanours,' and after years of travel he returned 'known for a swasher and a desperate Dick, a carder and a dicer, a professor of the seven damnable sciences, if ever man took degrees in them.' Through his 'old intimacy' with Tony Foster he became a retainer of Richard Varney, and but for his 'accursed custom' of drinking and swaggering, he might have climbed 'as high as Varney himself.' For he was 'a pestilent clever fellow withal.' *Kenilworth.*

LAMBSBEY. One of the men in Varney's service, sent out with Killigrew to scour the country in quest of Wayland Smith. *Kenilworth.*

LAMBSKIN, MRS. ALICE. Mrs. Bethune Baliol's principal female attendant. She might, 'from the gravity and dignity of her appearance, have sufficed to matronize a whole boarding-school, instead of one maiden lady of eighty and upwards.' She accompanied her mistress on a Highland tour with Donald MacLeish as guide. *The Highland Widow.*

LAMINGTON. One of Sir Geoffrey Peveril's menservants. *Peveril of the Peak.*

LAMMERMOOR SHEPHERDESS. The name given in derision to Lucy Ashton by her mother to indicate 'that the more plebeian blood of her father predominated in Lucy's veins.' *The Bride of Lammermoor.*

LAMPLUGH, WILL. One of the gang of men who took the *Jumping Jenny's* cargo to Goodman Grist's mill. *Redgauntlet.*

LANCELOT, DR. *See* TOURNIQUET.

LANEHAM, MASTER ROBERT. Clerk of Queen Elizabeth's council-chamber door, 'by the interest of Lord Leicester.' He attended the pageants at Kenilworth Castle and sent an account of them to a friend in London, 'written in a style of the most intolerable affectation, both in point of composition and orthography.' *Kenilworth.*

LANEHAM, SIBYL. Master Robert's wife. She had 'played the devil ere now, in a Mystery in Queen Mary's time.' *Kenilworth.*

LANG LINKER. One of the few who knew the secret cave to which Edie Ochiltree guided Lovel after his duel with Hector McIntyre. *The Antiquary.*

LANGCALE, LAIRD OF. A small proprietor: at first one of the 'honest and rational' party in the Covenanters' council, he was afterwards 'seduced' by Kettledrummle. He 'cannot be suitably or preceesely termed either fish, or flesh, or gude red herring— whoever has the stronger party has Langcale.' *Old Mortality.*

LANGLEY, SIR FREDERICK. 'A proud, dark, ambitious man; a caballer against the state; infamous for his avarice and severity; a bad son, a bad brother, unkind and ungenerous to all his relatives.' This was the man whom, under compulsion by her father, Isabel Vere would have married but for the Black Dwarf's interposition at the beginning of the ceremony. *The Black Dwarf.*

LANGTALE, MR. The advocate engaged for Effie Deans' defence. He had 'brought folk through waur snappers than a' this,' but a sudden call 'to the county of which he was Sheriff' obliged him to find a substitute in Mr. Fairbrother. *The Heart of Midlothian.* (*Snappers*, stumbles.)

LAPRAIK, LAURIE. The 'sly tod' from whom Steenie Steenson borrowed money to pay his arrears. When the payment was called in question Steenie could get nothing but hard words from him: 'thief, beggar, dyvour, were the saftest terms.' *Redgauntlet.*
(*Tod*, a fox. *Dyvour*, a bankrupt.)

LASCARIS. One of the 'politicians' who watched Tancred's little squadron approach the imperial city from Scutari. 'Rushing down towards the lists at the head of a crowd half desperate with fear, they hastily propagated the appalling news, that the Latins were coming back from Asia with the purpose of landing in arms, pillaging, and burning the city.' *Count Robert of Paris.*

LATHERUM. A barber: one of the Sunday guests of Jonathan Brown. *Rob Roy.*

LATIMER, DARSIE. *See* REDGAUNTLET, SIR ARTHUR DARSIE.

LATIMER, RALPH. A Westmoreland gentleman mentioned by Mr. Herries to Mr. Saunders Fairford as Darsie's father. *Redgauntlet.*

LAU, MONSEIGNEUR DE. One of the exiled French nobles whose presence in Peronne gave Louis a sense of insecurity and caused him to ask to be lodged in the castle during his stay. *Quentin Durward.*

LAUDERDALE, DUKE OF. President of the Scottish Privy Council, when Harry Morton, Cuddie Headrigg, and Ephraim Macbriar were tried. *Old Mortality.*

LAUNCELOT. Bard to the household of Aspramonte. When Bertha was threatened with banishment, Brenhilda maintained she would go too and ' Launcelot, the bard, shall follow with my spear and shield.' *Count Robert of Paris.*

LAURIE, BAILIE. One of the Dumfries magistrates. If Provost Crosbie were late for the Council meeting he would be ' trying some of his manœuvres.' *Redgauntlet.*

LAW, THE MAN OF. See MEIKLEWHAM, MR.

LAWFORD, MR. Town clerk of Middlemas. He helped Dr. Gray through the difficulties raised by the arrival of M. de Monçada, and acted as joint guardian to Richard Middlemas. A man ' of sense and humanity.' *The Surgeon's Daughter.*

LAWSON, SANDIE. Landlord of the Fox Hotel, St. Ronan's: ' the bankrupt body' who did not pay ' a bawbee of four terms' rent.' *St. Ronan's Well.*

(*Bawbee*, a halfpenny.)

LEAN, ALICE BEAN. Daughter of Donald: a strapping Highland lass who was, in Evan Maccombich's opinion, both *canny* and *fendy*, and ' to the boot of all that the best dancer of a strathspey in the whole strath.' She delivered to Edward Waverley the letters from his Colonel and Major which her father had suppressed. *Waverley.*

(*Canny*, prudent. *Fendy*, resourceful.)

LEAN, DONALD BEAN (*i.e.* WHITE). A Highland robber from whose depredations Tully-Veolan had for a time been saved by the payment of blackmail from Bailie MacWheeble to Fergus MacIvor. During Edward Waverley's visit to his cave Donald possessed himself of Edward's seal, and with this as a token, he managed under the name of Will Ruthven or Wily Will to stir up disaffection amongst Edward's troop in Dundee.

' He certainly possesses talents beyond the rude sphere in which he moves,' and is ' neither destitute of ambition nor encumbered with scruples.' *Waverley.*

LEE, SIR HENRY. An officer in attendance on Queen Elizabeth during the audience she gave to the Earls of Leicester and Sussex. *Kenilworth.*

LEE, ALBERT. Son of Sir Henry of Ditchley. Following his father closely ' in the race of loyalty' he guided King Charles to Woodstock Lodge after the defeat at Worcester, completed all plans for the King's escape by sea, and finally gained time for his flight by assuming the King's disguise and keeping Cromwell and his soldiers at bay in the labyrinth of the Lodge. ' You . . . have marked your fidelity by a hundred proofs.' *Woodstock.*

LEE, ALICE. Daughter of Sir Henry of Ditchley, ' the fairest gem of all': ' a good and kindly daughter,' patient and dutiful under her father's impatience and contradiction. ' She had been bred up chiefly with her brother and cousin, so that she had an unfearing and unsuspicious frankness of manner' which seemed for a time to encourage Louis Kerneguy's gallantry. But she rejected all his flattery with dignity, saved him from the consequences of his thoughtless passion by preventing his duel with Markham Everard, and gladly guided him in his hurried flight from the Lodge. 'A good girl, a wise girl, a virtuous girl, one of those whose price is above rubies.' *Woodstock.*

LEE, SIR HENRY, KNIGHT OF DITCHLEY. Ranger of the Royal Park of Woodstock : representative of a family who had lived there, 'father and son, these five hundred years.' Of a 'fiery, high, and unbending character,' ' he resisted every proposal of submitting himself to the existing government, and was . . . enrolled in the list of stubborn and irreclaimable malignants.' Markham Everard's influence with Cromwell saved him from the worst consequences of this, but ' age and misfortunes . . . had given to the good knight's passions a wayward irritability' which embittered his love for Markham with unjust and ill-natured suspicions. His loyalty to the King burnt all the stronger for disaster and ill-fate. To secure Charles' escape from Woodstock Lodge when Dr. Rochecliffe's secret had been betrayed by Tomkins, he spared neither Albert nor Alice, and himself faced death ' with a free bosom.' Adapting his favourite 'Will,' he said—
' As gentle and as jocund as to rest,
Go I to death—truth hath a quiet breast.'
Woodstock.

LEE, VICTOR. An ancestor, a painting of whom dominated Sir Henry's sitting-room. 'What although old Victor Lee was a sacrilegious man, as common report goes, and brewed ale in the font which he brought from the ancient palace of Holyrood, while church and building were in flames ? And what although his eldest son was when a child scalded to death in the same vessel ? ' Behind his picture there was a secret opening 'to the labyrinth of private apartments or hiding places' which enabled Dr. Rochecliffe to play his tricks on the Lords Commissioners, and Albert Lee to waste Cromwell's time whilst Louis Kerneguy made good his escape. *Woodstock.*

LEE, SIR SIMON [LOCKHART OF]. ' A considerable figure in the reigns of Robert the Bruce and of his son David.' While fighting against the Saracens he received as part of an Emir's ransom a sacred Talisman, which under the name of the Lee-penny became celebrated for its healing virtues. In *The Talisman* Kenneth of Scotland is said to have received it from Saladin as a wedding present, and afterwards given it to Sir Simon. *The Talisman.*

LEICESTER, EARL OF. One of the knights who with King Richard 'held a tournament after the taking of St. John-de-Acre, as

challengers against all comers.'
Brian de Bois-Guilbert was
amongst the unsuccessful assailants.
  The other challengers were Sir
Thomas Multon, Sir Foulk Doilly,
Sir Edwin Turneham, and Wilfred
of Ivanhoe. *Ivanhoe.*

LEICESTER, EARL OF. Robert Dudley, the rival of Sussex in Queen
Elizabeth's favour. ' His minute
and studied acquaintance with her
humours ' made him aware of the
many ' shoals, breakers, and reefs
of rocks' amongst which he
carried ' so high and so venturous
a sail,' and at times after his secret
marriage with Amy Robsart he
was ' well-nigh resolved to tempt
the sea no farther.' But Varney,
'a faithful and a good pilot,' was
ever at hand, and ambition ' had
become so woven in with every
purpose and action of his life'
that he played the traitor to his
love.
  'All that would sink another
ten fathom deep, seems but to
make him float the more easily.'
Kenilworth.

LELAND. The learned antiquary
who ' lost his senses on witnessing
the destruction of the conventual
libraries in England.' *The Antiquary.*

LENNOXES, THE. One of the clans
' a' mounted and in order' to
make war against puir Rob. ' It's
weel kend their quarrel—and I
dinna blame them—naebody likes
to lose his kye.' *Rob Roy.*
(*Kye*, cows.)

LEOPARD, KNIGHT OF THE. See
KENNETH OF SCOTLAND.

LEOPOLD, ARCHDUKE OF AUSTRIA.
An ally of Richard Cœur de Lion
and Philip of France against
Saladin. ' He was rather a weak
and a vain than an ambitious or
tyrannical prince,' and deeply resented the ill-concealed contempt
with which King Richard met his
attempts to gain his ' friendship
and intimacy.' The discord between them was fanned by King
Philip and Conrade of Montserrat,
as a means of ' dissolving, or
loosening at least, the league of the
Crusaders.' Having ' in all that
mass of flesh no bolder animation
than is afforded by the peevishness of a wasp, and the courage of
a wren,' he was a pliant tool for
their schemes. ' His character
has been stained in history on
account of one action of violence
and perfidy . . . the shame of
having made Richard a prisoner
when he returned through his
dominions, unattended and in
disguise.' *The Talisman.*

LESLEY, MR. ' A friend of Captain
McIntyre's ' who acted as his
second in the duel with Lovel.
The Antiquary.

LESLIE, GENERAL DAVID. Commander of the army sent into
England by the Scottish Convention of Estates to help the
Parliamentary army against
Charles I. To him and to the
Scottish cavalry ' as well as to
Cromwell's brigade of Independents ' belongs the honour of the
victory on Marston Moor in 1644.
In September, 1645, he closed
Montrose's series of brilliant victories by surprising and routing

him at Philiphaugh. *A Legend of Montrose.*

LESLIE, NORMAN. The chief actor in the murder of Cardinal Beaton. 'A true bloodhound.' *The Monastery.*

LESLIE, RALPH. Leader of the men who had a street encounter with the Seytons at the Tron, as Roland Graeme and Adam Woodcock were riding along to Holyrood. *The Abbot.*

LESLY, LUDOVIC, LE BALAFRÉ. A tried member of Louis' Scottish Guard : Quentin's maternal uncle. His courage and fidelity were beyond dispute, but he had never been promoted to an important command, and his 'unripe' nephew's 'favourable commencement of service' gave him 'a sense of wounded or diminished self-importance.' But he supported Quentin loyally at all times, and refused the prize which fell to him for finishing Quentin's 'bit of work' with De La Marck.

'A keen soldier, hardened, selfish, and narrow-minded ; active and bold in the discharge of his duty, but acknowledging few objects beyond it, except the formal observance of a careless devotion, relieved by an occasional debauch with Brother Boniface, his comrade and confessor.' *Quentin Durward.*

LETHAM, MISTRESS JOAN. Harry Gow's pretty cousin from Dundee. Henbane Dwining pretended that he recognised her in Louise when he met Harry on St. Valentine's Day with Louise on his arm. But Dwining 'took care that two or three of the most notorious gossips in Curfew Street, who liked not to hear Catharine called the Fair Maid of Perth, should be possessed of this story of her faithful Valentine.' *The Fair Maid of Perth.*

LEVEN, EARL OF. One of the Scottish generals at Marston Moor. He 'was driven out of the field by the impetuous charge of Prince Rupert, and was thirty miles distant, in full flight towards Scotland, when he was overtaken by the news that his party had gained a complete victory.' *A Legend of Montrose.*

LEVITT, FRANK. One of the two footpads who had promised to rob Jeanie Deans and 'send her begging back to her own beggarly country.' Partly on account of Jim Ratcliffe's 'pass,' and partly to show that he was 'master' over Tyburn Tom and Meg Murdockson, he would not allow 'a hair of her head' to be touched. *The Heart of Midlothian.*

LICKITUP, THE LAIRD OF. 'Him that was the laird.' 'He was a gude customer' at Niel Blane's 'Howff' 'anes in a day, and wants naething but means to be a gude ane again —he likes drink as weel as e'er he did.' *Old Mortality.*

(*Howff*, haunt.)

LICKPELF, LAIRD OF. Father of the lady whom the Laird of Dumbiedikes married after being refused by Jeanie Deans. *The Heart of Midlothian.*

LIÈGE, BISHOP OF. Louis of Bourbon. On the fourth night after Quentin Durward's arrival at his

Castle of Schonwaldt with the Ladies of Croye, he was murdered by William de la Marck, who with the men of Liège stormed the castle. 'A generous and kind-hearted prince ... who ... had uniformly maintained the frank and honourable character of the House of Bourbon.' *Quentin Durward.*
Note.—The murder of the Bishop is antedated by about fifteen years.

LIGHTBODY, JEAN. Gibbie Girder's wife: 'a bonny young quean.' *The Bride of Lammermoor.*
(Quean, a young woman.)

LIGHTBODY, MARION. Jean's mother: wife of him 'that was in the steading of Loup-the-Dyke.' She was an old friend of Caleb Balderstone, and took full responsibility for his raid on the christening dinner at Gibbie Girder's. 'I gied them to an acquaintance of mine,' she said of the roast goose and wild ducks, 'and what about it now?' *The Bride of Lammermoor.*

LIGHTFOOT, DR. One of Andrew Fairservice's 'worthy' divines. *Rob Roy.*

LIGHTOHEEL, JANET. Mother of the youth known as Godfrey Bertram Hewit. *Guy Mannering.*

LILTUP, JEAN. Second cousin to Dandy Dinmont's mother's half-sister: 'Auld Singleside's housekeeper and the mother of these twa young ladies that are gane.'
'He acknowledged a marriage, and satisfied the Kirk.' *Guy Mannering.*

LILY OF ST. LEONARD'S. *See* DEANS, EFFIE.

LIMMERFIELD, LAIRD O'. 'A near cousin' of Bailie Nicol Jarvie's Mattie. *Rob Roy.*

LINCOLN, BISHOP. One of the gentlemen in attendance on the Queen when Raleigh ventured to defend his action in refusing admittance to Dr. Masters while the patient slept. *Kenilworth.*

LINCOLN, DEAN OF. Father of the heiress whom Bishop Mannering wished Guy to marry. *Guy Mannering.*

LINDESAY. One of the band of Louis' Scottish Guard who were prepared to defend Quentin after his escape from the hands of Trois-Eschelles and Petit-André. *Quentin Durward.*

LINDESAY, LORD. One of the nobles sent by the Secret Council to Lochleven Castle in order to secure Queen Mary's signature to the deed of abdication. 'A man of the old world, rough and honest, though untaught,' he did not spare the Queen any of the indignities of her position, but he was touched in the end by the 'manliness' of her surrender. 'I would I had as deep cause,' he said, 'to be this lady's friend as I have to be her enemy—thou shouldst see if I spared limb and life in her quarrel.' *The Abbot.*

LINDSAY, DAVID. *See* CRAWFORD, EARL OF.

LINDSAY, MR. Member of Parliament for Edinburgh at the time of the Porteous Riot. While the riot was in progress he 'volunteered the perilous task of carrying a verbal message from the Lord Provost to Colonel Moyle' that he should force the Netherbow Port. But in the absence of a written requisition, the Colonel 'declined to encounter the risk.' *The Heart of Midlothian.*

LINKLATER, LAURIE. One of the yeomen of the King's kitchen: the friend through whom Richie Moniplies twice gained access to the royal person. He also admitted Lord Nigel to Greenwich Park on the occasion when the King imagined that Nigel made an attack on his life. *The Fortunes of Nigel.*

LINKLETTER, LAWRENCE. The old cousin who left Claud Halcro the 'wee bit island.' Cultmalindie was as near to him as Claud, but he 'loved wit, though he had little of his own.' *The Pirate.*

LITTLE JOHN. Robin Hood's lieutenant, 'absent on an expedition as far as the borders of Scotland'; a friend who, 'not content with advising, will needs direct thy motions, and look miserable when thou dost presume to act for thyself.' *Ivanhoe.*

LITTLEJOHN, BAILIE. The magistrate before whom Edie Ochiltree appeared when accused of robbing and assaulting Dousterswivel: 'a tall, portly magistrate on whom corporation crusts had not been conferred in vain.' *The Antiquary.*

LITTLEWORTH, LUCKIE. The tenant of the 'laigh cellar' in one of the properties owned by Peter Peebles before his misfortunes. *Redgauntlet.*

LIVINGSTONE, JOHN. 'A sailor in Borrowstounness' and a 'judicious Christian.' 'He thought Scotland was a Gehennah of wickedness when he was at home, yet when he was abroad he accounted it ane paradise; for the evils of Scotland he found everywhere, and the good of Scotland he found nowhere.' *Heart of Midlothian.*

LIZETTE. The maid who attended Anne of Geierstein at Graffs-lust. *Anne of Geierstein.*

LOCHIEL, CAMERON OF. One of the Highland chiefs who joined the young Chevalier. 'Gallant and accomplished.' *Waverley.*

LOCHIEL, EVAN DHU OF. See EVAN DHU.

LOCHLEVEN, LADY OF. See DOUGLAS, LADY MARGARET.

LOCKHARD, MR. Sir William Ashton's confidential servant. He attended Sir William and Lucy during their enforced stay at Wolf's Crag. 'A man of trust and consequence.' *The Bride of Lammermoor.*

LOCKSLEY. 'Diccon Bend-the-Bow,' leader of a band of outlaws who, though 'arrant thieves,' lived under strict laws of their own, and were 'regularly and equitably governed' by their chief. He was champion archer in the passage-of-arms at Ashby-de-la-Zouch, and afterwards he and his men, under the leadership of the Black Knight, relieved the prisoners in Front-de-Bœuf's castle. 'Call me no longer Locksley, my Liege,' he said, 'but know me under the name which, I fear, fame hath blown too widely not to have reached even your royal ears—I am Robin Hood of Sherwood Forest.' *Ivanhoe.*

LOGANHOUSE, LADY OF. *See* JOCK OF MILCH.

LONG ALLEN. One of the 'reckless warders' who amused themselves by tormenting the Charegite, and were deceived by his pretence of drunkenness. *The Talisman.*

LONG DICKIE. Christie of the Clinthill's horse. *The Monastery.*

LONGSWORD. *See* SALISBURY, EARL OF.

LONGUEVILLE, THOMAS DE. The 'Red Rover' who founded the family to which Sir Patrick Charteris belonged. During a voyage to France 'the celebrated patriot Sir William Wallace' was attacked by the rover, but saved his ship, and defeated the pirate in a hand-to-hand fight. The rover thereafter attached himself to Wallace, came to Scotland with him, married the heiress of the Charteris family, and settled in the Castle of Kinfauns. *The Fair Maid of Perth.*

LOOTIES. Indian banditti, 'always on the watch for prey.' Vanbeest Brown fell into their hands after his duel with Colonel Mannering. *Guy Mannering.*

LOPEZ, MRS. The old attendant whom General Witherington could trust with his wife when, after a nervous attack, she spoke 'about distressing occurrences in an early period of life.' *The Surgeon's Daughter.*

LOREDANI, GIACOMO. The interpreter who translated Saladin's letters for King Richard's perusal. *The Talisman.*

LORIMER. A servant who attended to Dalgetty's wants during his stay at Ardenvohr. *A Legend of Montrose.*

LORRAINE, DUKE OF. *See* VAUDEMONT, FERRAND DE.

LOUIS. The youngest of Julian Avenel's Border-riders: 'ready enough to sing.' *The Monastery.*

LOUIS XI OF FRANCE. (1) 'Brave enough for every useful and political purpose, Louis had not a spark of that romantic valour, or of the pride generally associated with it, which fought on for the point of honour, when the point of utility had been long gained. Calm, crafty, and profoundly attentive to his own interest, he made every sacrifice, both of pride and passion, which could interfere with it. He was careful in disguising his real sentiments and purposes from all who approached him, and frequently used the expressions, "that the king knew not how to reign who knew not how to dissemble; and that, for himself, if he thought his very cap knew his secrets, he would throw it into the fire." No man of his own, or of any other time, better understood how to avail himself of the frailties of others, and when to avoid giving any advantage by the untimely indulgence of his own.' No effort was too great, no policy too dangerous if it ministered to 'the peace and welfare of France.' 'The remorse arising from his evil actions Louis never endeavoured to appease by any relaxation in his Machiavellian stratagems, but laboured, in vain, to soothe and silence that painful feeling by superstitious observances, severe penance, and profuse gifts to the ecclesiastics.' But, by means of his ' powerful and prudent, though most unamiable character,' there were restored ' to the great French nation the benefits of civil government, which, at the time of his accession, they had nearly lost.'

See also PIERRE, MAÎTRE, and BURGUNDY, DUKE OF.

(2) Many members of the Swiss Confederation 'were also privately instigated to arms by the largesses of Louis XI, who spared neither intrigues nor gold to effect a breach betwixt these dauntless confederates and his formidable enemy, Charles the Bold.' Similarly, when an English army landed in France, 'the money of Louis . . . found noble hands willing to clutch it.' (1) *Quentin Durward*. (2) *Anne of Geierstein*.

LOUIS OF BOURBON. *See* LIÈGE, BISHOP OF.

LOUIS OF LUXEMBOURG. Count of St. Paul and High Constable of France. 'False and perjured both to France and Burgundy— one who hath ever endeavoured to fan into a flame our frequent differences, and that with the purpose of giving himself the airs of a mediator.' *Quentin Durward*.

LOUISE. A strolling glee-woman who, ' beneath the royal windows and in the cloister of the Dominicans,' was publicly honoured by the Duke of Rothesay with ' a kiss of approbation.' Placed by him under Harry Gow's protection that she might escape the wrath of Douglas' men, she brought some scandal to Harry's name. But in Falkland Castle, whither she was taken by Sir John Ramorny for the Duke's amusement, she proved ' a humble and accommodating companion' to Catharine Glover.

' Ah, poor Louise ! small cause to pine
Had'st thou for treasures of the mine ;
For peace of mind, that gift divine,
And spotless innocence, were thine,
   Ah, poor Louise !

' Ah, poor Louise ! Thy treasure's reft !
I know not if by force or theft,
Or part by violence, part by gift ;
But misery is all that's left
   To poor Louise.'
  The Fair Maid of Perth.

LOUPENGIRTH, LEDDY. Lady Binks' mother. ' The lad would fain hae louped back, but the auld leddy held him to his tackle.' *St. Ronan's Well*.

(*Loup*, to spring.)

LOUPONHEIGHT, LAIRD OF. The gallant laird who danced with Menie Gray ' the greater part of the evening' at the Hunters' Ball, Richard Middlemas and Adam Hartley watching from the music gallery. *The Surgeon's Daughter*.

LOVEL, MR. A young man ' of genteel appearance,' ' who is touched with some strain of a better spirit than belongs to these giddy-paced times—reveres his elders, and has a pretty notion of the classics.' He was ' not destitute of spirit neither,' and his ultimate identification with the distinguished Major Neville justified the Antiquary's good opinion. The further discovery that he was Lord William Geraldin, heir to the Earl of Glenallan, removed all barriers to his marriage with Isabella Wardour.

'I would as soon wish my hand to be as callous as horn, that it might escape an occasional cut or scratch,' he said, ' as I would be ambitious of the stoicism which should render my heart like a piece of the nether mill-stone.' *The Antiquary.*

LOWESTOFFE, REGINALD. The young Templar who sheltered Nigel after his attack on Lord Dalgarno and introduced him to ' Alsatia.' He was also a ' noble friend' to Richie Moniplies when Richie was secretly putting his master's affairs to rights. 'Shrewd, alert, and well acquainted with the town through all its recesses, but in a sort of disrespectable way.' *The Fortunes of Nigel.*

LOWRIE, TAM. Landlord of the Black Bull, Marchthorn, where Frank Tyrrel stayed during his temporary disappearance. *St. Ronan's Well.*

LOWTHER, JACK. One of the gang of men who took the *Jumping Jenny's* cargo to Goodman Grist's mill. *Redgauntlet.*

LOWTHER, LOURIE. A friend of Dandy Dinmont, with whom he stayed 'the drinking of twa cheerers,' after leaving Tib Mumps'. *Guy Mannering.*

LOWTHER, SHERIFF OF CUMBER-

LAND. The officer of Queen Mary's 'loving sister' who preferred 'a safe asylum from the rebels' after their success at Langside. *The Abbot.*

LOYALTY'S REWARD. The horse given to Dalgetty by Montrose to supply the place of the 'famed Gustavus.' *A Legend of Montrose.*

LUCK-IN-A-BAG. A notorious freebooter who held a command under Douglas in the 1715 rebellion. *The Black Dwarf.*

LUCY. A black spaniel bitch recommended ' with his last breath ' by John Osbaldistone to Frank. *Rob Roy.*

LUGLEATHER. One of the good burghers who witnessed Adam Woodcock's chastisement by the stranger page (Henry Seyton) at the Hostelry of St. Michael's. *The Abbot.*

LUMLEY, CAPTAIN. The officer who led Harry Morton before the Duke of Monmouth, when he went to learn his Grace's decision regarding the 'Remonstrance and Supplication' sent by the Covenanters through Lord Evandale. *Old Mortality.*

LUNDIN, DOCTOR LUKE. The Lady of Lochleven's Chamberlain in Kinross. 'Bred to the venerable study of medicine,' he ornamented his discourse with scraps of learning which rendered it 'almost universally unintelligible.' He was summoned to the castle when Queen Mary was thought to have been poisoned, but it was her ' good fortune' not to need his skill. In the town, however, his power was supreme, and ' woe betide the family of the rich boor who presumed to depart this life without a passport from Dr. Luke Lundin!' *The Abbot.*

LUNDIN, SIR LOUIS. Town Clerk of Perth. He suggested during the enquiry into the circumstances of Oliver Proudfute's death that the widow should claim bier-right. *The Fair Maid of Perth.*

Note.—Bier-right, the right by which the relatives of a murdered man could claim that accused persons should pass one by one before the bier, and in a solemn, prescribed form, assert their innocence. It was held that the near presence of the murderer awoke 'some imperfect life' in the dead body, and opened the fatal wounds afresh.

LUTESTRING, MASTER. The mercer of Chesterfield. *Peveril of the Peak.*

LUTIN. Lord Dalgarno's page: 'fit for every element—prompt to execute every command, good, bad, or indifferent—unmatched in his tribe, as rogue, thief, and liar.' *The Fortunes of Nigel.*

LYLE, ANNOT. Daughter and heiress of the Knight of Ardenvohr. As a child she was carried off from her father's tower by the Children of the Mist, her life being spared by Ranald MacEagh 'out of compassion.' Similarly she was spared by Allan McAulay in one of his expeditions against the Children of the Mist, and was brought up at Darnlinvarach rather as a sister than a dependent. Menteith was fascinated 'by the ingenuity, liveliness, and sweetness of her disposition,' while to Allan, even in his gloomiest moods, she became 'a sunbeam on a sullen sea.' But she 'dreaded' Allan 'as much as gratitude ... could permit her to do.' *A Legend of Montrose.*

LYSIMACHUS. 'A somewhat slight-made, but alert-looking man ... by profession a designer.' Like his patron Stephanos, he was one of the discontented citizens who lent their ears to the conspiracy, planned by Nicephorus, Achilles Tatius, and Agelastes. *Count Robert of Paris.*

M

McALPIN, JANET. The Sergeant's sister: 'a little, neat old woman, with a Highland curch and tartan plaid, watching the very looks of her brother, to her the greatest man upon earth.' *A Legend of Montrose.*

(*Curch*, a covering for a woman's head.)

McALPIN, SERGEANT MORE. 'One of the most honoured inhabitants of Gandercleugh.' He had served in various quarters of the world, and delighted to relate not only his own adventures, but 'numerous Highland traditions' learnt during his youth. His ancestors had served in Montrose's wars, and he was able to give to Peter Pattieson much information concerning these 'civil commotions' which 'reflect the highest honour upon the Highlanders.' *A Legend of Montrose.*

MACALPIN, PETER. An old man who had attended to the town clock of

Dumfries, but was dismissed by Provost Crosbie for making himself 'too busy for a person in office,' drinking 'healths and so forth which it became no man to drink or pledge.' But Mrs. Crosbie maintained he was 'the only hand to set a clock.' *Redgauntlet.*

McALPIN, RORY. The old Highlander who used to sing songs out of Ossian to Hector McIntyre. 'He must have taken very unwarrantable liberties with the original.' *The Antiquary.*

MACALPINE, CORPORAL. One of the guard that hauled Madge Wildfire to the guard house 'ae morning.' Her little dog attacked him, and the Corporal 'killed the bit faithfu' thing wi' his Lochaber axe.' *The Heart of Midlothian.*

MACALPINE, JEANIE. Landlady of the public-house in Aberfoil where Bailie Nicol Jarvie and Frank Osbaldistone expected to meet Rob Roy. 'Between sogers and Saxons, and caterans and cattle-lifters, and hership and bluidshed, an honest woman wad live quieter in hell than on the Highland line.' *Rob Roy.*

(*Caterans*, Highland robbers. *Hership*, plundering.)

MACANALEISTER, EACHIN. Rob Roy's lieutenant. *Rob Roy.*

McAULAY, ALLAN. Younger brother of Angus. Born under tragic circumstances, he was a shy, gloomy child, but after his mother's death he assumed 'a total independence of character and impatience of control,' and lived only to wreak vengeance on the Children of the Mist. He passed many years 'like a tamed lion' without 'contradiction or even expostulation,' and was ill-fitted to control his passion for Annot Lyle when it brought him into conflict with his friend Menteith. But in ordinary matters he had great 'acuteness and sense,' and his apparent 'predictions' were, 'in reality, the result of judgment and reflection.' *A Legend of Montrose.*

McAULAY, ANGUS. Laird of Darnlinvarach. He took a prominent part in Montrose's Highland gathering, yet in answer to his friend Sir Duncan Campbell his 'careless and cheerful' mind could find no justification for his action save that 'the iron hand of destiny branded our fate upon our forehead long ere we could form a wish, or raise a finger in our own behalf.' *A Legend of Montrose.*

McAULAY, LAIRD KENNETH. An ancestor of Angus and Allan. *A Legend of Montrose.*

MACAULEY, SIR AULEY. *See* TREBLEPLUMB, LADY.

MACBETHS. *See* MORAYS.

MACBRIAR, EPHRAIM. A youthful preacher of hardly twenty years who 'had been twice imprisoned for several months and suffered many severities.' He was one of the most uncompromising members of the Covenanters' council, and took the leading part in the cross-examination of Harry Morton at Drumshinnel. His religious zeal triumphed over his bodily weakness and infirmity, and he underwent torture and death 'with the same enthusiastic firmness which his whole life had evinced.' *Old Mortality.*

MACBRIAR, JOHN. The old deaf man 'that never understood a single question' the officers 'pat till him, and sae lost his life for ack o' hearing.' *Old Mortality.*

MACBRIAR, REV. AARON. Chaplain to Donohoe Bertram's mother. He was turned out of doors by Donohoe after a quarrel about the good graces of a milkmaid. *Guy Mannering.*

MACCALLUM, DOUGAL. Sir Robert Redgauntlet's butler. He had followed Sir Robert ' through gude and ill, thick and thin, pool and stream,' and ' could turn his master round his finger.' He was present when Steenie Steenson paid his rent, but on the night before Sir Robert's funeral he died while answering his master's silver whistle. 'Though death breaks service,' he said to Hutcheon, 'it shall never break my service to Sir Robert.' *Redgauntlet.*
See also WEIR, MAJOR.

MACCALLUM MORE. Gaelic title of the Dukes of Argyle : ' Great Colin's Son.'

MACCANDLISH, BAILIE. Mrs. MacCandlish's husband : ' dead and gone.' *Guy Mannering.*
(*Bailie,* the magistrate second in rank in a royal burgh.)

MACCANDLISH, MRS. Landlady of the *Gordon Arms.* Her ' natural sagacity and acquired suspicion ' were keen, and ' long habit had given Mrs. MacCandlish an acute tact in ascertaining the quality of her visitors, and proportioning her reception accordingly.' *Guy Mannering.*

MACCASQUIL. One of Mistress Bertram's disappointed relatives : ' formerly of Drumquag.' ' His hopes on the present occasion are founded on a very distant relationship, upon his sitting in the same pew with the deceased every Sunday, and upon his playing at cribbage with her regularly on the Saturday evenings—taking great care never to come off a winner.' *Guy Mannering.*

MACCLURE, AILY, OF DEEPHEUGH. One of Reuben Butler's parishioners. She practised ' abominations, spaeing folks' fortunes wi' egg-shells, and mutton-banes, and dreams, and divinations whilk is a scandal to ony Christian land to suffer sic a wretch to live.' *The Heart of Midlothian.*

(*To spae,* to foretell.)

MACCOMBICH, EVAN DHU. The foster-brother of Fergus MacIvor, and one of the most devoted of his clansmen.

' I was only ganging to say, my lord,' said Evan, in what he meant to be an insinuating manner, ' that if your excellent honour and the honourable Court would let Vich Ian Vohr go free just this once, and let him gae back to France, and no to trouble King George's government again, that [*sic*] ony six o' the very best of his clan will be willing to be justified in his stead ; and if you'll just let me gae down to Glennaquoich, I'll fetch them up to ye mysell, to head or hang, and you may begin wi' me the very first man!' *Waverley.*

McCOMBICH, JANET. Robin's aunt. As Robin was leaving Doune for his last journey into England she foresaw 'English blood' on his hand. Her certainty of an ill fate was so great that he gave his dirk into Hugh Morrison's keeping. Few of his aunt's words fell to the ground.' *The Two Drovers.*

McCOMBICH, LACHLAN. Robin's father. He had been called McCombich ('or *son of my friend*, his actual clan surname being McGregor') by 'the celebrated Rob Roy, because of the particular friendship which had subsisted between the grandsire of Robin and that renowned cateran.' *The Two Drovers.*
(*Cateran*, freebooter.)

McCOMBICH, ROBIN 'OIG' (*i.e.* YOUNG). One of the two drovers. For three years Harry Wakefield had been his 'chosen friend' on the journeys between the Scottish and the English markets, till on one occasion chance gave Robin the better claim to a coveted piece of pasture. At the first sign of misunderstanding he offered to share the ground 'for the sake of peace and good neighbourhood'; he remained patient when his offer 'was rejected with scorn'; he still tried to get away 'in peace' from a 'torrent of general ridicule' at Heskett's alehouse. But after he was 'struck down, and beaten' by his English friend, his 'wild untutored justice' demanded Harry's death. He wrought his revenge with 'deliberate determination' and showed no less 'resolution' and 'firmness' when the law exacted its penalty. 'I give a life for the life I took,' he said. *The Two Drovers.*

MACCORKINDALE, MRS. *See* DUTTON, DOLLY.

MACCOULS. *See* STEWARTS OF APPIN.

MACCRAW, MARGARET. The maiden name of Meg Murdockson. *The Heart of Midlothian.*

MACCRIBB. A friend of the Antiquary, with whom he had a controversy upon Ossian's poems. It 'began in smooth, oily, ladylike terms, but is now waxing more sour and eager.' *The Antiquary.*

MACCROSKIE. One of Mrs. Howden's neighbours. He suggested that the King and Queen would be better 'back at their German kaleyard.' *The Heart of Midlothian.*

MACCROSKY. The owner of 'a very bonny family o' bairns,' the sight of which revived Mistress Bertram's regret for the lost heir of Ellangowan, and increased her spite against Lucy. *Guy Mannering.*

MACCROSSKIE, DEACON. The Dumfries weaver. *Guy Mannering.*

MACCROSSKIE OF CREOCHSTONE. Son of the Deacon: Ellangowan's rival for 'the front gallery facing the minister.' *Guy Mannering.*

MACDINGAWAIE. The family name of Ellangowan's ancestors before they adopted the Norman surname of Bertram. *Guy Mannering.*

MacDingawaie, Arthur. A famous ancestor of the Bertrams, regarded by Meg Merrilies as the only equal of young Harry. *Guy Mannering.*

MacDingawaie, Donagild. An ancestor of the Bertram family who gave his name to one of the towers of the old castle. *Guy Mannering.*

MacDingawaie, Hanlon. An ancestor of the Bertram family who during the times of Galwegian independence ' murdered his brother and sovereign in order to usurp the principality from his infant nephew.' *Guy Mannering.*

MacDingawaie, Knarth. The brother and sovereign of Hanlon. *Guy Mannering.*

Macdonell, Alaster. ' Young Colkitto ' : leader of a body of the Earl of Antrim's people who joined Montrose. ' Brave to intrepidity . . . very strong and active in person, completely master of his weapons,' he was at the same time ' inexperienced in military tactics, and of a jealous and presumptuous disposition.' Yet his ' feats of strength and courage . . . seem to have made a stronger impression upon the minds of the Highlanders than the military skill and chivalrous spirit ' of Montrose. *A Legend of Montrose.*

Macdonell of Glengarry. *See* Vich Alister More.

MacDonought, Mr. Duncan. Reuben Butler's predecessor as minister of Knocktarlitie. *The Heart of Midlothian.*

McDougal of Lorn. One of the Highland chiefs who attended the gathering at Darnlinvarach, and put themselves under Montrose. *A Legend of Montrose.*

MacEagh, Kenneth. Ranald's grandsons, dearer than ' ten sons who are mouldering in earth, or are preyed on by the fowls of the air.' To him Ranald left the ideal of his race : ' Live free—requite kindness—avenge the injuries of thy race ! ' *A Legend of Montrose.*

MacEagh, Ranald. One of the Children of the Mist : the Highland freebooter who destroyed the Knight of Ardenvohr's castle. Dalgetty found him a prisoner almost without hope, in the dungeon of Inverary Castle, but together they were able to outwit the supposed Murdoch Campbell and make good their escape. Under Dalgetty's protection he joined Montrose as a guide, and at the battle of Inverlochy found an opportunity of wreaking vengeance on Sir Duncan Campbell. Mortally wounded by Allan McAulay, he revealed the secret of Annot Lyle's birth that he might thereby set Allan at enmity with Menteith. Like his forefathers, he died ' ere infirmity, disease or age ' had broken his spirit. *A Legend of Montrose.*

MacEvoy, Bessie. A relative of Janet. Her ' coodman, puir creature, died of the frost, being a shairman, for a' the whisky he could drink to keep it out o' his stamoch—and—' *The Highland Widow.*

MacEvoy, Janet. The honest Highland landlady with whom

Mr. Croftangry lodged in the Canongate when availing himself of the sanctuary of Holyrood to evade his creditors. 'The little busy, prating, important old woman' was promoted to be his housekeeper, when he returned in prosperous old age. *The Highland Widow.*

MACFARLANE, ELSPETH. Bailie Nicol Jarvie's mother. *Rob Roy.*

MACFARLANE, MAGGY. Parlane's surviving daughter, and wife of Duncan MacNab: 'the auld wife ayont the fire at Stuckavrallachan that made some mixture' of Bailie Nicol Jarvie's blood and Rob Roy's. *Rob Roy.*

MACFARLANE, PARLANE. Elspeth's father. He 'stood as near' Rob Roy 'as in the fourth degree of kindred.' *Rob Roy.*

MACFARLANES. One of the Highland clans that joined the young Chevalier. *Waverley.*

MACFIE. Laird of Gudgeonford : the owner of 'a great number of kain hens—that's hens that the tenant pays to the landlord—like a sort of rent in kind.' *Guy Mannering.*

MACFIN, MILES. The caddie into whose charge Dominie Sampson was put during his stay in Edinburgh. He had a 'happy indifference as to kirk or market, meeting or court of justice, or—any other place whatever.' *Guy Mannering.*

MACFIN, MR. THOMAS. Fiancé of Alison MacVittie. *Rob Roy.*

MCFITTOCH, MR. 'A dancing-master, who, itinerant during the summer, became stationary in the winter season, and afforded the youth of Middlemas the benefit of his instructions at the rate of twenty lessons for five shillings sterling.' *The Surgeon's Daughter.*

MACGILLIE CHATTANACH. The 'high-mettled Chief' of Clan Chattan. He was little disturbed by Ferquhard Day's desertion, he himself being 'man enough for two of the Clan Quhele.' But in Harry Gow he found a substitute who, he soon saw, was worthy of his ranks. 'His grey eye gleamed with a wild light expressive of valour and ferocity mingled; but wisdom and experience dwelt on the expression of his forehead, eyebrows, and lips.' *The Fair Maid of Perth.*

MACGILLIGAN, DUNCAN. 'A braw weel-grown lad of a nevoy,' whom Duncan Knock wished to advance by Lady Staunton's favour. *The Heart of Midlothian.*

MACGILLIHURON, RANALD. The name assumed by Ranald MacEagh when serving under Montrose. *A Legend of Montrose.*

MACGIVAN, SANDY. A friend of Margaret Ramsay's 'drudge' Janet. *The Fortunes of Nigel.*

MACGRAINER, MAISTER. The minister of the Anti-burghers in Kippletringan. *Guy Mannering.* (*Anti-burghers*, a religious sect who refused to take the burgess oath.)

MACGREGOR, HAMISH. One of Rob Roy's sons. 'They dinna ken the very multiplication table itself, whilk is the root of a' usefu' knowledge, and they did naething but laugh and fleer at me when I tauld them my mind on their ignorance.' *Rob Roy.*

(*To fleer*, to make wry faces.)

MacGregor, Helen (*née* Helen Campbell.) Rob Roy's wife. She was ' nane o' the maist douce maidens, nor meekest wives neither, and folk say that Rob himsell stands in awe o' her.' She had ' deep wrongs to avenge,' and showed by her reckless cruelty to Morris how strong her thirst for vengeance was. ' An incarnate devil when her bluid's up.' *Rob Roy.*

MacGregor, Robert. One of Rob Roy's sons. ' They are as ignorant as the kyloes ye used to drive to market, or the very English churls that ye sauld them to, and can do naething whatever to purpose.' *Rob Roy.*

(*Kyloes*, Highland cattle.)

MacGregor, Robert or Robin. ' Robert Campbell,' ' Rob Roy,' or ' Red Gregarach.' ' Robin was anes a weel-doing, painstaking drover . . . and he was baith civil and just in his dealings. . . . But the times cam hard, and Rob was venturesome. . . . And the creditors, mair especially some grit neighbours o' his, grippit to his living and land . . . sae . . . he took to the brae-side.' ' He's sic an auld-farran, lang-headed chield as never took up the trade o' cateran in our time ; mony a daft reik he has played—mair than wad fill a book, and a queer ane it wad be—as gude as Robin Hood, or William Wallace—a' fu' o' venturesome deeds and escapes, sic as folk tell ower at a winter-ingle in the daft days.' *Rob Roy.*

(*Auld-farran,* sagacious. *Cateran,* robber. *Reik,* exploit. *Daft days,* holidays.)

MacGruthar, Sandy. The victim of an affair that was politically unlucky for Ellangowan. David MacGuffog kept him ' twa or three days up yonder at the auld castle, just till they could get conveniency to send him to the county jail.' *Guy Mannering.*

MacGuffog. ' The thief-taker ' : keeper of the prison at Portanferry, and later, under-turnkey in the county jail. He profited without scruple from the prisoners' necessities.

' But mark ye me, friend,' he said to Vanbeest Brown, ' that we may have nae colly-shangie afterhend, these are the fees that I always charge a swell that must have his lib-ken to himsell—Thirty shillings a-week for lodgings, and a guinea for garnish ; half-a-guinea a-week for a single bed. . . . Then for meat and liquor, ye may have the best, and I never charge abune twenty per cent ower tavern price for pleasing a gentleman that way—and that's little eneugh for sending in and sending out, and wearing the lassie's shoon out.' *Guy Mannering.*

(*Colly-shangie,* squabble. *Lib-ken,* a cell.)

MacGuffog, David. The constable who kept Sandy MacGruthar three days in the ' auld castle ' : uncle of MacGuffog, ' the thief-taker.' *Guy Mannering.*

MacGuffog, Mrs. Wife of the prison-keeper : ' an awful spectacle, being a woman for strength and resolution capable of maintaining order among her riotous inmates, and of administering the discipline of the house, as it was called, during the absence of her husband, or when he chanced to have taken an overdose of the creature.' *Guy Mannering.*

MacIan, Gilchrist. Chief of Clan Quhele : Ian Eachin's father. Shortly before Eachin's birth he lost seven sons in battle with Clan Chattan. Eachin was born ' under a bush of holly and suckled by a white doe.' But his existence brought little comfort to the chief until after eighteen years Torquil persuaded the elders of the clan that Eachin's presence was necessary to secure the success of Clan Quhele in the combat with Clan Chattan. Gilchrist died before the combat took place, leaving Eachin to face a struggle for which his previous life had given him little training. *The Fair Maid of Perth.*

MacIan, Ian Eachin (Hector). Son of Gilchrist MacIan : ' Dault an Neigh Dheil, or foster-child of the White Doe.' On account of ' the ominous presage attending his birth and nurture,' he was brought up in obscurity as Simon Glover's apprentice Conachar. But the threatened defection of Torquil and his eight sons from the struggle with Clan Chattan made his recall imperative. ' More prone to quarrel than to fight,' he was conscious of an ' overpowering faint-heartedness,' and under the stress of ' a quick fancy that over-estimates danger,' he confessed his cowardice to Simon Glover and to Torquil. Simon could not give him the stimulus which the promise of Catharine's hand would have been, but in the heat of the struggle the devotion of Torquil and his stalwart sons kept his courage alive until he was left alone, face to face with his deadly enemy, Henry Gow. Then ' his heart sickened, his eyes darkened, his ears tingled, his brain turned giddy '—he turned and fled. *The Fair Maid of Perth.*

McIlduy. The patronymic title (' descendant of Black Donald ') of the Chief of the Camerons. *A Legend of Montrose.*

Macindallaghers, Chief of. One of the Highland chiefs who joined the young Chevalier. *Waverley.*

MacIntosh, Brigadier, of Borlun. Commanding officer of the detachment of Highlanders with whom Diana Vernon and her father travelled during the rebellion of 1715. *Rob Roy.*

McIntyre, Donald. Strathtudlem's seventh son : ' an honest writer.' *The Antiquary.*

McIntyre, Captain. Husband of the Antiquary's younger sister. He had no other fortune than his commission and a Highland pedigree. During an expedition against Hyder Ali, his detachment was cut off and was never heard of again. *The Antiquary.*

McIntyre, Captain Hector. The Antiquary's nephew : ' with his long pedigree and his airs of family, very much of a jackanapes.' He was ' a good lad notwithstanding,' and astonished the Antiquary by his military efficiency on the occasion of the false alarm of invasion at Fairport. *The Antiquary.*

McINTYRE, MARIA. The Antiquary's 'most exquisite niece,' 'as light-headed a goose as womankind affords.' She had 'an air of *espièglerie* which became her very well,' and from time to time acted as peacemaker between the Antiquary and her brother. 'People talk of a marriage between Miss McIntyre and Captain Wardour.' *The Antiquary.*

McINTYRE, MRS. The Antiquary's younger sister, who had 'sunk under the accumulated load of grief and uncertainty' concerning her husband's fate. *The Antiquary.*

MacIVOR, EVAN. *See* MACCOMBICH, EVAN DHU.

MacIVOR, FERGUS, VICH IAN VOHR (*i.e.* SON OF JOHN THE GREAT). A Highland chieftain, 'the most active, subtle, and desperate Jacobite in Scotland.' His father had taken part in the rebellion of 1715, and he himself was one of the prime movers in 1745.

'Regardless of danger, and sanguine from temper, youth, and ambition, he saw in imagination all his prospects crowned with success, and was totally indifferent to the probable alternative of a soldier's grave.' *Waverley.*

MacIVOR, FLORA. Sister of Fergus, and like him devotedly attached to the house of Stewart. But her loyalty 'burnt pure and unmixed with any selfish feeling,' and, though 'wildly enthusiastic,' 'disdained to avail itself of any indirect means of supporting the cause to which she was devoted.' For her brother's fate she blamed herself. 'Oh that I could recollect that I had but once said to him, He that striketh with the sword shall die by the sword; that I had but once said, Remain at home; reserve yourself, your vassals, your life, for enterprises within the reach of man. But, O, Mr. Waverley, I spurred his fiery temper, and half of his ruin at least lies with his sister!' *Waverley.*

MacIVOR, IAN. The founder of the family to which Fergus and Flora belonged. He erected a famous stone tower, and from this was called Ian nan Chaistel, or John of the Tower. All succeeding chiefs took the name, Vich Ian Vohr, or Son of John the Great. *Waverley.*

MacIZZARD, DOLLY. An Edinburgh lady whose voice, as it 'mingled in the psalmody at the Old Greyfriars' Church,' enamoured Darsie Latimer. *Redgauntlet.*

MACKAY. Viscount Dundee's opponent at Killiecrankie. *Old Mortality.*

MACKELL, QUINTIN, OF IRONGRAY. The name which acted as a 'password' when Harry Morton applied to Widow Maclure for news of Balfour of Burley. *Old Mortality.*

MACKELLAR. One of the 'faithful friends' who met Father Buonaventure at Joe Crackenthorp's inn: a countryman of Redgauntlet, like him he had little to lose. 'They that took my land the last time may take my life this,' he said. *Redgauntlet.*

MACKENZIE, YOUNG. One of the counsel suggested by Saddletree for Effie Deans' defence, but rejected by her father as the nephew of Bluidy Mackenzie, 'that has the blood of the saints at his fingers' ends.' *The Heart of Midlothian.*

MACKERRIS, COLONEL. The 'excellent friend and neighbour' who supplied to the author all 'these hard words about India.' 'One of the best fellows who ever trode a Highland moor, or dived into an Indian jungle.' *The Surgeon's Daughter.*

Note.—Colonel James Ferguson of Huntly Burn was the friend alluded to.

MACKITCHINSON. The fat, gouty, pursy landlord of the Queensferry inn, at which the Antiquary and Lovel dined on the first day of their acquaintance. *The Antiquary.*

MACLAREN, DUNCAN. See INVERASHALLOCH.

MACLEAN, NEIL. A fellow-prisoner who walked next in file to Sir Harry Redgauntlet and Pate-in-Peril, 'but had the luck to escape the gallows by some sleight-of-hand trick or other.' *Redgauntlet.*

MCLEAN, SIR HECTOR. One of the Highland chiefs who attended the gathering at Darnlinvarach, and put themselves under Montrose. *A Legend of Montrose.*

MACLEARY, LUCKIE. The mistress of the small inn where, on a memorable occasion, soon after Edward Waverley's arrival at Tully-Veolan, the Baron of Bradwardine and his friends drank their stirrup-cup. *Waverley.*

(*Luckie*, a designation given to an elderly woman.)

MACLEISH, DONALD. The cicerone who was, during Mrs. Bethune Baliol's Highland tour, 'not only our faithful attendant and steady servant, but our humble and obliging friend.' Their route from Dalmally to Oban took them past Elspat MacTavish's hut, and there, in view of the lonely figure at the foot of the oak-tree, Donald told her story. *The Highland Widow.*

MACLEUCHAR, MRS. The sharp-looking old dame at whose shop-door the Queensferry Diligence started from Edinburgh. Its unpunctuality greatly irritated the Antiquary. 'Woman . . . answer,' he said to her, 'and for once in thy long, useless, and evil life, let it be in the words of truth and sincerity—hast thou such a coach?' *The Antiquary.*

MACLEWIS. Captain of King Robert's guard of Brandanes. *The Fair Maid of Perth.*

Note.—*Brandanes*, the men of Bute. 'The territory of Bute was the King's own patrimony, and its natives his personal followers.'

MACLURE, NINIAN and JOHNNIE. Widow Maclure's sons. 'The tane fell wi' sword in hand, fighting for a broken national Covenant; the tother—O, they took him and shot him dead on the green before his mother's face!' *Old Mortality.*

MACLURE, PEGGY. Widow Maclure's grand-daughter. She guided Harry Morton to Balfour's retreat at the Linn, where she often went alone ' wi' milk and meal.' *Old Mortality.*

MACLURE, WIDOW BESSIE. The ' old woman wrapped in a red cloak ' who warned Balfour of Burley against going up the pass, on the night of the wappenschaw, thereby forcing him to ask shelter from Harry Morton. Humane to friend and foe alike, she sheltered Lord Evandale after his flight from Drumclog, but for this got ill-will ' amang some o' our ain folk.' Basil Olifant's enmity robbed her of all the comforts Lord Evandale's gratitude had bestowed, and when Harry Morton visited her after his return from exile he found her poor, blind, and lonely, yet uttering no word of complaint. ' I can bear my ain burden patiently,' she said, ' and warld's loss is the least part o't.' *Old Mortality.*

MACMORLAN, MR. Sheriff-substitute of the county : ' an active, honest, and intelligent man,' who showed Lucy Bertram great kindness. *Guy Mannering.*

MACMORLAN, MRS. Wife of the Sheriff-substitute : ' a ladylike person, and well qualified by birth and manners to receive the visit, and to make her house agreeable to Miss Bertram.' *Guy Mannering.*

MACMURROUGH NAN FONN (*i.e.* OF THE SONGS). The bard of Glennaquoich. *Waverley.*

MCNAB, CLAN. Part of a reinforcement raised by Colkitto after Montrose had retired from Aberdeen. *A Legend of Montrose.*

MACPHADRAICK, MILES. The man who brought ambiguous tidings to Elspat MacTavish after Hamish Bean had left her in anger. ' A cautious man,' he had so far encouraged MacTavish Mhor as occasionally to buy cattle from him ; to Hamish Bean he seemed wise, though ' crafty and worldly, after the fashion of the Sassenach.' By his advice Hamish joined Barcaldine's troop, in order to ' mend our estate in the world.' *The Highland Widow.*

MACPHERSON, CLUNY. The leader of a fine clan regiment from Badenoch, which, with Fergus MacIvor's men, was overtaken at Clifton by the English army. *Waverley.*

MACPHERSON, SECUNDUS, ESQ., OF GLENFORGEN. The translator of Annot Lyle's ballads. His version ' will be found nearly as genuine as the version of Ossian by his celebrated namesake.' *A Legend of Montrose.*

MACRAND, RORY. One of Reuben Butler's parishioners. He and Margery Kittleside ' southered sin wi' marriage.' *The Heart of Midlothian.*

(*Southered*, soldered.)

MACRAW, FRANCIE. The Earl of Glenallan's porter : an old soldier to whom Edie Ochiltree had been ' front-rank-man ' at Fontenoy. *The Antiquary.*

MACRAW, PETER. ' The old piper of Stornoway, who had a seal that flapped its tail to the tune of *Caberfae*, and acknowledged no other whatever.' *The Pirate.*

(*Caberfae* or Buckshead, the name given to the Chief of the MacKenzies. The MacRaws were followers of the MacKenzies.)

MACREADY, ARCHY. Mrs. Bethune Baliol's porter : ' a lame old man, tall, grave, and thin . . . an old soldier . . . saturnine, silent, and slow,' with ' an occasional partiality . . . to a dram.' *The Highland Widow.*

MACREADY, PATE. ' A far-awa' cousin ' of Andrew Fairservice : the ' travelling merchant ' who brought to Osbaldistone Hall news of the discussion in the Houses of Parliament about the theft of Morris' portmanteau. *Rob Roy.*

MACRIMMON. Hereditary piper to the Chief of MacLeod. *Rob Roy.*

MACTAVISH, ELSPAT. ' The Highland Widow ' : ' the Woman of the Tree.' Thinking always of her husband as ' of a hero who had fallen in his proper trade of war,' she reared her boy in the passionate hope that he would one day emulate his father's fame. When he ' made repeated steps towards independence ' of judgment and action, her restless and impetuous love drove her to ' all the vehemence of impotent and yet unrestrained passion.' Her heart's desire was to save him from ' the death-sleep of the soul, which is brought on by what she regarded as slavery,' but in her headlong ignorance she drove him to death. Strong and fierce in her agony as in her love, she spent her lonely days at the foot of the old oak tree, a weird figure, whose face showed ' the stern abstraction of hopeless and overpowering sorrow.' *The Highland Widow.*

MACTAVISH, HAMISH. Elspat's husband : a ' daring cateran,' whose ' strength and feats of prowess ' had gained him the title of MacTavish Mhor. After the failure of ' The Forty-five,' ' he was outlawed both as a traitor to the state and as a robber and cateran,' and finally shot after a desperate resistance in which Elspat took an heroic part. *The Highland Widow.*

(*Cateran*, a freebooter. *Mhor*, great.)

MACTAVISH, HAMISH BEAN (FAIRHAIRED). Elspat's son. Unlike his mother, he saw, ' when he mixed with the world, that the trade of the cateran was now alike dangerous and discreditable, and that if he were to emulate his father's prowess, it must be in some other line of warfare, more consonant to the opinions of the present day.' He enlisted, but in the clash of their wills which followed, he was conquered by subterfuge. His sense of honour forbade flight, and he determined ' to abide his destiny.' But she was still blind to all views of honour save her own, and at the moment of arrest she goaded him to bitterness beyond bearing. He shot Allan Cameron and sealed his own fate. ' If I weep,' he said to her, ' it is not for myself, but for you, for my sufferings will soon be over ; but yours—O, who but Heaven shall set a boundary to them !' *The Highland Widow.*

MACTRICKIT, WYLIE. A writer who 'was very pressing and spak very civilly' to Mrs. Wilson, after she inherited the life-rent of Milnwood. She, however, thought herself 'ower failed to tak a helpmate.' *Old Mortality.*

MACTURK, CAPTAIN MUNGO (or HECTOR). A member of the Committee of Management in 'the infant republic of St. Ronan's Well': 'the Man of Peace.' As general referee in all quarrels he gained 'a good deal of respect at the Well, for he was precisely that sort of person who is ready to fight with anyone—whom no one can find an apology for declining to fight with—in fighting with whom considerable danger was incurred, for he was ever and anon showing that he could snuff a candle with a pistol ball—and lastly, through fighting with whom no *éclat* or credit could redound to the antagonist.' 'As cankered ... as an auld Hieland terrier that snaps at whatever comes near it.' *St. Ronan's Well.*

(*Cankered,* cross, ill-conditioned.)

MACVITTIE, MISS ALISON. Daughter of Mr. Ephraim. 'She'll hae a hantle siller, if she's no that bonny.' *Rob Roy.*

(*Hantle,* a considerable quantity.)

MACVITTIE, MR. EPHRAIM. Partner in the firm MacVittie, MacFin & Co. : a man of 'starched and severe aspect.'

'Speak till him, then,' Fairservice advised, '—he'll gie ye a decent answer f r as rich as he is, unless ye were wanting siller frae him—they say he's dour to draw his purse.' *Rob Roy.*

MACVITTIE, MRS. Wife of Mr. Ephraim. *Rob Roy.*

MACVITTIE, MACFIN & Co. A firm of Glasgow merchants with whom Osbaldistone and Tresham did business. As long as prosperity lasted they made 'long-winded professions of regard,' but when Owen personally applied for assistance in the temporary difficulties of his master's house, they met him 'with a counter-demand of instant security against imminent hazard of eventual loss.' For this Mr. Osbaldistone afterwards 'refused every tender of apology and accommodation.' *Rob Roy.*

MACWHEEBLE, DUNCAN. Bailie, or 'prime minister,' to the Baron of Bradwardine.

'The Bailie was a man of earthly mould, after all ; a good deal of dirt and dross about him, undoubtedly, but some kindly and just feelings he had, especially where the Baron or his young mistress were concerned.' *Waverley.*

MAD TOM. One of the Earl of Glenallan's stallions. *The Antiquary.*

MADELON. Wife of La Jeunesse. *Quentin Durward.*

MADGE WILDFIRE. *See* ROBERTSON, GEORGE, and MURDOCKSON, MADGE.

MAGOR-MISSABIB. The name taken to himself by Habakkuk Mucklewrath 'because I am made a terror unto myself and unto all that are around me.' *Old Mortality.*

MAHONY, DUGALD. One of the Highland gillies who, with Evan Dhu, accompanied Edward Waverley on his expedition from Tully-Veolan to Glennaquoich. He protected Colonel Talbot after he was taken prisoner at Gladsmuir.
'He carried aye an axe on his shouther.' *Waverley.*

MAHOUND. An old Arab horse, 'with a temper as vicious as that of a fiend,' which Raoul generally rode when travelling in his wife's company. *The Betrothed.*

MAILSETTER, DAVIE. The nine-year-old son of the Mailsetters: the 'express' sent on the butcher's pony to deliver Mr. Lovel's letter at Monkbarns.
'I'm no gaun to let naebody see the letter,' sobbed the boy, 'till I gie't to Mr. Lovel, for I am a faithfu' servant o' the office—if it werena for the powny.' *The Antiquary.*

MAILSETTER, MR. The postmaster at Fairport. The state of the office was 'notorious.' 'Ye ken my gudeman likes to ride the expresses himsell . . . it's a red half-guinea to him every time he munts his mear—and I dare say he'll be in sune—or I dare to say, it's the same thing whether the gentleman gets the express this night or early next morning.' *The Antiquary.*

MAILSETTER, MRS. The postmaster's wife.

'I wad aye be obliging and neighbourly, and I'm no again your looking at the outside of a letter neither.' *The Antiquary.*

MALACHI. The young man instructed by Tom Trumbull to continue family worship, when Tom was interrupted by Alan Fairford. *Redgauntlet.*

MALAGROWTHER, SIR MUNGO, OF GIRNIGO CASTLE. An embittered hanger-on at court. When a youth he acted as 'whipping-boy' to King James, 'but when he grew too big to be whipped he had no other means of rendering himself acceptable.' 'A bitter, caustic, and backbiting humour, a malicious wit, and an envy of others more prosperous,' than himself kept him without friends or favour, and in his old age he 'was barely endured by James.' 'So deaf he can never hear good of anyone, and so wise that he can never believe it.' *The Fortunes of Nigel.*

MALCOLM, THE USURPER ('MISTICOT' or 'MISBEGOT'). Eldest son of Sybil Knockwinnock. On the death of Sir Richard Wardour, his mother's husband, he took forcible possession, but, after being defeated in the lists by Sir Richard's eldest son, he became a monk and retired to the priory. There he died soon after 'of pure despite and vexation.' His grave was unknown, and a legend ran that when it was found, the lands of Knockwinnock would be 'lost and won.' *The Antiquary.*

MALISE, EARL OF STRATHERN. An ancestor of Roland Graeme. The blood of the Seyton family sprang from 'no higher source.' *The Abbot.*

MALKIN. The Prior of St. Botolph's 'ambling jennet.' With 'grave advices and facetious jests,' the Prior lent her to Ivanhoe when he insisted on following the Black Knight. 'A beast of judgment.' *Ivanhoe.*

MALLY. One of the maid-servants at Shaws Castle. *St. Ronan's Well.*

MALVOISIN, ALBERT DE. Philip's brother: Preceptor of the establishment of Templestowe. 'Dissolute and unprincipled . . . he knew how to throw over his vices and his ambition the veil of hypocrisy. . . . Had not the arrival of the Grand Master been so unexpectedly sudden, he would have seen nothing at Templestowe which might have appeared to argue any relaxation of discipline.' *Ivanhoe.*

MALVOISIN, PHILIP DE. A Norman noble living in the neighbourhood of Cedric the Saxon: one of the challengers defeated by the Disinherited Knight in the lists at Ashby-de-la-Zouch. For his share in Prince John's conspiracy he suffered the death he had 'well deserved by many acts of falsehood, cruelty, and oppression.' *Ivanhoe.*

MANGERTON, LAIRD OF. *See* ARMSTRONG, JOHN.

MANGLEMAN, MUNGO. The surgeon at Greenock in whose mortar Mr. Archibald 'pounded for six months' of his youth. *The Heart of Midlothian.*

MANNERING FAMILY, THE.
— SIR MILES. An ancestor of Guy, renowned in the French wars.

— MANNERING & MARSHALL. The Lombard Street firm of which one of Guy Mannering's uncles was a partner.

— BISHOP MANNERING. An uncle of Guy who wished him to take orders. The arrangement of his 'venerable library' was Dominie Sampson's happy task at Woodbourne.

— SIR PAUL. The rich uncle who left Guy his fortune.

— GUY. The successful Indian colonel who 'relieved Cuddieburn and defended Chingalore and defeated the great Mahratta chief, Ram Jolli Bundleman.' To himself his career seemed one 'of difficulties, and doubts, and errors,' the circumstances which led to the death of his wife having left 'a perpetual aloes in the draught of existence.' 'His pride of arms and of ancestry, his chivalrous point of honour, his high talents, and his abstruse and mystic studies' erected a barrier between him and his daughter, while at the same time he was 'too proud to vindicate the affection and confidence' which he thought should be given 'without solicitation.' But he found it within his power to atone for the injustice he had done to Vanbeest Brown, and so reached a 'thorough understanding' with both him and Julia.

— MRS. MANNERING. Sophia Wellwood: the Colonel's wife. She

was as innocent as gay, and as gay as innocent, but she 'called her husband in her heart a tyrant until she feared him as such, and read romances until she became so enamoured of the complicated intrigues which they contain, as to assume the management of a little family novel of her own, and constitute her daughter, a girl of sixteen, the principal heroine. She delighted in petty mystery, and intrigue, and secrets, and yet trembled at the indignation which these paltry manœuvres excited in her husband's mind.'

— JULIA. Daughter of the Colonel and the object of Vanbeest Brown's affections. She was 'generous and romantic,' with 'too much of her own dear papa's disposition to be curbed in any of her humours.' Her letters to Matilda Marchmont 'throw light upon natural good sense, principle, and feelings, blemished by an imperfect education and the folly of a misjudging mother.' *Guy Mannering.*

MANSEL, LADY. Sir Edward's wife. In spite of the 'earnest prayers, tears, and entreaties' of Margaret Ramsay, the supposed page, she sent her to share Nigel's confinement, knowing that the King wanted to test him by listening unseen to their conversation. *The Fortunes of Nigel.*

MANSEL, SIR EDWARD. Lieutenant of the Tower during Nigel's confinement there. 'A punctilious old soldier and courtier.' *The Fortunes of Nigel.*

MAR, EARL OF. One of the leaders of the 1715 Rebellion. *Guy Mannering.*

MARCH, EARL OF. See DUNBAR, EARL OF.

MARCHMONT, MATILDA. A school-friend of Julia Mannering: the correspondent to whom she wrote 'six sheets a week' when staying with Mr. and Mrs. Mervyn. *Guy Mannering.*

MARCIAN. Armourer to Count Robert of Paris. *Count Robert of Paris.*

MARCK, WILLIAM DE LA. 'The Wild Boar of Ardennes.' 'The most notorious robber and murderer on all the frontiers—excommunicated by the Pope for a thousand crimes,' he made himself formidable to both the Duke of Burgundy and the Bishop of Liège with the help of supplies sent secretly by Louis. It was to his 'protection' that Louis would have consigned the Countess of Croye, but in Peronne Louis disclaimed all intercourse with him. His head became the price by which the Countess' hand should be won. *Quentin Durward.*

See also CROYE, COUNTESS HAMELINE DE.

MARESCHAL, RALPH, OF MARESCHAL WELLS. A kinsman of Ellieslaw, and a guest at the castle. He was the first to 'leap the ditch' at the meeting called to plan a Jacobite rising.

'I love this poor exiled King with all my heart,' he said, '... and I long to see some amends on the Unionist courtiers, that have bought and sold old Scotland, whose crown has been so long independent.' *The Black Dwarf.*

MARGARET OF ANJOU. Daughter of King René, and 'the dauntless widow of Henry the Sixth who, so long and in such desperate circumstances, upheld, by unyielding courage and deep policy, the sinking cause of her feeble husband.' Wearied by the 'humbler sources of solace' which her father enjoyed in his court at Aix, she tried, through her faithful follower, Seignor Philipson, to engage the aid of Charles the Bold against the 'usurper' Edward of York. But not all her promises to secure her father's abdication and his disavowal of her nephew's claim to Lorraine had power against Charles' passion for the conquest of Switzerland.

'If thou didst hoist too high a sail in prosperity, never lived there princess who defied more proudly the storms of adversity, or bore up against them with such dauntless nobility of determination.' *Anne of Geierstein.*

Note.—Scott's representation of Margaret's death is fictitious. She survived her father, and died in 1481.

MARGARET OF SCOTLAND. First wife of Louis XI: 'done to death by slanderous tongues in her husband's court.' *Quentin Durward.*

MARGERY, DAME. Eveline Berenger's nurse. Her mother, an old Saxon dame, had left the house of Baldringham with Eveline's grandmother, and from her Eveline learnt the story of Red-finger. 'Mannerly Margery,' as Dame Gillian called her, 'affected a little the character of the devotee.' *The Betrothed.*

MARKHAM. 'The most celebrated author on farriery': 'the very Alcoran of the savage tribe' at Osbaldistone Hall. *Rob Roy.*

MARKHAM. One of the gentlemen in attendance on the Earl of Sussex. *Kenilworth.*

MARMOR OF CLOCHNABEN, THE. A remote ancestor of the Geraldins. *The Antiquary.*

MARSHAL, ROBERT, OF STARRY SHAW. A backslider after marriage. 'His thriving days' were done, his wife's ill overcoming his good. *The Heart of Midlothian.*

MARSPORT, MUNGO. Prosecutor of Captain Lackland 'for coming on his lands of Marsport with hawks, lying dogs, etc.,' 'the said defender not being ane qualified person . . . not having ane ploughgate of land.' *The Heart of Midlothian.*

MARTHA. The old housekeeper at Osbaldistone Hall. She was bribed with a cup of tea to give Frank 'countenance' when he wished to spend an evening with Diana in the library. *Rob Roy.*

MARTHA. Clara Mowbray's 'immediate attendant.' *St. Ronan's Well.*

MARTHA. The name given by the Lady of Aspramonte to the Saxon Ulrica as being less 'uncouth' and 'heathenish.' *Count Robert of Paris.*

Martha, Abbess of Elcho. A kinswoman of Catharine Glover's mother. She and Father Francis 'joined in singing the same song. "Remain in the world," said they, "and thy father and thou shall be brought to trial as heretics—assume the veil, and the errors of both shall be forgiven and cancelled."' *The Fair Maid of Perth.*

Marthon. 'The traitorous waiting-woman' who accompanied the Ladies of Croye. A daughter of the tribe of Zamet and Hayraddin, she introduced them to the Countess Hameline, over whom, 'by their pretended knowledge in soothsaying and astrology,' they gained a great ascendency. Countess Isabelle said of her, 'That hypocritical Marthon often seemed to foster every seed of petty jealousy or discontent betwixt my poor kinswoman and myself, whilst she always mixed with flattery, addressed to the individual who was present, whatever could prejudice her against her absent kinswoman.' *Quentin Durward.*

Marthon. The old cook who prepared supper when Anne of Geierstein entertained Arthur Philipson in Arnheim Castle. *Anne of Geierstein.*

Martigny, Marie, Comptesse de. Mother of Frank Tyrrel by a secret marriage with the fifth Earl of Etherington, while still Lord Oakendale. *St. Ronan's Well.*

Martin. The verderer under Sir Henry Lee, a score of years older than Sir Henry, but 'as fresh as an old oak.' He was chosen to guide Charles II in his hurried flight from Woodstock Lodge, 'for no fox that ever earthed in the Chase knows the country so well for seven leagues around.' *Woodstock.*

Martin, Dame. 'The presiding matron' of Brokenburn foot dance. 'The queen of the revels,' she found Darsie Latimer 'prime at it.' She was 'a buxom dame of about thirty, her fingers loaded with many a silver ring, and three or four of gold; her ankles liberally displayed from under her numerous blue, white, and scarlet short petticoats, and attired in hose of the finest and whitest lamb's-wool, which arose from shoes of Spanish cordwain, fastened with silver buckles.' *Redgauntlet.*

Martin, Luckie. Mistress of the change-house in which Adam Woodcock was 'formally elected ... in solemn chapter' as Abbot of Unreason. *The Abbot.*

Martingale. One of Saddletree's customers who seemed likely to 'break on our hands, and lose us gude sixty pounds.' *The Heart of Midlothian.*

Martingale, Jamie. The contractor who furnished the 'naigs' for the Queensferry Diligence. *The Antiquary.*

Martival, Stephen de. One of the marshals of the field in the Passage of Arms at Ashby-de-la-Zouch. *Ivanhoe.*

Martivalle (Marti, or Martius) Galeotti. A celebrated astrologer who had long flourished at the court of Matthias Corvinus, King of Hungary, and was enticed by Louis to France. Dissatisfied with Louis' rewards, he betrayed confidences to John of Balue, and 'at once made a prisoner and a dupe' of Louis. But his 'audacious courage and readiness of wit' saved him from the King's contemplated revenge; 'for,' he predicted, 'from the moment my last groan is drawn, only twenty-four hours will remain to you for confession and penitence.' *Quentin Durward.*

MARY. A widowed daughter of the Empress Irene, who at the moment of the Emperor's death 'took a black robe from one of her own wardrobes and presented it to her mother.' *Count Robert of Paris.*

MARY, QUEEN OF SCOTS. 'The Mistress of Scottish beauty.' Her countenance seemed 'at once to combine our ideas of the majestic, the pleasing, and the brilliant, leaving us to doubt whether they express most happily the queen, the beauty, or the accomplished woman.' But the reign of this 'most illustrious—most unhappy lady' was 'such a tragedy of losses, disasters, civil dissensions, and foreign wars, that the like is not to be found in our chronicles.' 'God hath refused her the gift of hearkening to wise counsel,' one of her rebel barons urged; and again, 'the land may not brook the rule of one who cannot rule herself.' Yet for the sake of her beauty, her dignity, and her charm, 'true men' were ever ready to sacrifice all. *The Abbot.* See also MURRAY, EARL OF, *and* LINDESAY, LORD.

MASS, JOHN. The parish minister who was summoned to the Laird of Dumbiedikes' deathbed. The Laird wanted him to 'rattle ower some bit short prayer' in return for all the stipends and tiends he had paid 'ever sin the aughty-nine.' *The Heart of Midlothian.*

MASTER O' MORPHIE, THE. A patron of Gibbie Golightly. *The Antiquary.*

MASTERS, DR. Physician-in-ordinary to Queen Elizabeth. Sent by the Queen to attend the Earl of Sussex during a dangerous illness, he was refused admittance by Raleigh, and returned to court 'in high dudgeon.' Raleigh's ready tact soon removed the unfavourable effects of this from the Queen's mind. But the poor doctor 'caught cold on the river.' *Kenilworth.*

MATTHEW OF DONCASTER. 'A bowyer . . . remarkable for the great toughness and strength of the weapons which he made.' Seignor Philipson recognised his mark on the bow with which Arthur convinced the Swiss youths at Geierstein that he was no mean sportsman. *Anne of Geierstein.*

MATTIE. Bailie Nicol Jarvie's servant, 'considerate and officious.' She was a 'far-awa' cousin o' the Laird o' Limmerfield,' and was eventually promoted by the Bailie 'from her wheel by the kitchen fire to the upper end of his table.' *Rob Roy.*

Mattocks, Saunders. The sexton who helped Captain Clutterbuck and the Benedictine monk to find the 'inestimable treasure' buried in a side wall of the Abbey. *The Monastery.*

Matty. One of Mrs. Flockhart's maids. The 'limmer' went off with one of Hawley's dragoons. *Waverley.*

(*Limmer*, a woman of loose manners.)

Maugrabin. *See* Zamet and Hayraddin.

Mauleverer, Count Stephen. *See* Aldrovand, Father.

Mauleverer, Giles de. Lord of Middleham, and Prior Aymer's brother. *Ivanhoe.*

Mauley, Sir Edward. The Black Dwarf, 'born to great wealth which his parents designed should become greater by his union with a kinswoman.' He was supplanted in her affections by his treacherous friend Ellieslaw, who consigned his body 'to chains, his hand to guilt, and his soul to misery.' For Isabel Vere's sake he withheld his vengeance, and expiated his guilt by making her marriage with young Earnscliff possible. *The Black Dwarf.*

See also Vere, Letitia.

Maulstatute, Master. The Justice of the Peace before whom Julian Peveril was taken after wounding Jack Jenkins. 'Very honest in his intentions, very bounded in his talents, and rather timid in his disposition,' this legal sage shared to an unreasonable degree the popular dread of the 'Papists.' He lost all semblance of dignity and justice when he learnt Julian's parentage. *Peveril of the Peak.*

Maultext. Mr. Melchisedek. One of the preachers from whom Anthony Foster derived consolation. *Kenilworth.*

Mauthe Dog. 'A fiend or demon in the shape of a large, shaggy, black mastiff' supposed to haunt Peel Castle. *Peveril of the Peak.*

Maxwell, Mr., of Summertrees. 'Pate-in-Peril,' 'an old forty-five man,' and 'as black a Jacobite as the auld leaven can make him; but a sonsy, merry companion, that none of us think it worth while to break wi' for all his brags and his clavers.' Through Provost Crosbie's influence—Pate finding it necessary to humour him occasionally—he gave Alan Fairford a letter to Redgauntlet, and pledged his honour that Alan should suffer no 'personal illusage.' But he suggested 'a short captivity . . . till this business of the good Father B—— is safely blown over.' *Redgauntlet.*

('*Father B——,*' Buonaventure, the young Chevalier.)

Maxwell, Sawney. One of the gentlemen-ushers of the King's chamber. He had 'lang lugs.' *The Fortunes of Nigel.*

(*Lug*, ear.)

Maxwell, William. Lord Evandale, a young nobleman who fought with gallantry under Claverhouse at Drumclog, and afterwards helped Major Bellenden in the defence of Tillietudlem.

Between him and Harry Morton there was a keen rivalry. They were the final competitors for honour in the popinjay contest at the wappenschaw; they both loved Edith Bellenden; and they took opposite sides in the struggle of the Covenanters against Government. Yet each saved the other's life, and both would have welcomed a peaceful solution of the political and religious difficulties. During the years of Harry's exile Lord Evandale helped Lady Margaret and Edith Bellenden with a faithfulness and a generosity that might well have conquered Edith's youthful love. 'Never man . . . since the days of the patriarch Jacob, served sae lang and sae sair for a wife as gude Lord Evandale has dune.' *Old Mortality.*

MAYFLOWER, PHŒBE. Alice Lee's maid. 'The lightest-footed and lightest-hearted wench that ever tripped the sod in Woodstock Park,' she was faithful and capable and 'knew the world much better than her mistress.' Under Dr. Rochecliffe's and Jocelin's directions she played a part in the devices which frightened the Commissioners from the Lodge. She mistrusted and hated Joseph Tomkins, to whose wooing, 'sacred or profane, metaphysical or physical,' she listened only under compulsion, fearing that 'to offend him might endanger the security of the family.' *Woodstock.*

MEDICINE, THE MAN OF. *See* QUACKLEBEN, DR. QUENTIN.

MEIGALLOT, BARON. Owner of the drawbridge across the Tweed of which Peter of the Brig was warden. He maintained that the monks' right of free crossing had lapsed for fifty years. *The Monastery.*

MEIGALLOT, CHARLES OF. Great-great-grandfather of the Baron. In 1137 he granted a deed to Abbot Ailford giving to the ecclesiastics of St. Mary's, and to every pilgrim going there, the right to cross the bridge free of charge. *The Monastery.*

MEIKLEHOSE, ISAAC. One of the elders at Knocktarlite. He counselled caution when David Deans consulted him about the possibility of improving Duncan Knock's behaviour in church. 'He suld hae a lang-shankit spune,' he said, 'that wad sup kail wi' the de'il.' *The Heart of Midlothian.*

MEIKLEWHAM, MR. SAUNDERS. A member of the Committee of Management in 'the infant republic of St. Ronan's Well': 'the Man of Law.' He 'managed the affairs of the Squire much to the profit of one or other,' calling himself 'the friend and servant' of the Mowbray family. 'Thou art a rare counsellor in time of need, and hast as happy a manner of reconciling a man's conscience with his necessities, as might set up a score of casuists.' *St. Ronan's Well.*

MELCHIOR. The novice in whose garments the Black Priest of St. Paul's disguised Arthur Philipson when sending him from La Ferette to meet the Swiss embassy. Melchior attended the Black Priest and Seignor Philipson during their journey down the banks of the Rhine. *Anne of Geierstein.*

MELVILLE, CAPTAIN. The name assumed by Harry Morton in Holland, where on various occasions his services were 'distinguished by his Royal Highness.' *Old Mortality.*

MELVILLE, MAJOR WILLIAM. The laird of Cairnvreckan : one of 'the most respectable gentlemen, and best friends of government north of the Forth.'
'He was vigilant by profession, and cautious from experience, had met with much evil in the world, and therefore, though himself an upright magistrate and an honourable man, his opinions of others were always strict, and sometimes unjustly severe.' *Waverley.*

MELVILLE, SIR ROBERT. The noble who accompanied Lord Lindesay and Lord Ruthven to Lochleven Castle 'as a mediator.' *The Abbot.*

MENELAUS. Ralph Fisher's uncle. *The Abbot.*

MENGS, IAN. Landlord of the 'Golden Fleece,' the inn to which the Black Priest of St. Paul's recommended Seignor Philipson after their journey down the banks of the Rhine. 'This man's brow was like a tragic volume, in which you were as unlikely to find anything of jest or amusement as in a hermit's breviary. His answers were short, sudden, and repulsive, and the air and manner with which they were delivered was as surly as their tenor.' To Philipson, before the arrival of the Black Priest, he was even more 'coarse and insolent' than to his ordinary guests, but under the Priest's influence his manners changed, and he himself conducted his guest to the bedroom from which Philipson was taken during the night to stand his trial before the Judges of the Vehmgericht. *Anne of Geierstein.*

MENTEITH, EARL OF. A kinsman and trusted friend of Montrose. They travelled together, Montrose as Menteith's attendant, from the King to the gathering of Highlanders at Darnlinvarach, where Montrose's commission was read and the royal standard unfurled. Menteith took an active part in the campaign until disabled by Allan McAulay's frenzied attack after the battle of Inverlochy.
'There was conspicuous' in him 'a flash of the generous, romantic, disinterested chivalry of the old heroic times.' *A Legend of Montrose.*

MENZIES, CHRISTIAN. *See* DEANS, CHRISTIAN.

MERCER, MAJOR. An officer from whom Adam Hartley heard some particulars concerning Madame Montreville's life : 'a great deal of a gossip.' *The Surgeon's Daughter.*

MEREDITH. A Welshman who brought tidings to Sir John de Walton on Palm Sunday that the Earl of Pembroke had been defeated by Bruce at Loudon Hill, thereby placing Sir John 'at liberty to take measures for the safety of the Lady of Berkeley' by surrendering the castle. *Castle Dangerous.*

Note.—The battle of Loudon Hill was fought on 10th May, 1307. Palm Sunday fell in that year on 19th March.

MEREDITH, MR. One of the 'faithful friends' who met Father Buonaventure at Joe Crackenthorp's inn: a Welsh squire. 'When was Wales last in the race of honour?' *Redgauntlet.*

MEREDITH, MR. MICHAEL. A member of the Committee of Management in 'the infant republic of St. Ronan's Well': 'the Man of Mirth.' He was 'for the present obliged to absent himself,' having 'passed some jest upon Captain MacTurk which cut . . . to the quick.' *St. Ronan's Well.*

MERRILIES, MEG. 'A kind o' queen amang the gipsies.' Dominie Sampson described her as 'Beelzebub's post-mistress,' 'a harlot, thief, witch, and gipsy.' 'She was full six feet high,' 'her dark elf-locks shot out like the snakes of the gorgon,' 'while her eye had a wild roll that indicated something like real or affected insanity.'

'It is to rebuild the auld house—it is to lay the corner-stone—and did I not warn him?—I tell'd him I was born to do it, if my father's head had been the stepping-stane, let alane his. I was doomed—still I kept my purpose in the cage and in the stocks;—I was banished—I kept it in an unco' land;—I was scourged—I was branded—My resolution lay deeper than scourge or red iron could reach—and now the hour is come.' *Guy Mannering.*

MERTOUN, BASIL. The 'retired and gloomy' stranger whose 'secret seemed impenetrable' to the folks of Jarlshof. As young Vaughan, he had been Ulla Troil's lover. After her father's tragic death he fled to Hispaniola, and in time 'want came to aid despair and a troubled conscience.' He became a corsair, and trained his son Clement in the same 'desperate trade.' Hearing that Clement had been marooned by a rebellious crew, he was seized with remorse, and resolved 'to do penance in the wild islands of Zetland' for the rest of his life. He took his son Mordaunt with him as 'the living memorial' of his misery and guilt, and pondered over both till reason often 'trembled on her throne.' *The Pirate.*

MERTOUN, MORDAUNT. Son of Basil Mertoun (or Vaughan) and Louisa Gonzago. 'Of a bold, active, and daring character,' he excelled in the dangerous exploits of the islanders, and felt, when struggling with the elements, 'that the exertion necessary to subdue them is in itself a kind of elevating triumph.' In 'softer and lighter amusement,' too, 'no youth added more spirit to the dance or glee to the revel.' His mind was full of 'generous and high feeling,' and remained unchanged alike under his father's 'hasty churlishness,' Magnus Troil's unmerited coldness, and Cleveland's 'persevering enmity.' *The Pirate.*

MERVYN. *See* GWENWYN.

MERVYN, ARTHUR. A college friend of Guy Mannering, nicknamed 'Downright Dunstable.' Julia stayed for a time in his home in Westmoreland while her father went to Scotland.
'He is fat and good-natured, gifted with strong, shrewd sense and some powers of humour.' *Guy Mannering.*

MERVYN, MRS. Wife of Arthur Mervyn, Esq., 'Ladylike and housewifely.' *Guy Mannering.*

MICHAEL AGELASTES. *See* AGELASTES.

MICHAEL CANTACUZENE. Grand Sewer to the Emperor Alexius Comnenus. He 'arranged the strangers with his gold wand' at the banquet given to Count Robert and Brenhilda. *Count Robert of Paris.*

MICHAEL WING-THE-WIND. Adam Woodcock's friend in Holyrood Palace : 'a favourite old domestic who was admitted nearer to the Regent's person and privacy than many whose posts were more ostensible.' *The Abbot.*

MIDDLEBURGH, MR. An Edinburgh magistrate : 'acute, patient, and upright . . . very happily qualified to support the respectability of the office which he held.' When Mr. Sharpitlaw came to the court with a report of his expedition to Muschat's Cairn, 'Mr. Middleburgh had just taken his seat, and was debating in an animated manner, with one of his colleagues, the doubtful chances of a game at golf which they had played the day before.' *The Heart of Midlothian.*

MIDDLEHAM, HILDA OF. Prior Aymer's 'respected grandmother.' *Ivanhoe.*

MIDDLEHAM, ULFGAR, LORD OF. The Saxon noble dispossessed by Giles de Mauleverer. *Ivanhoe.*

MIDDLEMAS, LUCKIE. The mistress of an inn, to the Highlander on whose signboard Callum Beg likened Edward Waverley. *Waverley.*
(*Luckie*, a designation given to an elderly woman.)

MIDDLEMAS, MAUSE. The maiden name of Mause Headrigg. *Old Mortality.*
See also AUNTIE MEG.

MIDDLEMAS, RICHARD. Son of Zilia de Monçada and Richard Tresham. Left as an infant to the guardianship of Dr. Gray and Mr. Lawford, he was trained to be a doctor, but Nurse Jamieson had filled his mind with 'the most ambitious visions,' and 'his soul' revolted from 'the obscure lot' this seemed to involve. Embittered by the continued neglect of his parents, he pushed his way in India with an 'obstinacy of selfishness' which banished him from official life and led him into the path of involved intrigue. He planned to secure his own advance in Tippoo Sahib's favour by the sacrifice of Menie Gray, but was foiled by Adam Hartley, betrayed by his confederate Madame Montreville, and done to death by Hyder Ali. *The Surgeon's Daughter.*

MIDDLETON, GAULTIER OF. One of Front-de-Bœuf's companions-at-arms. Locksley's outlaws tied him to an oak tree, and compelled him to 'sing a mass while they were rifling his mails and his wallets.' *Ivanhoe.*

MIDDLETON, RALPH. *See* WETHERAL, STEPHEN.

MILAN, GALEASSE, DUKE OF. A 'wily Italian' whose aid Seignor Philipson had tried in vain to secure for Margaret of Anjou before approaching Charles the Bold. *Anne of Geierstein.*

MILLER, HOB. *See* WENLOCK.

MILLER, RAFF. One of Dorcas' sweethearts. *Redgauntlet.*

MILLER, THE. One of Locksley's men. He met his match in quarter-staff play when Gurth was defending his own and his master's gold. *Ivanhoe.*

MIMES, EMPEROR OF. 'King of Caperers, and Grand Duke of the Dark Hours': the titles assumed by the Duke of Rothesay as head of the band of Shrove Tuesday revellers who handled Oliver Proudfute roughly. *The Fair Maid of Perth.*

MINCING, MRS. Julia Mannering's maid. *Guy Mannering.*

MIRIAM. Daughter of the celebrated doctor Rabbi Manasses of Byzantium. She loved Rebecca as her own child, and made her skilful in the art of healing. But she fell a 'sacrifice to the fanaticism of the times.' 'Her body was burnt at a stake, and her ashes were scattered to the four winds.' *Ivanhoe.*

MIRTH, THE MAN OF. *See* MEREDITH, MR.

MIST, CHILDREN OF THE. The Mac-Eaghs, 'a particular race' of the MacGregors, so called 'from their houseless state and their incessantly wandering among the mountains and glens.' A deadly feud existed between them and the McAulays on account of their cruel murder of the McAulays' maternal uncle. 'A fierce and hardy people, with all the irritability, and wild and vengeful passions, proper to men who have never known the restraint of civilised society.' *A Legend of Montrose.*

MISTICOT. *See* MALCOLM THE USURPER.

MITFORD, COLONEL DICK. An old friend of Sir Geoffrey Peveril. The young lady whom Sir Geoffrey found under his wife's care when he returned from prison was said by Lady Peveril to be the Colonel's daughter. *Peveril of the Peak.*

MIXIT, DR. A doctor of medicine: one of the Sunday guests of Jonathan Brown. *Rob Roy.*

MOFFAT, MABEL. The elderly woman who served the Laird of the Solway Lochs in Brokenburn. With Cristal Nixon she attended Lilias Redgauntlet to the country dance at which Darsie Latimer played the fiddle instead of Rob the Rambler. 'Her looks were singularly forbidding.' *Redgauntlet.*

MONASTRAS. Captain of a tribe of Syrians who had attached themselves to Alexius Comnenus during his campaign against Jezdegerd. *Count Robert of Paris.*

MONÇADA, MATTHIAS DE. Zilia's father. Enraged by her flight with Tresham he informed the Government of Tresham's correspondence with Charles Edward Stewart, and secured a warrant for their arrest on high treason. Tresham was warned, and on arriving at Dr. Gray's house M. de Monçada secured Zilia alone. He obliged her to leave her child to the guardianship of Dr. Gray and Mr. Lawford, and while supplying money as need arose he rejected all appeals for recognition from Dr. Gray and Richard Middlemas alike. 'A dour chield.' *The Surgeon's Daughter.*

MONÇADA, ZILIA DE. *See* WITHERINGTON, MRS.

MONCRIEFF OF TIPPERMALLOCH. A 'popish' laird present at the Kinross fair. 'He would be sure to make a break-out,' Hob Anster urged, 'if the officers meddled with the auld popish witch-wife, who was sae weel friended.' *The Abbot.*

MONIPLIES, MUNGO. 'The flesher at the West Port' of Edinburgh: Richie's father. *The Fortunes of Nigel.*

MONIPLIES, RICHIE. Lord Nigel Glenvarloch's serving-man : 'of the old and honourable house of Castle Collop, weel kend at the West Port of Edinburgh.' Having a conceited consciousness of superior wisdom,' he did not hesitate to lecture his master when he thought him going astray. But he remained faithful and devoted, and with Martha Trapbois' help contrived a successful issue out of Nigel's financial misfortunes. 'He is truly honest, and has a heart and hand that make amends for some folly.' *The Fortunes of Nigel.*

MONKBARNS, LAIRD OF. *See* OLDBUCK, JONATHAN.

MONKBARNS, PROVOST. The Antiquary's father. In 1745, while Sir Anthony Wardour talked and hesitated, the sturdy provost ' sallied from his ancient burgh, heading a body of whig-burghers, and seized at once, in the name of George II, upon the Castle of Knockwinnock, and on the four carriage-horses, and person of the proprietor.' *The Antiquary.*

MONMOUTH, DUKE OF. Commander of the forces sent against the Covenanters after their success at Drumclog. 'The manly beauty of Monmouth's face was occasionally rendered less striking by an air of vacillation and uncertainty which seemed to imply hesitation and doubt at moments when decisive resolution was most necessary.' *Old Mortality.*

MONNA PAULA. *See* PAULINE, MADEMOISELLE.

MONTEMARE, ADELAIDE DE. The woman who taught Brian de Bois-Guilbert 'cruelty.' 'Her name was known wherever deeds of arms were done,' and when he returned with his 'dear-bought honours' and found her wedded to a Gascon squire, he revenged himself bitterly for her broken faith. *Ivanhoe.*

MONTENAY, SIR PHILIP DE. An old knight who acted as seneschal of Douglas Castle. Kept waiting at the gate in the 'raw air of a wet spring evening,' when he returned from the hunting party with Sir

John de Walton, he 'peevishly' blamed Sir Aymer de Valence for extreme martial punctiliousness. *Castle Dangerous.*

MONT-FITCHET, CONRADE. A Brother of the Order of the Temple : the ' dear companion ' of the Grand Master's ' battles and toils.' To his ear alone could the Master confide his ' sorrows.' He counselled caution in the reformation of the Order. *Ivanhoe.*

MONTGOMERY. One of those Covenanters who, once ' King James' greatest foes,' were on his side after the Revolution. *Old Mortality.*

MONTGOMERY, CAPTAIN. An officer in the Scots Guards of France, under whom Bothwell served. *Old Mortality.*

MONTHERMER, GUY DE. ' An elderly and stately knight ' sent by King Henry to summon Eveline Berenger ' to admit the King's forces into her castle and to deliver up the body of a false traitor, called Damian de Lacy.' *The Betrothed.*

MONT-JOIE. The French herald who announced Louis' approaching visit to Charles the Bold in Peronne. *Quentin Durward.*

MONTREVILLE, MADAME ADELA. A ' Semiramis-looking person ' who raised Richard Middlemas from an ' abyss of misery ' to share her wealth and affections. Her ' bolder genius ' then conceived the ' abominable plan ' concerning Menie Gray. Attended by Richard in the disguise of a black servant, Sadoc, she met Menie in Madras and conveyed her to Bangalore, there to be bartered to Tippoo Sahib in their ' traffic for greatness.' But she saw that the ' double-dyed villain ' intended to betray Tippoo, ' in policy alike and in love,' and rather than be a mere tool of his ambition, she gave Hyder Ali warning of his schemes. *The Surgeon's Daughter.*

MONTROSE, JAMES GRAHAME, EARL OF. (1) ' The Great Marquis.' Though at first ' violently attached to the Covenant,' he eventually espoused the King's cause, and in 1644, during General Leslie's absence in England, he raised the royal standard in Scotland. Partly through his own personal influence, and partly through their common animosity against the Marquis of Argyle, he rallied the Highland clans around him, and with the further aid of an Irish contingent under Colkitto, he gained a series of brilliant successes.

(2) ' The bravest, the most loyal, the most heroic spirit among our Scottish nobility.' ' His soul looked through his eyes with all the energy and fire of genius.' (1) *Old Mortality.* (2) *A Legend of Montrose.*

MONTSERRAT, CONRADE, MARQUIS OF. (1) A ' powerful and wily ' Italian baron who, in pursuit of his own personal ambitions, wished to dissolve the league of European princes. By taunts and innuendoes he roused Leopold of Austria to plant his banner on St. George's Mount beside the English standard ; he stole the English banner when Kenneth of Scotland had been seduced from his post by Nectabanus; detected by Roswal's 'noble instinct,' he maintained his innocence 'in despite . . . of man and brute, king or dog'; but he was wounded by Kenneth in the trial by combat, and finally destroyed by his friend the Grand Master of the Templars, even a 'worse traitor' than he.

(2) A friend of Bois-Guilbert in Palestine. Bois-Guilbert tried to persuade Rebecca that they should together join Conrade—'a friend free as myself from the doting scruples which fetter our free-born reason.' (1) *The Talisman.* (2) *Ivanhoe.*

Note.—Scott's account of Conrade's death is fictitious.

MOONSHINE, SAUNDERS. A zealous elder in Mr. Bide-the-Bent's church when on shore, and when on board his brig 'as bold a smuggler as ever ran out a sliding bowsprit to the winds that blow betwixt Campvere and the east coast of Scotland.' He promised to Mr. Bide-the-Bent that Lucy Ashton's letter should be safely conveyed to the Master of Ravenswood. *The Bride of Lammermoor.*

MOONSHINE, TOM. One of Frank Levitt's friends. Frank proposed to put Jeanie Deans on board Tom's lugger, and 'keep her out of the way three or four weeks.' *The Heart of Midlothian.*

MOORE, THOMAS, MERCHANT. Clerk of the jury which tried Effie Deans. *The Heart of Midlothian.*

MOORKOFF. The horse on which Harry Morton rode from Widow Maclure's to Glasgow in order to get Wittenbold's support against Basil Olifant. *Old Mortality.*

MORA. *See* SADHU SING.

MORAYS. One of the Highland clans which joined the young Chevalier. With them went the Macbeths, their 'subjects.' *Waverley.*

MORDAUNT. Secretary to Margaret of Anjou. *Anne of Geierstein.*

MORGAN. One of Gwenwyn's most celebrated soldiers, 'distinguished for strength, courage, and ferocity.' He disapproved of the proposed marriage with Eveline Berenger. *The Betrothed.*

MORNAY. The Seneschal who attended Louis to his apartments in Peronne Castle. *Quentin Durward.*

MOROLT, DENNIS. Sir Raymond Berenger's favourite squire. 'His was not the casuistry which could release his master from the fetters with which his unwary confidence had bound him.' He could but plead to be allowed to share his rashness: 'the poor esquire has no business to be thought wiser than his master.' When he saw Sir Raymond struck down by Gwenwyn, 'his own force seemed by sympathy to abandon him.' *The Betrothed.*

MORRIS. A fellow-traveller with Frank Osbaldistone on his way to Northumberland, and along with Frank and 'Mr. Campbell' one of Jonathan Brown's Sunday guests. He accused Frank of stealing his portmanteau, but did not dare to mention Rob Roy. Later, he was used by Rashleigh Osbaldistone to decoy Rob Roy, and for this paid the penalty with his life. By Helen MacGregor's orders, he was drowned like a dog. 'A twa-leggit creature wi' a goose's nead and a hen's heart.' *Rob Roy.*

MORRIS. One of the Earl of Derby's servants. *Peveril of the Peak.*

MORRISON, HUGH. The drover into whose keeping Robin McCombich gave his dirk, in order to allay his aunt's fears. By pretending that he had enlisted, Robin regained possession of it, in order to work his revenge on Harry Wakefield. *The Two Drovers.*

MORTAR. See PESTLE.

MORTCLOKE, MR. The undertaker at Mistress Bertram's funeral. He distributed 'among the pallbearers little cards, assigning their respective situations in attendance upon the coffin,' but, 'however skilful a master of these lugubrious ceremonies, did not escape giving some offence.' *Guy Mannering.*

MORTEMAR, ALBERICK OF. See THEODORICK.

MORTON, EARL OF. See DOUGLAS, JAMES.

MORTON, MR. The pastor of Cairnvreckan. 'I have never been able to discover which he belonged to, the evangelical, or the moderate party in the Kirk!' Owing to the 'mixture of faith and practice in his doctrine,' 'his memory has formed a sort of era in the annals of Cairnvreckan.' *Waverley.*

MORTON, COLONEL SILAS. Harry's father: 'the famous old roundhead, cool, resolute, soldierly and inflexible in his cursed principles.' Harry 'idolized' his memory. *Old Mortality.*

MORTON, HENRY (or HARRY). Son of Silas Morton and nephew of old Milnwood: 'a lad of fire, zeal, and education.' His friendship with Major Bellenden taught him 'that goodness and worth were not limited to those of any single form of religious observance,' and he condemned 'each party as its excesses fell under his eyes.' But the treatment meted out to him after he gave food and shelter to his father's old friend Balfour of Burley roused him to resist the authority that 'tyrannically' invaded his 'chartered rights as a freeman.' He threw in his lot with the Covenanters and tried to introduce greater moderation into their ranks. In the face of danger and unpopularity, he remained bold and determined, relinquishing his efforts only when captured and exiled. *Old Mortality.*

See also MELVILLE, CAPTAIN.

MORTON, MR., OF MILNWOOD. The uncle by whom Harry was brought up: 'an infirm, hypochondriac old man, who never meddles with politics, and loves his money-bags and bonds better than anything else in the world.' His ruling passion was strong even in death, his last words being 'something we cou'dna mak out, about a dipped candle being gude eneugh to see to dee wi.' *Old Mortality.*

(A *dipped candle* was one of easy, home make.)

MORTSHEUGH, JOHNNIE. Sexton of the Hermitage churchyard, where Alice Gray was buried. In his youth he had been trumpeter at Ravenswood Castle, but for the family he had neither gratitude nor regret. 'Me, that's an auld man, living in yon miserable cabin, that's fitter for the dead than the quick, and killed wi' rheumatise, and John Smith in my dainty bit mailing, and his window glazen, and a' because Ravenswood guided his gear like a fule!' *The Bride of Lammermoor.*
(*Mailing*, a farm.)

MOTHER BLOOD. The name given by Frank Levitt to Meg Murdockson. *The Heart of Midlothian.*

MOTHER REDCAP. A woman of like occupation to Dame Suddlechop. She dealt 'in comforting young creatures' and 'may do very well for skippers' wives, chandlers' daughters, and such like.' *The Fortunes of Nigel.*

MOUAT, MR., OF THE CRAMES. The seller of blue bonnets 'of the Prince's pattern.' *Waverley.*

MOWBRAY FAMILY, THE. *St. Ronan's Well.*

— SIR REGINALD. A seventeenth-century representative of the Mowbrays of St. Ronan's, 'at one time a very powerful family . . . allied to and friends of the house of Douglas.' He distinguished himself by an 'obstinate defence of the castle against the arms of Cromwell.'

— LAWRENCE. Laird of St. Ronan's about the middle of the eighteenth century. In his day the decay of the family began.

— MR. MOWBRAY. Father of John and Clara. He 'thought of nothing but his sports,' and knew of Clara's romantic meetings with Frank Tyrrel only after their affections were deeply engaged. His interposition drove the lovers to the use of Valentine Bulmer as intermediary, this with dire results to all.

— JOHN. Laird of St. Ronan's, and leader of Sir Bingo Binks' set at the Spa. An inmate rather of the hotel than of his own castle, he courted the 'inconstant jade, Fortune,' hoping always by gambling and betting to retrieve the decayed fortunes of his family. But he wanted 'both judgment and temper,' and had no skill with which to meet the subtler schemes of Lord Etherington. 'He loved his sister as much as he was capable of loving anything but himself,' yet he treated her as a mere stake in his game, gave her no real opportunity of justifying herself against light gossip, and drove her from him by his unreasonable fear of 'dishonour.'

— CLARA. John's sister. Unwittingly married as a girl to Valentine Bulmer at the moment when romantic happiness seemed within her reach, she grew morbid with years of 'grief and solitude.' She lived in a whimsical alternation of levity and sadness, for John 'has taught me to tremble at his frown,' she confessed to Frank Tyrrel, ' . . . . and I try to go down amongst them yonder, and to endure their folly, and, all things considered, I do carry on the farce of life wonderfully well.' When she saw herself the subject of John's 'plots and schemes' with Lord Etherington she made unavailing appeals to his better self, but was driven to death by the frenzy which demanded that at all costs her supposed 'dishonour' should be *hid*.

— REGINALD SCROGIE. Originally Ronald Scrogie : maternal uncle of the fifth Earl of Etherington and father of Peregrine Touchwood. He disinherited his son, who 'undutifully laughed' at his dislike of 'the vulgar name of Scrogie.' He settled his estate on his grand-nephew, on condition that before attaining the age of twenty-five complete the heir should 'take . . . in holy wedlock, a young lady of good fame of the name of Mowbray, and by preference of the house of St. Ronan's.' *St. Ronan's Well*.

MOYLE, COLONEL. Commander of a regiment of infantry quartered in the Canongate on the night of the Porteous Riot. By securing possession of the Netherbow Port the rioters prevented interference from the troops. *The Heart of Midlothian*.

MUCKLEBACKIT, ELSPETH (ELSPETH CHEYNE). Mother of Saunders : a confidential servant of the Countess of Glenallan. Hating what her mistress hated, she suggested the lie by which the Countess ruined her son's life. For twenty years she kept silence : 'none shall say that I betrayed my mistress, though it were to save my soul !' *The Antiquary*.

MUCKLEBACKIT, JENNY. One of Maggie's daughters. 'A nondescript animal.' *The Antiquary*.

MUCKLEBACKIT, MAGGIE. The Antiquary's fish-wife : wife of Saunders, and absolute mistress of the family.

'Show me a word my Saunders daur speak, or a turn he daur do about the house, without it be just to tak his meat, and his drink, and his diversion, like ony o' the weans.' *The Antiquary*.

MUCKLEBACKIT, PATIE. Saunders' youngest and favourite child. 'Ye'll be a bra' fallow,' his father said to him, 'an ye be spared, Patie—but ye'll never be—never can be—what he was to me !' *The Antiquary*.

MUCKLEBACKIT, SAUNDERS. Son of Elspeth and husband of Maggie. The ill-fortune of the family seemed to reach its climax when Steenie was drowned before his eyes.

'There is a curse either on me or on this auld black bitch of a boat, that I have hauled up high and dry and patched and clouted sae mony years, that she might drown my poor Steenie at the end of them, an' be d—d to her !' *The Antiquary*.

MUCKLEBACKIT, SIMON. Elspeth's husband, 'an unco' bit beneath hersell.' *The Antiquary*.

MUCKLEBACKIT, STEENIE. Eldest son of Saunders and Maggie, drowned before his father's eyes.

'But, O dear, my poor Steenie, the pride o' my very heart, that was sae handsome and comely, and a help to his family, and a comfort to us a', and a pleasure to a' that lookit on him!—O my bairn, my bairn, my bairn! what for is thou lying there, and eh! what for am I left to greet for ye!' *The Antiquary.*

(*To greet*, to weep.)

MUCKLEWHAME, PROVOST. A Fairport provost who ' chose to assume the privileges of gentlemen,' and challenged the town clerk. *The Antiquary.*

MUCKLEWRATH, HABAKKUK. An insane preacher ' whom the enemy have long detained in captivity in forts and castles, until his understanding hath departed from him. . . . Nevertheless, our violent brethren will have it that he speaketh of the spirit, and that they fructify by his pouring forth.' His violent invectives did much to lessen Harry Morton's influence and to foster the dissensions that proved so disastrous at Bothwell Bridge. He died a violent death in the hut at Drumshinnel, denouncing Claverhouse with his last breath. *Old Mortality.*

See also MAGOR, MISSABIB.

MUCKLEWRATH, JOHN. The blacksmith of Cairnvreckan: a professor of religion to such an extent that ' he would drive a nail for no man on the Sabbath, or kirk-fast, unless it were in a case of absolute necessity, for which he always charged sixpence each shoe.' *Waverley.*

MUCKLEWRATH, MRS. Wife of John: an ' exulting Bacchante ' with Jacobite leanings. *Waverley.*

MUGGLETON, OBADIAH. One of Captain Bangtext's men. *The Heart of Midlothian.*

MUIRHEAD, JACK. 'The breaker' who failed to bring the spaniel Juno under command. *The Antiquary.*

MULTON, SIR THOMAS. *See* LEICESTER, EARL OF (p. 151), *and* BOHUN, HENRY.

MULTON, RALPH DE. The son whom Sir Thomas ' left training his little Galloway nag on the banks of the Irthing.' Thoughts of him softened the stout English baron's heart as he delivered sentence of instant death to Sir Kenneth. *The Talisman.*

MULTON, THOMAS DE. Lord of Gilsland or Lord de Vaux: a faithful baron from Cumberland who, during King Richard's illness, ' dared alone to come between the dragon and his wrath, and quietly but firmly maintained a control which no other dared assume over the dangerous invalid.' ' His love and devotion to the King was like the vivid affection of the old English mastiff to his master, leaving him churlish and inaccessible to all others, even towards those to whom he was indifferent, and rough and dangerous to any against whom he entertained a prejudice.' But his ' nobleness of disposition ' overcame his national prejudice against Kenneth of Scotland. *The Talisman.*

MUMBLAZEN, MASTER MICHAEL. An old bachelor related to the House of Robsart, who had honoured Lidcote Hall with his residence for twenty years. With a ' profound learning' of heraldry and genealogy, he combined sagacity, brevity, and discretion concerning the modern world. He supplied the means which enabled Edmund Tressilian to present Sir Hugh Robsart's suit at court. *Kenilworth.*

MUMPS, TIB. The landlady of the Cumberland alehouse in which Vanbeest Brown and Dandy Dinmont met for the first time.

'Tib's no muckle to lippen to neither, and I would advise ye on no account to stay in the house a' nicht.' *Guy Mannering.*

MURDIESON, MEG. The 'ill-faur'd cuttie,' who was going to be married to Cuddie Headrigg's successor at Tillietudlem. *Old Mortality.*

(*Cuttie*, a worthless girl.)

MURDOCH. The party to whom a disputed watch was awarded by Fergus MacIvor after Gladsmuir. The disappointed party consoled himself by observing : ' She (*i.e.* the watch, which he took for a living animal) died the very night Vich Ian Vohr gave her to Murdoch.' *Waverley.*

MURDOCKSON, DONALD. Meg's husband, described on his gravestone in Willingham churchyard as ' a sincere Christian, a brave soldier, and a faithful servant ' to the Rev. Robert Staunton. *The Heart of Midlothian.*

MURDOCKSON, MADGE. ' Madge Wildfire ' : Meg's daughter : ' a beautiful but very giddy girl ' whose mind was ' totally alienated ' by George Staunton's treatment. ' Far past reasonable folks' motives,' she was the sport of every accidental suggestion, yet through all her mixed ramblings and freakish outbursts she retained a vague feeling that she had fallen on evil days. *The Heart of Midlothian.*

MURDOCKSON, MEG. Donald Murdockson's wife : George Staunton's foster - mother. After Madge's ' misfortune,' mother and daughter fell into disgrace and were driven from Willingham. In Edinburgh they came across Staunton, then living under the name of George Robertson. While in prison with Wilson, he put Effie Deans in their care, but Meg, who lived only to revenge her daughter's wrong, secretly disposed of Effie's child to Annaple Bailzou, and later tried to intercept Jeanie on her journey to London. She died at the hangman's hands, ' a bluidy-fingered thief and murderess.' *The Heart of Midlothian.*

MURRAY, EARL OF. (1) Lord James Stewart : Queen Mary's halfbrother. Though delayed in the west too long to prevent bloodshed between Sir John Foster and the Community of St. Mary's, he was able, on his arrival with Morton, to adjust the conflicting interests and prevent an open rupture with England. The ' coxcomb ' Sir Piercie Shafton was banished, and St. Mary's was left ' provisionally in no worse situation than before.'

' Brave among the bravest, fair in presence and in favour, skilful to manage the most intricate affairs, to attach to himself those who were doubtful, to stun and overwhelm, by the suddenness and intrepidity of his enterprises, those who were resolute in resistance, he attained, and as to personal merit certainly deserved, the highest place in the kingdom.'

(2) Regent in room of his nephew, the infant James VI. He led the army which defeated Queen Mary at Langside after her escape from Lochleven Castle.

'Men shall say, when they read my story, that if it were my cruel hap to rise to power by the dethronement of a sister, I employed it, when gained, for the benefit of the commonweal.' (1) *The Monastery.* (2) *The Abbot.*

MURRAY, MISS NICKIE. The 'patroness' of the Edinburgh balls to which Darsie Latimer 'sometimes made his way.' *Redgauntlet.*

MURRAYS, THE. One of the clans 'peculiarly zealous in the royal cause.' *A Legend of Montrose.*

MUSCHAT, NICHOL. 'A debauched and profligate wretch' who planned with 'another brutal libertine and gambler,' Campbell of Burnbank, to destroy his wife's character. Having failed in this, and also in an attempt to poison her, he cut her throat in the King's Park. The spot was marked by a cairn, and was long supposed to be haunted. It was there Jeanie Deans met Robertson at midnight. *The Heart of Midlothian.*

MUSGRAVE, MRS. One of Justice Inglewood's neighbours. *Rob Roy.*

MUSGRAVE, SIR MILES. A gentleman 'of name and quality' from the north of England. He attended the Highland gathering at Darnlinvarach, and afterwards took part in Montrose's campaign. *A Legend of Montrose.*

MUSTARD AND PEPPER. The generic names of Dandy Dinmont's breed of terriers.

'There's auld Pepper and auld Mustard, and young Pepper and young Mustard, and little Pepper and little Mustard.' *Guy Mannering.*

MYRBEAU, SIRE DE. One of the four nobles deputed by the Estates of Burgundy to inform Charles the Bold that they opposed 'new imposts and exactions ... for the raising of additional bands of hired soldiers.' *Anne of Geierstein.*

MYSIE. Lady Bellenden's 'principal female attendant.' *Old Mortality.*

MYSIE. The solitary female domestic at the Wolf's Crag. *The Bride of Lammermoor.*

MYSIE OF THE MILL. See HAPPER, MYSIE.

N

NAEMMO, YOUNG. One of the counsel suggested by Saddletree for Effie Deans' defence, but rejected by her father as 'naething at a'.' *The Heart of Midlothian.*

NANTZ. One of Dirk Hatteraick's crew. *Guy Mannering.*

NARSES. A slave at the court of Alexius Comnenus. From him Achilles Tatius heard that 'a large sum of gold had been abandoned' to Bohemond of Tarentum. *Count Robert of Paris.*

NATHAN, BEN ISRAEL. A Rabbi with whom Isaac stayed for a night when overcome by fatigue on his way to Templestowe. He received 'his suffering countryman with that kindness which the law prescribed, and which the Jews practised to each other.' *Ivanhoe.*

NATHAN, BEN SAMUEL. A rich Rabbi whom two of Higg's brethren served. *Ivanhoe.*

NEAL. A gentleman in attendance on the Marquis of Argyle when he received Dalgetty at Inverary Castle. *A Legend of Montrose.*

NECTABANUS and GUENEVRA. The two dwarfs presented to Queen Berengaria by the dethroned Queen of Jerusalem. 'As deformed and as crazy . . . as any queen could have desired,' they were the instruments of Queen Berengaria's idle amusements. They tested Sir Kenneth's nerves by their fantastic appearance in the chapel at Engaddi; Nectabanus was afterwards the bearer of the message which enticed Kenneth from his guardianship of the English banner. Falling into disfavour, the dwarfs were presented to Saladin, and as a member of the Sultan's retinue at the trial by combat Nectabanus witnessed the treachery of the Grand Master of the Templars to Conrade of Montserrat. *The Talisman.*

NEEDHAM, JACK. A highwayman: a 'Beggar's Opera' hero. *Rob Roy.*

NEIPPERG, LAWRENZ. The Blue Cavalier who distinguished himself by his 'air of authority' at the secret rendezvous of the Bâlese youths with Rudolph of Donnerhugel, near Graffs-lust. He justified the execution of von Hagenbach in La Ferette. *Anne of Geierstein.*

See also VAUDEMONT, FERRAND DE.

NELL. One of the servants who ran from Martindale Castle to tell Lance Outram of Sir Geoffrey's and Julian's arrest. *Peveril of the Peak.*

NELLY. One of Mrs. Dinmont's maids. *Guy Mannering.*

NELLY, DAME. *See* CHRISTIE, DAME NELLY.

NEPTUNE. One of John Davies' dogs. *Redgauntlet.*

NETHERSTANE, EDIE. The miller at Grindleburn with whom Triptolemus Yellowley used to quarrel over the grinding of his corn. 'And now,' Barbara urged in Zetland, ' naething less will serve you than to bring in the very same fashery on a wheen puir bodies, that big ilk ane a mill for themselves, sic as it is ? ' *The Pirate.*

(*Fashery*, trouble. *Wheen*, a number. *Big*, build.)

NETHERSTANES, SANDIE. The miller. *The Antiquary.*

NEVILLE, EDWARD GERALDIN. Younger son of the Countess of Glenallan, and inheritor of his father's estate in Yorkshire. On the night of Eveline Neville's death he carried off her child with the help of Teresa d'Acunha, and brought him up as his own natural son. *The Antiquary.*

Neville, Eveline. 'Daughter of a cousin-german and intimate friend' of the Countess of Glenallan's husband. She was brought up by the Countess, but was obliged to take refuge from her growing dislike, with Sir Arthur Wardour and his lady. After the Countess' tale concerning her parentage, she was overcome by the horror of her position and tried to drown herself. Shortly before her death she gave birth to a son ('Mr. Lovel'), whose likeness in later years to 'the unfortunate Eveline' led the Antiquary to say 'I felt my heart warm to him from the first.' *The Antiquary.*

Neville, Major. *See* Lovel, Mr.

Neville, Sir Henry. A knight from Westmoreland, frank and 'debonnair': chamberlain to King Richard. He tried to dissuade the King from trusting Zohauk, 'this juggling slave of Saladin,' but his interference was found to be 'presumptuous and unmannerly.' He conducted the slave to his private interview with Edith of Plantagenet. *The Talisman.*

Newcastle, Duke of. The Minister responsible for Captain Porteous' reprieve. *The Heart of Midlothian.*

Newcastle, The Mayor of. The nearest acting justice in the neighbourhood of Osbaldistone Hall before Squire Inglewood's appointment. 'Being rather inclined to the consumption of the game when properly dressed than to its preservation when alive,' he was more partial to the poacher than to the sportsman. *Rob Roy.*

Newcome, Johnny. A name applied in derision to Gibbie Girder by Caleb Balderstone: one of the causes of Gibbie's ill-will. *The Bride of Lammermoor.*

Nicanor. The Protospathaire, or 'First Swordsman.' He and Achilles Tatius being 'of separate factions in the army, and on indifferent terms with each other,' their mutual ill-will was utilised by the Emperor in guarding against the outbreak of conspiracy. *Count Robert of Paris.*

Nicephorus Briennius. Husband of Anna Comnena. Dissatisfied that 'the policy of Alexius had interposed more than one person of condition' between the imperial rank and his own, and wearied somewhat by his wife's 'erudition,' he found relief with Agelastes and Achilles Tatius. When their conspiracy was discovered, he could allege nothing in excuse of his 'folly and ingratitude.' But the Emperor was 'trained on' till he 'sacrificed justice and true policy to uxorious compassion and paternal tenderness of heart,' and forgave him. Nicephorus was, however, detained as a prisoner in the palace for twenty-four hours, and was thus hindered from fulfilling the challenge to which his amorous advances to Brenhilda had led. *Count Robert of Paris.*

Note. — 'His eminent qualities, both in peace and war, are acknowledged by Gibbon,' and his four books of Memoirs are 'valuable as being the work of an eye-witness of the most important events which he describes.'

NICHOLAS, FATHER. (1) An aged monk in St. Mary's. When Father Eustace prayed the Lord Abbot to assign him suitable penance for having gloried in his own wisdom, he was ordered to choose for his companion ' our reverend Brother Nicholas, and without interruption or impatience, to listen for a stricken hour to his narration, concerning those things which befell in the times of our venerable predecessor, Abbot Ingilram.'

(2) One of the 'more aged brethren' who 'had sunk under the pressure of the times.' (1) *The Monastery.* (2) *The Abbot.*

NICNEVEN, MOTHER. The name by which Magdalen Graeme was known in Kinross, she being supposed to be a sorceress. *The Abbot.*

NICODEMUS. One of General Harrison's servants. He was retained by Tomkins as a companion on the night when Dick Robison's ghost had created general alarm. *Woodstock.*

NIELSON, CHRISTOPHER. The 'surgeon and apothecary' who dressed the wound that Frank Osbaldistone received from Rashleigh.

' If it werena for hot blood and ill blood, what would become of the twa learned faculties ? ' *Rob Roy.*

NIGEL, LORD. See OLIFAUNT, NIGEL.

NIHIL NAMELESS. The writer of a letter informing young Mareschal that the vessels of ' James & Company, late merchants in London, now in Dunkirk,' had been driven off the coast, and that ' the west country partners have resolved to withdraw their name from the firm.' *The Black Dwarf.*

NIXON, CRISTAL. Redgauntlet's confidential servant. An ' old brutal desperado whose face and mind are a libel upon human nature,' he acted as jailer to his master's nephew and niece with ' that cynicism which is especially entertained with human misery.' He insinuated himself into all his master's secrets, being conceived by him ' to possess the qualities most requisite for a conspirator— undaunted courage, imperturbable coolness and address, and inviolable fidelity.' But when Redgauntlet sent him to Nanty Ewart with instructions for the young Chevalier's escape, he thought he knew a ' better trick ' — valued at thirty thousand pounds—and planned to catch ' the old fox and his cubs in the same trap.' *Redgauntlet.*

NIXON, MARTHA. The Earl of Oxford's nurse : ' a northern woman and full of superstitions.' ' She was wont to say that any sudden and causeless change of a man's nature . . . indicates an immediate change of his fortune.' This old woman's fancy recurred strongly to the Earl's mind when Charles the Bold asked him to forego his duel with Campo-Basso. *Anne of Geierstein.*

NOBLE, HOBBIE. ' A celebrated English outlaw . . . who . . . became a follower, or rather a brother-in-arms, to the renowned Laird's Jock.' He bequeathed his famous two-handed sword to Jock. *Death of the Laird's Jock.*

NOLL. Oliver Cromwell's nickname. *Woodstock.*

NORMAN. One of Sir William Ashon's foresters. He served the Ravenswoods as a boy, and found the change of master little to his liking. 'We hae lost a' sense of wood-craft,' he said, 'on this side of the hill.' *The Bride of Lammermoor.*

NORMAN NAN ORD (OF THE HAMMER). One of Torquil's sons. Harry Gow gave him the best mail harness he ever wrought, on condition that after the contest of Palm Sunday Norman would bring Eachin into a fair field to fight with Harry. But to Torquil, and to Eachin who wore it, it proved an 'accursed mail.' *The Fair Maid of Perth.*

NORNA OF THE FITFUL-HEAD. Ulla Troil: cousin of Magnus Troil and mother of Clement Vaughan. Of a brooding and superstitious nature, and trained by her father in the legendary lore of the old Norse sagas, she felt that by the catastrophe of her father's death she was 'taken from humanity, to be something pre-eminently powerful, pre-eminently wretched.' She claimed to be the 'Sovereign of the Seas and Winds,' and she 'performed her part with such undoubting confidence, and such striking dignity of look and action, and evinced at the same time such strength of language and energy of purpose,' that her claims were generally acknowledged. But her sagacity and resource failed her with regard to Mordaunt Mertoun, and the shock of discovering that the hated pirate, Cleveland, against whom she had persistently schemed, was her own son, freed her mind from its worst frenzies. *The Pirate.*

NORTHAMPTON, EARL OF. One of the Earl of Huntinglen's friends: 'that celebrated putter-down of pretended prophecies, Lord Henry Howard.' He had gained Queen Elizabeth's favour by his *Defensative against the Poison of supposed Prophecies* in 1583, and towards the close of her reign became one of James' most ardent partisans. *The Fortunes of Nigel.*

NORTHUMBERLAND, EARL OF. 'A sworn upholder' of the Catholic faith, understood to have taken the Community of St. Mary's under his protection. He devised with Sir Piercie Shafton and some others of 'the choice and picked spirits of the age,' how and by what means the Catholic religion might be restored. When, however, his plot was discovered, he laid 'the burden of all this trafficking' upon Sir Piercie's back, and Sir Piercie sought refuge at St. Mary's. *The Monastery.*

NOSEBAG, MRS. 'Originally the helpmate of a pawnbroker,' and afterwards the wife of the adjutant and riding-master of a dragoon regiment: Edward Waverley's travelling companion in the Northern Diligence.

'That gimlet-eyed jade — mother adjutant, as we call her—

is a greater plague to the regiment than prevot - marshal, serjeant-major, and old Hubble-de-Shuff, the Colonel, into the bargain.' *Waverley.*

NOVIT, NICHIL. (1) 'Procurator before the Sheriff court.' When summoned to the Laird of Dumbiedikes' deathbed, he 'recommended, as an opiate for the agonised conscience of the Laird, reparation of the injuries he had done' to Widow Butler and Davie Deans.

(2) Son of the above : 'amaist as gleg as his father.' He was employed by the young Laird of Dumbiedikes to 'agent Effie's plea,' and ' do what carnal wisdom' could for her. (1) and (2) *The Heart of Midlothian.*

(*Gleg*, clever.)

NOWEL, GOVERNOR. Minister in the Isle of Man under the young Earl of Derby. *Peveril of the Peak.*

O

OAKENDALE, LORD. The title of the heir to the Earldom of Etherington. *St. Ronan's Well.*

OATES, DR. TITUS. One of Sir Geoffrey Peveril's accusers : the notorious alarmist who for nearly two years kept the country in a fever of apprehension by his accounts of the supposed great Popish plot. ' This singular man . . . had no other talent for imposture than an impudence which set conviction and shame alike at defiance.' *Peveril of the Peak.*

OCHILTREE, EDIE. One of the King's ' bedesmen ' : a travelling beggar who was on terms of outspoken intimacy with gentle and simple alike. Full of local knowledge and experience, he was able to play an important part in several critical times. He had no mean opinion of his own position.

' And then what wad a' the country about do for want o' auld Edie Ochiltree, that brings news and country cracks frae ae farmsteading to anither, and gingerbread to the lasses, and helps the lads to mend their fiddles, and the gudewives to clout their pans, and plaits rush-swords and grenadier caps for the weans, and busks the laird's flees, and has skill o' cowills and horse-ills, and kens mair auld sangs and tales than a' the barony besides, and gars ilka body laugh wherever he comes ?— troth, my leddy, I canna lay down my vocation ; it would be a public loss.' *The Antiquary.*

(*Bedesman*, a pauper enjoying royal bounty. *To clout*, to patch. *To busk*, to prepare.)

OGLETHORPE, THEOPHILUS. A boon companion of Donohoe Bertram. *Guy Mannering.*

O'KEAN, LIEUTENANT. A lover of Mistress Bertram. Tied up with his love-letters there was found his bond for two hundred pounds, ' upon which *no* interest whatever appeared to have been paid.' *Guy Mannering.*

OLAUS, OLAVE, or OLLAW. ' The celebrated Monarch of Norway, who, rather by the edge of his sword than any milder argument, introduced Christianity into those isles, and was respected as the patron of Kirkwall some time before he shared that honour with Saint Magnus the Martyr.' He gave his name to the great fair held at Kirkwall on the third of August, 'being Saint Olla's day.' *The Pirate.*

'OLD ADAM.' The soldiers' name for Colonel Gardiner. *Waverley.*

OLD ALICE. *See* GRAY, ALICE.

OLD GILBERT. One of Sir William Ashton's menservants. *The Bride of Lammermoor.*

OLD MILNWOOD. *See* MORTON, MR.

OLD MORTALITY. A religious enthusiast who 'left his house, his home, and his kindred, and wandered about until the day of his death.' For about thirty years he spent his life in repairing and erecting gravestones to the memory of the persecuted Covenanters, 'cleaning the moss from the grey stones, renewing with his chisel the half-defaced inscriptions, and repairing the emblems of death with which these simple monuments are usually adorned.' 'To talk of the exploits of the Covenanters was his delight.' Mr. Pattieson embodied his anecdotes 'into one compressed narrative,' but was at the same time 'far from adopting' Old Mortality's 'style, his opinions, or even his facts.' *Old Mortality.*

Note. — Robert Paterson, well-known by the title of 'Old Mortality,' was born in Dumfriesshire in 1715. About 1758 he left his wife and family, and adopted the life described above. He was mainly supported by the hospitality of the Cameronians, and though very poor in his old age, he was so more by choice than through necessity. He died in 1801.

OLD ROWLEY. *See* CHARLES II.

'OLD TRUE-PENNY.' A name given to Edie Ochiltree by the Antiquary. *The Antiquary.*

OLDBUCK, GRISELDA. The Antiquary's 'most discreet' sister, who was 'sometimes apt to *jibb* when he pulled the reins too tight.' In appearance she closely resembled her brother, but she was rendered ridiculous by her grotesque *coiffure*, her inappropriate attire, and her garrulous conversation. *The Antiquary.*

OLDBUCK (OLDENBUCK, OLDINBUCK), JONATHAN. 'The Antiquary': Laird of Monkbarns. 'Learning, wit, drollery, the more poignant that they were a little marked by the peculiarities of an old bachelor; a soundness of thought rendered more forcible by an occasional quaintness of expression'—these were his chief characteristics. He was 'snell and dure enough in casting up their nonsense' to other folk 'as if he had nane o' his ain,' but his bark was 'muckle waur than his bite.' To the poor he was 'aye kind and neighbourly.' *The Antiquary.*

Note.—He takes part in the meeting of shareholders described in the Introduction to *The Betrothed* as being held 'to form a joint-stock company, united for the purpose of writing and publishing the class of works called the *Waverley Novels.*'

OLDBUCK, WILLIE - WALD. The Antiquary's elder brother. He 'marched out of the world on a pair of damp feet caught in the Kittlefittingmoss.' *The Antiquary.*

OLDENBUCK, ALDOBRAND. The Antiquary's great-great-great-grandfather. For printing the Augsburg Confession 'that eminent man was expelled from his ungrateful country, and driven to establish his household gods even here at Monkbarns.' His ghost was supposed to haunt the Green Room. *The Antiquary.*

OLDENBUCK, WOLFBRAND. One of the Antiquary's ancestors: the Westphalian printer who in December, 1493, 'accomplished the printing of the great Chronicle of Nuremberg.'
' That great restorer of learning.' *The Antiquary.*

OLIFANT, BASIL. Male heir to the last Earl of Torwood. 'Disaffected to Government from his claim to the estate being set aside in favour of Lady Margaret Bellenden,' he was prepared to join the Covenanters after their victory at Drumclog, but when they were defeated at Bothwell Bridge, he placed himself and his men at Claverhouse's disposal. In King James' day he 'turned papist to please the managers,' and got Tillietudlem Castle and lands; 'on the back o' that came the Revolution, and wha to turn coat faster than the laird?' He was shot by Cuddie Headrigg when proceeding to arrest Lord Evandale. *Old Mortality.*

OLIFAUNT, LADY MAUD. Lady Hermione's mother. *The Fortunes of Nigel.*

OLIFAUNT, NIGEL, LORD GLENVARLOCH. The representative of an old Scottish house 'that stood by King and country five hundred years.' But his fortunes were decayed, and powerful enemies at court delayed the satisfaction of his just claims. 'Surrounded by snares of different kinds ingeniously contrived to ruin his character, destroy his estate, and perhaps to reach even his life,' he soon found himself in a 'perilous labyrinth,' from which escape seemed almost impossible. But he was a 'braw lad,' and when he had overcome the fear of ridicule, the native strength of his character asserted itself. *The Fortunes of Nigel.*

OLIFAUNT, RALPH. A cadet of the house of Glenvarloch: Lady Hermione's maternal grandfather. He left Scotland in the train of Francis, Earl of Bothwell, and settled in Barcelona. *The Fortunes of Nigel.*

OLIFAUNT, RANDAL, LORD GLENVARLOCH. Nigel's father. In troubled times he had stood by King James 'with heart, sword, and fortune,' and advanced large loans 'in the King's utmost emergencies.' He had also befriended George Heriot, who, when he discovered Nigel's plight in London, used his influence with the King on Nigel's behalf. *The Fortunes of Nigel.*

OLIVER, JACK. A friend of Darsie Latimer and Alan Fairford, 'who produces with such happy complacence his fardel of small talk, and who, as he never doubts his own powers of affording amusement, passes them current with every pretty woman he approaches, and fills up the intervals of chat by his complete acquaintance with the exercise of the fan, the *flacon*, and the other duties of the *Cavaliere Serviente.*' *Redgauntlet.*

OLIVER, THE DEVIL'S. *See* DAIN, OLIVER.

O'QUILLIGAN. Major of a regiment in which Dalgetty served abroad. After a private dispute, Dalgetty explained, ' it pleased him the next day to deliver his orders to me with the point of his baton advanced and held aloof, instead of declining and trailing the same.' Upon this matter they fought. The Major receiving the lighter punishment from their colonel, Dalgetty exchanged his commission. *A Legend of Montrose.*

ORLEANS, DUKE OF. The first Prince of the blood royal, and, failing the King's offspring, heir to the kingdom of France. 'Of a gentle, mild, and beneficent disposition,' he suffered 'extreme dejection' from the 'degraded and almost captive state' in which he was kept at court, and 'alike denied employment and countenance.' This dejection was greatly increased by the prospect of being compelled 'to give his hand to the Princess Joan of France, the younger daughter of Louis, to whom he had been contracted in infancy, but whose deformed person rendered the insisting upon such an agreement an act of abominable rigour.' *Quentin Durward.*

ORMOND, DUKE OF, JAMES BUTLER. A 'celebrated noble,' between whom and Buckingham there existed a 'constant and almost mortal quarrel.' But his 'faithful services, high rank, and acknowledged worth and virtue' secured him some influence with the King. This he used to urge the cause of the Peverils and the Countess of Derby. *Peveril of the Peak.*

ORMSTON, JOCK. *See* ORROCK, PUGGIE.

ORROCK, PUGGIE. One of the two sheriff-officers who marshalled Edie Ochiltree before Bailie Littlejohn. He and Jock Ormston were objects of the children's 'alternate dread and sport.' *The Antiquary.*

ORTHEN, GILES. A wealthy burgess whose house was offered to Louis during his stay in Peronne. *Quentin Durward.*

OSBALDISTONE FAMILY, THE.

— SIR HENRY. Fifth baron of the name. He carried off the fair maid of Fairington and kept her against all the power of mighty Scottish chiefs.

— SIR HILDEBRAND. The owner of Osbaldistone Hall, 'Cub Castle' as it was called by the neighbours. He was knighted by James II and after the Revolution spent a sequestered life upon his native domains in Northumberland with his six sons and his niece Diana Vernon. But in 1715 he was persuaded to join the rebellion. After Preston he was taken prisoner and died in Newgate, 'beaten down to the very earth by his family calamities.'

OSBALDISTONE FAMILY, THE.

— ARCHIE. Sir Hildebrand's eldest son. When he 'came to a bad end, in that unlucky affair of Sir John Fenwick's, old Hildebrand used to hollow out his name as readily as any of the remaining six, and then complain that he could not recollect which of his sons had been hanged.'

— PERCY. Sir Hildebrand's heir. He had 'more of the sot than of the gamekeeper, bully, horse-jockey, or fool.' He died as the result of a wager with Brandy Swalewell as to which of them should drink 'the largest cup of strong liquor when King James was proclaimed by the insurgents at Morpeth.'

— THORNCLIFF. Sir Hildebrand's favourite son. Jealous of his cousin Frank's intimacy with Diana Vernon, he was, in her opinion, 'more of the bully than the sot, gamekeeper, jockey, or fool.' He joined the rebellion of 1715 and was killed in a duel, fought on a question of precedence with a gentleman 'as fierce and intractable as himself.'

— JOHN. One of Sir Hildebrand's sons. He 'sleeps whole weeks amongst the hills' and 'has most of the gamekeeper.' At the battle of Preston he 'behaved very boldly' and received several wounds, of which he died, a prisoner in Newgate.

— DICK. One of Sir Hildebrand's sons. 'The jockey is powerful with Dickon, who rides two hundred miles by day and night to be bought and sold at a horse-race.' He broke his neck 'in an attempt to show off a foundered bloodmare, which he wished to palm upon a Manchester merchant who had joined the insurgents.'

— WILFRED. One of Sir Hildebrand's sons. 'The fool predominates so much over Wilfred's other qualities, that he may be termed a fool positive.' He 'had the best fortune of the family,' being slain at Preston while 'fighting with great bravery, though I have heard he was never able exactly to comprehend the cause of quarrel, and did not uniformly remember on which king's side he was engaged.'

— RASHLEIGH. Sir Hildebrand's youngest son. He was without physical attractions such as his brothers had, but nature gave him 'a mouthful of common sense, and the priest has added a bushelful of learning.' Subtle and scheming, he was 'better acquainted with men's minds than with the moral principles that ought to regulate them,' and without hesitation or regret he played the traitor to all his friends: to his cousin Diana and her father, to his cousin Frank and his uncle in London, to Rob Roy, to the

Pretender for whom he had plotted, and even to his own father and brothers. 'A detestable villain.'

OSBALDISTONE FAMILY, THE.

— WILLIAM. Sir Hildebrand's brother: leading partner in the great London house, Osbaldistone and Tresham. Annoyed at his son Frank's persistent refusal to join him in business, he sent him to Osbaldistone Hall, and in his stead received Rashleigh into the counting-house. During his uncle's absence in Holland Rashleigh disappeared, taking with him valuable assets, the want of which seriously threatened the stability of the house. It was in an attempt to restore his father's credit that Frank met with his adventures in Rob Roy's country.

— FRANK. The old man who writes to his friend Will Tresham these Memoirs of 'the hazards and difficulties' of his youth. The only son of the leading partner in the great London house Osbaldistone & Tresham, he refused to join his father in business, being unwilling 'to submit to labour and limitations' unpleasant to his taste and temper. His experiences in Northumberland and Scotland showed him to be 'a kind-hearted and an honourable youth,' and one who understood 'that which is due to the feelings of a man of honour.' But to Diana Vernon he frequently 'spoke nothing but the paltry gossip which simpletons repeat from play-books and romances, till they give mere cant a real and powerful influence over their minds.' *Rob Roy.*

OSBALDISTONE & TRESHAM. A London house which had bought lands in the Highlands and granted bills in payment. 'If these bills are not paid,' the Bailie urged, ' the Glasgow merchant comes on the Hieland lairds, whae hae deil a boddle o' siller, and will like ill to spew up what is item a' spent—They will turn desperate—five hundred will rise that might hae sitten at hame—the deil will gae ower Jock Wabster—and the stopping of your father's house will hasten the outbreak that's been sae lang biding us.' *Rob Roy.*

(*Boddle,* a copper coin worth two pennies Scots, or the third of an English penny.)

OSBORNE. The dealer who paid twenty pounds to Davy Wilson for the *Game of Chess,* 1474, Davy having picked it up in Holland for twopence. *The Antiquary.*

OSMUND. 'A trusty old soldier' bound to Hereward ' by long kindness and confidence.' He was commissioned to accompany Bertha to the Crusaders' camp at Scutari. *Count Robert of Paris.*

OSTLER, DICK. One of Mrs. Bickerton's menservants : 'a queer, knowing, shambling animal, with a hatchet face, a squint, a game-arm, and a limp.' He recognised the ' pass' which Jim Ratcliffe had given Jeanie Deans, and assured her that ' ony gentleman, as keeps the road o' this side Stamford will respect Jim's pass.' *The Heart of Midlothian.*

OSTLER, JOHN. Meg Dods' 'aged hostler.' Like the maidservants he thought he saw a ghost when Frank Tyrrel returned. *St. Ronan's Well.*

OSWALD. Cedric's cup-bearer. When searching for Wilfred after it was discovered that he was the Disinherited Knight, he recognised Gurth and 'deemed it his duty' to secure him 'as a fugitive of whose fate his master was to judge.' *Ivanhoe.*

OTRANTO, PRINCE OF. *See* TANCRED.

OUTRAM, LANCE. Park-keeper at Martindale Castle: Mistress Ellesmere's nephew: Deborah Debbitch's lover in youth. Though without 'skill in war' or 'the right spirit for a soldier,' he led the attack on Moultrassie Hall which set Julian Peveril at liberty. Thereafter, partly from fear of Deborah and partly from love of Julian, 'he was resolved to follow Master Julian to the death.' 'Whenever Peveril was in a broil,' he said, 'Outram was in a stew; so I will never bear a base mind, but even hold a part with you, as my fathers have done with yours, for four generations, whatever more.' *Peveril of the Peak.*

OVENS. One of Mrs. MacCandlish's neighbours. *Guy Mannering.*

OVERDEES, ROWLEY. *See* CULLOCH, SAWNEY.

OVERSTITCH. *See* SHAFTON OF WILVERTON.

OVERTON, COLONEL. One of the officers to whom Mr. Gordon was 'holding forth' during Wildrake's interview with Cromwell in Windsor Castle. *Woodstock.*

OWEN. The head clerk in the house of Osbaldistone & Tresham. When the firm's credit was endangered by Rashleigh's treachery, he was sent to Glasgow to arrange matters, but through the sharp practice of MacVittie, MacFin & Co. he soon found himself in prison. There he was secretly visited by Frank Osbaldistone, Rob Roy, and Bailie Nicol Jarvie, who together made plans to defeat Rashleigh's schemes.

'Clear-headed in his own routine . . . not very acute in comprehending what lay beyond that sphere.' *Rob Roy.*

OWEN, SAM. The manservant who accompanied Darsie Latimer to Dumfries and Shepherd's Bush. *Redgauntlet.*

OXFORD, BISHOP OF. One of the bishops in attendance on the King: 'equally willing to become food for fagots in defence of the Latinity of the university, as for any article of his religious creed.' *The Fortunes of Nigel.*

OXFORD, COUNTESS OF. Wife of John de Vere, Earl of Oxford. She found refuge for some years in Bretagne, but joined her husband when he retired to Switzerland after the death of Charles the Bold. *Anne of Geierstein.*

OXFORD, EARL OF. *See* PHILIPSON, SEIGNOR.

OXFORD, LORD OF. 'A young unthrift, whom Foster had more than once accommodated with loans on usurious interest.' He testified to Queen Elizabeth that the certificate declaring Amy Robsart unfit to attend at Kenilworth

Castle was in Foster's handwriting. *Kenilworth.*

OYLEY, BALDWIN DE. Squire to the redoubted knight Brian de Bois-Guilbert. *Ivanhoe.*

P

PACIFICATOR. One of the Antiquary's *noms-de-guerre*. *The Antiquary.*

PAGET, LADY. One of Queen Elizabeth's dames of honour. ' Prosaic from her cradle upwards,' she left to her royal mistress the task of completing the couplet which Raleigh had begun.

> 'Fain would I climb, but that I fear to fall.'
> 'If thy mind fail thee, do not climb at all.'

Kenilworth.

PALMER, THE. Wilfred, knight of Ivanhoe, in disguise. He guided Bois-Guilbert and Prior Aymer to Rotherwood, and on the following morning earned lasting gratitude from Isaac of York by saving him from Bois-Guilbert's plans. *Ivanhoe.*

PAREIRA, JOSEPH. The armourer of Milan from whom had come the armour worn by Wilfred of Ivanhoe in the passage-of-arms. *Ivanhoe.*

PARIS, BRENHILDA, COUNTESS OF. Wife of Count Robert. ' From a girl, she despised the pursuits of her sex,' and as the Lady of Aspramonte challenged her suitors to meet her in the lists. ' Unhorsed and unhelmed, and stretched on the earth ' by Count Robert, she wedded him in the church of his patroness, Our Lady of the Broken Lances, and thereafter shared his military exploits. Separated from her husband after their banquet in the palace of Alexius Comnenus, she was taken to the garden house of Agelastes, whom she soon discovered to be an 'arch-deceiver,' bent on furthering the amorous advances of Nicephorus. She staked her honour on a combat in the lists with him. To Agelastes she justified her unwomanly life in these words :

' One hour of life, crowded to the full with glorious action, and filled with noble risks, is worth whole years of those mean observances of paltry decorum, in which men steal through existence, like sluggish waters through a marsh, without either honour or observation.' *Count Robert of Paris.*

PARIS, COUNT ROBERT OF. One of the leaders of the first Crusade. During the ceremony of paying allegiance to Alexius Comnenus he seated himself on the Emperor's throne, afterwards doing homage ' with as little waste and delay of time ' as possible. In spite of this personal affront to the Emperor, he remained in Constantinople ; was enticed by Agelastes to his ' poor habitation ' ; accompanied the imperial ladies to the palace, and during a banquet there drank freely of the Emperor's wine. On waking from his drugged sleep, he found himself in a dungeon with a chained tiger. After killing the animal, he made acquaintance with Ursel in the next dungeon ; wounded Sylvanus when he came down with Ursel's pittance of food; killed the warder Sebastes; and attacked Hereward, who came to the rescue. A truce having been made between the two, Hereward helped Count Robert to escape, on condition that he would afterwards 'meet him in fair fight.' Their mutual antagonism was satisfied by the combat, in which Hereward took the place of Nicephorus. *Count Robert of Paris.*

Note.—Anna Comnena 'has recorded the bold usurpation of the Emperor's seat by this haughty chieftain,' whom she calls 'Robert of Paris, a haughty barbarian.' Authorities differ concerning his identity.

PARKER, MISS. One of the visitors to the Well. *St. Ronan's Well.*

PASLEY, PEG. The seamstress whom Mrs. MacCandlish employed to make 'half a dozen ruffled sarks' for Vanbeest Brown. *Guy Mannering.*

PATE-IN-PERIL. The name given to Mr. Maxwell of Summertrees in memory of his daring escape when handcuffed to Sir Henry Redgauntlet. *Redgauntlet.*

PATERSON. Landlord of Mr. Herries' 'old resting-place' in Edinburgh, 'at the head of the Horse Wynd.' *Redgauntlet.*

PATERSON, PATE. The little cripple-kneed foot-page sent by Bryce Snailsfoot for the Kirkwall officers when he feared Cleveland's revenge for the theft of the box left at Jarlshof. *The Pirate.*

PATERSON, WILL. A Zetlander shot by 'the Dutchman that he saved from sinking.' 'To fling a drowning man a plank or a tow may be the part of a Christian; but I say, keep hands aff him, if ye wad live and thrive free frae his danger.' *The Pirate.*

PATON OF MEADOWHEAD. One of the Covenanters' leaders at Drumclog: a man 'of military skill.' *Old Mortality.*

PATRICK. An old servant at Shaws Castle. 'There's nae post-cattle come into our stables,' he said on the night of Mr. Touchwood's arrival. 'What do we ken, but that they may be glandered, as the groom says?' *St. Ronan's Well.*

PATTIESON, PAUL. Brother to Peter. Jedediah Cleishbotham represents that he undertook to remove the 'grievous inconsistencies and other mistakes' from Peter's manuscripts of *Count Robert of Paris* and *Castle Dangerous.* But Paul preferred to send his brother's last labours 'down to posterity unscathed by the scalping-knife of alteration.' *Count Robert of Paris.*

PATTIESON, PETER or PATRICK. 'A young person' with whom Jedediah Cleishbotham had 'contracted for teaching the lower classes' in his school. He died young, leaving his papers to his 'learned friend and patron,' and amongst these the *Tales of my Landlord* were found. *The Black Dwarf.*

PATULLO, MRS. Lady Ashton's female attendant. *The Bride of Lammermoor.*

PAULETTI, ERMINIA. *See* HERMIONE, LADY.

PAULINE, MADEMOISELLE. Monna (Mistress) Paula, Lady Hermione's attendant. Her ' persevering enquiries ' discovered the place where Lady Hermione was confined after her mother's death, and her calmness protected Lady Hermione from the worst consequences of her husband's treachery. Accompanied by Margaret Ramsay dressed as a page, she presented Lady Hermione's petition to the King. *The Fortunes of Nigel.*

PAUPIAH. Steward to the President of the Council in Madras. He was in communication with the native courts, and ' carried on many mysterious intrigues.' When Richard Middlemas was in Madras disguised as Sadoc, he arranged with Paupiah for the betrayal of Bangalore as soon as Tippoo Sahib appointed him Governor. *The Surgeon's Daughter.*

PAVILLON, GERTRUDE (TRUDCHEN). The Syndic's daughter, ' a fair and smiling Flemish lass.' ' Admiring her personal charms, while she pitied her distress,' she showed to the Countess of Croye ' the zeal and affection of a sister,' and sent her own ' bachelor,' Hans Glover, to guide the Countess and Quentin Durward safe out of the territory. It was when saving her life during the pillage of Liège by the French and Burgundians that Quentin relinquished the high honour promised to him who ' brings us the head of the Wild Boar of Ardennes.' *Quentin Durward.*

PAVILLON, MRS. MABEL. The Syndic's wife. ' She was a jolly little roundabout woman, who had been pretty in her time, but whose principal characteristics for several years had been a red and sharp nose, a shrill voice, and a determination that the Syndic, in consideration of the authority which he exercised when abroad, should remain under the rule of due discipline at home.' *Quentin Durward.*

PAVILLON, SYNDIC HERMANN. One of the leaders of the discontented citizens in Liège. He helped Quentin Durward to escape from the excited crowd of Liègeois in the belief that Quentin had a message from Louis for his ear and Rouslaer's alone. During the attack on Schonwaldt Castle his life was saved by the ' lively young Archer,' who immediately secured his help in succouring the Countess Isabella. Though ' a hot-headed and intemperate zealot in politics,' he was a ' good-tempered, kind-hearted man . . . always well-meaning and benevolent,' and with Quentin as his squire and the Countess as his daughter, he braved the dangers of William de la Marck's revels. *Quentin Durward.*

See also ROUSLAER

PEACE, THE MAN OF. *See* MACTURK, CAPTAIN.

PEARSON, CAPTAIN GILBERT. An officer in close attendance on Cromwell. He accompanied Cromwell to Woodstock Lodge, superintended the placing of sentinels ''as Tomkins' scroll gave directions,' and finally discharged the mine at the foot of Love's Ladder, when the supposed king refused to surrender. 'A blunt soldier,' with 'little of grace but much of sincerity,' he was 'much more solicitous to anticipate the wishes of Oliver than to know the will of Heaven.' *Woodstock.*

PEDEN, ALEXANDER. A Cameronian minister in the ' auld and wrastling times.' *The Heart of Midlothian.*

PEEBLES, PETER. The plaintiff in the notable case *Peebles against Plainstanes*, which had been before the courts for fifteen years. Peter had meanwhile made ' shipwreck of time, means, and understanding,' and become 'the old scarecrow of Parliament House.' Alan Fairford seemed likely to bring the complicated business to an end had not his father made the mistake of giving him Provost Crosbie's letter in court amongst Peter's papers. But Peter could not have lived without his lawsuit. 'It is grandeur upon earth,' he told Joshua Geddes, ' to hear ane's name thunnered out along the long-arched roof of the Outer House — " *Poor* Peter Peebles against Plainstanes, *et per contra* " ; a' the best lawyers in the house fleeing like eagles to the prey ; some because they are in the cause, and some because they want to be thought engaged (for there are tricks in other trades by selling muslins)—to see the reporters mending their pens to take down the debate—the Lords themselves pooin' in their chairs, like folk sitting down to a gude dinner, and crying on the clerks for parts and pendicles of the process, who, puir bodies, can do little mair than cry on their closet-keepers to help them. To see a' this . . . and to ken that naething will be said or dune amang a' thae grand folk, for maybe the feck of three hours, saving what concerns you and your business—O, man, nae wonder that ye judge this to be earthly glory ! ' *Redgauntlet.*
(*Feck*, space.)

PEEL-THE-CAUSEWAY. An old man at Goodman Grist's mill. *Redgauntlet.*

PEGGY. Mrs. Saddletree's servant. *The Heart of Midlothian.*

PEGGY OF RAMSEY. 'A poor wretch ' who narrowly escaped being confined in the vault under the chapel of Castle Rushin, for a crime which ' in Cupid's courts would have been called a peccadillo.' *Peveril of the Peak.*

PEMBROKE, MR. A non-juring clergyman who acted as Sir Everard Waverley's chaplain and Edward's tutor. The presence of his political treatises amongst Edward's books helped to incriminate Edward in the eyes of the military authorities. On Sir Everard's arrest he deemed it prudent to retire to ' The Priest's Hole,' to which, unfortunately, the butler could venture with food only once a day. *Waverley.*

(*Non-juring clergyman*, one who refused to recognise the Revolution and the Hanoverian succession.)

PENFEATHER, LADY PENELOPE. The

'fanciful lady of rank' whose recovery from 'some imaginary complaint' by the use of St. Ronan's mineral spring brought it into fame. Posing as 'the presiding goddess of the region,' she drew round her 'painters and poets, and philosophers and men of science, and lecturers, and foreign adventurers,' without being herself discovered 'to be a fool, unless when she set up for being remarkably clever.' 'A woman of quality, and my patient,' Dr. Quackleben said, 'and such people always act charmingly.' But to Jack Mowbray she was 'a greedy, unconscionable jade, who has varnished over a selfish, spiteful heart, that is as hard as a flint, with a fine glossing of taste and sensibility.' *St. Ronan's Well.*

PENGWINION. One of the 'faithful friends' who met Father Buonaventure at Joe Crackenthorp's inn: 'a Cornish chough.' *Redgauntlet.*

(*Chough*, a Cornish crow.)

PENNY, JOCK. *See* CULLOCH, SAWNEY.

PEOLPHAN. 'The mighty Hunter of the North' whom Dousterswivel talked of seeing in St. Ruth's. 'He mimicked the motion of snuff-taking and its effects.' *The Antiquary.*

PEPPER. *See* MUSTARD AND PEPPER.

PEPPERCULL. *See* COLEPEPPER.

PERCY. *See* BOHUN, HENRY.

PERETTE, DAME. The name borne by Countess Hameline de Croye when staying under Louis' protection in Plessis-les-Tours. *Quentin Durward.*

PEST, COUNSELLOR. One of the legal celebrities in whose eyes Mr. Saunders Fairford wished Alan to stand well. *Redgauntlet.*

PESTLE and MORTAR. The two ponies which Dr. Gray 'exercised alternately' on his long rounds. *The Surgeon's Daughter.*

PETER, FATHER. 'A learned monk of Aberbrothick.' He was a guest at Glen-houlakin when it was harried by the Ogilvies, and was permitted to bind Quentin's wounds and remove him to a place of safety, on condition that the youth became a monk. *Quentin Durward.*

PETER OF THE BRIG. (1) The bridge-keeper: a dependent of the Baron of Meigallot. By keeping Peter's 'interest pitched in his view' Father Eustace 'got round' his heart, and compromised the long-standing quarrel concerning the right of monks and pilgrims to use the bridge free of charge.

(2) The bridge-keeper, rendered 'peevish through age and misfortune.' The changes of the times had 'reduced him to become the oppressed instead of playing the extortioner.' (1) *The Monastery.* (2) *The Abbot.*

PETER THE HERMIT. The man whose burning zeal fired Europe with the desire to free the Holy Land from the infidel Turks. He 'had a place in the council and possessed great weight' when the request brought by Bertha to the camp in Scutari was under discussion. *Count Robert of Paris.*

PETERS, HUGH. A famous divine. Sir Geoffrey had seen him, 'with a Bible in one hand and a pistol in the other, ride in triumph through the court door when Martindale was surrendered.' *Peveril of the Peak.*

PETERSON, PEREGRINE. 'The Conservator of Scottish Privileges at Campvere.' He held a mortgage over Lord Glenvarloch's estate. *The Fortunes of Nigel.*

PETIT-ANDRÉ. 'Jean-qui-rit': one of Tristan l'Hermite's subordinates, 'more utterly detested than, perhaps, any creatures of their kind, whether before or since.' Petit-André 'was a joyous-looking, round, active little fellow, who rolled about in execution of his duty as if it were the most diverting occupation in the world. He seemed to have a sort of fond affection for his victims, and always spoke of them in kindly and affectionate terms. . . . Petit-André seldom failed to refresh them with a jest or two, as if to induce them to pass from life as something that was ludicrous, contemptible, and not worthy of serious consideration.' *Quentin Durward.*

PETTIGREW, CLERK. *See* COSTLETT, CAPTAIN.

PEVERIL, JULIAN. Sir Geoffrey's son. 'Naturally bold and high-spirited,' he became, during the years he spent in the Countess of Derby's household, 'a gallant and accomplished youth,' 'strict in judging his duty and severely resolved in executing it.' He remained unshaken in his convictions, equally against the artful schemes of Ganlesse and the friendly advances of Major Bridgenorth.

'The spirit of his mother looks from his eye, and his stately step is as that of his father.' *Peveril of the Peak.*

PEVERIL, LADY (*née* MARGARET STANLEY). Sir Geoffrey's wife. Throughout her husband's varied fortunes she bore herself 'with prudence and with patience,' while by her compassionate kindness she bound Major Bridgenorth to her by a tie so strong that it baffled him in his deepest political scheming. Providence gave her a fair form, and 'tenanted that form with a mind as pure as the original frailty of our vile nature will permit.' *Peveril of the Peak.*

PEVERIL, SIR GEOFFREY. Head of the family in the time of Charles II. He had commanded a regiment for Charles I through the Civil War, had fought for Charles II at Wiggan Lane and Worcester, and had lived 'an obstinate malignant' through the Commonwealth, only to receive scanty favour at the Restoration and, towards the close of Charles' reign, to suffer imprisonment on suspicion of complicity in the great Popish plot. 'Proud from pedigree and brave by constitution,' he had 'an undaunted and persevering valour,' but it was combined with a 'blunt impetuosity' which sometimes marred his own interests. Had it not been for his wife's influence, he would have found in his Puritan neighbour Bridgenorth a 'powerful enemy' altogether without mercy. *Peveril of the Peak.*

PEVERIL, WILLIAM. (1) A bastard son of William the Conqueror, and founder of the ' opulent family of knightly rank,' the Peverils of the Peak.

(2) Head of the family in King John's ' stormy days.' He forfeited the fief of Castleton, but his descendants retained the title ' which served to mark their high descent and lofty pretensions.' (1) and (2) *Peveril of the Peak.*

PHIL. John Davies' boy. *Redgauntlet.*

PHILIP, FATHER. (1) Sacristan at St. Mary's. While returning from Glendearg, where he had confessed the Lady of Avenel and gained possession of her 'thick black volume with silver clasps,' he was the victim of one of the White Lady's visitations. He was well soused in the river by her, and returned to the convent with her rhymes hanging in his memory ' like a burr in a beggar's rags.'

(2) One of the monks who 'had sunk under the pressure of the times.' He left a written statement confessing that after having united Julian Avenel and Catherine Graeme 'in the holy sacrament of marriage,' he had been prevailed upon to ' conceal and disguise the same,' and to induce the damsel to believe 'that the ceremony had been performed by one not in holy orders, and having no authority to that effect.' (1) *The Monastery.* (2) *The Abbot.*

PHILIP OF FRANCE. 'The August':

King Richard's chief ally against Saladin. ' One of the most sagacious monarchs of the time, who, dreading the fiery and overbearing character of Richard, considering him as his natural rival, and feeling offended, moreover, at the dictatorial manner in which he, a vassal of France for his continental domains, conducted himself towards his liege lord, endeavoured to strengthen his own party, and weaken that of Richard, by uniting the crusading princes of inferior degree, in resistance to what he termed the usurping authority of the King of England.' ' With their diminished forces and civil discords,' the continuance of hostilities against Saladin became impossible. *The Talisman.*

PHILIPSON, ARTHUR. Son of John de Vere, Earl of Oxford. ' The faithful companion ' of his father's wanderings, he learnt to estimate danger ' by the measure of sound sense and reality ' and to ' expose himself frankly' to every toil and sacrifice which ' duty and allegiance ' demanded. From the moment when she saved him from an imminent death on the mountains, Anne of Geierstein engaged his tenderest romantic feelings, and these were only strengthened by her mysterious power in releasing him from the dungeon of La Ferette, and in guarding him on his way to Strasburg. ' When at Geierstein they looked but like another girl and bachelor,' yet in her ancestral halls of Arnheim Anne felt that he ' would break his own heart — the heart of anyone else—rather than make false his father's words.' But his deadly duel with Rudolph of Donnerhugel removed the last barrier between 'the high-born maiden' and himself. *Anne of Geierstein.*

PHILIPSON, SEIGNOR. John de Vere, the exiled Earl of Oxford: one of the most devoted adherents of the House of Lancaster and a 'faithful follower' of the widowed Queen, Margaret of Anjou. In his rôle of foreign merchant he acted as her emissary to Charles the Bold. While urging immediate action in her cause, he tried to dissuade Charles from making war against the Swiss, his intercourse with Landamman Biederman and the other deputies of the Confederation having given him an insight into their real worth and power. But he failed to convince Charles and was forced 'to look on the game and see how it might be won, while we are debarred by the caprice of others from the power of playing it according to our own skill.' 'A man of deep observation, of high thought and pretension,' he walked in 'the path of wisdom and rectitude,' and showed 'a dignified and unaltered composure' under all personal danger. Neither the power of Hagenbach nor of the Judges of the Secret Tribunal moved him, and when duty prompted unwelcome truths, he did not shrink from rousing the wrath of Charles the Bold. *Anne of Geierstein.*

PHŒBE. 'The beautiful animal' which Diana Vernon was riding the first time Frank Osbaldistone saw her. *Rob Roy.*

PHRAORTES. The Admiral who, with six ships of war, unsuccessfully opposed Tancred's return to Constantinople. *Count Robert of Paris.*

PIERRE, MAÎTRE. The elder of the two strangers with whom Quentin made acquaintance when approaching Plessis-les-Tours. In the character of a substantial merchant of Tours, he heard Quentin's frank opinion of himself, the King, as well as of the other leading European personages. *Quentin Durward.*

PIGAL, MONSIEUR DE. 'Half smuggler, half dancing-master,' he taught Alice Bridgenorth to dance. *Peveril of the Peak.*

PIKE, GIDEON. Major Bellenden's ancient valet. *Old Mortality.*

PINCH-MEASURE. The good host of the Fleur-de-Lys inn at Plessis-les-Tours. Under his roof Quentin and Jacqueline met for the first time. *Quentin Durward.*

PINDIVIDE. A great merchant of Paul's who 'had given the crows a pudding' and become bankrupt. *The Fortunes of Nigel.*

PINNIEWINKS, GAFFER. 'The trier of witches,' who should have put Wayland Smith ' to his probation.' *Kenilworth.*

PINNIT, ORSON. Keeper of Queen Elizabeth's royal bears. He complained 'that amidst the extreme delight with which men haunt the play-houses ... the manly amusement of bear-baiting is falling into comparative neglect.' *Kenilworth.*

PIPER, MR. The 'best of contractors who ever furnished four

frampal jades for public use.' Mr. Croftangry travelled by his mail coach when going to Lanarkshire to see Glentanner with a view to purchase. *The Highland Widow.*
(*Frampal*, unruly.)

PIRIE, JOHN. *See* STEENSON, SANDIE.

PIRNER, JOHN. ' Professed weaver and practical black-fisher in the Aultoun of St. Ronan's.' He usually attended Frank Tyrrel on his fishing expeditions. *St. Ronan's Well.*

PITCHPOST, THE MISSES. The timber merchant's daughters: well-dowered English ladies who married two Irishmen. *The Fortunes of Nigel.*

PIXIE. Sir Henry Lee's pony, 'diminutive but full of spirit.' ' Old Pixie and his old master have survived many a tall fellow, and many a great horse—neither of them good for much themselves.' *Woodstock.*

PLAINSTANES, PAUL. The defendant in the notable case *Peebles against Plainstanes*. During a partnership of twelve years, Peebles had ' become impoverished, while his partner (his former clerk), having no funds but his share of the same business, into which he had been admitted without any advance of stock, had become gradually more and more wealthy.' An amicable dissolution of the partnership proved impossible, and in the course of fifteen years ' the carelessness and blunders ' of solicitors converted the case ' into a huge chaotic mass of unintelligible technicality.' *Redgauntlet.*
See also TOUGH, MR.

PLANTAGENET, LADY EDITH OF. A kinswoman of King Richard: the lady of Sir Kenneth's love. To him she was ' a superior being, who was to move without watch or control, rejoice him by her appearance, or depress him by her absence, animate him by her kindness, or drive him to despair by her cruelty—all at her own free will, and without other importunity or remonstrance than that expressed by the most devoted services of the heart and sword of the champion, whose sole object in life was to fulfil her commands, and, by the splendour of his own achievements, to exalt her fame.' But, though worshipped as a divinity at a distance, she ' let this northern adventurer sit nearer her heart than prudence would sanction,' and braved King Richard's taunts to plead for him when ' fallen from his duty through a snare set for him in mere folly and idleness of spirit.' *The Talisman.*

PLATO. Colonel Mannering's favourite spaniel. *Guy Mannering.*

PLEYDELL, PAULUS. An Edinburgh advocate: Sheriff-depute of the county at the time of Frank Kennedy's death and young Harry Bertram's disappearance, and also when, sixteen years later, the mystery was solved.

' Mr. Pleydell was a lively, sharp-looking gentleman, with a professional shrewdness in his eye, and, generally speaking, a professional formality in his manners.

But this, like his three-tailed wig and black coat, he could slip off on a Saturday evening, when surrounded by a party of jolly companions, and disposed for what he called his altitudes.' *Guy Mannering.*

PLUMDAMAS, PETER. A shopkeeper in the Lawnmarket. Being 'a lover of peace and good neighbourhood,' he tried to smooth difficulties between Mrs. Howden and Miss Damahoy when their conversation became personal. *The Heart of Midlothian.*

PLUNKET, CAPTAIN. 'A prime fowler' who perished on the Scaw of Unst. His 'kist came ashore dry,' and gave Bryce Snailsfoot a supply of 'the primest o' powder.' *The Pirate.*

(*Kist*, travelling trunk.)

PLYEM, SIR PETER. Parliamentary candidate for a set of five burghs near Gandercleugh. On the day of the coach accident he had hired for electioneering work two pairs of horses from the landlord of the Wallace Inn, and this it was that lengthened the stay of Hardie, Halkit, and Dunover at the inn. *The Heart of Midlothian.*

POINDER, GEORGE. A city officer who accompanied Mr. Sharpitlaw and James Ratcliffe to Muschat's Cairn. He was 'not much desirous of a rencontre hand to hand, and at a distance from his comrades, with such an active and desperate fellow as Robertson.' *The Heart of Midlothian.*

POLICY, MRS. The housekeeper of Queen Mary's apartments in Holyrood, during Mr. Croftangry's residence in the Canongate. In gratitude for his timely assistance in stopping the efforts of Messrs. Scrub and Rub's agent, she allowed him to wander freely through the 'deserted halls.' *The Fair Maid of Perth.*

POLLOCK AND PEELMAN. A firm whose bill formed one of the assets carried off by Rashleigh Osbaldistone. *Rob Roy.*

POLWARTH, ALICK. Edward Waverley's servant during the march into England.

'A simple Edinburgh swain, who had mounted the white cockade in a fit of spleen and jealousy because Jenny Jop had danced a whole night with Corporal Bullock of the Fusileers.' *Waverley.*

POLYDORE. One of the youths whom Bertha encountered on her way to the Crusaders' camp at Scutari. *Count Robert of Paris.*

PONTOYS, STEPHEN. A companion of Ralph Genvil under Amelot when he tried to relieve Wenlock. 'He is as wily as an old fox, and neither hope nor fear will draw him a hair-breadth farther than judgment warrants.' *The Betrothed.*

PORTEOUS, CAPTAIN JOHN. A captain of the City Guards. 'He is said to have been a man of profligate habits, an unnatural son, and a brutal husband,' but he was 'useful in his station, and his harsh and fierce habits rendered him formidable to rioters or disturbers of the public peace.' To the Edinburgh mob, 'one of the fiercest which could be found in

Europe,' he was an object of great hatred, both on general grounds and on account of his conduct at Andrew Wilson's execution. Condemned to death for firing on the crowd and reprieved at the last moment, he died a victim to the mob's vengeance. *The Heart of Midlothian.*

PORTEOUS, MRS. Captain Porteous' widow: the 'elderly female in a black gown' whom Sir George Staunton accidentally met in Mrs. Saddletree's, fourteen years after the Porteous Riot. *The Heart of Midlothian.*

PORTER, SAM. David Ramsay's servant. He looked after the shop when the apprentices were otherwise engaged. *The Fortunes of Nigel.*

POTT, MR. 'Pharmacopolist as well as vender of literature and transmitter of letters.' *St. Ronan's Well.*

POTT, MRS. Mr. Pott's wife. Her 'person and manners were not ill-adapted to her situation, for she was good-looking, and vastly fine and affected.' *St. Ronan's Well.*

POUNDTEXT, PETER. The Presbyterian minister of Milnwood's parish. He had availed himself of the Government's 'indulgence,' and by complying with certain conditions was licensed to preach. After the battle of Drumclog he joined the Covenanters and was 'one of the honest and rational party' in their council. He helped Harry Morton to release Lord Evandale from Burley's hands, and to secure the safe conduct to Edinburgh of the defence party in Tillietudlem. *Old Mortality.*

POWHEID, LAZARUS. The old sexton of the kirk of Douglas from whom Sir Aymer de Valence tried in vain to get information concerning the horseman he had met in the deserted street of Douglas. 'A tall, thin man, emaciated by years and privations; his body was bent habitually by his occupation of grave-digging, and his eye naturally inclined downwards to the scene of his labours.' His features 'were strongly marked, sagacious, and venerable, indicating, at the same time, a certain air of dignity, which age, even mere poverty, may be found occasionally to bestow, as conferring that last melancholy species of independence proper to those whose situation can hardly, by any imaginable means, be rendered much worse than years and fortune have already made it.' *Castle Dangerous.*

POWYS, PRINCE OF. *See* GWENWYN.

POYNINGS. One of the spectators whose greeting the Earl of Leicester returned 'with such ready and condescending courtesy,' as he hurried from the council chamber 'to attend her Majesty to her barge.' *Kenilworth.*

PRANCE OF PADWORTH. One of Michael Lambourne's early comrades. 'Pranced off—made immortal ten years since . . . marry, sir, Oxford Castle and Goodman Thong, and a tenpennyworth of cord, best know how.' *Kenilworth.*

PRAYFORT, PETER. The owner of 'that pendicle or poffle of land called the Carlinescroft,' towards which Jedediah Cleishbotham turned longing eyes. *The Heart of Midlothian.*

PRENDERGAST, MR. Christie Steel's spiritual adviser. He was ' clear ' regarding the 'lawfulness' of her keeping a public-house. *The Highland Widow.*

PRESTON, GENERAL. Commander of the forces in Edinburgh Castle. *Waverley.*

PRITCHARD, CAPTAIN WILLIAM. Master and commander of his Majesty's sloop-of-war *Shark*. Acting on Frank Kennedy's information, he chased Dirk Hatteraick's lugger so close that Dirk fired her rather than be taken. *Guy Mannering.*

PROTOCOL, MR. PETER. An Edinburgh attorney and clerk to the signet. Mistress Margaret Bertram, 'having the fullest confidence in his capacity and integrity,' appointed him her trustee. *Guy Mannering.*

PROUDFUTE, MAUDIE. Oliver's wife. During his lifetime she was noticed only ' as a good-looking, black-haired woman, believed to be dink and disdainful to those whom she thought meaner or poorer than herself,' but after the tragedy of his death she became an imposing figure. The living centre of an enquiry which touched the fundamental relations between the nobles and the citizens, she bore herself alike in presence of the townsmen and of the King with a dignity born ' from the extremity of her distress.' *The Fair Maid of Perth.* (*Dink*, contemptuous.)

PROUDFUTE, OLIVER. The Bonnet-maker, ' a brisk, forward, rather corpulent little man, . . . reasonably wealthy and a leading man in his craft.' He took a prominent part amongst the citizens who brought the affray of St. Valentine's Eve to the notice of Sir Patrick Charteris, greatly magnifying his own share in the defence, and making himself still more ridiculous by his contest with the Devil's Dick. But his struggle ' to obtain the character of a fighting man,' and a gallant ' young blood,' cost him his life. Dressed in Harry Gow's buff-coat and cap of steel, and walking with Harry's swashing step and pibroch whistle, he was struck down by Bonthron in his friend's stead. ' Silly braggart . . . thy loves and thy battles are alike apocryphal.' *The Fair Maid of Perth.*

PROVEDITORE, VENETIAN. ' A little old man, dressed entirely in black . . . one of those deputies whom the Venetian Government sent into camps to overlook the conduct of the generals to whom the leading was consigned, and to maintain that jealous system of espial and control which had long distinguished the policy of the republic.' He protested against King Richard engaging in a trial by combat with Conrade of Montserrat until ' he shall have repaid the fifty thousand bezants which he is indebted to the republic.' *The Talisman.*

PUNCHEON, PETER. 'Cooper to the Queen's stores at the Timmer Burse at Leith.' Gibbie Girder's predecessor in office. *The Bride of Lammermoor.*

PUREFOY. Tutor to Joseph Albany and Nehemiah Holdenough at Cambridge University. *Woodstock.*

Q

QUACKLEBEN, DR. QUENTIN. A member of the Committee of Management in 'the infant republic of St. Ronan's Well': 'the Man of Medicine.' He had been 'first to proclaim and vindicate the merits of these healing fountains,' the waters having cured Lady Penelope Penfeather 'of her seventh attack upon the nerves, attended with febrile symptoms.' 'He resided nine months out of the twelve at St. Ronan's, and was supposed to make an indifferent good thing of it—especially as he played whist to admiration.' He also attached himself to Mrs. Blower. *St. Ronan's Well.*

QUACKLEBEN, MASS JOHN. An authority on spiritual matters approved of by Andrew Fairservice. *Rob Roy.*

QUHELE, CLAN. *See* CHATTAN AND QUHELE.

QUID, MR. One of Mistress Bertram's disappointed relatives: a tobacconist who, 'having a good stock-in-trade when the colonial war broke out, trebled the price of his commodity to all the world, Mrs. Bertram alone excepted, whose tortoiseshell snuff-box was weekly filled with the best rappee at the old prices.' *Guy Mannering.*

QUINCY, ROGER DE. Earl of Winchester. During his absence in Palestine Prince John occupied his Castle of Ashby, and 'disposed of his domains without scruple.' *Ivanhoe.*

QUITAM, MR. An attorney: one of the Sunday guests of Jonathan Brown. *Rob Roy.*

QUODLING. The Duke of Buckingham's 'little chaplain.' He declaimed the Duke's funeral sermon on Mother Cresswell. *Peveril of the Peak.*

R

RABAT, JAMES. Dean of Guild in Glasgow when the townsmen gathered together to withstand the destruction of their Cathedral by the reformers. 'And a gude mason he was himself, made him the keener to keep up the auld bigging.' *Rob Roy.*

RACHEL. 'A girl who acted occasionally' as Deborah Debbitch's assistant in attending to Alice Bridgenorth and Julian Peveril when children together in Martindale Castle. *Peveril of the Peak.*

RACKAM. One of the crew of the *Fortune's Favourite.* *The Pirate.*

RAINE, DAME. Roger's wife. When left a buxom widow she was 'so far incommoded by the exercise of her newly acquired independence that she had recourse upon all occasions to the advice of Matt Chamberlain.' But when Julian

Peveril appealed to her in his anxiety for his father her own instincts prevailed. *Peveril of the Peak.*

RAINE, ROGER. ' The drunken tapster of the Peveril Arms ' : one of the guests at Lady Peveril's Restoration Feast. He was also one of the men who, with Sir Geoffrey, escorted the Countess of Derby from Martindale Castle on her way to the Isle of Man. *Peveril of the Peak.*

RALEIGH, SIR WALTER. Blount's ' Wittypate ' : Queen Elizabeth's ' Squire Lack-Cloak,' ' to whom nature had taught intuitively, as it were, these courtly arts which many scarce acquire from long experience.' ' Accomplished in mind and body, with grace, gallantry, literature, and valour,' and showing in his expression ' the firmness of a decided, and the fire of an enterprising, character, the power of reflection and the promptitude of determination,' he rose rapidly in the Queen's favour.

' An eagle am I, that will never think of dull earth while there is a heaven to soar in, and a sun to gaze upon.' *Kenilworth.*

RAMORNY, SIR JOHN. Master of the House to David, Duke of Rothesay. Serving his master ' through vice and virtue,' he lost his hand by a blow from Henry Gow in the midnight turmoil on Saint Valentine's Eve. His revenge having miscarried, he was driven to the extremity of hatred against the Duke by the ' cautious and limited testimony ' given on his behalf to the King when enquiry was made concerning Oliver Proudfute's death. In league with the Duke of Albany, and served by Dwining and Bonthron, he became ' a willing agent in young Rothesay's destruction.' *The Fair Maid of Perth.*

RAMSAY, DAVID. ' Memory's Monitor, watchmaker and constructor of horloges to his most Sacred Majesty James I ' : ' an ingenious but whimsical and self-opinioned mechanic.' He ' was a civil neighbour, and a learned man, doubtless, and might be a rich man if he had common-sense to back his learning ; and, doubtless, for a Scot, neighbour Ramsay was nothing of a bad man, but he was so constantly grimed with smoke, gilded with brass filings, and smeared with lamp-black and oil, that Dame Simmons judged it would require his whole shopful of watches to induce any feasible woman to touch the said neighbour Ramsay with anything save a pair of tongs.' *The Fortunes of Nigel.*

RAMSAY, MARGARET. David's daughter. She ' was about twenty years old, very pretty, very demure, yet with lively black eyes, that ever and anon contradicted the expression of sobriety, to which silence, reserve, a plain velvet hood, and a cambric ruff had condemned Mistress Marget as the daughter of a quiet citizen.' She was in reality spoilt and indulged, and had ' a hundred freakish whims and humours,' but her ' excellent heart ' was touched by the sorrow in Nigel's voice and the 'misfortune in his melancholy smile.' Through the knowledge of his distresses she became a 'deep-thinking and impassioned woman, ready to make exertions alike and sacrifices, with all that vain devotion to a favourite object of affection, which is often so basely rewarded.' *The Fortunes of Nigel.*

RAMSAY, SIR WILLIAM, OF DALWOLSEY. The 'auld and honourable stock' from which, the King maintained, David Ramsay was descended. 'They all wrought wi' steel, man; only the auld knights drilled holes wi' their swords in their enemies' corselets, and he saws nicks in his brass wheels.' *The Fortunes of Nigel.*

RAND, JOCK. One of the Mucklebackits' friends. *The Antiquary.*

RAND, TAM. The miller's man: one of the 'few lads' Jenny Dennison knew 'to speak to.' *Old Mortality.*

RANDAL. One of the Lady of Lochleven's attendants. *The Abbot.*

RANGER. One of Frank Kennedy's dogs. *Guy Mannering.*

RANNLETREE, CAPTAIN. The visitor whose lodgings at the Well, Mr. Winterblossom thought, might suit Frank Tyrrel. He 'seems disposed to resign the folding-bed at Lilliput Hall, on account of his finding it rather deficient in length.' *St. Ronan's Well.*

RAOUL. 'An old and almost invalided huntsman, whose more active services in the field and the chase had been for some time chiefly limited to the superintendence' of Sir Raymond Berenger's kennels. Cross-grained and rheumatic, he was at constant war with his wife, Dame Gillian. *The Betrothed.*

RAREDRENCH, MR. The apothecary who attended to Richie Moniplies' wounds in David Ramsay's shop. 'This gentleman, as sometimes happens to those of the learned professions, had rather more lore than knowledge.' *The Fortunes of Nigel.*

RASPER, JAMES. Mrs. Glass' shopman. *The Heart of Midlothian.*

RATCLIFFE, HUBERT. The 'humble friend' through whose exertions Sir Edward Mauley regained his freedom and the management of his own property. As an inmate of Ellieslaw Castle, and at the same time the channel through which Sir Edward's liberality flowed, he exercised almost complete control over Ellieslaw's affairs. 'A grave, steady, reserved man,' he remained to the end Sir Edward's 'sole confidant.' *The Black Dwarf.*

RATCLIFFE, JAMES. 'Daddie Ratton': a 'most notorious thief,' well known in Highlands and Lowlands, 'forby England and Holland.' Though lying under sentence of death, he did not take advantage of the Porteous Riot to escape from the Tolbooth, having, he said, 'ta'en a fancy to leave aff trade, and set up for an honest man.' He recognised George Robertson under his disguise as 'Madge Wildfire,' and with this information ingratiated himself into the magistrates' favour, and became a turnkey. 'If sac be that he's disposed to turn his knowledge to the city's service,' said the Procurator Fiscal, ' ye'll no find a better man. Ye'll get nae saints to be searchers for uncustomed goods or for thieves and sic like—and your decent sort of men . . . can do nae gude ava.' *The Heart of Midlothian.*

RATCLIFFE, THOMAS. *See* SUSSEX, EARL OF.

RATTRAY, SIR RULLION, OF RANAGULLION. The opponent who in mortal combat cut off three of the fingers of Sir Mungo Malagrowther's right hand. *The Fortunes of Nigel.*

RAVENSWOOD FAMILY, THE.

— SIR MALISE. ' The Revenger ' : a thirteenth-century ancestor of the Ravenswood family. By a well-timed attack on a powerful usurper, he gave the family its motto, ' I bide my time.'

— RAYMOND. The ancestor of the Ravenswood family around whom centred the legend concerning the Mermaid's Well. The family dated its decay from his time. He was killed on the Field of Flodden. *See also* ZACHARY, FATHER.

— LORD RAVENSWOOD (THE 11TH). ' Called the Skipper, from his delight in naval matters.' He encouraged the trade of Wolf's-hope by building the pier, and for this ' it had been matter of understanding, that he was to have the first stone of butter after the calving of every cow within the barony, and the first egg, thence called the Monday's egg, laid by every hen on every Monday in the year.'

RAVENSWOOD FAMILY, THE.

— LORD RANDAL. Edgar's great-grandfather, seen and remembered by Caleb Balderstone.

— ' AULD ' RAVENSWOOD. Allan's father. ' He raised his militia to caper awa' to Bothwell Brigg against the wrang-headed wastland whigs.'

— ALLAN. Edgar's father. He fought with the militia against the Covenanters at Bothwell Bridge, and in the Revolution of 1688 ' espoused the sinking side.' For this his blood ' had been attainted and his title abolished.' Of a ' hot, fiery, and imprudent character,' he ' fought every point to the last ' in his lawsuits with Sir William Ashton, and ' resisted every effort at compromise ' with a ' determined and dogged obstinacy.' He died ' during a fit of violent and impotent fury,' breathing curses on his successful adversary.

— EDGAR, MASTER OF RAVENSWOOD. Son of Allan, Lord Ravenswood. The brooding spirit of his father's legacy of vengeance ' had quenched the light and ingenuous vivacity of youth in a countenance singularly fitted to display both, and it was not easy to gaze ' on him ' without a secret impression either of pity or awe.' But his vows of vengeance were beguiled from his mind by Sir William Ashton's plausible pretences, and in spite of all warnings and portents he ' abandoned himself ' to the pleasure of Lucy's society. Unable to realise the difficulties of her position during his absence and blinded by his turbulent passions when he sought her on his return, he himself dealt the last blow to her tottering reason. His wild unreasonableness snapped the tie that bound her to life. *The Bride of Lammermoor.*

RAYMOND OF TOULOUSE. One of the leaders of the first Crusade. With Tancred, he refrained from paying allegiance to Alexius Comnenus when passing through Constantinople. *Count Robert of Paris.*

REBECCA. Isaac's beautiful daughter. Though born of a despised race, she ' bore herself with a proud humility,' believing it was the especial duty of the children of Zion ' to suffer without sinning.' Reflection had trained her judgment, and she was prepared, ' by habits of thought and by natural strength of mind,' to control her tenderness for Ivanhoe and at the same time to encounter the dangers to which Bois-Guilbert's passion exposed her. ' In that strong reliance on Heaven natural to great and generous characters,' she remained unmoved alike by his threats and his entreaties. Death was at all times the least of her apprehensions, and when it seemed imminent she said to Guilbert, ' When we enter those fatal lists, thou to fight and I to suffer, I feel the strong assurance within me, that my courage shall mount higher than thine.' *Ivanhoe.*

REBECCA, MRS. Mistress Bertram's maid.
' But I hope my mistress's is a good will for a' that, for it would be hard on me to lose the wee bit legacy—I served for little fee and bountith, weel I wot.' *Guy Mannering.*

RECLUSE, THE. *See* BLACK DWARF, THE.

RED-FINGER. *See* VANDA.

REDGAUNTLET FAMILY, THE.

— ALBERICK. A valiant knight called Fitz-Aldin, who won his name ' from the great slaughter which he had made of the Southron ' in the wars for Scottish Independence. During a headlong pursuit of the ' minion ' Baliol, he unhorsed his son Edward, and ' without pausing to enquire whether young Edward was wounded, he dashed his spurs into his horse. . . . The steed made indeed a bound forward, but was unable to clear the body of the youth, and with its hind foot struck him in the forehead, as he was in the act of rising. The blow was mortal.' After this unnatural crime the Redgauntlets were marked by ' a singular indenture of the forehead ' resembling a miniature horse-shoe. Heaven also ' decreed that the valour of his race should always be fruitless, and that the cause which they espoused should never prosper.'

— EDWARD. Alberick's elder son. He ' shared so much the haughty spirit of his father, that he became impatient of domestic control, resisted paternal authority, and finally fled from his father's house, renounced his political opinions, and awakened his mortal displeasure by joining the adherents of Baliol.'

REDGAUNTLET FAMILY. THE.
— SIR ROBERT. The hero of Wandering Willie's tale. He fought for Charles II in Montrose's time, and 'was aye for the strong hand; and his name is kend as wide in the country as Claverhouse's or Tam Dalyell's.' But he was 'disturbed in his grave' by Steenie Steenson's curses, and in his hall of 'ghastly revellers,' gave Steenie his receipt, telling him, 'There is your receipt, ye pitiful cur; and for the money, my dog-whelp of a son may go look for it in the Cat's Cradle.'

See also WEIR, MAJOR.

— SIR JOHN. Sir Robert's son. 'Some thought it was easier counting with the auld rough knight than the fair-spoken young ane'; in the absence of both receipt and money he told Steenie Steenson to 'pay or flit.' When, after Steenie's night in Pitmurkie Wood, they were found, he 'made up his story about the jackanape as he liked himself.'

— SIR REDWALD. Sir John's only son: 'the last of the honourable house.' Willie Steenson spent 'mony a merry year wi' him, but . . . he gaed out with other pretty men in the forty-five.'

Note.—The relationship between Sir Redwald and Sir Henry is not clear. When giving Alan Fairford an account of his own escape, Mr. Maxwell of Summertrees refers to Willie's devotion to his 'master,' Sir Henry, in Carlisle prison. This seems to identify Sir Redwald with Sir Henry, but for the fact that Sir Henry was not an only son. If, on the other hand, Sir Redwald was a predecessor of Sir Henry, he was not 'the last' of the house.

REDGAUNTLET FAMILY, THE.
— SIR HENRY. 'Chief of his name' in the time of the 'Forty-five.' He distinguished himself at Culloden, but was captured, and suffered death at Carlisle.

— EDWARD HUGH. Sir Henry's younger brother: uncle of Darsie Latimer. 'A political enthusiast of the most dangerous character,' he was undismayed by the failure of the 'Forty-five,' and in his various spheres as 'Laird of the Solway Lochs,' 'Herries of Birrenswork,' and 'Squire Ingoldsby,' spent his life endeavouring, 'in contempt of every danger . . . to awaken the courage of a broken party.' Proud, passionate, and unscrupulous, he felt, while trying to bring Darsie as well as Lilias into subjection to his will, that the spirit of his ancestor, Sir Alberick, was alive within him, and that he was ready, should Darsie oppose him, to earn a 'new doom.' But the young Chevalier's hereditary obstinacy, combined with Cristal Nixon's treachery, brought all his schemes to nought.

See also HUGO, FATHER.

— LADY DARSIE. Sir Henry's wife. She blamed his brother's 'insane political enthusiasm' for her husband's death, and was 'irresistibly anxious' to save her children from their uncle's guardianship. But he discovered her retreat and kidnapped Lilias. Arthur was saved from a similar fate, and was sent after his mother's death, to Edinburgh, where he was brought up as Darsie Latimer, being kept in ignorance of his parentage, in accordance with his mother's last instructions to Samuel Griffiths.

REDGAUNTLET FAMILY, THE.

— SIR ARTHUR DARSIE. Son of Sir Henry and Lady Darsie. Educated in Edinburgh as Darsie Latimer, he tried, while an inmate of Mr. Fairford's house, to devote himself, like Alan, to the study of law. But he was of a 'romantic' and 'unsettled' disposition, and set off on a tour to the South of Scotland in the vague wish to be as near as possible to his 'native England.' There his identity was discovered by the Laird of the Solway Lochs, who caused him to be seized and conveyed into Cumberland that the legal guardianship appointed by Sir Henry might be assumed. Darsie bore the apparent unreasonableness of his captivity with spirit, and overcame his uncle's violent determination that he should throw in his lot with the young Chevalier by following Lilias' advice to 'temporise . . . and let the bubble burst of itself.'

— LILIAS. Daughter of Sir Henry and Lady Darsie. She was kidnapped in childhood by her uncle, and after being educated abroad, travelled throughout England and Scotland with him, virtually a prisoner. She witnessed many of his 'strange and desperate machinations,' and in view of his 'rashness and enthusiasm,' soon learnt to keep her own 'liberal opinions' secret. As 'Green Mantle' she stirred the romantic feelings of Alan Fairford and Darsie Latimer: of Alan, as the mysterious lady who, with a 'mixture of grace and timidity,' warned him of Darsie's danger, and of Darsie, as the 'sweet and gentle-speaking creature,' 'severe in youthful wisdom,' who tried to put him on his guard, and afterwards, during his captivity in Cumberland, kept hope alive within him. *Redgauntlet.*

RED GREGARACH. *See* MACGREGOR, ROBERT or ROBIN.

RED-HAND. *See* WARDOUR, SIR RICHARD.

REDMAN, SIR MAGNUS. English Warden of the Eastern Marches: one of Harry Gow's customers. *The Fair Maid of Perth.*

REDMANTLE (CLOGHT-DEARG). The evil spirit supposed to haunt the glen in which Elspat MacTavish accosted the Rev. Michael Tyrie as he returned from his attendance at Hamish's execution. *The Highland Widow.*

RED REIVER. *See* WILLIE OF WESTBURNFLAT.

RED ROTTEN. A gipsy warned off by Dunbog. *Guy Mannering.*

REINOLD. An ancient Norman esquire, Sir Raymond Berenger's butler. *The Betrothed.*

RELIGION, THE MAN OF. *See* CHATTERLY, SIMON.

RENÉ OF ANJOU. 'King of both the Sicilies, Naples, Aragon, and Jerusalem.' 'His daughter is dethroned, his dominions crumbling to pieces, his family on the eve of becoming extinct, his grandson driven from one lurking-place to another, and expelled from his mother's inheritance—and he can find amusement in these fopperies!' He 'feasted and received guests, danced, sung, composed poetry, used the pencil or brush with no small skill, devised and conducted festivals and processions, and studying to promote, as far as possible, the immediate mirth and good-humour of his subjects, if he could not materially enlarge their more permanent prosperity, was never mentioned by them, excepting as *Le Bon Roi René*, a distinction conferred on him down to the present day, and due to him certainly by the qualities of his heart, if not by those of his head.' *Anne of Geierstein*.

RENTOWEL, JABESH. A youthful preacher in the little town to which Callum Beg convoyed Edward Waverley from Glennaquoich. *Waverley*.

RENWICK, MR. JAMES. 'A blessed martyr' for the Covenant, executed in 1688. *The Heart of Midlothian*.

REUBEN. 'A dark-browed and black-bearded Israelite' in attendance on Isaac and Rebecca in Ashby-de-la-Zouch. He helped to carry Wilfred of Ivanhoe to their home after he fainted from his wounds in the Passage of Arms. *Ivanhoe*.

REUBEN OF TADCASTER. One of Isaac's wealthy friends. From him, Isaac assured Bois-Guilbert, 'the very gaberdine I wear is borrowed.' *Ivanhoe*.

REWCASTLE, JOHN. A Jedburgh smuggler who attended the Jacobite gathering at Ellieslaw Castle. *The Black Dwarf*.

RICE, THOMAS AP. A 'thorough-paced' Welshman in attendance on the Earl of Sussex. On the occasion of the Queen's unexpected visit to Say's Court, Raleigh feared she should find him breakfasting off his 'leek porridge and toasted cheese—and she detests, they say, all coarse meats, evil smells, and strong wines.' *Kenilworth*.

RICHARD CŒUR DE LION. (1) Son of Henry II. He accompanied his father to the siege of the castle of Garde Doloureuse, and took it by storm. 'As much too hot as his brother is too cold.'

(2) The Crusader King of England. Possessing 'stern resolution and restless activity' as well as 'that ardour of mind which wooed danger as a bride,' he was chief of the allied princes in 'courage, hardihood, and military talents.' But his 'reckless impatience,' his 'uncurbed haughtiness,' and 'unveiled contempt for his brother sovereigns' caused constant discord with Philip of France and Leopold of Austria, and led eventually to the abandonment of the enterprise. 'Alas! that a creature so noble as thou art—so accomplished in princely thoughts and princely daring—so

fitted to honour Christendom by thy actions, and, in thy calmer mood, to rule her by thy wisdom, should yet have the brute and wild fury of the lion mingled with the dignity and courage of that king of the forest!'

(3) As the Black Knight of the Fetterlock, he successfully intervened to help Ivanhoe at a critical juncture in the Passage of Arms at Ashby-de-la-Zouch, and afterwards directed the attack of Locksley and his men on Front-de-Bœuf's castle. 'Gay, good-humoured, and fond of manhood in every rank of life,' he had a mind ' unapt to apprehend danger and prompt to defy it when most imminent.' ' A generous, but rash and romantic monarch.' (1) *The Betrothed.* (2) *The Talisman.* (3) *Ivanhoe.*

RICHARD, DUKE OF GLOUCESTER. Brother to Edward IV, during whose reign he held various high offices: afterwards Richard III. 'The savage Richard': 'the blood-drinker.' *Anne of Geierstein.*

RICKETS, MABEL. The old Northumbrian nurse who poured herself forth to Frank Osbaldistone's infant ears 'in descriptions of the scenes of her youth, and long narratives of the events which tradition declared to have passed amongst them.' *Rob Roy.*

RIMEGAP, JOE. A miner from the Bonadventure mine, who was ' shot as dead as a buck in season ' during Lance Outram's attack on Moultrassie Hall. *Peveril of the Peak.*

RINGAN. *See* ANTON.

RINGHORSE, SIR ROBERT. One of the old time lords who ' were decent, considerate men, that didna plague a puir herd callant muckle about a moorfowl or a mawkin, unless he turned common fowler.' *St. Ronan's Well.*

(*Callant,* a stripling. *Mawkin,* a hare.)

RINGWOOD, MASTER. Reginald Lowestoffe's cousin. One of Richie Moniplies' companions in trapping Captain Colepepper at Camlet Moat. *The Fortunes of Nigel.*

RINTHEROUT, JENNY. The Antiquary's female domestic. She ' vexed hersell ' about Steenie Mucklebackit, ' the silly tawpie, as if he wad ever hae lookit ower his shouther at the like o' her!' *The Antiquary.*

(*Tawpie,* a foolish woman.)

RINTHEROUT, TAM. Brother of Jenny. At Miss Grizzel's instigation the Antiquary took him on trial as a manservant for a time, but this was not a success.

'Why did he pilfer apples,' his master asked, ' take birds' nests, break glasses, and ultimately steal my spectacles, except that he felt that noble emulation which swells in the bosom of the masculine sex, which has conducted him to Flanders with a musket on his shoulder, and doubtless will promote him to a glorious halbert, or even to the gallows ?' *The Antiquary.*

RIVANE. *See* RUTHVEN, WILL.

RIVIÈRE, SIRE PENCIL. One of the exiled French nobles whose presence in Peronne gave Louis a sense of insecurity, and caused him to ask to be lodged in the Castle during his stay. *Quentin Durward.*

ROAN ROBIN. The horse which Darsie Latimer rode to Dumfries. *Redgauntlet.*

ROB ROY. *See* MACGREGOR, ROBERT or ROBIN.

ROB THE RAMBLER. Wandering Willie's comrade. On the day of the dance at Brokenburn, having 'got to the lee-side of some smuggler's punch-bowl,' he failed to meet Willie at the rendezvous. Darsie Latimer then played the 'mad frolic' of taking his place. Rob and Willie were at Joe Crackenthorp's during the critical interview between 'Father Buonaventure' and his leading adherents, and warned them of treachery by playing 'The Campbells are coming.' *Redgauntlet.*

ROB THE RANTER. One of Madge Wildfire's 'joes.' *The Heart of Midlothian.*

(*Jo,* a sweetheart.)

ROBB, DUNCAN. The grocer at Kippletringan. He 'has aye a sum to make up, and either wants ready money, or a short-dated bill.' *Guy Mannering.*

ROBERT. One of Sir Arthur Wardour's menservants. Under the strain of Sir Arthur's ill-temper, he referred to unpaid wages, and was dismissed. 'Never answer a master that speaks to you in a passion.' *The Antiquary.*

ROBERT, DUKE OF NORMANDY. Son of William the Conqueror: one of the leaders of the first Crusade who, when passing through Constantinople, promised allegiance to Alexius Comnenus. 'A valiant, though extravagant, thoughtless, and weak man.' *Count Robert of Paris.*

ROBERT III OF SCOTLAND. Greatgrandson of Robert the Bruce, and 'second of the ill-fated family of Stewart.' 'The King of so fierce a people as the Scots then were ought to have been warlike, prompt, and active, liberal in rewarding services, strict in punishing crimes; one whose conduct should make him feared as well as beloved. The qualities of Robert the Third were the reverse of all these.' His good-nature was 'so great as to approach to defenceless simplicity or weakness of character,' and 'according to the interest which had been last exerted over his flexible mind, the King would change from an indulgent to a strict and even cruel father—from a confiding to a jealous brother—or from a benignant and bountiful to a grasping and encroaching Sovereign.' Unable to discipline his wayward son, David, Duke of Rothesay, who, in spite of wilfulness, was the light of his eyes and the darling of his heart, he entrusted the young Duke to the care of the Duke of Albany. David's death, followed by the capture of young Prince James by Henry IV of England, broke the King's heart. *The Fair Maid of Perth.*

ROBERTS. George Heriot's cashkeeper. 'Roberts, like Sir Mungo himself, was a little deaf, and like Sir Mungo, knew also how to make the most of it.' *The Fortunes of Nigel.*

ROBERTS, JOHN. The man who stood at the wheel of the *Jumping Jenny* under Nanty Ewart : 'a bald-pated, grizzled old fellow, whose whole life had been spent in evading the revenue laws, with now and then the relaxation of a few months' imprisonment, for deforcing officers, resisting seizures, and the like offences.' *Redgauntlet.*

ROBERTSON, DR. One of the 'preachers whose talents have done such honour' to Scotland. *Guy Mannering.*

See also HUME, DAVID.

ROBERTSON, GEORGE ('GENTLEMAN GEORDIE'). Andrew Wilson's accomplice. With several old associates he would have rescued Wilson 'from the very noose that dangled over his head,' had not the Edinburgh magistrates 'anticipated, by half an hour, the ordinary period for execution.' His hatred was then directed against 'the beast, Porteous, who kept firing on the people long after it had ceased to be necessary,' and some months later, as 'Madge Wildfire,' he directed the Porteous Riot and gained his revenge. He hoped at the same time to effect Effie Deans' escape from the Tolbooth, but in this he failed, as he did in his later attempt to induce Jeanie to save her sister's life by telling a lie. *The Heart of Midlothian.*

See also STAUNTON, GEORGE.

ROBERTSONS OF ATHOLE. *See* DONNOCHY.

ROBIN. 'Butler, valet-de-chambre, footman, gardener, and what-not, in the house of Milnwood.' *Old Mortality.*

ROBIN. Horse-boy in the Castle of Garde Douloureuse. *The Betrothed.*

ROBIN OF REDCASTLE. One of Julian Avenel's men. He 'spoiled a good gelding in chasing' Halbert Glendinning after his escape from Julian's castle. *The Monastery.*

ROBINS, ZERUBBABEL. Chief of four soldiers left by Cromwell in Dr. Rochecliffe's chamber to help Humgudgeon in preventing the supposed king's flight from Love's Ladder. He and Merciful Strickalthrow seized Albert Lee after his perilous leap. *Woodstock.*

ROBISON, DICK. 'The player whose ghost haunted Harrison.' 'He served for his old master, Charles, in Mohun's troop, and was murdered by this butcher's dog . . . after surrender at the battle of Naseby Field.' Tomkins, knowing Harrison's fanatical fears, instructed Jocelin Joliffe to play the part of Robison's ghost. *Woodstock.*

ROBSART, AMY. Daughter of Sir Hugh Robsart : Countess of Leicester. After her runaway marriage she was 'mewed up like some foreign slave' in Cumnor Place, but she bore her solitude 'with pleasure' as long as she was sure her lord loved her. When Richard Varney would have compromised her honour, however, she showed 'a spirit and temper as apprehensive as lightning, and as swift n execution,' and by her energy and earnestness she almost persuaded Leicester to forsake the 'crooked policies' which were 'so repugnant to her noble nature.' Yet she was left defenceless against Varney's deadly revenge. *Kenilworth.*

ROBSART, SIR HUGH. The 'jovial knight' of Lidcote Hall who 'hath loved hospitality and open housekeeping more than the present fashion, which lays as much gold lace on the seams of a doublet as would feed a dozen of tall fellows with beef and ale for a twelvemonth.' But when Amy, 'the principal joy' of the house, went secretly away, his spirit was broken. 'My poor head,' he confessed to Tressilian, 'forgets all it should remember, and remembers only what it would most willingly forget.' *Kenilworth.*

ROBSART, SIR ROGER. Sir Hugh's father. He 'valiantly took part with Henry VII.' in the battle of Stoke, and protected Edmund Tressilian's grandfather from the King's vengeance when he was taken, fighting for Lambert Simnel. *Kenilworth.*

ROCCOMBOLE, MARQUIS DE. A dear friend to Mr. Touchwood who 'whistles all the time you talk to him. He says he learned it in the reign of terror when a man was glad to whistle to show his throat was whole.' *St. Ronan's Well.*

ROCHECLIFFE, DOCTOR JOSEPH ALBANY. The fictitious antiquarian in whose manuscripts Scott professed to have found the subject matter of this tale. Rector of Woodstock, and 'chaplain during most part of the Civil War, to Sir Henry Lee's regiment,' he had been 'a main limb in every thing that has been attempted since forty-two — penned declarations, conducted correspondence, communicated with chiefs, recruited followers, commissioned arms, levied money, appointed rendezvouses.' His knowledge of the labyrinth of passages in Woodstock Lodge made possible the tricks by which Desborough, Harrison, and Bletson were frightened from the spot, and a safe hiding place for Charles II secured. But in spite of his 'audacity, presence of mind, and depth of judgment,' he was 'goose enough to believe that such a fellow as Tomkins would value anything beyond the offer of the best bidder.' *Woodstock.*

See also ALBANY, JOSEPH.

RODERICK MAWR. *See* GWENWYN.

'ROGUE' HARRISON. The butcher in command of the 'three thousand Roundheads' against whom the Countess of Derby defended Latham House for six weeks. *Peveril of the Peak.*

ROLLOCK. One of the citizens who met together on St. Valentine's Day, 'for investigating the affray of the preceding evening.' *The Fair Maid of Perth.*

RONALDSON, NEIL. The Ranzelman 'who had the voice most potential in the deliberations of the township': one of Swertha's 'confederates' in making as much profit as possible out of Mr. Mertoun. He 'canna walk a mile to hear the minister, but he will hirple ten if he hears of a ship embayed.' He divided, 'with all due impartiality, the spoils of the wrecked vessel amongst the natives of the community; listening to and redressing their complaints of inequality; and (if the matter in hand had not been, from beginning to end, utterly unjust and indefensible) discharging the part of a wise and prudent magistrate, in all the details.' *The Pirate.*

(*Hirple*, to walk haltingly.)

RORY. One of the two Highlanders who attended Rob Roy when he went to keep his tryst with Rashleigh Osbaldistone. *Rob Roy.*

RORY BEAN. The Laird of Dumbiedikes' 'Highland Pegasus.' 'My powny,' the Laird once said at Davie Deans' house, 'winna for the life o' me gang ony other road than just frae Dumbiedikes to this house-end, and sae straight back again.' *The Heart of Midlothian.*

RORY DALL. One of the last harpers of the Western Highlands: teacher of Flora MacIvor. *Waverley.*

ROSABELLE. Queen Mary's favourite horse. 'Never matched in Scotland for swiftness, for ease of motion, and for sureness of foot.' *The Abbot.*

ROSAMUND, FAIR. Daughter of Walter de Clifford, and mistress of Henry II. The Tower built for her by her royal lover 'was traditionally said to have been accessible only by a sort of small drawbridge, which might be dropped at pleasure from a little portal near the summit of the turret, to the battlements of another tower of the same construction, but twenty feet lower, and containing only a winding staircase, called in *Woodstock* Love's Ladder.' The famous labyrinth 'round which successive Monarchs had erected a Hunting seat or Lodge' was also planned to ensure her safety; so that, 'if at any time her lodging were laid about by the Queen, she might easily avoid peril imminent.' But 'our records say she was poisoned by the injured Queen.' The labyrinth, tower, and turret are made to serve Dr. Rochecliffe's purposes, and Albert Lee's more effectually. *Woodstock.*

For ROSAMUND see also SALISBURY, EARL OF.

Ross, LORD. Commander of the Government forces lying at Glasgow. Claverhouse joined him after the defeat at Drumclog, and together they resisted a spirited attack led by Harry Morton. *Old Mortality.*

ROSSBALLOH, AULD. See TAMLOWRIE, LAIRD OF.

ROSWAL. Sir Kenneth's stag greyhound, 'of the noblest Northern breed—deep in the chest, strong in the stern, black colour, and brindled on breast and legs—not spotted with white, but just shaded into grey—strength to pull down a bull—swiftness to cote an antelope.' Severely wounded when protecting the English standard during his master's absence from duty, he was cured by Adonbec's sacred talisman, and by his 'noble instinct' detected Conrade of Montserrat as his assailant, while Conrade was in the act of paying public honour to the flag he had violated. *The Talisman.*

ROTHESAY, DAVID, DUKE OF. Robert III's eldest son, 'a young man of spirit and talent.' Married against his inclinations to Marjory Douglas, he 'took his own mode of venting his displeasure, by neglecting his wife, contemning his formidable and dangerous father-in-law, and showing little respect to the authority of the King himself, and none whatever to the remonstrances of Albany, his uncle, whom he looked upon as his confirmed enemy.' After the death of his mother, Queen Annabella, he gave himself up to 'fugitive amours and extravagant revels,' scrupling at 'no extremities which may promise to gratify an idle passion.' Forwarded in his vicious course by Sir John Ramorny, and dogged by the Duke of Albany, he was early blighted, like 'a flower exhausted from having been made to bloom too soon.' *The Fair Maid of Perth.*

Note.—He died in 1402, not in 1396 as Scott indicates.

ROTHESAY, DUCHESS. *See* DOUGLAS, MARJORY.

ROUGE SANGLIER. The name assumed by Hayraddin when he came to the court of Charles the Bold disguised as a herald from William de la Marck. *Quentin Durward.*

ROUGEDRAGON, LADY RACHEL. 'A meagre old Scottish lady of high rank.' Lilias Redgauntlet lived with her for a time after leaving the Parisian convent. 'She was not ill-tempered,' Lilias told Darsie, nor very covetous — neither beat me nor starved me—but she was so completely trammelled by rank and prejudices, so awfully profound in genealogy, and so bitterly keen, poor lady, in British politics, that I sometimes thought it pity that the Hanoverians, who murdered, as she used to tell me, her poor dear father, had left his dear daughter in the land of the living.' *Redgauntlet.*

ROUGH RALPH. Lance Outram's 'helper' in the care of the park at Martindale Castle. *Peveril of the Peak.*

ROUSILLON, RAYMOND and MARGARET DE. *See* CABESTAINY, WILLIAM.

ROUSLAER, SYNDIC. One of the leaders of the discontented citizens in Liège. In open communication with William de la Marck, he was also a 'very busy and bustling' friend to Louis. He and Pavillon accosted Quentin Durward in Liège as an envoy from Louis, having recognised the badge of the Scottish Guard which Quentin wore. *Quentin Durward.*

See also PAVILLON, SYNDIC.

ROVER, THE RED. *See* LONGUEVILLE, THOMAS DE.

ROWENA, LADY OF HARGOTTSTANDSTEDE. Cedric's ward. She 'drew her descent from Alfred,' and Cedric hoped to 'forward the restoration of Saxon independence' by her union with Athelstane.

But he accustomed her to so much deference and homage that she exercised not only 'free will, but despotic authority,' and was 'disposed both to resist and to resent any attempt to control her affections.' She did not try 'to conceal her avowed preference of Wilfred of Ivanhoe.' But 'her disposition was naturally . . . mild, timid, and gentle.' In her countenance there reigned 'gentleness and goodness,' Rebecca said; ' and if a tinge of the world's pride or vanities may mix with an expression so lovely, how should we chide what is of the earth for bearing some colour of its original?' *Ivanhoe.*

ROWLEY. One of Julian Avenel's Border-riders: 'constant at his feast,' he fled at the fray. *The Monastery.*

RUBEMPRÉ, MONSEIGNEUR DE. One of the nobles of Burgundy who assembled 'to superintend the defence of the country' when Charles the Bold retired to Upper Burgundy after the defeat at Morat. *Anne of Geierstein.*

RUBRICK, MR. A non-juring clergyman: a guest of the Baron of Bradwardine. 'A particularly good man, who had a very quiet and peaceful conscience, *that never did him any harm.*' *Waverley.*

(*Non-juring clergyman,* one who refused to recognise the Revolution and the Hanoverian succession.)

RUBRICK OF DUCHRAN. See DUCHRAN.

RUBRICK, THE MISSES. 'She of the four Miss Rubricks who chanced to be next Rose was sure to recollect that her thimble, or her scissors, were at the other end of the room, in order to leave the seat nearest to Miss Bradwardine vacant for his occupation.' *Waverley.*

RUMBLEBERRY, RICHARD. A young preacher from the Glen of Bengonnar 'who suffered martyrdom in the Grassmarket.' 'They say he gaed singing and rejoicing till't.' *Old Mortality.*

RUMMELAER, COMMODORE. One of Magnus Troil's friends who had been 'down in the Bay of Honduras and all thereabouts,' and who held that 'there is never peace with Spaniards beyond the Line.' *The Pirate.*

RUSSEL, JAMES. 'A person of exceeding and punctilious zeal': one of the slayers of the Archbishop of St. Andrews. He gave 'his testimony with great warmth even against' the payment of freights at public ferries as being an unlawful 'subjection to constituted authority.' *The Heart of Midlothian.*

RUTHVEN (*also* RIVANE, RUFFIN), WILL. See LEAN, DONALD BEAN.

RUTHVEN, WILLIAM, LORD. One of the nobles sent by the Secret Council to Lochleven Castle to secure Queen Mary's signature to the deed of abdication. With his father he had taken part in David Rizzio's murder, and his presence in Lochleven Castle gave Queen Mary an 'instinctive terror.' But, throughout the interview, he remained unmoved, 'like a polished corselet of steel.' 'The son of an ill-fated sire, and the father of a yet more unfortunate family.' *The Abbot.*

RUTHWIN, YOUNG. Alice of Bower's lover, 'slain for her love the last spring.' *The Black Dwarf.*

RUTLAND, COUNTESS OF. One of Queen Elizabeth's dames of honour : ever a good friend to the Earl of Leicester. *Kenilworth.*

RUTLEDGE, ARCHIE. A constable. *Rob Roy.*

RUTLEDGE, GAFFER. The farmer of Grime's Hill. A letter purporting to come from him drew Mr. Jobson opportunely away from Inglewood Place when the charge of highway robbery made by Morris against Frank Osbaldistone was being investigated. *Rob Roy.*

RUTLEDGE, JOB. The smuggler under whose care Alan Fairford was left amongst the subterranean vaults while Tom Trumbull went to fetch ' what little baggage ' Alan should need for his journey to Redgauntlet. *Redgauntlet.*

RUTLEDGE, KITTY. A rival of Dorcas in her fellow-servant John's affections. *Redgauntlet.*

RYMAR, MR. ROBERT. One of the visitors to the Well : author of a ' New Tale of Chivalry.' *St. Ronan's Well.*

S

SADDLETREE, BARTOLINE. The owner of ' an excellent and highly-esteemed shop for harness, saddles, etc., etc., at the sign of the Golden Nag, at the head of Bess Wynd.' He left the management of the business to his wife, and as a hanger-on at the courts picked up scraps of Latin with odds and ends of legal knowledge, the possession of which highly exalted him in his own esteem. ' If my father had had the sense to send me to Leyden and Utrecht to learn the Substitutes and Pandex—!' *The Heart of Midlothian.*

SADDLETREE, MRS. Bartoline's careful helpmate : a ' far awa' cousin ' of the Deans, and Effie's mistress after Effie left home. She was ' an observing, shrewd, notable woman,' ' of an ordinary and worldly way of thinking.' She ' had been tender a' the summer,' and as a result Effie was left to her own resources. *The Heart of Midlothian.*

(*Tender*, sickly.)

SADHU SING. A soldier and freebooter whose reason was unhinged when his bride Mora was carried off by a tiger. Four or five years later Adam Hartley saw him still seated, 'with his eyes fixed on a small and rude tomb,' ' among the trophies of his grief and his vengeance ' : — ' a tiger's skull and bones—with a sabre almost consumed by rust.' *The Surgeon's Daughter.*

SADOC. Richard Middlemas disguised as Madame Montreville's black servant. *The Surgeon's Daughter.*

ST. ASAPH'S, DEAN OF. ' An eminent Puritan,' in attendance on Queen Elizabeth. *Kenilworth.*

ST. AUBIN, LUCY. Though ' one of the most beautiful and wealthy matches,' she lived and died a maid for the sake of young William Waverley.

'You would have thought, Edward, that the very trees mourned for her, for their leaves dropped around her without a gust of wind.' *Waverley.*

ST. BOTOLPH, PRIOR OF. A venerable father who received the wounded Ivanhoe after the Castle of Torquilstone was destroyed. He had 'the good cause of Old England' at heart. *Ivanhoe.*

SAINT CLAIR, MASTER OF. One of the reprieved prisoners mentioned by Mrs. Saddletree to Jeanie Deans. He 'shot the twa Shaws.' *The Heart of Midlothian.*

SAINT-CYR, HUGH DE. Seneschal to King René in his palace at Aix. *Anne of Geierstein.*

ST. DUTHAC. Abbot of Aberbrothock. The golden goblet termed the Blessed Bear of Bradwardine was his gift to the Baron of his time, in gratitude for a valiant defence of the patrimony of the monastery. *Waverley.*

ST. EDMUND'S, ABBOT OF. *See* WOLFRAM.

SAINT MAUR. One of Front-de-Bœuf's servants. With the others, he was deaf to his master's cries when the castle was on fire. *Ivanhoe.*

ST. PAUL'S, BLACK PRIEST OF. *See* GEIERSTEIN, ALBERT OF.

SAINT RINGANS, LADY. One of the 'set' who went about 'wasting their decayed lungs in puffing' Doctor Damiotti. *My Aunt Margaret's Mirror.*

ST. RONAN'S, LAIRD OF. *See* MOWBRAY, JOHN.

SAINT ROQUE, ABBESS OF. *See* FOLJAMBE, LADY.

ST. WITHOLD'S, ABBOT OF. *See* WALTHEOFF.

SALADIN. The renowned Sultan of Egypt and Syria, 'than whom no greater name is recorded in Eastern history.' 'A generous and valiant enemy,' 'true-hearted and loyal,' he was in points of chivalry a worthy opponent to Richard: each loved and honoured the other —'as noble adversaries ever love each other.' But his policy was deeper and his prudence greater than Richard's. Disguised as Sheerkohf or Ilderim of Kurdistan, he guided Kenneth of Scotland to the hermit of Engaddi; returned to camp with him as Adonbec, physician to Saladin's 'own person'; cured the squire Strauchan, King Richard, and the faithful hound Roswal by his sacred talisman; revived Kenneth from despair; conceived the plan by which the knight regained his honour, and, in all his wealth and glory as Sultan, presided over the trial by combat at the Diamond of the Desert. *The Talisman.*

SALISBURY, EARL OF. (1) The 'most goodly person' in King Richard's army, 'his own natural brother, William with the Long Sword . . . the offspring of Henry the Second's amour with the celebrated Rosamund of Woodstock.' He followed the King to St. George's Mount when he went to avenge the dishonour done to the English flag, and attended him again when the allied forces saluted the flag ' in sign of regard and amity.'

(2) ' One of the good lances who accompanied King Richard to Palestine, and who are now straggling homeward.' Fitzurse suggested that the Black Knight might be he. (1) *The Talisman.* (2) *Ivanhoe.*

See also BOHUN, HENRY.

SALMON, PATRICO. The opponent of the gipsies in a ' great fight ' when Meg Merrilies did good service. ' If I had not helped you with these very fambles (holding up her hands), Jean Baillie would have frummagem'd you, ye feckless do-little ! ' *Guy Mannering.*

(*Frummagem'd,* throttled.)

SAMPSON. Junior tapster in Dame Crane's inn, Marlborough. *Kenilworth.*

SAMPSON, DOMINIE (ABEL). A ' stickit minister.' For many years he enjoyed the hospitality of Ellangowan, and after the Laird's death he acted as librarian to Colonel Mannering. His eccentric appearance, combined with his absent-mindedness, exposed him to ignorant ridicule, but his ' simplicity and benevolence of character ' gained the esteem of those who knew him best. To the Bertram family he showed a whole-hearted devotion.

' No, Miss Lucy Bertram,' he said in the time of trouble, ' while I live I will not separate from you. I'll be no burden—I have thought how to prevent that. But, as Ruth said unto Naomi, Entreat me not to leave thee, nor to depart from thee ; for whither thou goest I will go, and where thou dwellest I will dwell.' *Guy Mannering.*

SAMPSON, WILL. The horse-hirer in Candlemaker Row from whom Mr. Saunders Fairford heard that ' Alan had been looking for a good hack to go to the country for a few days.' *Redgauntlet.*

SANG, TAM. Driver of the Fairport coach, ' Royal Charlotte,' in which Dousterswivel tried to take ' the wings of the morning.' *The Antiquary.*

SATAN. ' The vicious devil of a brown Galloway nag ' which Adam Woodcock loved for its very wildness. *The Abbot.*

SAUNDERS. Son of the old woman at whose house Halbert Glendinning met the pedlar who acted as his guide to the Earl of Murray's detachment of horse. *The Monastery.*

SAUNDERS. One of Sir Geoffrey Peveril's grooms. He was one of the Countess of Derby's escort from Martindale Castle on her way to the Isle of Man. *Peveril of the Peak.*

SAUNDERSON, MR. SAUNDERS. The major-domo, or ' second officer of state ' in the barony of Bradwardine. Commonly called *Alexander ab Alexandro* by his master. *Waverley.*

SAVILLE, LORD. The ' fashionable gallant ' to whom Chiffinch ' blabbed ' at a wayside inn concerning his and Edward Christian's scheme that Alice Bridgenorth should supplant the Duchess of Portsmouth in the King's favour.

Saville played 'the rogue' and informed the Duchess, and she persuaded Buckingham to interfere. *Peveril of the Peak.*

SAVIOLA, VINCENTIO. Sir Piercie Shafton's instructor: 'the first master of the first school of fence that our Royal England affords.' 'Truly noble and all-unutterably skilful.' *The Monastery.*

SAVOY, ROMONT, COUNT OF. A 'strict ally and adviser' of Charles the Bold, from whom, the Swiss deputies maintained, 'many injuries' had been received. But 'he has already felt with whom he has to contend.' *Anne of Geierstein.*

SAWYERS, DEACON. The joiner employed to 'put on ane or twa o' the doors' of the Tolbooth which were broken down during the Porteous Riot. *The Heart of Midlothian.*

SAYINGS, THE SAYER OF. A 'man of conversation' who attended Leopold of Austria. His capacity was 'somewhat betwixt that of a minstrel and a counsellor; he was by turns a flatterer, a poet, and an orator; and those who desired to be well with the Duke generally studied to gain the goodwill of the *spruch-sprecher.*' With Jonas Schwanker, the court jester, he kept up a running commentary of 'grave and comic nonsense' which Conrade of Montserrat utilised for his own purposes when dining with the Archduke. *The Talisman.*

SCAMBESTER, ERIC. Magnus Troil's butler: 'a grey-headed domestic . . . in the dress of a Dantzic skipper,' 'known far and wide through the isles by the name of the Punch-maker.' *The Pirate.*

SCATHLOCK. One of Robin Hood's men. When Richard was making merry with the outlaws, Robin ordered Scathlock to wind such a blast of his horn as would break up the banquet. Robin feared 'lest it trenched upon hours of dearer import than to be thus dallied with.' *Ivanhoe.*

SCHEYTER, SEBALDUS. Patron of Wolfbrand Oldenbuck. *The Antiquary.*

SCHINDERHAUSEN, OLEARIUS. 'A learned professor at the famous University of Leyden.' Henry Warden proposed that Roland Graeme should be sent to him with letters of recommendation for the post of under-janitor. There, 'besides gratis instruction,' Warden told the Lady of Avenel, 'if God give him the grace to seek it, he will enjoy five marks by the year, and the professor's cast-off suit, which he disparts with biennially.' *The Abbot.*

SCHOEFFERBACH, NICHOLAUS. 'That gifted man' from whom Jasper Dryfesdale learnt the doctrine that 'he cannot sin who doth but execute that which is predestined.' *The Abbot.*

SCHOLEY, LAURENCE. One of the servants who attended Magnus Troil and his daughters when they visited Norna: 'an alert and ready-witted fellow.' It was owing to his sharpness of observation that they found shelter in the deserted hut. *The Pirate.*

SCHONFELDT, LIEUTENANT. The

officer ordered by Governor von Hagenbach to collect his men quietly at the eastern gate in anticipation of the arrival of the Swiss embassy in La Ferette. *Anne of Geierstein.*

SCHRECKENWALD, ITAL. The 'cruel and interested steward' of Count Albert of Geierstein, and a 'faithful though unscrupulous follower.' His 'singular indifference to danger' saved him from paying the penalty of his insolence when he delivered Anne of Geierstein to her uncle's care—her father 'having on his hands wars and other affairs of weight.' But 'the air of command' seemed so natural to Anne in the Castle of Arnheim, that he who kept 'every other person in awe with his stern looks and cross words,' was forced by her orders to allow Arthur Philipson to accompany Anne to Strasburg. *Anne of Geierstein.*

SCHWANKER, JONAS. Court jester to Leopold of Austria. *The Talisman.*
See also SAYINGS, THE SAYER OF.

SCOTT OF SCOTSTARVET. Author of *The Staggering State of Scots Statesmen.* Sir William Ashton was warned by the Marquis of A—'s emissary that this 'curious memoir . . . has been outstaggered in our time.' *The Bride of Lammermoor.*

SCRABELSTONE, SIR ANTHONY OF. The name given by Friar Tuck to Locksley as that of the Black Knight, when Locksley found them making merry together. *Ivanhoe.*

SCRIEVER, JOCK. The apprentice or 'servitor' of Bailie MacWheeble. *Waverley.*

SCROGGS, LORD CHIEF JUSTICE. Presiding judge at the Peverils' trial. 'A calm, dignified, judicial demeanour was at no time the characteristic of his official conduct. He always ranted and roared either on the one side or the other.' *Peveril of the Peak.*

SCROGIE, RONALD. See MOWBRAY, REGINALD SCROGIE.

SCROW, MR. Glossin's clerk. *Guy Mannering.*

SCRUB & RUB, MESSRS. The owners of an 'Infallible Detergent Elixir.' Their agent, 'a cockney from London,' wished to convince Mrs. Policy of its efficacy by removing the two hundred and fifty years old stain of Rizzio's blood from the floor of Queen Mary's apartment in Holyrood. *The Fair Maid of Perth.*

SCRUTATOR. One of the Antiquary's noms-de-guerre. *The Antiquary.*

SEAFORTH, EARL OF. Commander of one of the armies opposed to Montrose. But Montrose hoped that the victory at Inverlochy would win him to the King's party, for 'it is not disloyalty,' he said, 'but despair of the good cause, that has induced him to take arms against us.' *A Legend of Montrose.*

SEBASTES OF MITYLENE. One of the soldiers on guard at the Golden Gate when Hereward fell asleep 'on the shady side of the grand porch.' Sebastes had already been 'a pirate five years at sea, and a robber three years now in the hills,' and for the sake of Hereward's silver he was ready 'to take the only part which is worth a brave man's while to resort to in a pressing affair.' But Hereward escaped his dagger. His meditated revenge was prevented by his own death in Count Robert's dungeon. *Count Robert of Paris.*

SEBASTIAN. 'A favoured servant' of Queen Mary, who married one of her female attendants. The Queen's absence from the Kirk of Field on the night of Darnley's murder was due to her 'attending on a masque at Holyrood, given by her to grace the marriage.' *The Abbot.*

SEDLEY, SIR CHARLES. One of the nobles of Charles II's court from whom the Duke of Buckingham won a bet of a thousand pounds for his funeral sermon on Mother Cresswell. *Peveril of the Peak.*

SEELENCOOPER, CAPTAIN. Governor of the hospital of Ryde in which Richard Middlemas found himself after being robbed by Tom Hillary. 'He had all the air of having been originally a turnkey in some ill-regulated jail—a stout, short, bandy-legged man, with one eye, and a double portion of ferocity in that which remained.' *The Surgeon's Daughter.*

SELBY. An officer on duty at court on the night when Sir Geoffrey Hudson accused Buckingham of treachery. *Peveril of the Peak.*

SELBY. Servant to the Misses Arthuret at Fairladies. *Redgauntlet.*

SELLOK, CIS. One of the servants who ran from Martindale Castle to tell Lance Outram of Sir Geoffrey's and Julian's arrest. She ran back to the Castle for Lady Peveril's orders to Lance, and kindled the beacon with which the fortunes of the Peverils seemed to be identified. *Peveril of the Peak.*

SEMPLE, JOHN. Minister of Carsphairn, in Galloway: 'a Presbyterian clergyman of singular piety and great zeal.' *The Heart of Midlothian.*

SEMPLE, MRS. The Duchess of Argyle's 'own woman.' *The Heart of Midlothian.*

SETH. An attendant of Isaac and Rebecca. He helped to carry Wilfred of Ivanhoe to their house in Ashby-de-la-Zouch after he fainted from his wounds in the Passage of Arms. *Ivanhoe.*

SETOUN, EUPHEMIA. The name assumed for Effie Deans by Sir George and Lady Staunton when they tried to give fashionable details concerning her Scottish parentage. *The Heart of Midlothian.*

SETTLE, ELKANA. One of the poets who attended the Duke of Buckingham's Levée: 'the unworthy scribbler whom the envy of Rochester and others tried to raise to public estimation as a rival to Dryden.' *Peveril of the Peak.*

SEYTON, CATHERINE. 'Waiting-damsel' to Queen Mary. Endowed with her father's 'lofty pride' and her mother's 'high spirit,' she had at the same time a 'light heart and lively humour,' and was unwearied in exercising her 'inventive imagination' to relieve the tedium of her mistress' confinement. To Roland Graeme there was in all she did a touch of wildness, as of a 'wild young lark' which 'would like best to sing under God's free sky.' But there lurked in her bosom 'deep and serious feeling' and when she enthusiastically devoted him to 'the good cause,' she fired him with a zeal as keen as her own. *The Abbot.*

SEYTON, DICK, OF WINDYGOWL. One of the young men who took part in the street encounter with the Leslies, when the cry 'Seyton' drew Roland Graeme into the fray. *The Abbot.*

SEYTON, GEORGE, LORD. Catherine's father, 'one of Scotland's proudest, as well as most worthy, barons.' He was of a family 'which of all others has ever been devoted' to Queen Mary, and he led the vanguard at Langside. 'Wise, true, and valiant.' *The Abbot.*

SEYTON, HENRY. Catherine's twin-brother. So close was their resemblance 'in form and features' that Roland Graeme gave Catherine 'the credit' of some of her brother's 'mad pranks.' Henry had much of 'that angry and heady spirit which evil times' had encouraged amongst the young nobles, and in spite of their common devotion to Queen Mary, he treated Roland with a haughty distrust. But as Roland tended him on the field of Langside, he confessed, 'I love thee better dying than ever I thought to have done while in life.' *The Abbot.*

SHAFTESBURY, EARL OF. Anthony Ashley Cooper, a 'politician and intriguer' of the period. 'Patron' of the great Popish Plot, he 'would not hesitate to sacrifice to the popular Moloch of the day whatsoever, or whomsoever—whose ruin could propitiate the deity.' *Peveril of the Peak.*

SHAFTON, NED. One of the Newgate prisoners after the 1715 rebellion. *Rob Roy.*

SHAFTON, SIR PIERCIE. A relative of the Duke of Northumberland whose residence in the Halidome of St. Mary's led eventually to Sir John Foster's inroad. 'A devout servant of the fair sex, a witty-brained, prompt, and accomplished courtier,' he was forced by political reasons to exchange 'the smiles of those beauties who form a galaxy around the throne of England for the cold courtesy of an untaught damsel and the bewildered stare of a miller's maiden.' In spite of his Euphuistic affectations, however, he was capable of genuine energy of mind, and his chivalrous companionship with Mysie of the Mill proved him worthy of her simple devotion. *The Monastery.*

SHAFTON OF WILVERTON. Sir Piercie's father, 'who, men say, was akin to the Piercie on the wrong side of the blanket.' He married Moll Overstitch, 'the prettiest wench in those parts' and daughter of Old Overstitch, the tailor. Hence Sir Piercie's ungovernable rage when Halbert Glendinning showed him the White Lady' bodkin. *The Monastery.*

SHAGRAM. The old pony on which Mary Avenel rode ' gipsy-fashion . . . betwixt two bundles of bedding,' when the exiled family went across the moors to Glendearg. *The Monastery.*

SHAKEBAG, DICK. One of Captain Colepepper's companions in the attack on Lord Dalgarno at Camlet Moat. *The Fortunes of Nigel.*

SHAKESPEARE, WILL. One of the spectators whose greeting the Earl of Leicester returned ' with such ready and condescending courtesy,' as he hurried from the council-chamber ' to attend her Majesty to her barge.' ' Wild Will . . . we will have thee hanged for the veriest wizard in Europe.' *Kenilworth.*

Note. — Shakespeare was only eleven years of age in 1575.

SHARKER, CAPTAIN. Captain of the vessel in which Jenkin Vincent intended to sail for America before Richie Moniplies saved him from despair. *The Fortunes of Nigel.*

SHARPE. An old pirate of the ' true breed' under whom Hawkins and Derrick had served. *The Pirate.*

SHARPER. The cutler in whose shop Sir Geoffrey Peveril and Julian, with Sir Geoffrey Hudson, found refuge from the Strand mob. After freeing them of their swords by a ruse, he imprisoned them and left them to the mercy of Major Bridgenorth. *Peveril of the Peak.*

SHARPITLAW, GIDEON. ' Procurator Fiscal, upon whom the duties of superintendent of police devolved.' It was chiefly on his advice that Ratcliffe was taken into the town's service. ' Like all rogues, he was a great calumniator of the fair sex,' and blamed the women, instead of Ratcliffe's double dealing, when his expedition to Muschat's Cairn failed. *The Heart of Midlothian.*

SHAVINGS. The Fairport carpenter. *The Antiquary.*

SHAW, WILLIAM. One of Sir William Ashton's menservants. *The Bride of Lammermoor.*

SHEERKOHF. *See* SALADIN.

SHEMUS AN SNACHAD (*i.e.* JAMES OF THE NEEDLE). The hereditary tailor of Vich Ian Vohr. ' A man of his word, when whisky was no party to the contract.' *Waverley.*

SHEMUS BEG (' LITTLE '). A blind harper who visited Donald Bean Lean. *Waverley.*

SHEVA. A brother of Isaac's tribe. He had the key of Isaac's warehouses in York, and was ordered to pay a thousand crowns to Locksley's messenger as ransom. *Ivanhoe.*

SHOOLBRED, LUCKIE. Harry Gow's housekeeper. He persuaded her to ' risk the honest name ' she had kept for sixty years by taking care of Louise, the glee-woman, for a night. *The Fair Maid of Perth.* (*Luckie*, an old woman.)

SHORTCAKE, MRS. The Fairport baker's ' lady ' : one of Mrs. Mailsetter's friends. *The Antiquary.*

SHORTELL, MR. The Liverpool mercer from whose door Charles Topham started on his journey to Derbyshire to arrest Sir Geoffrey Peveril. *Peveril of the Peak.*

SHORTYARD. The mercer. The money with which he paid his bill was ' by ill chance ' in Jenkin Vincent's pocket during one of his gambling escapades, and proved the cause of poor Jin ' blemishing his honesty.' *The Fortunes of Nigel.*

SHOWER, MR. The minister to whose chapel Frank Osbaldistone was taken in his youth. *Rob Roy.*

SHREWSBURY, COUNTESS OF. The lady entrusted with the care of Queen Elizabeth's ' unhappy sister of Scotland.' *Kenilworth.*

SHREWSBURY, LORD. Earl Marshal of England. *Kenilworth.*

SIBBALD. The servant who accompanied Montrose and Menteith from England to Darnlinvarach. *A Legend of Montrose.*

SIDIER DHU. The black soldiers : ' the independent companies that were raised to keep peace and law in the Highlands.' *Waverley.*

SIDIER ROY. The red soldiers : King George's men. *Waverley.*

SILVERQUILL, SAM. One of Vanbeest Brown's fellow-prisoners in Portanferry jail : ' an idle apprentice ' charged with forgery. *Guy Mannering.*

SIM, AILIE. The keeper of a ' public ' to which Edie Ochiltree turned his steps after his interview with the Earl of Glenallan. *The Antiquary.*

SIMMIE. The turnspit at Glendearg. ' Good-for-nothing Simmie—thy wits are harrying birds' nests.' *The Monastery.*

SIMMONS, WIDOW. David Ramsay's old neighbour, ' the sempstress who had served in her day the very tip-top revellers of the Temple with ruffs, cuffs, and bands.' *The Fortunes of Nigel.*

SIMON OF HACKBURN. One of Hobbie Elliot's friends most eager in the pursuit after Grace Armstrong had been kidnapped.
' I'se quarrel wi' ony body I like, except the King, or the laird I live under.' *The Black Dwarf.*

SIMON OF SOWPORT. A ' pipe and tabor bastard ' who supplied the music at the Brokenburn dance until Wandering Willie and Darsie Latimer arrived. *Redgauntlet.*

SIMONSON, SIMON. A Liverpool friend of Major Bridgenorth. Julian Peveril was offered a letter of introduction to him when Major Bridgenorth tried to persuade him to escape from Moultrassie Hall in order to avoid trial with his father. *Peveril of the Peak.*

SIMPSON, MATTIE. The mistress of the Trinlay-knowe alehouse : one of Andrew Fairservice's friends. *Rob Roy.*

SIMSON, JEAN. One of the old women who competed to announce to Dr. Gray the approach of interesting strangers. She was installed as sick nurse to the delicate lady, Zilia de Monçada. *The Surgeon's Daughter.*

SIMSON, TAM. *See* CHATTERLY, SIMON.

SINCLAIR. Father of Magnus Troil's wife : ' a noble chief ' from the Highlands of Sutherland ' who, driven from his own country during the feuds of the seventeenth century, had found shelter in those peaceful islands.' *The Pirate.*

SINCLAIR, PATE. The pilot sent to help Triptolemus Yellowley when he was chosen by the Kirkwall magistrates to be a hostage in the pirates' hands. *The Pirate.*

SIN-DESPISE, DOUBLE-KNOCK. One of Captain Bangtext's men. *The Heart of Midlothian.*

SINGLESWORD, YOUNG. One of the reprieved prisoners instanced by Mrs. Saddletree to Jeanie Deans. He 'stickit the Laird of Ballencleuch . . . I'se warrant there's mercy, an folk could win at it.' *The Heart of Midlothian.*

SKELTON, SAM. One of the gang of men who met the *Jumping Jenny* to unload her. 'Being a Papist' he knew Fairladies, and accompanied Nanty Ewart when taking Alan Fairford there. *Redgauntlet.*

SKREIGH, MR. Clerk and precentor of the parish: 'the Letter-Gae of haly rhyme.'

'His story, however, found faith with the worthy Mr. Skreigh, and other lovers of the marvellous, who still hold that the Enemy of Mankind brought these two wretches together upon that night, by supernatural interference, that they might fill up the cup of their guilt and receive its meed, by murder and suicide.' *Guy Mannering.*

SKURLIEWHITTER, ANDREW. A 'smooth-tongued, lank-haired, buckram-suited, Scottish scrivener': a protégé of George Heriot. But Lord Dalgarno was also his patron, and for him he did 'foul practice.' At the same time he was in league with Captain Colepepper, was accessory to the murder of old Trapbois, and gave Colepepper the information which sent him to Camlet Moat after Lord Dalgarno's gold. 'That fellow, by his visage, should either be a saint or a most hypocritical rogue.' *The Fortunes of Nigel.*

SLICING DICK OF PADDINGTON. *See* BLOWSELINDA.

SLIPPRYTONGUE. A merchant whose bill formed one of the assets carried off by Rashleigh Osbaldistone. *Rob Roy.*

SLOETHORN. Father of the heiress whom Guy Mannering's merchant uncle wished him to marry. 'Rich enough to play at span-counter with moidores, and make threadpapers of bank-notes.' *Guy Mannering.*

SLOTH. Wilkin Flammock's 'strong Flanderkin elephant of a horse.' *The Betrothed.*

SLOUNGING JOCK. One of MacGuffog's helpers in the capture of Jans Jansen. *Guy Mannering.*

SLUDGE, DICKIE. 'Flibbertigibbet,' the 'queer, shambling, ill-made urchin' who led Edmund Tressilian to Wayland Smith's forge on the moor. 'Nature never packed a shrewder wit into a more ungainly casket,' and Master Holyday thought him worthy to take part in the great pageant at Kenilworth Castle. When Wayland Smith evaded all his enquiries concerning the lady who travelled under his care, he took effective measures to show his resentment. These brought him into unexpected prominence, and his 'acute genius raised him to favour and distinction.'

'' 'Tis a very devil for mischief, yet not an ill-natured devil either.' *Kenilworth.*

SLUDGE, GAMMER. Dickie's mother. She entertained Master Erasmus Holyday in return for the pains which the dominie bestowed ' on the top and bottom of her hopeful heir' in making him ' travel through the accidence.' *Kenilworth.*

SMACKAWA, LAIRD OF. One of Jedediah Cleishbotham's guests, ' wont to prefer my Prophet's Chamber even to the sanded chamber of dais in the Wallace Inn.' *Old Mortality.*

(*Chamber of dais*, the best room.)

SMA' TRASH, EPPIE. Keeper of the change-house at Wolf's-hope. She had lived all her life under the Ravenswood family, and when Caleb Balderstone was trying to provide for the entertainment of Bucklaw at Wolf's Crag, he thought he could ' work a wee drap out o' her by fair means or foul.' *The Bride of Lammermoor.*

SMITH, ADAM, ESQ. *See* HUME, DAVID.

SMITH, GENERAL. Commander of a British army destined by Paupiah and Richard Middlemas to take possession of Bangalore after Middlemas' intended betrayal of Tippoo Sahib. *The Surgeon's Daughter.*

SMITH, HENRY. *See* GOW, HENRY.

SMITH, JOHN. *See* MORTSHEUGH, JOHNNIE.

SMITH, LUCKIE. ' The howdie, that suffered in the year saxteen hundred and seventy-nine.' Hers was a case like Effie Deans', of ' presumptive murder.' After her execution the law regarding it fell into abeyance until the frequency of child-murder caused its revival in Effie's time. *The Heart of Midlothian.*

(*Luckie*, a designation given to an elderly woman. *Howdie*, midwife.)

SMITH, WAYLAND. Dickie Sludge's ' old playfellow ' : Edmund Tressilian's attendant and confidential servant. In turn, blacksmith, juggler, actor, and physicianer, he had acquired, as Dr. Doboobie's servant, a knowledge of the curative arts which enabled him to counteract Alasco's concoctions, and so save both the Earl of Sussex and Amy Robsart. As a pedlar he gained access to Amy in Cumnor Place, and afterwards escorted her to Kenilworth Castle. He had ' the sharp, keen expression of inventive genius and prompt intellect,' and protected the unhappy Countess with ' shrewdness, alertness of understanding, and variety of resource.' *Kenilworth.*

SMITH, WILL. The name under which Chiffinch entertained Ganlesse and Julian Peveril after their journey from Altringham. *Peveril of the Peak.*

SMOTHERWELL, STEPHEN. The executioner : Dwining's ' confederate ' in saving Bonthron from death on the gallows. He adjusted the noose round the broad steel collar which supported the ' sundry other conveniences for easing the patient.' *The Fair Maid of Perth.*

SNAIL, COLLECTOR. An 'honest man,' who could 'sing his sang, and take his drink, and draw his salary,' and 'never fashes ony body.' *Guy Mannering.* (*To fash,* to trouble.)

SNAILSFOOT, BRYCE. A jagger, or pedlar : ' a stout, vulgar little man with green, goggling, and gain-descrying' eyes. 'The mounting of his pack depended less upon the warehouses of Lerwick or Kirkwall,' than on ' the lawful spoil of the Egyptians' sent up by the sea. Plausible and double-dealing, he knew no justice but the justice of his trade, and readily played false to his friends. 'My conscience,' he said, 'Maister Mordaunt, is as tender as ony man's in my degree ; but she is something of a timorsome nature, cannot abide angry folk, and can never speak above her breath, when there is aught of a fray going forward. Indeed, she hath at all times a small and low voice.' *The Pirate.*

SNAP. Madge Wildfire's little dog. 'It suffered baith cauld and hunger when it was living, and in the grave there is rest for a' things.' *The Heart of Midlothian.*

SNOREHOUT, HANS. Minister of a Dutch congregation which Edward Christian expected would join the outbreak planned by him and the Duke of Buckingham. *Peveril of the Peak.*

SNUFFY DAVY. *See* WILSON, DAVY.

SOLES. The shoemaker who measured the footmarks on the mud at Warroch after the murder of Frank Kennedy. Many years later he was able to testify before Mr. Pleydell that his measurements fitted the boots of Hatteraick and his mate Brown. *Guy Mannering.*

SOLITARY, THE. *See* BLACK DWARF, THE.

SOLMES. Confidential valet to the Earl of Etherington. A business delinquency having put him in Mr. Touchwood's power, he purchased freedom by keeping Mr. Touchwood informed of his master's plans. 'A deep villain—and now he proves traitor to boot.' *St. Ronan's Well.*

SOLOMON. Joshua Geddes' ' useful iron-grey galloway.' To be a helpless spectator while the ' doomed gallows-bird ' Benjie Coltherd misused his patient animal proved more than Joshua's self-control could bear. So, too, with Solomon, under Benjie's treatment. He galloped home ' at a swift and furious pace, and flung the child Benjie from his back, upon the heap of dung which is in the stableyard.' *Redgauntlet.*

SOLSGRACE, MASTER NEHEMIAH. The Presbyterian minister of Martindale *cum* Moultrassie : ' though a very good man in the main, was particularly and illiberally tenacious of the petty distinctions which his sect adopted.' *Peveril of the Peak.*

SOLWAY LOCHS, LAIRD OF THE. One of the names by which Edward Hugh Redgauntlet was known. He possessed great influence over

the 'wild communities' of sailors and fishermen dwelling on the Solway, and incited them to the destruction of Joshua Geddes' salmon nets in order that in the general confusion he might get forcible possession of Darsie Latimer. *Redgauntlet.*
  Note.—The pools of salt water left by the tide among the sands are called the *Lochs of Solway.*

SOMMERVILLE, MISS NELLY. The young lady who nursed Mr. Sommerville when 'suffering the incapacities of the paralytic.' 'The young person, who had naturally a resigned, Madonna-like expression of countenance, listened to his impatient chiding with the most humble submission . . . and gradually, by the sweet and soft tone of her voice, soothed to rest the spirit of causeless irritation.' *The Highland Widow.*

SOMMERVILLE, MR. The advocate who brought order into young Chrystal Croftangry's affairs, and enabled him to leave his refuge in the Canongate. He 'had repeatedly prevented, by his benevolent and manly exertions, the triumphs of selfish cunning over simplicity and folly.' *The Highland Widow.*

SORREL. Sir Hugh Robsart's hunter. *Kenilworth.*

SOUPLE SAM. The hack—'it belanged to the George at Dumfries'—that Guy rode on his first visit to Ellangowan. 'It was a blood-bay beast, very ill o' the spavin.' *Guy Mannering.*

SOUPLE, TAM. The three-legged palfrey' with which Andrew Fairservice thought to take his journey into Rob Roy's country. *Rob Roy.*

SOUPLEJAW, SAUNDERS. The 'second-sighted' town-souter of Glen-houlakim, 'worth Galeotti or Gallipotty or whatever you call him, twice told, for a prophet.' He foretold that Ludovic Lesly should be 'made' by marriage—which 'hath not yet come to pass.' *Quentin Durward.*
  (*Souter*, a shoemaker.)

SOWERBROWST, MR. The maltster: 'a pleasant, sensible man, and a sponsible man in the world,' whom Dr. Quackleben regarded as a possible rival for Mrs. Blower's hand. *St. Ronan's Well.*

SPEARS OF SPYINGHOW. *See* WETHERAL, STEPHEN.

SPENSER, MASTER EDMUND. One of the spectators whose greeting the Earl of Leicester returned 'with such ready and condescending courtesy,' as he hurried from the council-chamber 'to attend her Majesty to her barge.' *Kenilworth.*

SPIGOTS. Sir Geoffrey Peveril's old butler. He 'was shot dead on the north-west turret with a blackjack in his hand.' *Peveril of the Peak.*
  (*Black-jack*, a huge tankard made of leather.)

SPITFIRE. *See* SPITTAL.

SPITTAL (commonly SPITFIRE). Markham Everard's page, 'a little gipsy-looking boy . . . somewhat stinted in size, but active both in intelligence and in limb.' When

Cromwell arrived unexpectedly at Markham's lodgings, Wildrake managed to warn the inmates of Woodstock Lodge by sending off Spitfire with a woodcock's feather 'as a token to Mistress Lee.' *Woodstock.*

SPONTOON. Confidential servant of Colonel Talbot. He travelled north as far as Huntingdon with Edward Waverley.

'Accustomed to submit to discipline,' he ' was rigid in enforcing it.' *Waverley.*

SPRENGER, LOUIS (or MARTIN). Annette Veilchen's bachelor. *Anne of Geierstein.*

SPUR 'EM, DICK. One of MacGuffog's helpers in the capture of Jans Jansen. *Guy Mannering.*

SQUALLIT, JOHN. The town-crier of Perth. He was wounded in the defence during which the old Kempe of Kinfauns gave Simon Glover a lesson in courage. *The Fair Maid of Perth.*
(Kempe, champion.)

STAIR, EARL OF. 'The celebrated Earl.' He sent from Flanders to Lady Forester information concerning 'the melancholy event of a duel between Sir Philip Forester and his wife's half-brother, Captain Falconer.' *My Aunt Margaret's Mirror.*

STANCHELLS, CAPTAIN. Principal jailer in Glasgow Tolbooth. *Rob Roy.*

STAND-FAST-IN-FAITH GIPPS. One of Captain Bangtext's men. *The Heart of Midlothian.*

STANDISH, SQUIRE. 'A justice with a zeal for King George and the Protestant succession.' Mr. Jobson, as his clerk, had more occasion to restrain than to stimulate him. *Rob Roy.*

STANLEY. Gentleman of the bedchamber to the Earl of Sussex. *Kenilworth.*

STANLEY, FRANK. Nephew of Colonel Talbot. Edward Waverley travelled north under the protection of his passport. *Waverley.*

STANLEY, MARGARET. *See* PEVERIL, LADY.

STAPLES, LAWRENCE. 'The upperwarder, or in common phrase, the first jailer of Kenilworth Castle.' 'I love my prisoners,' he said, when protecting the Countess from Michael Lambourne. 'No man shall abuse or insult my prisoners; they are my jewels, and I lock them in a safe casket accordingly.' *Kenilworth.*

STAUNTON, GEORGE. Son of the rector of Willingham. Born in the West Indies, and spoilt by a doting mother, he received into his mind during his childhood 'all the seeds of those evil weeds which afterwards grew apace.' After a profligate youth, in the course of which he ruined Madge Murdockson, he was cast off by his father. 'The chances of a wandering life' took him to Scotland, and there, as George Robertson, he continued his evil course. After Effie Deans' release he married her, and in a few years, as Sir George and Lady Staunton, they took a prominent place in London society. He died by the hand of the young savage known as 'The Whistler,' who was his own and Effie's son.

'Experience teaches us ... that mischief shall hunt the violent man, and that the bloodthirsty man shall not live half his days.' *The Heart of Midlothian.*

STAUNTON, REV. ROBERT. Rector of Willingham : George's father. In early life an officer in the West Indies, he had married the heiress of a wealthy planter there. His attempts to counteract 'the baneful effects of his wife's system' of bringing up their son had the effect of causing George to regard him, even in childhood, as 'a rigid censor.' Jeanie Deans said of him, 'Though he read his discourse, and wore that surplice ... I cannot but think he must be a very worthy, God-fearing man.' *The Heart of Midlothian.*

STAUNTON, SIR EDMUND. The Willingham Squire. *The Heart of Midlothian.*

STAUNTON, SIR WILLIAM. Rev. Robert's brother. He presented the family living to Robert. *The Heart of Midlothian.*

STEED, SAUNDERS. Andrew Arnot's groom. *Quentin Durward.*

STEELE, CHRISTIE. Landlady of the Treddles Arms. A devoted servant to Chrystal Croftangry's mother, she had viewed his 'foibles and vices with abhorrence and without a grain of allowance,' and after twenty years could not be tempted into forgiveness by the suggestion of his return to the estate. *The Highland Widow.*

STEELHEART. *See* WETHERAL, STEPHEN.

STEENIE. *See* BUCKINGHAM, DUKE OF (THE 1ST).

STEENSON, JAMIE. The name assumed by Callum Beg in the hope of allaying the suspicions of Ebenezer Cruickshanks. *Waverley.*

STEENSON, MAGGIE. Willie's wife. At times her tongue made the sightless Willie 'tire of the blessing of hearing.' *Redgauntlet.*
See also AINSLIE, EPPS.

STEENSON, SANDIE. One of Bailie Nicol Jarvie's friends. With the Bailie and John Pirie, he advanced sums sufficient to secure the credit of Osbaldistone and Tresham. *Rob Roy.*

STEENSON, STEENIE. Wandering Willie's grandfather. 'Being obliged to follow Sir Robert in hunting and hosting, watching and warding, he saw muckle mischief, and maybe did some, that he couldna avoid.' He was 'a kind of favourite' with his master, but in the peaceful days after the Revolution fell into arrears with his rent, and only by dint of much scraping found the money when threatened with extreme measures. But no sooner had he 'set doun the siller, and just as his honour Sir Robert, that's gaen, drew it till him to count it, and write out the receipt, he was ta'en wi' the pains that removed him.' Besides this, the money disappeared, and the 'haill world was like to regard' Steenie as a thief and a cheat. But one dark night, as he was going to ride home through the wood of Pitmurkie 'that is a' fou of black firs,' being 'bauld wi' brandy and desperate wi' distress ... he had courage to go to the gate of hell, and a step farther, for that receipt.' *Redgauntlet.*

See also WEIR, MAJOR, *and* TIBBIE FAW.

STEENSON, WILLIE. 'Wandering Willie,' the blind fiddler with whom Darsie Latimer went to the country dance at Brokenburn, in place of Rob the Rambler. Born of a family which had lived under the Redgauntlets 'since the riding days and lang before,' he was brought up in Sir Redwald's household, and was taught music by 'the best teachers baith England and Scotland could gie.' After his master's death, his 'head never settled weel,' and he became a strolling fiddler. When he tired of 'scraping thairm or singing ballants,' he could 'make a tale serve the turn among the country bodies,' and to Darsie, as they tramped together across the lea, he told the true tale of Sir Robert Redgauntlet and his own grandfather. He cheered Darsie's captivity in Cumberland with well-chosen national airs, finishing, as Cristal Nixon approached him in the courtyard, with—

'Leave thee—leave thee, lad—
I'll never leave thee;
The stars shall gae withershins
Ere I will leave thee.'
Redgauntlet.

(*Thairm,* fiddlestring. *Withershins,* the wrong way about.)

STEINERNHERZ, FRANCIS. Executioner to Governor von Hagenbach, under whom he enjoyed 'constant practice.' Omens pointed to Seignor Philipson as the nobleman whose execution would complete the number necessary to give Francis 'his freedom from taxes and his nobility by patent.' But he proved equally ready to gain his freedom and his title *von Blut-sacker* by exercising his skill on the Governor himself. He had also sufficient presence of mind to take from the dead body Seignor Philipson's precious necklace of diamonds. *Anne of Geierstein.*

STEINFELDT, BARONESS OF. 'An old lady, notorious for playing in private society the part of a malicious fairy in a minstrel's tale ... famous ... for her insatiable curiosity and overweening pride.' 'She was engaged in a bitter quarrel' with Hermione, Baroness von Arnheim, and was suspected of causing her death by poison. *Anne of Geierstein.*

STEINSONS, THE THREE. Three of the 'few lads' Jenny Dennison knew 'to speak to.' *Old Mortality.*

STEPHANOS THE WRESTLER. 'A magnificent-looking man in form ... but ... clownish and peasantlike in the expression of his features.' Like 'his admirer and flatterer' Lysimachus, he was one of the discontented citizens who lent their ears to the conspiracy planned by Nicephorus, Achilles Tatius, and Agelastes. It gnawed his heart 'like the worm that dieth not' to see Hereward, 'this beggarly foreigner,' bring the conspiracy to nought and move off with 'praise, honour, and preferment.' *Count Robert of Paris.*

STEPHEN. One of Front-de-Bœuf's servants. With the others, he was deaf to his master's cries when the castle was on fire. *Ivanhoe.*

STEPHEN, COUNT. Count Crèvecœur's nephew. He was left in charge of the reconnoitring party which had encountered the Countess of Croye and Quentin Durward, while the Count escorted the two quasi-prisoners to Charles the Bold in Peronne. *Quentin Durward.*

STEVENS. The messenger who arrived at Lidcote Hall with a letter from the Earl of Sussex urging Edmund Tressilian's presence in London. *Kenilworth.*

STEVENSON, JOCK. Auld Jock ' was at the cock ' while Vanbeest Brown and Jock Jabos watched the curlers. *Guy Mannering.*

(*Cock*, the mark for which curlers play.)

STEWART, ALLAN, OF IVERACH. One of the Highlanders whom Bailie Nicol Jarvie and Frank Osbaldistone met in Jeanie MacAlpine's public-house. In his encounter with the Bailie his plaid was burnt by a red-hot poker which the Bailie used as his weapon. *Rob Roy.*

STEWART, DONALD. Governor of the Castle of Doune, and lieutenant-colonel in the service of His Royal Highness Prince Charles Edward. ' A plain country gentleman.' *Waverley.*

STEWART, FRANCIS. *See* BOTHWELL, FRANCIS, EARL OF (1).

STEWART, LORD JAMES. *See* MURRAY, EARL OF.

STEWART, PRINCE CHARLES EDWARD. (1) The young Chevalier : ' the gallant and handsome young Prince ' ' whose form and manners as well as the spirit he displayed ' in the ill-fated and desperate undertaking of 1745 made him ' rather like a hero of romance than a calculating politician.' ' A prince to live and die under,' ' his station is amongst those, a certain brilliant portion of whose life forms a remarkable contrast to all which precedes and all which follows it.'

(2) ' Father Buonaventure.' ' He was a man of middle life, about forty or upwards ; but either care, or fatigue, or indulgence, had brought on the appearance of premature old age, and given to his fine features a cast of seriousness, or even sadness.' ' Yet there was something of majesty, depressed indeed, and overclouded, but still grand and imposing, in the manner and words of Father Buonaventure,' which impressed Alan Fairford, in spite of his ' preconceived opinions ' regarding Catholic priests in general. In an upper loft of Joe Crackenthorp's inn, ' with a dignified courtesy which at once supplied whatever was deficient in external pomp,' he met ' his faithful friends once more—not, perhaps, with his former gay hopes which undervalued danger, but with the same determined contempt of the worst which can befall him, in claiming his own rights and those of his country.' Yet his will was adamant against the suggestion that he should dismiss the lady whose

companionship was judged fatal to all political ambition. (1) *Waverley*. (2) *Redgauntlet*.

STEWARTS OF APPIN. (1) Part of a reinforcement raised by Colkitto after Montrose had retired from Aberdeen.

(2) One of the Highland clans that joined the young Chevalier. With them went the MacCouls, their 'hereditary servants.' (1) *A Legend of Montrose*. (2) *Waverley*.

STEWARTS OF ATHOLE. One of the clans 'peculiarly zealous in the royal cause.' *A Legend of Montrose*.

STILES, DAVID. Clerk to his Majesty's Signet. Cuthbert Clutterbuck's tutors and curators wished to bind him apprentice to old David. *The Monastery*.

STIMBISTER, BET. The maid whose broken vows were the cause of Claud Halcro leaving Zetland in his youth. In his poem of farewell he called her 'Mary' 'for the sound's sake.' *The Pirate*.

STITCHELL, JAMES. Maxwell's maternal grandfather: 'a master fashioner of honest repute,' as Sir Mungo Malagrowther took pleasure in reminding Maxwell at court. *The Fortunes of Nigel*.

STORLSON, ULLA. A young Zetlander who 'used to go, day by day, to the top of Vossdale Head to look for her lover's ship that was never to return.' Brenda Troil dreaded that her fate would also be Minna's. *The Pirate*.

STORMHEAVEN, BOANERGES. David Deans' favourite preacher. *The Heart of Midlothian*.

STRACHAN, ELIAS. The Covenanter who bought Dalgetty's 'natural hereditament of Drumthwacket.' In later years Sir Dugald acquired possession of his paternal estate ' by a pacific intermarriage with Hannah Strachan, a matron somewhat stricken in years,' and widow of Elias. *A Legend of Montrose*.

STRAUCHAN. The trusty armour-bearer for whose life Kenneth of Scotland undertook his pilgrimage to Engaddi. Cured by Adonbec's sacred talisman, he was sent off to Scotland when his master thought his own death certain. But he found means to inform Thomas of Gilsland concerning his master's identity. *The Talisman*.

STRICKALTHROW, MERCIFUL. One of the soldiers left by Cromwell in Dr. Rochecliffe's chamber to help Humgudgeon in preventing the escape of the supposed king from Love's Ladder. When Albert Lee leapt into the chamber Merciful wished to ' strike this son of a wicked father under the fifth rib,' but Robins counselled delay. *Woodstock*.

STRUMPFER, NICK. Norna's ' Pacolet ': ' a square-made dwarf, about four feet five inches high, with a head of most portentous size, and features correspondent— namely, a huge mouth, a tremendous nose, with large black nostrils, which seemed to have been slit upwards, blubber lips of an unconscionable size, and huge wall-eyes, with which he leered, sneered, grinned, and goggled.' *The Pirate*.

(*Pacolet*, a dwarf in an old romance, said to have a magical horse of wood by which he could convey himself to any place desired.)

STUBBS, CECILIA. Daughter of the Squire : a 'presumptuous damsel' who, for a little, seemed likely to win Edward Waverley's affection. She earned his Aunt Rachel's gratitude by contenting herself with the steward's son. *Waverley.*

STUBBS, MR. The Willingham beadle. 'Cash? that is always what you think of, Stubbs.' *The Heart of Midlothian.*

STUBBS, SQUIRE. A neighbour of Sir Everard Waverley, and one of the series of readers to whom his *Weekly Intelligencer* was passed on. *Waverley.*

STUKELY. A distinguished gallant of the time. He married an heiress, squandered her fortune, and then deserted her for a life of adventure on the Continent. *The Monastery.*

STURMTHAL, MELCHIOR. Banner-bearer of Berne : one of the deputies sent by the Swiss Confederation to remonstrate with the Duke of Burgundy on the aggressions and exactions of von Hagenbach. Like Adam Zimmerman, he 'seemed to hold the consequences of war more lightly than they were viewed' by Arnold Biederman and Nicholas Bonstetten. *Anne of Geierstein.*

SUDDLECHOP, BENJAMIN. 'The most renowned barber in all Fleet Street.' 'Besides trimming locks and beards . . . besides also occasionally letting blood . . . extracting a stump, and performing other actions of petty pharmacy . . . he could, on occasion, draw a cup of beer as well as a tooth, tap a hogshead as well as a vein, and wash, with a draught of good ale, the moustaches which his art had just trimmed.' *The Fortunes of Nigel.*

SUDDLECHOP, DAME URSULA. Benjamin's wife. 'Busy and important far beyond her ostensible situation in society,' she could, amongst her 'multifarious practices,' 'be useful to the impassioned and the frail in the rise, progress, and consequences of their passion.' 'Muffled gallants and masked females' came to her for help, but she 'was never known to betray any transaction intrusted to her, unless she had either been indifferently paid for her service, or that someone found it convenient to give her a double douceur to make her disgorge the secret.' She was 'luxurious and genial in her habits' and had 'an infinite desire to be of service to her fellow-creatures.' *The Fortunes of Nigel.*

SUFFOLK, LADY. One of Queen Caroline's principal attendants : 'an ambitious rival.' *The Heart of Midlothian.*

SUMACK & Co. The nursery gardeners of Newcastle from whom Saunders Saunderson received his training. *Waverley.*

SUNDERLAND, CICELY. Adam Woodcock's 'favourite.' *The Abbot.*

SUSSEX, EARL OF. Thomas Ratcliffe, the rival of Leicester in

Elizabeth's favour. He was 'esteemed and honoured by his Sovereign' for his 'military services, high blood, and frank bearing,' but in 'person, features, and address' he was at a disadvantage when compared with Leicester. *Kenilworth.*

SWALEWELL, BRANDY. The 'gentleman' with whom Percy Osbaldistone took the wager that resulted in his death. *Rob Roy.*

SWANSTON. One of the men who helped Job Rutledge to get the *Jumping Jenny* ready for the morning tide. *Redgauntlet.*

SWARTASTER. One of the young Islanders who were favourite guests at Magnus Troil's. *The Pirate.*

SWASHING WILL OF WALLINGFORD. One of Michael Lambourne's early comrades. 'He died the death of a fat buck ... being shot with a crossbow bolt, by old Thatcham, the Duke's stout park-keeper at Donnington Castle.' *Kenilworth.*

SWEEPCLEAN, SAUNDERS. The bailiff deputed to take forcible possession at Sir Arthur Wardour's.

'One of those dogs who are not too scornful to eat dirty puddings.' *The Antiquary.*

SWERTHA. Mr. Mertoun's housekeeper. 'The withered and selfish heart of the poor old woman' was filled ' with greed and avarice,' and she was equally anxious to profit at her master's expense, to get a share of the spoil from the sea, and to drive a hard bargain with Bryce Snailsfoot. *The Pirate.*

SWINEFORD, DAME. Sir Hugh Robsart's housekeeper. *Kenilworth.*

SYDDALL, ANTHONY. The aged butler and major-domo at Osbaldistone Hall : the 'confidant' of Diana Vernon and her father. *Rob Roy.*

SYLVANUS. An orang-outang 'trained to be useful in the wards of the prison' of Alexius Comnenus. Sent down to the dungeons with Ursel's supply of food and water, he was attacked and wounded by Count Robert. When in pity Count Robert bound his wounds 'the creature seemed sensible of his clemency.' Roaming in the garden of Agelastes, he was the cause of the shriek which brought Bertha and Hereward together again ; and in the same garden a blow on his wounded paw roused him to crush Agelastes to death. *Count Robert of Paris.*

T

TACKET, MARTIN. The shepherd with whom the Lady of Avenel took refuge when the English plundered her mansion and lands. In Glendearg he 'yielded obedience to both mistresses,' and grew to love the children as his own. It satisfied him to think ' there is use for the grey hairs on the old scalp, were it but to instruct the green head by precept and by example.' *The Monastery.*

TACKET, TIBB. Martin's wife : ' in better days' bower-woman to the Lady of Avenel. She 'diligently served the united family' in Glendearg, and when differences arose between her and Dame Glendinning, Tibb, 'though she often gave the first provocation, had generally the sense to be the first in relinquishing the argument.' *The Monastery.*

TAFFRIL, LIEUTENANT. Jenny Caxon's lover : Lovel's second in the duel with Hector McIntyre. He allowed Lovel to escape in his gun-brig, and afterwards to employ some of his men in depositing the supposed treasure-trove in the ruins of St. Ruth's Priory. *The Antiquary.*

TALBOT, COLONEL. The husband of Lady Emily Blandeville. His life was saved by Edward Waverley at Gladsmuir, and some months later he saved Edward from a rebel's fate.

'An English gentleman and soldier, manly, open, and generous, but not unsusceptible of prejudice against those of a different country, or who opposed him in political tenets.' *Waverley.*

TALLBOY. Abbot Boniface's forester. He waxed 'dim-eyed, and hath twice spoiled a noble buck, by hitting him unwarily on the haunch . . . a foul fault.' *The Monastery.*

TALLY, TOM. A friend of Lord Dalgarno who 'played a hand at put for a wager with Quinze le Va, the Frenchman, during morning prayers in Saint Paul's ; the morning was misty, and the parson drowsy, and the whole audience consisted of themselves and a blind woman, and so they escaped detection.' *The Fortunes of Nigel.*

(*Put*, a game with cards.)

TAM O' TODSHAW. One of Dandy Dinmont's neighbours in Liddesdale. *Guy Mannering.*

TAM O' WHITTRAM. One of the last who had known all about 'the lawful mode of following a fray across the Border.' 'He died in the hard winter.' *The Black Dwarf.*

TAMLOWRIE, LAIRD OF. One of a party of friends who met at the Queensferry inn for an afternoon's conviviality. But to the landlord's chagrin the Antiquary, with some of his 'auld-warld stories, that the mind o' man canna resist, whirled them to the back o' beyont to look at the auld Roman camp.'

The others of the party were Sir Gilbert Grizzlecleugh, auld Rossballoh, and the Bailie. *The Antiquary.*

TANCRED, PRINCE OF OTRANTO. A kinsman of Bohemond : one of the leaders of the first Crusade who did not promise allegiance to Alexius Comnenus when passing through Constantinople. In response to Bertha's appeal to the Crusaders he returned from Scutari accompanied by 'fifty lances, with their furniture and following,' in order to see 'fair play' in the combat between Nicephorus and Count Robert. The Greek ships of war having unsuccessfully opposed his landing, the Emperor received him graciously, and appointed him to act with Nicanor as Field Marshal of the lists.

'The noblest knight of the Christian chivalry.' *Count Robert of Paris.*

TAPEITOUT, MR. The minister's assistant and successor : suggested by Tom Hillary as a substitute for Richard Middlemas in Menie Gray's affections. *The Surgeon's Daughter.*

TAPSTER, JOHN. One of the 'myrmidons of the bonny Black Bear' in Cumnor. *Kenilworth.*

TARRAS. Hobbie Elliot's horse. *The Black Dwarf.*

TASTE, THE MAN OF. *See* WINTERBLOSSOM, MR.

TAYLOR, JOHN. 'The water-poet who keeps both a sculler and a pair of oars': maintained by the King's royal grace. *The Fortunes of Nigel.*

TEARUM. 'The gaunt, half-starved mastiff' that kept watch at Portanferry jail. *Guy Mannering.*

TELFORD, TOBY. *See* HODGE.

TEMPLARS. Members of the famous Order of the Temple. This Order was formed early in the twelfth century to protect pilgrims to the Holy Land from the Saracens, and its members bound themselves by a solemn vow to a life of chastity, poverty, and obedience. They were at the same time monks and knights, and fought with a courage and devotion almost unparalleled in the history of the world. But abuses crept in ; the wealth and luxury of the Order created powerful enemies, and confessions of infamy were wrung from many members by cruelty and torture. The Order was finally suppressed by a Papal bull in 1312. *Ivanhoe.*

TEMPLARS, GRAND MASTER OF THE (*The Talisman*). *See* AMAURY, GILES.

TEMPLARS, GRAND MASTER OF THE (*Ivanhoe*). *See* BEAUMANOIR, LUCAS DE.

TEMPLETON, LAURENCE. The fictitious writer of the epistle dedicating *Ivanhoe* to Dr. Dryasdust. He professed to have found the materials of the tale in an Anglo-Norman MS. belonging to Sir Arthur Wardour. He takes part in the meeting of shareholders described in the Introduction to *The Betrothed*, as being held 'to form a joint-stock company united for the purpose of writing and publishing the class of works called the *Waverley Novels.*' *Ivanhoe.*

TENNANT & CO. A Fairport firm that received twelve letters by one post.

'Thae folk do mair business than a' the rest o' the burgh.' *The Antiquary.*

TERNOTTE. One of the attendants who accompanied Eveline Berenger to the House of Baldringham. *The Betrothed.*

THACKHAM, JANE. The lady who 'jumped out of the shot-window of old Gaffer Thackham's grange' to go to the parish church and become Dame Goldthred. The palfrey, 'bonny Bayard,' which the mercer had intended for her use was taken possession of by Wayland Smith at a critical moment in his journey with the Countess of Leicester to Kenilworth Castle. Goldthred made what peace he could with the disappointed bride, 'a picture of Lot's wife.' *Kenilworth.*

THATCHAM. See SWASHING WILL OF WALLINGFORD.

THEODORICK OF ENGADDI. Formerly Alberick of Mortemar, 'noble in birth, high in fortune, strong in arms, wise in counsel.' For twenty years 'mean, abject, and despairing, fluctuating between madness and misery,' he did penance in the vaults of Engaddi over the grave of a fallen nun ' whose guilt was avenged by self-murder.' But his spirit was at the same time 'active, shrewd, and piercing to advocate the cause of the Church of Jerusalem,' and by his fits of frenzy he gained 'favour and reverence from the Paynimrie, who regard madmen as the inspired of Heaven.' Honoured at the same time by the Christians for the severity of his penance, he acted as intermediary between Saladin and the allied Princes. *The Talisman.*

THERESA, SISTER. Flora MacIvor's companion when she left Carlisle for France. 'An elderly woman, apparently a foreigner.' *Waverley.*

THETIS. One of John Davies' dogs. *Redgauntlet.*

THIBAULT OF MONTIGNI. 'One of the challengers at the Passage of Haflinghem' held in honour of the Countess Hameline of Croye 'while in the very earliest bloom.' 'He was the kindest soul alive, and not only was he never so discourteous as to lift hand against his lady, but, by our good dame, he who beat all enemies without doors, found a fair foe who could belabour him within.' *Quentin Durward.*

THICKSCULL and DUNDERMORE, FATHERS. 'Two good brethren of the convent of Lindores' under whose care, the fictitious Waltheof's letter said, Catharine Glover had been sent to the Highlands. *The Fair Maid of Perth.*

THIEBAULT. A trooper, a Provençal by birth, who acted as Arthur Philipson's guide from Dijon to Aix, and thence to the convent of Saint-Victoire. He afterwards accompanied Arthur and his father to the Duke of Burgundy's retreat in Upper Burgundy, and attended them on the field of Nancy, proving always a 'trusty attendant.' *Anne of Geierstein.*

THIMBLETHWAITE, TIMOTHY. "The Master Fashioner' with whom Claud Halcro lodged when in London. 'He made for all the wits,' 'was a person of wit himself,' and introduced Claud to the Wits' Coffeehouse, and the 'glorious John Dryden.' *The Pirate.*

THOMAS THE RHYMER. Author of the prophecy :—

'When the last Laird of Ravenswood to Ravenswood shall ride,
And woo a dead maiden to be his bride,
He shall stable his steed in the Kelpie's flow,
And his name shall be lost for evermore!'

The Bride of Lammermoor.

See also ERCELDOUN, THOMAS OF.

THOMSON, PEG. One of the old women who competed to announce to Dr. Gray the approach of interesting strangers. She 'was permitted the privilege of recom mending her good-daughter Bet Jamieson to be wet-nurse' to Zilia de Monçada's child. *The Surgeon's Daughter.*

THONG, GOODMAN. *See* PRANCE OF PADWORTH.

THORNTON, CAPTAIN. The officer who arrested Bailie Nicol Jarvie and Frank Osbaldistone at Aberfoil. On the following day he was led into an ambush by 'the Dougal creature,' and defeated by Helen MacGregor ' wi' a wheen auld carles that are past fighting, and bairns that are no come till't, and wives wi' their rocks and distaffs, the very wally-draigles o' the countryside.' *Rob Roy.*

(*Wheen*, a number. *Carles*, men. *Wally-draigles*, feeble folk.)

THREE-PLIE, DEACON. 'The rape-spinner,' one of whose ropes, Bailie Nicol Jarvie feared, would be Rob Roy's 'last cravat.' *Rob Roy.*

THRYME. A large aged wolf-dog belonging to the Lady of Baldringham. 'The hound . . . excepting the red glare of his eyes, might have seemed a hieroglyphical emblem, lying at the feet of some ancient priestess of Woden or Freya.' *The Betrothed.*

THWACKER, QUARTERMASTER. The 'shark,' who with twenty men was waiting for the *Jumping Jenny* on the Cumberland coast. He had a 'kindness' for Doll Crackenthorp, else Joe had never got down to give Nanty Ewart warning. *Redgauntlet.*

TIB. The hen-wife at Tillietudlem. *Old Mortality.*

TIB. Mr. Bindloose's maid. *St. Ronan's Well.*

TIBBIE FAW. An ostler wife who kept a little lonely change-house on the edge of the common by Pitmurkie Wood. Steenie Steenson drank a mutchkin of brandy there on his way home after Laurie Lapraik had put him 'far beyond the bounds of patience.' *Redgauntlet.*

(*Faw*, fate. *Mutchkin*, a measure equal to an English pint.)

TICKLING TOM. The waterman into whose wherry Alice Bridgenorth was said to have been forced by one of the Duke of Buckingham's men when Julian was fighting Jenkins. *Peveril of the Peak.*

TIDER, ROBIN. The man whom Varney took to replace Lambourne when he carried off the Countess from Kenilworth Castle. 'Neither quite so prompt nor altogether so profligate as Lambourne.' *Kenilworth.*

TIDESLY. One of the 'open debauchers and ruffianly swordsmen' who were 'a terror to peaceable men and a scandal' to the Earl of Leicester's service. They 'bear gallows in their face and murder in their right hand.' *Kenilworth.*

TILLIBARDINE, KNIGHT OF. The common relative of the Master of Ravenswood and the Marquis of A—. *The Bride of Lammermoor.*

TIM. One of Duke Hildebrod's tapsters. *The Fortunes of Nigel.*

TIMMS, CORPORAL. A non-commissioned officer in Edward Waverley's troop. He was misled by

Will Ruthven, and after trial by court-martial, was shot for stirring up mutiny in the company. *Waverley*.

TIMOTHY. The aged waiter who, 'with many a weary sigh and many a groan,' served Ian Meng's guests. *Anne of Geierstein*.

TIMOTHY, BROTHER. One of the Brethren at St. Mary's. When told to saddle Benedict for the Abbot's journey to Glendearg he 'stared, thinking ... that his ears had scarce done him justice.' *The Monastery*.

TINTO, DICK. (1) An artist friend of Peter Pattieson who stayed for some time at the Wallace Inn, Gandercleugh. He maintained that the characters in Peter's *Tales* 'patter too much,' and urged him to make the narratives 'rather descriptive than dramatic.' Towards this end, he supplied Peter with the materials out of which *The Bride of Lammermoor* grew.

(2) The 'celebrated' painter who restored Meg Dods' sign, gilding the Bishop's crook and augmenting 'the horrors of the Devil's aspect.' 'An auld used hand.' (1) *The Bride of Lammermoor*. (2) *St. Ronan's Well*.

TIPPERHEWIT, GIRNIGO OF. The 'natural heir and seventh cousin' of Girnigo of Killancureit, but displaced by Bullsegg. *Waverley*.

TIPPOO SAHIB. Hyder Ali's son: 'vice-regent of his newly-conquered territory of Bangalore.' He had 'the cunning of his father and his military talents, but he lacks his cautious wisdom.' Having conceived an 'outrageous passion for a portrait' of Menie Gray, he was led to honour Richard Middlemas by the prospect of receiving 'the original within his power.' He failed to discover that Richard's ultimate object was to betray him to the English. *The Surgeon's Daughter*.

TIRLSNECK, JOHNNIE. The beadle. With his 'stern brow and well-known voice' he tried to keep order amongst the crowd of children at the gate of Shaws Castle on the day of the 'dramaticals' there. *St. Ronan's Well*.

TOBY. One of the attendants at the table d'hôte in the Fox Hotel: 'a lumpish lad' whom Mr. Winterblossom 'permitted to wait on no one till, as the hymn says, "All his wants were well supplied."' *St. Ronan's Well*.

TOD GABBIE. *See* BAILLIE, GABRIEL.

TOINETTE. One of Galeotti's 'abettors of lavish expense.' But 'the stars never told him that honest Ludovic Lesly used to help yonder wench of his to spend the fair ducats he flings into her lap.' *Quentin Durward*.

TOISON D'OR. (1) The herald who accompanied Count Crèvecœur to the French court at Plessis-les Tours. In presence of Louis and the Duke of Burgundy sitting together in council in Peronne, he exposed Hayraddin, the professed herald of William de la Marck.

(2) 'Herald of the order of the Golden Fleece.' He acted as master of ceremonies in Dijon when Charles the Bold received members of the Estates of Bur-

gundy, and immediately afterwards the deputies from Switzerland. (1) *Quentin Durward.* (2) *Anne of Geierstein.*

Tom. A manservant of Sir Robert Hazlewood. *Guy Mannering.*

Tom. One of the watermen who gave Julian Peveril information about Alice Bridgenorth's fate while Julian fought Jenkins. *Peveril of the Peak.*

Tom with the Tod's Tail. The Lord Abbot's ranger. *The Monastery.*

(*Tod*, fox.)

Tomanrait. The old man from whom Edward Waverley received hospitality after his accident at the Highland hunting party. 'A relic of primitive simplicity!' *Waverley.*

Tomb, Knight of the. The disguise in which Sir James Douglas acted as guide to Augusta of Berkley after Margaret de Hautlieu had taken her to the haunts of the Douglas and his friends. *Castle Dangerous.*

Tomkins, Joseph. 'Honest Joe,' 'Trusty Tomkins,' 'Fibbet': 'a bitter Independent, and a secretary, or clerk, or something or other, to the regicide dog Desborough ... a wild ranter in religious opinions, but in private affairs far-sighted, cunning, and interested even as any rogue of them': 'an artful and thorough-paced agent.' Known in youth to Dr. Rochecliffe and Jocelin Joliffe as Phil Hazeldine, he was to some extent trusted by them; he helped them to carry out the scheme by which the Lords Commissioners were frightened from Woodstock Lodge; he acted 'as a sort of ambassador for his worthy masters' after their departure; he knew the secret of Louis Kerneguy's disguise; and, but for the ill-timed advances to Phœbe Mayflower which caused his death, he could have led Cromwell to the 'side of Charles Stewart's bed, ere he had slept off the last night's claret.' *Woodstock.*

Topham, Charles. An officer of the Black Rod of the House of Commons sent 'to pursue and seize upon the persons of certain individuals' accused of complicity in the great Popish Plot. Sir Geoffrey Peveril was one of those arrested by him.

'Pompous and stupid.' *Peveril of the Peak.*

Torfe, Provost George. Chief Magistrate of Kirkwall. He was deaf to all Minna Troil's appeals that he should set Cleveland free in order to secure her father's safety. 'His duty was imperious and must be obeyed.' *The Pirate.*

Tormot. Torquil's 'youngest and dearest' son, and the last of the eight to fall. *The Fair Maid of Perth.*

Torquil of the Oak. An old forester: foster father to Eachin MacIan. 'Incapable from the formation of his own temper' of believing that Eachin was a 'personal coward,' he regarded the young chief's dread of the combat with Clan Chattan as due to 'enchantment.' With his eight sons he surrounded Eachin in the combat, keeping him as 'safe as in a castle,' until one after the other they all lay dead on the field—he the last to fall. Then, in accord with the prophecy which had kept Torquil's faith alive, Eachin escaped, 'without either scar or scratch, wem or wound.' *The Fair Maid of Perth.*

TORRENCE and WALDIE. 'Resurrection women.' 'Rather than disappoint the evening lecture of the students, they stole a live child, murdered it, and sold the body for three shillings and sixpence! *Guy Mannering.*

TORWOOD, EARL OF. Lady Margaret Bellenden's father. He left his own estate to her. *Old Mortality.*

TORWOOD, FERGUS, 3RD EARL OF. Lady Margaret Bellenden's grandfather, 'the handsomest man of his time.' His second lady, Countess Jane, had, on the other hand, 'a hump back and only one eye.' 'Marriage went by destiny.' *Old Mortality.*

TOSHACH BEG (*i.e.* LITTLE). The 'second' of MacGillie Chattanach. He objected to Torquil's proposal that Eachin MacIan should withdraw from the contest between the clans in order to equalise the number after Ferquhard Day's desertion. 'The life of the Chief,' he said, 'is to the clan the breath of our nostrils, nor will we ever consent that our Chief shall be exposed to dangers which the Captain of Clan Quhele does not share.' *The Fair Maid of Perth.*

TOUCHWOOD, MR. The partner of Ronald Scrogie's father 'in the great firm of Touchwood, Scrogie & Co.' *St. Ronan's Well.*

TOUCHWOOD, MR. PEREGRINE SCROGIE. Reginald Scrogie Mowbray's disinherited son, and cousin of the 5th Earl of Etherington. Disgusted with the Hotel at the Well as 'the very fountainhead of folly and coxcombry—a Babel for noise and a Vanity-fair for nonsense,' he took up his abode with Meg Dods. There he was kept informed by Solmes of Lord Etherington's schemes. A 'fidgety, fiery old Nabob,' he spoke and acted 'in all the dignity of dollars,' and wished to put matters to rights for Frank Tyrrel and the Mowbrays. But he failed to save Clara from John's passion. 'He often talks of his disappointments, but can never be made to understand, or at least to admit, that they were in some measure precipitated by his own talent for intrigue and manœuvring.' *St. Ronan's Well.*

TOUGH, MR. The defendant's counsel in the case *Peebles against Plainstanes*. On the second day after Alan Fairford's departure he was heard in answer to the opening counsel. 'Deep-mouthed, long-breathed, and pertinacious, taking a pinch of snuff betwixt every sentence, which otherwise seemed interminable—the veteran pleader prosed over all the themes which had been treated so luminously by Fairford; he quietly and imperceptibly replaced all the rubbish which the other had cleared away; and succeeded in restoring the veil of obscurity and unintelligibility which had for many years darkened the case of Peebles against Plainstanes.' *Redgauntlet.*

TOUGHYARN, MASTER. The inhabitant of Woodstock who drew up the memorial presented to the Earl of Leicester during his short visit to the town. He 'took six months to draw it up . . . and see if the Earl hath not knocked the marrow out of it in twenty-four hours!' *Kenilworth.*

TOURNIQUET and LANCELOT, DOCTORS. The doctors who failed to save Reuben Witherington's life when he was attacked by smallpox. 'What avails the reputation of the physician when the patient perisheth?' *The Surgeon's Daughter.*

TOUTHOPE, MR. 'A canny chield at Loughmaben, a bit writer ad,' whom Andrew Fairservice expected to square his accounts with Thorncliff Osbaldistone. But he had been appointed 'clerk to the peace of the county' in Andrew's absence, and found it his duty to 'arrest' Thorncliff's mare. He was persuaded not to detain Andrew himself, and made him a present of a broken-winded and spavined pony on which to continue his journey. *Rob Roy.*

(*Canny*, cautious.)

TOXARTIS. A mercenary soldier whom Brenhilda killed 'by what seemed a mere fillip on the head,' he having insulted her as she walked along the shore of the Propontis with Agelastes and her husband. *Count Robert of Paris.*

TRACY. One of the gentlemen in attendance on the Earl of Sussex. On the occasion of the Queen's unexpected visit to Say's Court, Raleigh feared she should find Tracy breakfasting off his 'beastly black puddings and Rhenish'; 'and she detests, they say, all coarse meats, evil smells, and strong wines.' *Kenilworth.*

TRAGENDECK, CAPTAIN. One of Magnus Troil's friends who had been 'down in the Bay of Honduras and all thereabouts,' and who held that 'there is never peace with Spaniards beyond the Line.' *The Pirate.*

TRAMP, GAFFER. One of the crowd that watched Meg Murdockson being hung. *The Heart of Midlothian.*

TRAPBOIS, 'GOLDEN.' A usurer of some notoriety who was believed 'to understand the plucking of a pigeon as well as, or better than, any man of Alsatia.' Nigel was assigned as a guest for his 'poor apartment.' He was murdered during the attempted robbery by Colepepper and Skurliewhitter, Nigel shooting their companion, Jack Hempsfield. *The Fortunes of Nigel.*

TRAPBOIS, MARTHA. Old Trapbois' unprepossessing daughter. Though she held her father's avarice in horror, she pitied the old man and served him faithfully to the end. In gratitude to Nigel for his protection she furnished Richie Moniplies with the money necessary to redeem Glenvarloch, and afterwards accepted Richie as her permanent 'protector.' *The Fortunes of Nigel.*

TREBLEPLUMB, LADY. 'Sir Thomas Trebleplumb the great Turkey merchant's widow,' who married the Scotsman Sir Auley Macauley. *The Fortunes of Nigel.*

TREDDLES, MR. 'A cautious money-making person' who bought Glentanner when Mr. Croftangry was obliged to sell it. But his son speculated 'boldly and unfortunately,' and the estate with its new house, 'a huge lumping four-square pile of freestone,' again came into the market. *The Highland Widow.*

TREE, THE WOMAN OF THE. See MACTAVISH, ELSPAT.

TREMOUILLE, CHARLOTTE DE LA. See DERBY, COUNTESS OF.

TREMOUILLE, DUKE DE LA. Father of the Countess of Derby. 'The house of my father,' the Countess boasted, 'was the most famous school of chivalry in France; nor have I degenerated from him, or suffered any relaxation in that noble discipline which trained young gentlemen to do honour to their race.' *Peveril of the Peak.*

TRESHAM, MR. The sleeping partner in the firm Osbaldistone & Tresham. It was he who informed Frank of Rashleigh's treachery during his temporary management of affairs. At his request Frank joined Owen in Glasgow. *Rob Roy.*

TRESHAM, RICHARD. See WITHERINGTON, GENERAL.

TRESHAM, WILL. Son of the sleeping partner in the great London house, Osbaldistone and Tresham. At his request Frank Osbaldistone wrote the Memoirs of his adventurous youth. *Rob Roy.*

TRESHAM & TRENT. The firm out of which Osbaldistone & Tresham grew. *Rob Roy.*

TRESSILIAN, EDMUND. Amy Robsart's accepted suitor while she was still 'the principal joy' of her father's house. Serious and reflective by nature, he was deeply moved by her supposed entanglement with Richard Varney, and made constant but unavailing efforts to restore her to her father. After her tragic death 'neither the prospect of rural independence, nor the promises of favour which Elizabeth held out to induce him to follow the Court, could remove his profound melancholy.' He died before his day, 'young in years, but old in grief.'

'Never breathed mortal man more free of whatever was base, false, or selfish.' *Kenilworth.*

TREVANION & TREGUILLIAM. A mining firm in Cornwall with whom Osbaldistone and Tresham did business. *Rob Roy.*

TRIMMEL, MR. 'A neighbour' recommended as a possible publisher to Mr. Pembroke by Jonathan Grubbet. 'He is a bachelor, and leaving off business, so a voyage in a western barge would not inconvenience him.' *Waverley.*

TRIMMER. John Mowbray's favourite hound 'that has beat the whole country.' *St. Ronan's Well.*

TRISTAN L'HERMITE. Provost-Marshal of the Royal Household, and one of Louis' low-born favourites. As chief hangman he was an unscrupulous tool in Louis' hands, so zealous in his despatch that he had 'now and then mistaken the criminal and strung up in his place an honest labourer.' Like his subordinates Trois-Eschelles and Petit-André, he had 'a sort of professional delight' in his 'horrid office,' and was the object of the deepest hatred and execration. *Quentin Durward.*

TRODDEN, GERTRUDE. A dame whose fate foreshadowed that of Martin Waldeck. *The Antiquary.*

TROIL FAMILY, THE.

— RIBOLT. One of the remote ancestors of Magnus, 'renowned for deeds of valorous enterprise in the fifteenth century.' He was buried in the old Kirk of Saint Ringan (or Ninian), and from his coffin Norna took, 'with much caution and apparent awe,' a piece of lead which afterwards played a part in her mystic treatment of Minna Troil's ailment.

— ROLFE. Father of Erland and Olave, 'the most rich and well estated of any who descended from the old Norse stock.'

— ERLAND. Ulla's father. He died on the night when she left him to join the 'fatal stranger.' 'I left the house at midnight,' she told Minna and Brenda, 'I had to pass my father's door, and I perceived it was open—I thought he watched us; and, that the sound of my steps might not break his slumbers, I closed the fatal door—a light and trivial action—but, God in Heaven! what were the consequences!—At morn the room was full of suffocating vapour—my father was dead—dead through my act—dead through my disobedience—dead through my infamy!'

TROIL FAMILY, THE.

— OLAVE. Brother of Erland and father of Magnus. The discord which arose between the brothers regarding the division of their father's land would have been healed by the marriage of Magnus and Ulla, had not Ulla been infatuated by a 'fatal stranger.'

— MAGNUS. A descendant of the ancient Earls of Orkney: 'the principal proprietor, as well as the *Fowd,* or provincial judge, of his district.' 'He was an honest, plain Zetland gentleman, somewhat passionate ... and somewhat over-convivial in his habits ... but frank-tempered and generous to his people and kind and hospitable to strangers.' Proud of his two beautiful daughters, and jealous of their Norse descent, he with difficulty consented to Brenda's marriage with Mordaunt Mertoun. But 'in scornful allusion to the Highland and Border families, to whom Zetland owes many respectable landholders,' he said at last 'as well his daughter married the son of an English pirate as of a Scottish thief.'

— ULLA. *See* NORNA.

— MINNA. Magnus Troil's elder daughter. 'The lover of solitude, and of those paths of knowledge in which men walk best without company—the enemy of light mirth, the friend of musing melancholy, and the frequenter of fountain-heads and pathless glens,' she was captivated by the 'daring gallantry' of Captain Cleveland. She had been bred 'in such remote simplicity and utter ignorance of what is evil,' that she compared his ' occupation with that of the old Norsemen who . . . took the name of Sea-Kings.' When disillusionment came, she spared reproaches and used her power to direct Cleveland to the path of ' good or glorious action,' while she herself ' learned to exchange the visions of wild enthusiasm . . . for a truer and purer connection with the world beyond us.'

TROIL FAMILY, THE.
— BRENDA. Magnus Troil's younger daughter. ' Equally lovely and equally innocent,' she differed from Minna in ' character, taste, and expression.' She was bright and vivacious; 'her eye seemed to look on every object with pleasure'; her 'guileless and open-hearted simplicity . . . cast an enchantment over everything which she did or said.' ' In recompense for a less portion of imagination than her sister,' she ' was gifted with sound common sense,' was not so ' easily deceived in people,' and did not quit her ' own thoughts of an innocent friend for the gossip of the island.' *The Pirate.*

TROIS - ESCHELLES. ' Jean - qui - pleure': one of Tristan l'Hermite's subordinates ' more utterly detested than, perhaps, any creatures of their kind, whether before or since.' ' Trois-Eschelles was a tall, thin, ghastly man, with a peculiar gravity of visage, and a large rosary round his neck, the use of which he was accustomed piously to offer to those sufferers on whom he did his duty. He had one or two Latin texts continually in his mouth on the nothingness and vanity of human life; and, had it been regular to have enjoyed such a plurality, he might have held the office of confessor to the jail *in commendam* with that of executioner.' *Quentin Durward.*

TROLLD. A dwarf famous in the northern Sagas, supposed to have made the Dwarfie Stone for his residence. Ulla Troil believed that he appeared to her there and promised to give her the power ' o'er tempest and wave ' which she coveted. But not, he said,

' Till thou reave thy life's giver
Of the gift which he gave.'
The Pirate.

TROTCOSEY, ABBOT. The ' mitred abbot' of the parish in which Monkbarns and Knockwinnock lay. His name was to be seen ' at the head of the rolls of Parliament in the fourteenth and fifteenth centuries.' *The Antiquary.*

TROTTER, NELLY. ' The fishwoman whose cart formed the only neutral channel of communication between the Auld Town and the Well, and who was in favour with Meg because, as Nelly passed her door on her way to the Well, she always had the first choice of her fish.' Through her Meg Dods sent a 'bit picture' of Frank Tyrrel's drawing to the connoisseurs at the Well that they might see 'the merits of her lodger as an artist.' *St. Ronan's Well.*

TRUEMAN. 'The quaker': 'that formal ass,' the Earl of Etherington said, when giving Solmes directions concerning a certain postal packet, ' who addresses me by my Christian and family name, Francis Tyrrel.' *St. Ronan's Well.*

TRUMBULL, BAILIE. The representative of justice in whose stable Thorncliff Osbaldistone's mare was detained by Mr. Touthope. *Rob Roy.*

TRUMBULL, TOM. 'Tam Turnpenny,' the 'grizzled hypocrite' at Annan to whom Maxwell of Summertrees directed Alan Fairford for knowledge of Redgauntlet's whereabouts. 'The lines, or rather, as Quin said of Macklin, the cordage, of his countenance were so sternly adapted to a devotional and even ascetic expression, that they left no room for any indication of reckless daring or sly dissimulation.' But his works ' of necessity and mercy ' took him ' all in the way of business ' into close partnership with smugglers and outlaws. He put Alan under Nanty Ewart's care. *Redgauntlet.*

TRUSTY TOMKINS. *See* TOMKINS, JOSEPH.

TUCK, FRIAR. The Clerk of Copmanhurst: a hermit and one of Locksley's men. 'The jolly Clerk of Copmanhurst is a known man, and kills half the deer that are stolen in this walk.' When his tried friend, the Black Knight, proved to be the King and offered to retain him as a yeoman of the guard, he could but plead 'how the sin of laziness has beset me.' ' Saint Dunstan,' he said, ' stands quiet in his niche . . . never complains—a quiet master he is and a peaceful . . . but to be a yeoman in attendance on my Sovereign the King . . . good, my Liege, I pray you to leave me as you found me.' *Ivanhoe.*

TUCK, THOMAS. 'Tyburn Tom': one of the two footpads who promised to rob Jeanie Deans ' and send her begging back to her own beggarly country.' He worked in company with Frank Levitt and Meg Murdockson, and with Meg urged that strong measures be taken against Jeanie, in spite of Ratcliffe's ' pass.' *The Heart of Midlothian.*

TUGMUTTON, TIMOTHY. The name which Dick Fletcher signed on his and Frederick Altamont's letter to the Magistrates of Kirkwall, as ' Fletcher was the most crabbed word to spell . . . in the whole dictionary.' *The Pirate.*

TUISCO. A comrade of Hayraddin, who accompanied Heinrick to take part in the seizure of the Ladies of Croye. *Quentin Durward.*

TULL, RAB. Town clerk of Fairport at the time of the grand law-plea between the Oldbucks and the feuars at Musselcraig. The ' Green Room ' ghost appeared to him and led him to the spot where the missing charter was to be found.

'A just-living man for a country writer.' *The Antiquary.*

TULLIBARDINE, MARQUIS OF. One of the Highland chieftains who joined the young Chevalier. *Waverley.*

TULLIELLUM, LAIRD OF. Maternal grandfather of the Baron of Bradwardine. *Waverley.*

TUNSTALL, FRANK. One of David Ramsay's 'sharp-witted, active, able-bodied, and well-voiced apprentices.' He was of more aristocratic descent than his companion Vincent and at the same time 'of a much more staid and composed temper,' and applied himself to learn the 'abstract principles of science connected with the trade.' 'He lived on the best terms with his companion and readily stood by him' when engaged in one of his 'street skirmishes,' but for himself, he 'had not a word to throw at a dog.' *The Fortunes of Nigel.*

TURNBULL, DICK. A friend with whom Hobbie Elliot had an unsettled quarrel. *The Black Dwarf.*

TURNBULL, MICHAEL. 'The bold borderer' who refused to drink the health of the English King at Sir John de Walton's hunting party. He afterwards acted as 'the honourable escort of Augusta de Berkley bearing a letter explaining the terms' on which Sir James Douglas was willing to set her free. But he was mortally wounded by Sir John de Walton, who was roused to fury by Lady Augusta's appeal for help, and acted 'almost at unawares.' 'Methinks,' he said, as he lay dying, 'this gay English knight would not have come off with such advantage had the ground on which we stood been alike indifferent to both, or had I been aware of his onset.' *Castle Dangerous.*

TURNEHAM, SIR EDWIN. *See* LEICESTER, EARL OF (p. 151).

TURNER, MRS. Dame Suddlechop's 'honoured patroness': 'half-milliner, half-procuress, and secret agent in all manner of proceedings.' 'She had the ill-luck to meddle in the matter of Somerset and Overbury, and so the great Earl and his lady slipped their necks out of the collar, and left her and some half-dozen others to suffer in their stead.' *The Fortunes of Nigel.*

Note.—Mrs. Turner figured in the State trials that arose out of the poisoning of Sir Thomas Overbury in the Tower. Both Lady Essex (afterwards Countess of Somerset) and the Earl of Somerset were condemned, but they were pardoned by James I, while the subordinate actors were put to death.

TURNER, SIR JAMES. A boon companion of Donohoe Bertram. *Guy Mannering.*

TURNPENNY, TAM. *See* TRUMBULL, TOM.

TURNPENNY, TAM. A banker: one of Clara Mowbray's trustees. *St. Ronan's Well.*

TURNTIPPET, LORD. A Privy Councillor who had 'complied wi' a' compliances, tane a' manner of tests, abjured all that was to be abjured, and sworn a' that was to be sworn for these thirty years bypast.' *The Bride of Lammermoor.*

TURN-TO-THE-RIGHT THWACKAWAY. One of Captain Bangtext's men. *The Heart of Midlothian.*

TWIGTYTHE, REV. MR. The clergyman who married Ned Williams and Cicely Jopson. He took an interest in the supposed student of divinity and brought him newspapers. *Waverley.*

TWINEALL. The clerk whom Frank's father sent to Osbaldistone Hall to arrange that Frank should change places with one of Sir Hildebrand's sons. *Rob Roy.*

TYBURN, TOM. *See* TUCK, THOMAS.

TYRE, ARCHBISHOP. A 'sagacious prelate,' 'both loved and honoured' by King Richard. By some he was represented as 'a politic and unscrupulous person,' accessory to the secret plans of the allied princes for bringing the Crusade to an end. *The Talisman.*

TYRIE. One of the band of Louis' Scottish Guard who were prepared to defend Quentin after his escape from the hands of Trois-Eschelles and Petit-André. *Quentin Durward.*

TYRIE, REV. MICHAEL. The minister of Glenorquhy. From him, as he rode past his mother's hut, Hamish MacTavish heard convincing testimony that he was indeed 'undone' by his mother's mistaken love. The minister afterwards exerted himself on Hamish's behalf, and accompanied him to the scene of his death, but to the broken-hearted Elspat he could bring no comfort. *The Highland Widow.*

TYRREL, FRANK. The Earl of Etherington's elder brother. Blaming himself as the ultimate cause of Clara Mowbray's misery, he tried, with a whole-hearted devotion, to guard her against his brother's 'molestations.' To secure such tranquillity of mind as was still possible for her, he was ready to sacrifice not only his own claims to rank and fortune, but the honour of his dead mother, the Comptesse de Martigny. But he was shy and distrustful of others, and not all the 'rectitude of his purpose' availed to stop the march of events which might have been averted by a judicious frankness towards Peregrine Touchwood. *St. Ronan's Well.*

U

ULRICA. Torquil Wolfganger's daughter. While she was young and fair the elder Front-de-Bœuf stormed the castle of Torquilstone, killing her father and seven brothers. 'Ere their bodies were cold,' she told Rebecca, 'and ere their blood was dried, I had become the prey and the scorn of the conqueror.' 'Wretched and degraded,' she had her hours of revenge in nursing the 'unnatural hatred' between the elder Front-de-Bœuf and his son Reginald until it ended in the father's death. At last, as a 'decrepit old hag,' she helped the Black

Knight's attack on the castle by setting fire to it. She died in the ruins, exulting that Reginald should 'perish like a fox in his den, when the peasants have set fire to the cover around it.' *Ivanhoe.*

ULRICA. Bertha's mother: 'Martha' in the household of the Lady of Aspramonte. *Count Robert of Paris.*

UNA. One of Flora MacIvor's maids. *Waverley.*

UNDERTAKERS, THE FIFE. Lowlanders to whom James VI granted possession of Lewis, with a view to destroy the 'patriarchal power' of the Highland Chiefs. Most of the settlers were eventually put to the sword by the natives. *A Legend of Montrose.*

UNREASON, ABBOT OF. 'Father Howleglas, the learned Monk of Misrule': Adam Woodcock, leader of the revellers who went to St. Mary's in a mock representation of the appointment of Father Ambrose as Abbot. *The Abbot.*

(*Howleglas* for Owlglass or Eulenspiegel, the mediæval type of a knavish fool.)

URFRIED. The name assumed by Ulrica. *Ivanhoe.*

URRIE (or HURRY), SIR JOHN. An officer in joint command with General Baillie. 'A soldier of fortune,' he 'had already changed sides twice during the Civil War, and was destined to turn his coat a third time before it was ended.' *A Legend of Montrose.*

URSEL (ZEDEKIAS). A former rival of Alexius Comnenus for the throne of Greece. Betrayed by his confederates, he was imprisoned in one of the dungeons of the palace, and there discovered by Count Robert. As a means of propitiating those of the people who favoured the conspiracy of Nicephorus, Alexius restored him to liberty—his 'courage, liberality, and other popular virtues' being still 'fondly remembered.' *Count Robert of Paris.*

URSLEY, DAME. *See* SUDDLECHOP, DAME URSULA.

URSULA, SISTER. *See* HAUTLIEU, MARGARET DE.

V

VACONELDIABOLO, FATHER. Chaplain to Provost-Marshal Tristan l'Hermite. *Quentin Durward.*

VALENCE, SIR AYMER DE. Deputy-governor of Douglas Castle. His 'newly-dubbed dignity' was offended when Sir John de Walton spoke to him with 'authoritative emphasis' concerning his easy admission of Bertram to the castle. But he stood 'high in the roll of English chivalry,' and showed 'a great degree of acuteness and accuracy' in solving Augustine's secret. 'Yours is that happy brain, which, bold in youth as beseems a young knight, is in more advanced life the happy source of prudent counsel.' *Castle Dangerous.*

VANBEEST & VANBRUGGEN. The Middleburgh house with which Dirk Hatteraick had a trade connection. Vanbeest was a cousin of 'Lieutenant' Brown, and little Harry Bertram was handed to him as a footboy. But Harry 'got about the old man's heart,' was bred in the office, and sent to India. *Guy Mannering.*

VANDA. 'Red-finger,' the murdered Briton in whose chamber every female of the house of Baldringham was required to pass a night before attaining her twenty-first year. To Eveline Berenger she pronounced the doom :

'Widow'd wife, and wedded maid,
Betrothed, betrayer, and betray'd !'

But after Eveline had stood the test of time Vanda returned with smiling aspect, her spirit appeased and Baldrick's crime requited. *The Betrothed.*

VANDEWASH, BEN. The Dutch broker from whom Mr. Touchwood got the breed of 'right Chitty-gong fowl' for Meg Dods. *St. Ronan's Well.*

VANWELT, JAN. One of Wilkin Flammock's neighbours : the central figure in the parable by which Wilkin justified himself to Father Aldrovand regarding the defence of the castle. *The Betrothed.*

VARANES. Jezdegerd's brother. After Jezdegerd's death he took command of the Syrians, and with a large body of cavalry 'on horses unmatched either in speed or wind,' he tried to intercept Alexius Comnenus in his retreat to Laodicea. But the Varangian guard successfully interfered. *Count Robert of Paris.*

VARNEY, SIR RICHARD. The 'sworn man, and a close brother' of the Earl of Leicester's secret council. His master used to say of him that 'he knew no virtuous property save affection to his patron'; but he was an 'evil genius,' moved only by 'ambition and haughty hope of power, pleasure, and revenge.' After Amy Robsart's outspoken contempt and scorn of him, he could not look on her without such a mingling of 'fear, and hate, and fondness,' as drove him to destroy her power over the Earl. No treachery was too base for him, and he tricked her to death 'by means of her best affections.' *Kenilworth.*

VAUDEMONT, FERRAND DE. Son of King René's daughter Yolande. Claiming Lorraine in his mother's right, he made common cause with the Swiss against Charles the Bold. As Lawrenz Neipperg he took part in the disturbance in La Ferette, and after war broke out he became General of the Confederates' army. By his success he rendered futile the negotiations that were being conducted by Arthur Philipson between his aunt, Margaret of Anjou, and Charles the Bold. 'A young man of courage and spirit.' *Anne of Geierstein.*

VAUGHAN, BASIL. *See* MERTOUN, BASIL.

VAUGHAN, CLEMENT. *See* CLEVELAND, CAPTAIN.

VAUGHAN, FATHER. *See* VERNON, SIR FREDERICK.

VAUGHAN, HENRY. The servant sent by the Duke of Northumberland to tell Sir Piercie Shafton that he must seek safety in flight, the Duke having been obliged to issue letters for his imprisonment. *The Monastery.*

VAUGHAN, MORDAUNT. *See* MERTOUN, MORDAUNT.

VAUX, LORD DE. *See* MULTON, THOMAS DE.

VEHMGERICHTE. A Secret Tribunal based on ancient Germanic methods of tribal justice, which exercised great power during the middle ages. 'Their severe and secret vengeance often deterred the rapacity of the noble robber, and protected the humble suppliant; the extent, and even the abuse, of their authority was in some measure justified in an Empire divided into numerous independent jurisdictions, and not subjected to any paramount tribunal, able to administer impartial justice to the oppressed. But as the times improved, the Vehmic tribunals degenerated.' In the sixteenth century they were restricted to Westphalia and subordinated to the ordinary courts, and were finally dissolved in 1811 by Jerome Buonaparte. *Anne of Geierstein.*

VEILCHEN, ANNETTE. 'A girl who, though her attendance on Anne of Geierstein was in a menial capacity, was held in high estimation at Geierstein.' 'Merry' and at the same time 'resolute and sensible, though rather bold and free,' she would fain have had her mistress receive Arthur Philipson in Arnheim Castle with the warmth of 'any frank-hearted Swiss girl.'

'Half-nettled' by the stately futilities with which they entertained each other at table, she broke out at last, 'You have both been very merry, forsooth, at my expense, and all because I wished rather to rise and seek what I wanted, than wait till the poor fellow, who was kept trotting between the board and beauffet, found leisure to bring it to me. . . . But for all your new world fancies, I can tell you, you are but a couple of children, who do not know your own minds, and are jesting away the only leisure given you to provide for your own happiness.' *Anne of Geierstein.*

VERE, ISABEL. Daughter of the Laird of Ellieslaw. Possessed of 'beauty, wealth, station, accomplishments,' and threatened by 'their corresponding evils—unsuccessful love, crossed affections, the gloom of a convent, or an odious alliance,' she was preserved by her qualities of 'truth, virtue, and innocence.' *The Black Dwarf.*

VERE, LETITIA. Wife of the Laird of Ellieslaw. A relative of Sir Edward Mauley, she had been brought up by his parents to marry him. While Sir Edward was in prison paying the penalty for the fatal wound he gave in Ellieslaw's defence, Letitia was persuaded to transfer her affections. *The Black Dwarf.*

VERE, RICHARD. Laird of Ellieslaw: Isabel's father. In early life he was one of the two friends on whose 'faith and sincerity' Sir Edward Mauley relied 'implicitly,' but he acted with such treachery as almost shattered Sir Edward's belief in humanity. For Isabel's sake, Sir Edward showed him great liberality. This the Laird used only to further his political ambitions. Ignorant that Sir Edward lived in his neighbourhood as the *Black Dwarf*, and was kept informed of his schemes by Mr. Ratcliffe, he was left without 'subterfuge' when the Black Dwarf appeared to interrupt Isabel's marriage with Sir Frederick Langley. *The Black Dwarf.*

Vere, Arthur de. *See* Philipson, Arthur.

Vere, John de. *See* Philipson, Seignor.

Vermandois, Hugh, Count of. Hugh, the Great Count: brother of Philippe, King of France: one of the leaders of the first Crusade who promised allegiance to Alexius Comnenus. Wrecked on the shores of Greece, he had been taken as a prisoner to Constantinople, but was liberated on the intervention of 'the tremendous Godfrey of Bouillon.' *Count Robert of Paris.*

Vernon, Diana. The niece of Sir Hildebrand Osbaldistone's wife: 'the heath-bell of Cheviot, and the blossom of the Border.' She confided to Frank Osbaldistone that for three things she thought herself 'much to be pitied': 'I am a girl, and not a young fellow, and would be shut up in a madhouse if I did half the things I have a mind to . . . I belong to an oppressed sect and antiquated religion . . . I am by nature, as you may easily observe, of a frank and unreserved disposition—a plain, true-hearted girl . . . and yet fate has involved me in such a series of nets, and toils, and entanglements that I dare hardly speak a word for fear of consequences— not to myself, but to others.' Yet she bore herself with buoyant vivacity, and when filial duty seemed to necessitate her retirement to a convent, she approached this fate with an air ' of composed and submissive, but dauntless, resolution and constancy.' *Rob Roy.*

Vernon, Sir Frederick. Diana's father. For many years he was believed to be dead, but, as Father Vaughan, he worked actively for the Pretender from Osbaldistone Hall as his headquarters. His wife having been a relative of the Breadalbanes he had great influence with the Scottish chiefs, and 'was possessed of matter enough to have ruined half Scotland.' In order to secure his property, he had, soon after Diana's birth, made a compact with Sir Hildebrand Osbaldistone that she would either marry one of his sons or retire to a convent. *Rob Roy.*

Vernon, Sir Richard. One of Diana's ancestors: 'slain at Shrewsbury, and sorely slandered by a sad fellow called Will Shakespeare.' *Rob Roy.*

Vexhelia. Osmund's wife. She was Brenhilda's companion while Bertha was absent on her mission to the Crusaders at Scutari. *Count Robert of Paris.*

Vich Alister More (*i.e.* Son of

Alister the Great). Macdonell of Glengarry, one of the Highland chiefs who attended the gathering at Darnlinvarach, and put themselves under Montrose. He and his clan distinguished themselves at Inverlochy. *A Legend of Montrose.*

Vich Ian Vohr. *See* MacIvor, Fergus *and* Ian.

Vidal, Renault. *See* Cadwallon.

Vienne, Archbishop of. Chancellor of Burgundy. He tried to moderate the wrath roused in Charles the Bold by the refusal of the Estates to vote supplies, and again by the independent attitude of the Swiss deputies. *Anne of Geierstein.*

Viewforth. A neighbouring laird whose lineage compared unfavourably with Ellangowan's. *Guy Mannering.*

Villiers, George. *See* Buckingham, Dukes of.

Vincent, Jenkin. 'Jin Vin,' one of David Ramsay's 'sharp-witted, active, able-bodied and well-voiced apprentices.' Acting on Dame Suddlechop's advice with the object of winning Margaret Ramsay's favour as a gallant, he gave up 'skittles and trap-ball for tennis and bowls, good English ale for thin Bordeaux and sour Rhenish, roast beef and pudding for woodcocks and kickshaws—my bat for a sword, my cap for a beaver, my forsooth for a modish oath, my Christmas-box for a dice-box, my religion for the devil's matins, and mine honest name for—!' But he was honest at heart, helped Nigel to escape from 'Alsatia,' and acted with Richie Moniplies in trapping Colepepper. *The Fortunes of Nigel.*

Vincovincentem, Lord. 'A Lord of Session' whose judgments Saddletree quoted. *The Heart of Midlothian.*

Violante. One of the white-robed nymphs who acted 'as a species of living book-desk, to support and extend the parchment rolls in which the Princess recorded her own wisdom, or from which she quoted that of others.' *Count Robert of Paris.*

Vipont, Ralph de. A knight of St. John of Jerusalem: one of the challengers in the Passage of Arms at Ashby-de-la-Zouch. In his combat with the Disinherited Knight 'the poor Hospitaller was hurled from his saddle like a stone from a sling.' *Ivanhoe.*

Vorst, Peterkin. A Flemish sentinel. Finding him asleep at his post on the walls of the castle of Garde Douloureuse, Eveline Berenger and Rose Flammock took his duty upon themselves, and were the first to hear the approach of Hugo de Lacy's army. *The Betrothed.*

W

Wabster, Michael. One of the townsmen who hastened out to help Henry Gow in protecting Simon Glover's house on St. Valentine's Eve. *The Fair Maid of Perth.*

Wade, Field-Marshal. Commander of an army stationed upon the Borders to intercept the young Chevalier's advance. *Waverley.*

WAKEFIELD, HARRY. One of the two drovers. Giving way at the first moment of misunderstanding with Robin McCombich to a natural feeling of irritation, he allowed his resentment to be fanned by Fleecebumpkin and his friends at Heskett's alehouse, in spite of some revivals of 'respect' for his Highland friend. But his English sense of justice was satisfied when he had knocked Robin down. He was ready to 'shake hands' and 'be better friends than ever.' To Robin, however, the personal indignity was an unforgettable degradation. Two hours later he returned saying, 'You, Harry Waakfelt, showed me to-day how the Saxon churls fight—I show you now how the Highland Dunnie-wassel fights.' *The Two Drovers.*

(*Dunnie-wassel*, a well-born Highlander.)

WALDECK, MARTIN. The hero of a German legend 'taken down' by Isabella Wardour from Dousterswivel, and read aloud by Lovel on the occasion of the expedition to the ruins of St. Ruth's Priory. Martin was the youngest of three brothers who 'carried on the laborious and mean occupation of preparing charcoal for the smelting furnaces' in the Harz mountains. His fortunes show 'the miseries attendant upon wealth hastily attained and ill-employed.' *The Antiquary.*

WALDIE. *See* TORRENCE.

WALDIMIR, ABBOT. The fourteenth-century founder of Monkbarns—a residence for the bailiff of the abbey and a storehouse for the grain received by the monks as ground rent. *The Antiquary.*

WALDSTETTEN, COUNTESS. 'A lady of high rank and small fortune, the respectable widow of a Count of the Empire.' As a relative of Herman, Baron von Arnheim, she 'accepted an invitation to preside over her kinsman's domestic affairs, and remove, by her countenance, any suspicions which might arise from the presence of Hermione.' *Anne of Geierstein.*

WALKER. The owner of the inn where Mr. Pleydell celebrated the success of Harry Bertram's case with 'a glorious batch of claret.' *Guy Mannering.*

WALKER, PETER. 'By trade an itinerant merchant or pedlar': 'the most zealous and faithful collector and recorder of the actions and opinions of the Cameronians.' *The Heart of Midlothian.*

WALLACE, WILLIAM. The 'Champion of Scotland,' able to 'foil any two martial champions that ever drew sword.' His 'inimitable strength and agility' would have rescued Margaret de Hautlieu from her prison in St. Bride's, had not her father taken a 'fearful advantage' of Wallace's compassion in sparing his life. *Castle Dangerous.*

WALLENRODE, EARL. 'A gigantic warrior from the frontiers of Hungary.' On seeing King Richard trample on the Austrian flag, he struck a blow at him which 'might have proved fatal, had not the Scot intercepted and caught it on his shield.' *The Talisman.*

WALSINGHAM, SIR FRANCIS. One of Queen Elizabeth's secretaries of state: a statesman of 'penetrating and prospective sagacity,' whose favour was founded 'on Elizabeth's solid judgment, not on her partiality.' *Kenilworth.*

WALTHEOF. Abbot of St. Withold's at Burton-on-Trent. On their return journey from Ashby-de-la-Zouch Cedric and his party spent a night there and were received by the Abbot 'with the profuse and exuberant hospitality of their nation.' *Ivanhoe.*

WALTHEOFF. A Grey Friar: confessor to the Duchess of Rothesay. From Falkland Castle, Dwining wrote in his name a letter concerning Catharine Glover which imposed on 'the thick-witted Charteris,' and kept him away from the castle. *The Fair Maid of Perth.*

WALTHEOFF. Hereward's father. He and Engelred as leaders of the Foresters 'were among the last bold men who asserted the independence of the Saxon race of England.' William Rufus 'brought an overpowering force' upon their bands, and both the 'unfortunate chiefs remained dead on the field.' *Count Robert of Paris.*

WALTON, SIR JOHN DE. Governor of Douglas Castle: lover of the Lady Augusta of Berkley. In his anxiety 'to discharge perfectly a duty upon which must depend the accomplishment of all the hopes' she had permitted him to entertain, he became 'one of the most cautious and jealous men in the world'; his vigilance was 'marked with severity.' The 'caprice of the lady herself... engendered such a nest of mistakes' as helped, however, to further the Douglas' plans to regain his castle. *Castle Dangerous.*

Note.—Sir John de *Webtoun* is the name given by Barbour in his *Bruce* to the governor who was to be held worthy of his lady's love if he kept Douglas Castle for a year. Unlike Scott's hero, he did not surrender the castle, but making a sally was killed in an ambush laid by Douglas. His lady's letter was found in his pocket.

WAMBA. 'Son of Witless, who was the son of Weatherbrain, who was the son of an Alderman': Cedric's jester. The infirmity of his brain 'consisted chiefly in a kind of impatient irritability which suffered him not long to ... adhere to any certain train of ideas,' but he had wit enough to escape when his master was seized and carried off to Front-de-Bœuf's castle, and devotion enough to save Cedric's life at the risk of his own. *Ivanhoe.*

WAMPHRAY, LAIRD OF. *See* JOHNSTONE, DICK.

WANDERING WILLIE. *See* STEENSON, WILLIE.

WARD, JACK. One of the British prisoners entrusted by Hyder Ali to Richard Middlemas' charge.

He 'had the bastinado' for celebrating the merits of Richard and Madame Montreville in a couplet. *The Surgeon's Daughter.*

WARDEN, HENRY. (1) As 'Henry Wellwood' a college friend of Father Eustace: afterwards a preacher of the reformed doctrines. In consequence of his uncompromising zeal in reproving Julian Avenel for his treatment of Catherine, he fell into the power of Father Eustace. But while unable to 'fight side by side as friends,' they were at least able to act 'as generous enemies.'

(2) Resident minister in the Castle of Avenel. He 'engaged in a furious and acrimonious contest concerning the sacrifice of the mass ... with the Abbot Eustatius ... and his grave, stern, and absorbed deportment ... made his presence rather add to than diminish the gloom which hung over the Castle.' Though 'single-minded and benevolent,' he evinced at times a marked dislike' to Roland Graeme, and contributed by his public rebuke to the page's dismissal. (1) *The Monastery.* (2) *The Abbot.*

WARDLAW. The land steward at Osbaldistone Hall. *Rob Roy.*

WARDLAW, HENRY. Archbishop of St. Andrews and Primate of Scotland. Influenced by the Church party in league with the Duke of Albany, the King confirmed his nomination by the Pope, 'thus yielding to Rome those freedoms and immunities of the Scottish Church which his ancestors, from the time of Malcolm Canmore, have so boldly defended.' *The Fair Maid of Perth.*

WARDOUR, ISABELLA. Sir Arthur's daughter: the Antiquary's 'fair foe.' She was 'the wale o' the country for beauty' and 'one of the most accomplished as well as sensible girls.' After Mr. Lovel's departure from Fairport, when her heart was softened by approaching disaster, she found that her former repulse of his attentions 'had been dictated rather by duty than inclination.' *The Antiquary.*

(*Wale*, a person or thing chosen as the most excellent of its kind.)

WARDOUR, CAPTAIN REGINALD GAMELYN. Sir Arthur's son: a fellow-officer of Major Neville, the 'matchless friend' by whose generosity he was able to relieve his father's financial difficulties. 'People talk of marriage between Miss McIntyre and Captain Wardour.' *The Antiquary.*

WARDOUR, SIR ANTHONY. Sir Arthur's father. He was a Jacobite in principle, but in 1745 his 'zeal became a little more moderate just when its warmth was of most consequence.' 'His demi-pique saddle would suit only one of his horses, and that horse could by no means be brought to stand fire.' *The Antiquary.*

WARDOUR, SIR ARTHUR. A baronet of ancient descent and embarrassed fortune. He had some taste for antiquities, and was a crony of the Antiquary. Their views differed so widely as to cause frequent discord, but they were too necessary to each other to quarrel, and the reality of their friendship was seen when Dousterswivel had almost brought Sir Arthur to ruin.

'That I should have been such a miserable dolt—such an infatuated idiot—such a beast, endowed with thrice a beast's stupidity, to be led and driven and spur-galled by such a rascal, and under such ridiculous pretences—Mr. Oldbuck, I could tear myself when I think of it.' *The Antiquary.*

See also GUARDOVER, GAMELYN, and ADHEMAR, PRIOR.

Note.—Laurence Templeton professed to have found the materials for *Ivanhoe* 'in the singular Anglo-Norman MS. which Sir Arthur Wardour preserves with such jealous care.'

WARDOUR, SIR RICHARD. 'The first o' the name ever was in this country': 'Red-hand.' He married auld Knockwinnock's only daughter, Sybil, 'that was to have the castle and the land.' *The Antiquary.*

See also KNOCKWINNOCK, SYBIL and MALCOLM, THE USURPER.

WASP. Vanbeest Brown's 'rough terrier dog, his constant companion.' When Brown came to Dandy Dinmont's assistance on the Waste of Cumberland, Wasp 'acted gloriously during the skirmish, annoying the heels of the enemy, and repeatedly effecting a moment's diversion in his master's favour.' *Guy Mannering.*

WAT THE DEVIL. A Northumbrian freebooter in the days of Frank Osbaldistone's great-grandfather. *Rob Roy.*

WATKINS, WILL. The only member of his band of Shrove Tuesday revellers whom the Duke of Rothesay found sober after his visit to Sir John Ramorny. Being the only Englishman amongst the train, he found it best to keep sober when the Scots got drunk, 'seeing that they only endure me even when we are all sober, and if the wine were uppermost, I might tell them a piece of my mind, and be paid with as many stabs as there are skenes in the good company.' *The Fair Maid of Perth.*

(*Skenes,* knives.)

WATSON, JEAN. See GRAY, MRS.

WAVERLEY FAMILY, THE.

— WILIBERT. An ancestor of Edward. On his return from the Crusades, he found that his betrothed, believing him dead, was on the eve of wedding the hero who had protected her from insult. He generously gave up his claim, and retired to a monastery.

— SIR HILDEBRAND. An ancestor of Edward. From him also sprang the Waverleys of Highley Park, 'degenerate,' in the eyes of the main branch, since the great law-suit of 1670. They had further offended by union with the Bradshawe family.

— WILFRED. Eldest son of Sir Hildebrand.

— LADY ALICE. One of 'Aunt Rachel's' heroines. Rachel told 'how Charles had, after the field of Worcester, found a day's refuge at Waverley-Honour, and how, when a troop of cavalry were approaching to search the mansion, Lady Alice dismissed her youngest son with a handful of domestics, charging them to make good with their lives an hour's diversion, that the King might have that space for escape.'

WAVERLEY FAMILY, THE.
— SIR NIGEL. The elder son of Lady Alice, and great-grandfather of Edward.
— WILLIAM. Youngest son of Lady Alice, and lover of Lucy St. Aubin. He gave his life for Charles II.
— SIR GILES. Edward's grandfather.
— SIR EVERARD. The 'affectionate old uncle' to whose title and estates Edward was presumptive heir. The worthy representative of an ancestor who bore the device *Sans tache* on the field of Hastings, he at the same time 'inherited from his sires the whole train of Tory or High Church predilections and prejudices which had distinguished the House of Waverley since the Great Civil War.' But when his nephew, following his father's instructions, accepted a commission in a dragoon regiment, he concluded that 'when war was at hand, although it were shame to be on any side but one, it were worse shame to be idle than to be on the worse side, though blacker than usurpation could make it.'
— RICHARD. Edward's father. Dissatisfied with his prospects as Sir Everard's younger brother, he decided early that 'to succeed in the race of life, it was necessary he should carry as little weight as possible.' But his plans of wealth and ambition miscarried, and he was forced to retire from political life 'under the comfortable reflection that he had lost, at the same time, character, credit, and—what he at least equally deplored—emolument.'

WAVERLEY FAMILY, THE.
— RACHEL. Sister of Sir Everard, and like him one of 'the gentlest and kindest of the votaries of celibacy.' 'The benevolent features of the venerable spinster kindled into more majestic expression' as she told to her young nephew the family legends of honour and generosity.
— EDWARD. The central figure of the tale. 'His person promised firmness and agility,' 'his blue eye seemed of that kind which melted in love, and which kindled in war,' and he was 'gleg aneuch at the broadsword and target.' But he was 'blown about with every wind of doctrine,' and circumstances rather than convictions changed him from a captain in the King's army to a rebel under Prince Charles Edward Stewart.

'O, indolence and indecision of mind! if not in yourselves vices, to how much exquisite misery and mischief do you frequently prepare the way!'

(*Gleg*, clever.)

WAYLAND, LANCELOT. Wayland Smith's 'real name.' *Kenilworth*.

WEATHERSPORT, CAPTAIN. Captain of the *Halcyon*, the man-of-war which captured the *Fortune's Favourite*. He set Cleveland and Jack Bunce at liberty in virtue of their having protected two Spanish ladies of quality from the brutality of their followers when pillaging a village eight or nine years earlier. Regarding Goffe and the others he said, 'there will be ropes reeved for some of them, I think.' *The Pirate.*

WEDDELL, MISTRESS MARTHA. Lady Margaret Bellenden's 'lady-in-waiting.' *Old Mortality.*

WEIR, MAJOR. Sir Robert Redgauntlet's special pet, an 'ill-favoured jackanape ... a cankered beast it was, and mony an ill-natured trick it played—ill to please it was, and easily angered—ran about the haill castle, chattering and yowling, and pinching and biting folk, especially before ill weather, or disturbances in the State.' In the confusion of Sir Robert's sudden death the Major carried off Steenie Steenson's siller to the old turret called the Cat's Cradle, and took possession of the silver whistle with which old Dougal MacCallum was called to his death. *Redgauntlet.*

WEIVER. The minister of a congregation of Fifth-Monarchy men which Major Bridgenorth joined. On the day of the Peverils' acquittal the congregation assembled armed, ready to take part in the outbreak planned by Edward Christian and the Duke of Buckingham. *Peveril of the Peak.*

Note.—From *Woodstock:* 'Fifth-Monarchy men ... going even beyond the general fanaticism of the age, presumptuously interpreted the Book of the Revelations after their own fancies, considered that the second Advent of the Messiah and the Millenium, or reign of the Saints upon earth, was close at hand, and that they themselves, illuminated, as they believed, with the power of foreseeing these approaching events, were the chosen instruments for the establishment of the New Reign, or Fifth Monarchy, as it was called, and were fated also to win its honours, whether celestial or terrestrial.'

WELLWOOD, HENRY. *See* WARDEN, HENRY.

WELLWOOD, SOPHIA. *See* MANNERING, MRS.

WENLOCK. An Englishman besieged by the insurgent commons of the west in a village about ten miles from the Castle of Garde Douloureuse. Damian de Lacy had set out to relieve him when news of Eveline Berenger's capture by Dawfyd drew him to the Welsh mountains. This delay, combined with Damian's quarrel with Wenlock on account of 'some petty wrong he did to the miller's wife,' led to the belief that Damian favoured the commons. At the approach of Amelot and his little band the defenders surrendered, and Hob Miller sent Wenlock's head to the relief party as 'toll of the grist which he hath grinded.' *The Betrothed.*

WESTENHO, CAPTAIN. 'A soldier of fortune ... an old familiar of Craigengelt's.' 'By dint of exaggeration of real circumstances and coining of others,' he gave 'explicit testimony to the truth of Ravenswood's approaching marriage' with a lady abroad. *The Bride of Lammermoor.*

WETHERAL, STEPHEN, 'STEEL-HEART.' One of the men whom Fitzurse took with him to make his secret attack on Richard Cœur-de-Lion. The others were Broad Thoresby, and 'three northern men-at-arms' from Ralph Middleton's gang, called the Spears of Spyinghow. *Ivanhoe.*

WETZWEILER, TIEL. See GLORIEUX, LE.

WHACKBAIRN, MR. 'The principal teacher of the little parochial establishment' at Liberton, when Mr. Butler was engaged as assistant. 'Tolerably educated,' he 'retained some taste for classical lore.' *The Heart of Midlothian.*

WHACKER, MAJOR. One of the Government officers quartered on Mrs. Flockhart. 'A very ceevil gentleman.' *Waverley.*

WHALLEY, RICHARD. The hero of a story told by Major Bridgenorth to Julian Peveril. The story describes how an American village was saved from the Indians by an unknown leader who immediately afterwards disappeared. *Peveril of the Peak.*

Note.—Scott here confuses Edward Whalley, the regicide, with his father, *Richard.* Tradition generally ascribes the heroic delivery to William Goffe, also a regicide, who escaped to America with his father-in-law, Edward Whalley, after the Restoration.

WHILLIEWHAW. One of the counsel suggested by Saddletree for Effie Deans' defence, but rejected by her father as 'ony thing ye like.' *The Heart of Midlothian.*

WHISTLER. Balmawhapple's greyhound. *Waverley.*

WHISTLER, THE. A 'young savage' in Donacha Dhu's band: Effie Deans' child. He was sold by Meg Murdockson to Annaple Bailzou, and shared her wanderings and beggary till he was seven or eight. He was then sold to Donacha Dhu, who intended him for the American traders. But he soon showed himself 'a born imp of Satan, and *therefore*' Donacha Dhu could not part with him. After the affray in which both Donacha Dhu and Sir George Staunton lost their lives, the Butlers made attempts to reform The Whistler, but all in vain. *The Heart of Midlothian.*

WHITAKER, RICHARD. Sir Geoffrey Peveril's steward. 'You shall have all your directions punctually obeyed,' he said to Lady Peveril, when checked for his forwardness, 'but as an old servant, I cannot but speak my mind.' *Peveril of the Peak.*

WHITECRAFT, JOHN. Landlord and miller at the sign of the Cat and Fiddle near Altringham. Under his roof Julian Peveril met Ganlesse. 'I hears on nought,' the landlord said when asked for news, 'except this Plot, as they call it, that they are pursuing the Papishers about; but it brings water to my mill, as the saying is. Between expresses hurrying hither and thither, and guards and prisoners riding to and again, and the custom of the neighbours, that come to speak over the news of an evening, nightly I may say, instead of once a week, why the spigot is in use, gentlemen, and your land thrives.' *Peveril of the Peak.*

WHITECRAFT, MRS. John's wife. 'I do not understand these doings, not I,' she said; 'and if a hundred Jesuits came to hold a consult at my house, as they did at the White Horse Tavern, I should think it quite out of the line of business to bear witness against them, provided they drank well and paid their score.' *Peveril of the Peak.*

WHITE DOE, FOSTER-CHILD OF THE. *See* MACIAN, IAN EACHIN.

WHITEFISH, JOHN. One of the Wolf's-hope feuars who employed Davie Dingwall to upold their independence against Caleb Balderstone's requisitions. *The Bride of Lammermoor.*

WHITE LADY OF AVENEL. *See* AVENEL, WHITE LADY OF.

WHITELOCKE, LORD-KEEPER. Major Bridgenorth's ensample against the drinking of healths. 'At the table of the Chamberlain of the kingdom of Sweden he did positively refuse to pledge the health of his Queen, Christina, thereby giving great offence, and putting in peril the whole purpose of that voyage; which it is not to be thought so wise a man would have done, but that he held such compliance a thing not merely in-different, but rather sinful and damnable.' *Peveril of the Peak.*

WHITEROSE, CATHERINE. Dr. Dryasdust's cousin and housekeeper. *Peveril of the Peak.*

WHITEROSE, REV. GEORGE. A clergyman, 'in the Minster Close, York.' Lady Staunton instructed Jeanie to write to her 'under cover' to him. He is mentioned in *Peveril of the Peak* as the maternal uncle of Dr. Dryasdust. *The Heart of Midlothian.*

WIBBALD. *See* GILBERT.

WILDBLOOD. The horse Claverhouse rode to Drumshinnel. *Old Mortality.*

WILDBLOOD, DICK, OF THE DALE. One of the guests at Lady Peveril's Restoration feast. He was also one of the men who with Sir Geoffrey escorted the Countess of Derby from Martindale Castle on her way to the Isle of Man. *Peveril of the Peak.*

WILD BOAR OF ARDENNES, THE. *See* MARCK, WILLIAM DE LA.

WILD GOOSE, MR. Peter Peebles' eighth agent. *Redgauntlet.*

WILDRAKE, ROGER, OF SQUATTLESEA-MERE, LINCOLN. A chum of Markham Everard at college and at Lincoln's Inn. 'Not even politics' destroyed their friendship, and after the triumph of the Parliamentary party Roger lived under Markham's protection as his secretary. Markham held that Roger had at bottom 'as deep a principle of honour and feeling as ever governed a human heart,' but he was of a 'thoughtless, conceited, and reckless character,' 'with the whole vices of his faction' in himself individually. 'It is such fellows as he,' Albert Lee said, 'who, sunk from the license of their military habits into idle debauched ruffians, infest the land with riots and robberies, brawl in hedge alehouses and cellars, where strong waters are sold at midnight, and, with their deep oaths, their hot loyalty, and their drunken valour, make decent men abominate the very name of cavalier.' *Woodstock.*

WILFRED. Cedric's son, Knight of Ivanhoe : the Disinherited Knight who gained the championship in the Passage of Arms at Ashby-de-la-Zouch. Banished by his father because he refused to renounce his 'unreasonable passion' for Rowena, he gained fame in the Holy Land and became a favourite with Richard Cœur-de-Lion. He returned as a Palmer, was equipped for the tournament by Isaac of York, and afterwards nursed by Rebecca. His long-standing feud with Bois-Guilbert was closed when he fought as Rebecca's champion at Templestowe.

'If to maintain the honour of ancestry,' said Rebecca, 'it is sufficient to be wise in council and brave in execution—to be boldest among the bold, and gentlest among the gentle, I know no voice, save his father's—.' *Ivanhoe.*

WILKINSON, JAMES. Mr. Fairford's manservant. 'The attentive James . . . with his long face, lank hair, and very long pigtail in its leathern strap, was placed, as usual, at the back of my father's chair, upright as a wooden sentinel at the door of a puppet-show.' *Redgauntlet.*

WILKS, STEENIE. One of the men who helped in the rescue at Halket-head craigs. *The Antiquary.*

WILL. Gibbie Girder's foreman. *The Bride of Lammermoor.*

WILL O' THE FLAT. A Liddesdale farmer. *Guy Mannering.*

WILLIAM. A youth in attendance on Anne of Geierstein when, with Annette Veilchen as chaperon, she entertained Arthur Philipson in Arnheim Castle. The youth did the service 'debonairly,' 'with deftness and courtesy.' *Anne of Geierstein.*

WILLIAM. One of the 'pages and yeomen' told, at Sir John de Walton's hunting-party, to seize Michael Turnbull as a 'spy and traitor.' *Castle Dangerous.*

WILLIAM, PRINCE OF ORANGE. As Stadtholder he gave Harry Morton a commission in a Swiss regiment in a distant province. When he came to the British throne he 'grievously disappointed' those who expected to find in him a 'zealous Covenanted Monarch' by declaring that he would tolerate 'all forms of religion which were consistent with the safety of the State.' *Old Mortality.*

WILLIAMS, FARMER. Ned's father. Edward Waverley lived in hiding at his farm of Fasthwaite for some weeks. *Waverley.*

WILLIAMS, NED. Cicely Jopson's sweetheart. *Waverley.*

WILLIE. (1) Saddletree's apprentice boy. 'It's a fatherless bairn,' Mrs. Saddletree said, ' and motherless, whilk in some cases may be waur, and ane would take care o' him if they could—it's a Christian duty.'
(2) One of Ratcliffe's 'late companions in misfortune' who escaped from the Tolbooth during the Porteous Riot. (1) and (2) *The Heart of Midlothian.*

WILLIE. Andrew Skurliewhitter's boy. *The Fortunes of Nigel.*

WILLIE OF WESTBURNFLAT. William Graeme, the 'Red Reiver.' After being cured of a dangerous illness by the Black Dwarf he forgot all his 'promises of amendment,' and resumed his wild life. He burnt Hobbie Elliot's stackyard and steading, carried off Grace Armstrong, and afterwards Isabel Vere, while taking part at the same time with her father in the scheme for a Jacobite rising. 'The lads of Westburnflat, for ten lang descents . . . have all drunk hard, lived high, taking deep revenge for light offence, and never wanted gear for the winning.' *The Black Dwarf.*

WILLIE OF WINTON. One of Hobbie Elliot's friends : ' lowland-bred, poor fallow, and soon frighted for himsell.' *The Black Dwarf.*

WILLIESON, WILLIAM. 'Half-owner and sole skipper of a brig that made four voyages annually between Cockpool and Whitehaven': one of the plotters of a Jacobite rising. *The Black Dwarf.*

WILLOUGHBY, LORD. A 'noble courtier' who gave up his seat in the Queen's barge to her 'young Squire of the Cloak.' *Kenilworth.*

WILMOT, LORD. One of the 'witty and profligate youth of quality' by whom Charles was surrounded. The ring dropped into Alice Lee's pitcher at Rosamund's well by Charles when disguised as a gipsy woman, belonged to Wilmot. This was discovered by Markham Everard and led him to identify Louis Kerneguy with Wilmot until Charles disclosed himself in order to clear the misunderstanding between Markham and Alice. *Woodstock.*

WILMOT, MRS. Isabella Wardour's aunt. It was when staying with her in Yorkshire that Isabella made Mr. Lovel's acquaintance. *The Antiquary.*

WILSA. Dame Suddlechop's 'dingy Iris,' a little mulatto girl. *The Fortunes of Nigel.*

WILSON, ANDREW. Formerly a dragoon. Kettledrummle was riding his nag when trying to escape from an interrupted conventicle, but the more the minister 'spurred to win awa', the readier the dour beast ran to the dragoons when he saw them draw up.' *Old Mortality.*

(*Dour*, obstinate.)

WILSON, ANDREW. 'Handie Dandie': a smuggler in Fife. 'Possessed of great personal strength, courage, and cunning,' he was 'particularly obnoxious to the revenue officers,' and was at length 'totally ruined by repeated seizures.' 'As a fair and honourable reprisal' for this, he robbed the Collector of Customs. He was caught, and with his accomplice, George Robertson, condemned to death. Public interest in his case was strengthened by the fact that after the failure of a joint attempt at escape—the failure being due to his obstinacy—he succeeded in freeing Robertson by overpowering their guards. Hopes of a reprieve proved groundless, and immediately after his death there began the series of events which culminated in the Porteous Riot.

'Minds like Wilson's . . . sometimes retain the power of thinking and resolving with enthusiastic generosity.' *The Heart of Midlothian.*

WILSON, BOB. One of Sir William Ashton's men-servants. He brought Henry a new pony from the Mull of Galloway. *The Bride of Lammermoor.*

WILSON, CHRISTY. One of the party in the Wallace Inn who listened to Bauldie's stories about the Black Dwarf. *The Black Dwarf.*

WILSON, DAVY. 'Commonly called Snuffy Davy, from his inveterate addiction to black rappee, was the very prince of scouts for searching blind alleys, cellars, and stalls, for rare volumes.' *The Antiquary.*
See also OSBORNE.

WILSON, JOHN. Ellangowan's groom. John reported to his fellows 'that Meg appeared to the Laird as he was riding hame from Singleside, over Gibbie's-know, and threatened him wi' what she wad do to his family; but whether it was Meg, or something waur in her likeness, for it seemed bigger than ony mortal creature, John could not say.' *Guy Mannering.*

WILSON, MISTRESS ALISON. Old Milnwood's housekeeper. In spite of her overbearing ways, she 'loved her old and young master . . . better than anyone else in the world.' The auld laird left her the life-rent of Milnwood 'as he heard nought o' his nephew,' and she held 'the gear well thegither' during Harry's exile. *Old Mortality.*

WILSON, SANDIE. The 'Marshalsman' of Louis' Scottish Guard: 'as honest a man as ever tied noose upon hemp.' *Quentin Durward.*

WILY WILL. See LEAN, DONALD BEAN.

WINCHESTER, BISHOP OF. The clergyman who officiated at the marriage of Lady Hermione and Lord Dalgarno in the King's chapel. *The Fortunes of Nigel.*

WINCHESTER, EARL OF. See QUINCY, ROGER DE.

WINDSOR, MR. The clergyman who read prayers at George Heriot's on the occasion of Nigel's visit there. *The Fortunes of Nigel.*

WINGATE, JASPER. 'Steward, or master of the household,' in Avenel Castle: 'a man experienced . . . in the ways of great families.' 'To speak the truth when my Lady commands me,' he said, 'is in some measure my duty, Mistress Lilias; always providing for and excepting those cases in which it cannot be spoken without breeding mischief and inconvenience to myself or my fellow-servants.' *The Abbot.*

WINGFIELD. The feather-dresser. He testified before the magistrates that the revellers whom he saw treating Oliver Proudfute roughly on Shrove Tuesday 'wore the cinctures and coronals of painted feathers, which he himself had made by the order of the Prince's Master of the Horse.' *The Fair Maid of Perth.*

WINGFIELD, AMBROSE. One of the 'stout fellows' recommended by Andrew Fairservice to protect Osbaldistone Hall against any 'desperate enterprise' of Sir Rashleigh. 'As honest a man as lives.' *Rob Roy.*

WINGFIELD, LANCIE. One of the 'stout fellows' recommended by Andrew Fairservice to protect Osbaldistone Hall against any 'desperate enterprise' of Sir Rashleigh. 'A false knave ... a spy for Clerk Jobson.' *Rob Roy.*

WINKELBRAND, LOUIS. Maurice de Bracy's lieutenant. When a rumour of the attack on Front-de-Bœuf's castle reached York, Fitzurse ordered Winkelbrand to set out for the castle and 'do what yet may be done for the succour of our friends.' *Ivanhoe.*

WINKIE, WILLIE. The tinker who made the 'tin sconces' which served instead of silver candlesticks at Darnlinvarach. *A Legend of Montrose.*

WINNET, WILL. 'The bedral' with whom Edie Ochiltree worked for a summer. 'Then it cam a green Yule, and the folk died thick and fast ... sae aff I gaed, and left Will to delve his last dwellings by himsell for Edie.' *The Antiquary.* (*Bedral*, sexton.)

WINNIE, ANNIE. One of the three 'sibyls' who performed the last offices for Alice Gray. Later they watched Lucy Ashton's bridal procession, grumbling about the dole and longing rather for deaths than bridals. *The Bride of Lammermoor.*

WINTER. General Witherington's principal servant, 'a native of Northumberland like himself.' *The Surgeon's Daughter.*

WINTERBLOSSOM, MR. PHILIP. A member of the Committee of Management in 'the infant republic of St. Ronan's Well': 'the Man of Taste.' He was 'a civil sort of person, who was nicely precise in his address, wore his hair cued, and dressed with powder, had knee-buckles set with Bristol stones, and a seal-ring as large as Sir John Falstaff's. In his heyday he had a small estate, which he had spent like a gentleman, by mixing with the gay world. He was, in short, one of those respectable links that connect the coxcombs of the present day with those of the last age, and could compare, in his own experience, the follies of both. In latter days, he had sense enough to extricate himself from his course of dissipation, though with impaired health and impoverished fortune.' 'As perpetual president of the table d'hôte at the Well ... he used to amuse the Society by telling stories about

Garrick, Foote, Bonnel Thornton, and Lord Kelly, and delivering his opinions in matters of taste and vertu.' *St. Ronan's Well.*

WINTERFIELD, JACK. A friend of Squire Inglewood's youth. He was hanged at York 'despite family connections and great interest—all for easing a fat west-country grazier of the price of a few beasts.' *Rob Roy.*

WINTERTON. One of the leaders of the 1715 rebellion. *Rob Roy.*

WIN-THE-FIGHT, MASTER JOACHIM. An attorney in Chesterfield under whose care Major Bridgenorth left his affairs when he gave up residence in Moultrassie Hall. He supported Mr. Solsgrace in his opposition to Dr. Dummerar's reinstatement in the parish. 'Gloomy, important, and mysterious,' he seemed to Lady Peveril to wear 'a malicious and disobliging expression' when receiving the interest on the sum due by Sir Geoffrey to Major Bridgenorth. *Peveril of the Peak.*

WISE WIGHT OF MUCKLESTANE MOOR. See BLACK DWARF, THE.

WISEBEHIND, MR. An advocate whom Mr. Meiklewham consulted concerning the Mowbray entail. *St. Ronan's Well.*

WISHEART, DR. Montrose's military chaplain : ' A man very clever in his exercise, and who will do execution on your sins in less time than I could smoke a pipe of tobacco.' *A Legend of Montrose.*

WITHERINGTON, GENERAL. General of the East India Company's depôt in the Isle of Wight. As Richard Tresham he had been 'deeply engaged' in the service of Prince Charles Edward Stewart and escaped imprisonment for high treason only by deserting Zilia de Monçada in Dr. Gray's house and 'skulking' among friends in the Highlands till the affair blew over. In the East India Company's service he rose ' to riches and eminence,' and after fourteen years' separation married Zilia. But in the reproaches of Adam Hartley's protégé, Richard Middlemas, they heard ' Heaven speaking our condemnation by the voice of our own child.' *The Surgeon's Daughter.*

WITHERINGTON, MRS., *née* ZILIA DE MONÇADA. The General's wife : Richard Middlemas' mother. Torn from her child in the bitterness of her father's wrath and pledged after marriage to keep the fatal secret for ' honour's ' sake, she wore her years away in ' unutterable sorrow.' But all the feelings which she had ' subdued and cherished long were set afloat in full tide by the unexpected discovery of this son,' and nature had her revenge. *The Surgeon's Daughter.*

WITHERINGTON, REUBEN. Son of the General. Drs. Tourniquet and Lancelot having failed to save his life from an attack of smallpox, his mother persuaded the General to allow Adam Hartley to try the new method of treatment by giving ' the comforts of fresh air and cold water ' to his brother and sister. *The Surgeon's Daughter.*

WITIKIN. A fellow-countryman of Hereward, who on retiring from service 'spent the end of a long life in this city of Constantinople. ... The poor old man, in despair of something to pass his time, attended the lectures of the philosophers.' But he found that 'their theories . . . are built on the sand.' *Count Robert of Paris.*

WITTENBOLD ('WITTYBODY'). Commander of 'a wheen German horse down at Glasgow yonder': 'a very gude man too, for aught I see, that is, considering he is a sodger and a Dutchman.' With Harry Morton he arrived at Fairyknowe just too late to save Lord Evandale's life. *Old Mortality.*

(*A wheen,* a number.)

WODENSVOE, LORD OF. The cruel Lord who murdered his brother. Out of his gibbet irons had been wrought the lamp by whose light Norna told her tragic life-story to Minna and Brenda Troil. *The Pirate.*

WOGAN, CAPTAIN. A hero of Flora MacIvor. He 'renounced the service of the usurper Cromwell to join the standard of Charles II. . . . and at length died gloriously in the royal cause.' *Waverley.*

WOLF. The staghound which saved Roland Graeme from the loch of Avenel. Jealousy was a passion 'not unknown' to him. *The Abbot.*

WOLF-FANGER. The bloodhound which accompanied Rudolph of Donnerhugel and Arthur Philipson when they patrolled the neighbourhood of Graffs-lust: 'though usually employed in the pursuit of animals of chase . . . also excellent for discovering ambuscades.' *Anne of Geierstein.*

WOLFGANGER, TORQUIL. The Saxon nobleman dispossessed by the elder Front-de-Bœuf: Ulrica's father, and a friend of Cedric's father. *Ivanhoe.*

WOLFRAM, ABBOT. Abbot of St. Edmund's. For his treatment of Athelstane when he awoke from his deathlike trance, the Abbot and his monks were confined in the dungeons of Coningsburgh for 'three days on a meagre diet.' *Ivanhoe.*

WOLVERINE, JACK (or TOM). A mutual gambling friend to Lord Etherington and John Mowbray. Through a false report that he was 'too strong for Etherington at anything he could name' Mowbray was led to regard the Earl as a 'good subject of plunder,' he being able to beat Wolverine 'from the Land's End to Johnnie Groat's.' *St. Ronan's Well.*

WOOD, LUCKIE. Mistress of an alehouse in the Cowgate where Advocate Pleydell's clerk Driver was to be found 'at all times when he is off duty.' *Guy Mannering.*

(*Luckie,* a designation given to an elderly woman.)

WOODCOCK, ADAM. The falconer of Avenel, a 'canny' Yorkshireman, and, in spite of the page's arrogance, a good friend to Roland Graeme. 'He was a favourite in his department, jealous and conceited of his skill, as masters of the game usually are ; for the rest of his character, he was a jester and a parcel poet (qualities which by no means abated his natural conceit), a jolly fellow who, though a sound Protestant, loved a flagon of ale better than a long sermon, a stout man of his hands when need required, true to his master, and a little presuming on his interest with him.' *The Abbot.*

See also UNREASON, ABBOT OF. (*Parcel*, in part. *Archaic.*)

WOODSETTER. One of the counsel suggested by Saddletree for Effie Deans' defence, but rejected by her father as 'a Cocceian.' *The Heart of Midlothian.*

WOODSTALL, HENRY. One of the 'reckless warders' who amused themselves by tormenting the Charegite, and were deceived by his pretence of drunkenness. *The Talisman.*

WOODSTOCK, MAYOR OF. A 'zealous Presbyterian,' in whose 'goodly form . . . there was a bustling mixture of importance and embarrassment, like the deportment of a man who was conscious that he had an important part to act, if he could but exactly discover what that part was.' But being alike 'unwarlike' and 'unlearned,' he had no courage with which to contend against Independent soldiers in church nor spiritual apparitions in the Lodge. *Woodstock.*

WOODVILLE, FRANK, LORD. General Browne's host at Woodville Castle. Himself 'a complete sceptic on the subject of supernatural appearances' and knowing that the General's 'courage was indubitable,' he accommodated his guest in the tapestried chamber without giving any hint of its traditions. He hoped to make the room 'a useful part of the house,' and without destroying its air of antiquity, he had given it a 'modern air of comfort.' But the traditional ghost appeared in the night to the General. When on the following day he suddenly recognised the 'accursed hag' and her sacque dress amongst the family portraits, Lord Woodville came to the conclusion 'there can remain no longer any doubt of the horrible reality of your apparition.' *The Tapestried Chamber.*

WYLIE, ANDREW. One of MacVittie, MacFin & Co.'s clerks who had formerly been with Bailie Nicol Jarvie. 'He whiles drinks a gill on the Saturday afternoons wi' his auld master,' and the Bailie was able to make some 'perquisitions' through him. *Rob Roy.*

WYND, HAL OF THE. See GOW, HENRY.

WYNDHAM, SIR WILLIAM. The leader of the Tory party during the rebellion of 1715. In the pocket of his night-gown a letter from Sir Everard Waverley was found. *Waverley.*

WYVIL, WILLIAM DE. One of the marshals of the field in the Passage of Arms at Ashby-de-la-Zouch. *Ivanhoe.*

Y

YARICO. One of the Earl of Glenallan's brood mares. *The Antiquary.*

YARROW. Dandy Dinmont's sheepdog. *Guy Mannering.*

YELLOWLEY, BARBARA ('BABY'). Sister of Triptolemus. From her earliest infancy she showed the eager, narrow, pinching nature of the Clinkscales, but, in spite of all her scrapings and savings, 'the evil star of Triptolemus' (or rather 'his absurd speculations') predominated at Cauldacres. In Zetland she carried her economies so far that he grumbled 'when we have fire we are not to have food, and when we have food we are not to have fire, these being too great blessings to enjoy both in the same day!' But she had, at the same time, 'like all who possess marked character, some sparks of higher feeling, which made her sympathise with generous sentiments, though she thought it too expensive to entertain them at her own cost.' *The Pirate.*

YELLOWLEY, BARBARA (*née* CLINKSCALE). Jasper's wife: 'a woman of spirit' with a 'handsome fortune of two thousand marks at her own disposal.' 'The house of Clinkscale had at least as great a share of Scottish pride as of Scottish parsimony, and was amply endowed with both.' *The Pirate.*

YELLOWLEY, JASPER. Father of Triptolemus. He had been persuaded to leave his native Yorkshire for a farm in the Mearns, but 'it was in vain that the stout farmer set manfully to work, to counterbalance, by superior skill, the inconveniences arising from a cold soil and a weeping climate.' *The Pirate.*

YELLOWLEY, TRIPTOLEMUS. 'Factor of the High Chamberlain of the Isles of Orkney and Zetland,' deputed to increase his master's revenue by improving the culture of the Crown lands. Originally intended for the ministry, he had devoted his time at St. Andrews University to a study of 'such authors of antiquity as had made the improvement of the soil the object of their researches,' and gained such an insight into these mysteries that he 'laid down the law upon every given subject relating to rural economy.' But he found to his great surprise that the agriculturists in Zetland were 'so wretchedly blind as not to be sensible of their deplorable defects,' while they regarded him, with all his knowledge and good intentions, as 'a pedantic, fantastic, visionary schemer.' *The Pirate.*

YETTLIN, DEACON. A Glasgow smith. *Rob Roy.*

YOGLAN, ZACHARIAS. The Jewish chemist from whom Wayland Smith procured the last precious drug necessary for compounding 'the true orvietan, that noble medicine which is so seldom found genuine and effective within these realms of Europe.' *Kenilworth.*

(*Orvietan,* or Venice treacle,

was supposed to be a sovereign remedy against poison.)

YORK, DUKE OF. Afterwards James II. He rode by Charles II's side in the royal progress from Rochester to London. *Woodstock.*

YORKE, ROWLAND. One of the gallants of the time: 'a man of loose and dissolute behaviour, and desperately audacious.' He was famous for having 'brought into England the bold and dangerous way of fencing with the rapier in duelling.' *The Monastery.*

YOUNG, JOHN. A gipsy warned off by Dunbog. *Guy Mannering.*

YOUNGLAD, MR. A writer. *The Heart of Midlothian.*

YSEULTE. The 'good palfrey' which bore Eveline Berenger away from the house of Baldringham. *The Betrothed.*

Z

ZACHARY, FATHER. The hermit to whom Raymond of Ravenswood confessed his intercourse with the Naiad of the well. Regarding her as 'a limb of the kingdom of darkness,' he suggested the experiment which caused the fatal catastrophe. *The Bride of Lammermoor.*

ZAMET, MAUGRABIN. Hayraddin's brother: the 'Bohemian chatterer' whose body Quentin Durward cut down from the tree where Tristan l'Hermite had hung him. He had been employed by Louis to carry letters from the Countess of Croye to a kinsman in Burgundy, but played the traitor and informed the Duke. *Quentin Durward.*

(*Maugrabin*, the African Moor.)

ZAMOR. The horse Bois-Guilbert rode in the lists at Templestowe. Won in single fight from the Soldan of Trebizond, he 'never failed his rider.' *Ivanhoe.*

ZARAH. *See* FENELLA.

ZARETH. A friend of Isaac of York living in Sheffield. *Ivanhoe.*

ZEDEKIAH. One of the servants who helped General Harrison to his apartment in Woodstock Lodge when the frenzy roused by Dick Robison's ghost had spent itself. *Woodstock.*

ZIMMERMAN, ADAM. A burgess of Soleure, 'formal and important': one of the deputies sent by the Swiss Confederation to remonstrate with the Duke of Burgundy on the aggressions and exactions of von Hagenbach. Like Melchior Sturmthal, he 'seemed to hold the consequences of war more lightly than they were viewed' by Arnold Biederman and Nicholas Bonstetten. *Anne of Geierstein.*

ZOHAUK. *See* KENNETH OF SCOTLAND.

ZOSIMUS. The Patriarch, 'to whose high rank some license was allowed' in the imperial circle. He took part in the secret council which considered the treatment to be accorded to the Crusaders from the West, and was also present at the council of the imperial family which deliberated concerning Nicephorus' fate.

There he acted 'as a sort of mediator between a course of severity and a dangerous degree of levity.' *Count Robert of Paris.*

ZULICHIUM, PRINCESS OF. The heroine of the tale with which Agelastes ingratiated himself into the favour of Count Robert and Brenhilda. Enchanted by one of the old Magi whom she ridiculed after having enticed him into 'a fool's paradise,' she was wakened from her sleep by a kiss from the lips of Sir Artavan of Hautlieu. Her form was changed into that of a dragon, Sir Artavan not having 'courage to repeat his salute three times.' *Count Robert of Paris.*